The Lives and Times of the Forty Martyrs of England and Wales 1535–1680

The Lives and Times of the Forty Martyrs of England and Wales 1535–1680

Malcolm Pullan

ATHENA PRESS
LONDON

The Lives and Times of the Forty Martyrs of
England and Wales 1535–1680
Copyright © Malcolm Pullan 2008

All Rights Reserved

No part of this book may be reproduced in any form
by photocopying or by any electronic or mechanical means,
including information storage or retrieval systems,
without permission in writing from both the copyright
owner and the publisher of this book.

ISBN 978 1 84748 258 7

First Published 2008 by
ATHENA PRESS
Queen's House, 2 Holly Road
Twickenham TW1 4EG
United Kingdom

Printed for Athena Press

*Dedicated to the memory of ALL the Catholic martyrs
of England and Wales, known and unknown,
and Anna Dimascio (1950–1995) by whose hand
the ikon of the Forty Martyrs was written:
a rare talent snuffed out all too soon*

1. John Rigby
2. Philip Howard
3. Richard Gwyn
4. Philip Evans
5. John Lloyd
6. John Roberts
7. Alban Roe
8. Ambrose Barlow
9. Margaret Clitherow
10. Anne Line
11. Margaret Ward
12. John Houghton
13. Richard Reynolds
14. Robert Lawrence
15. Augustine Webster
16. David Lewis
17. John Jones
18. Robert Southwell
19. Nicholas Owen
20. Henry Walpole
21. John Wall
22. John Stone
23. Cuthbert Mayne
24. John Kemble
25. Edmund Gennings
26. Swithun Wells
27. Edmund Arrowsmith
28. John Southworth
29. Henry Morse
30. John Boste
31. John Almond
32. John Plessington
33. Luke Kirby
34. Thomas Garnet
35. Ralph Sherwin
36. Edmund Campion
37. Alexander Briant
38. Eustace White
39. Polydore Plasden
40. John Paine

Ikon of the Forty Martyrs of England and Wales

Contents

Canonization Homily of Pope Paul VI	xi
Preface	xiii
Introduction	xvii
CHAPTER ONE: The Henrician Martyrs and the Aftermath	24
CHAPTER TWO: Edward VI and Mary Tudor	55
CHAPTER THREE: The Elizabethan Persecution	65
CHAPTER FOUR: The Elizabethan Martyrs, 1577–1601	98
CHAPTER FIVE: The Jacobean Martyrs, 1603–1625	246
CHAPTER SIX: Charles I and the Civil War Martyrs, 1625–1649	280
CHAPTER SEVEN: Puritan Parliament and The Commonwealth	322
CHAPTER EIGHT: Charles II and the 'Popish Plot', 1660–1685	333
Epilogue	373
Appendix 1: The Ikon of the Forty Martyrs of England and Wales	377

Appendix 2: Prayer to the Forty Martyrs of	
England and Wales	378
List of Sources	379
Index of Persons	393

Canonization Homily of Pope Paul VI

> I saw under the altar the souls of those who had been killed because they had proclaimed God's word and had been faithful in their witnessing.
>
> Revelation 6:9

'To all those who are filled with admiration in reading the records of these Forty Martyrs it is perfectly clear that they are worthy to stand alongside the greatest martyrs of the past; and this is not merely because of their fearless faith and constancy, but by reason of their humility, simplicity and serenity, and above all the spiritual joy and that wondrously radiant love with which they accepted their condemnation and death.'

Homily of Pope Paul VI at the Canonization of the Forty Martyrs of England and Wales, 25 October 1970

Preface

> It hath been a laudable custom in all ages, from the beginning of Christ His Church, to publish and truly set forth the singular virtues of such her children as either in their lives by rare godliness did shine above the rest, or by their patient deaths most stoutly overcame all barbarous cruelty, and both by their lives and deaths glorified God, encouraged to like victories their faithful brethren, and with invincible fortitude confounded the persecuting tyrants.

So begins *A True Report of the Life and Martyrdom of Mrs Margaret Clitherow*; written by Father John Mush in 1586; and being so bold as to try and emulate that 'laudable custom', I have written this volume.

Why a book specifically about the lives and times of the Forty Martyrs of England and Wales, and why a book now? After all, the martyrs lived hundreds of years ago, so who is interested in them? What relevance do they have today when, in the interests of 'political correctness', it is de rigueur for religious differences to be played down? The fact is that I have discovered many people are curious to know about these canonized martyrs. I have been asked several times if I could recommend 'a book' that could be acquired and I have had to reply that I was unaware of the existence of any comprehensive volume on the subject. To which has come back the rhetorical riposte, 'Then why don't you write one?'

I have a personal interest in recusant history. My ancestral family, the Pulleyns of Yorkshire, whose coat of arms was the scallop shell of St James of Compostela, their crest the pelican in her piety, suffered greatly for their Catholic Faith in penal times. They were people of influence and standing enjoying considerable wealth and property. This was all gradually eaten away in fines and confiscations until they were ruined because of their refusal to 'conform'. In the list of Yorkshire Catholics compiled for James I in 1604 – an example of the spy system under which Catholics had to live – the Pulleyns and the families

Preface

connected to them by marriage are named. The Pulleyns gave seminary priests to the Church, among them the brothers Joshua and William, sons of James Pulleyn of Killinghall. Joshua, born in 1543, was at Douai with several future martyrs. Listed as *Josue Pullan*, he was ordained priest in 1578 alongside St Alexander Briant. He returned to England in the same year and later in life, in 1594, he joined the Jesuits. He died on 3 June 1607. William was ordained deacon in the same ceremony as his kinsman, Blessed Francis Ingleby, who will feature later in the life of St Margaret Clitherow. He was ordained priest in 1583 and served as a chaplain in Flanders where he died. The Pulleyns were allied to the Catholic Inglebys of Ripley Castle by marriage. They were also related to Guy Fawkes, he of Gunpowder Plot notoriety. The headmaster of York Grammar School where Guy was educated was John Pulleyn BA. Guy's mother remarried a Pulleyn of Scotton and the boy and his sisters were partly raised in their stepfather's house – but we don't often mention that!

I have spent over thirty years studying the lives of the martyrs, trying to make them better known and loved, to keep their memory alive and encouraging devotion to them. Unlike our Catholic forebears, to whom stories of the martyrs were familiar, new generations have grown up knowing little or nothing about these heroes and heroines of the Old Faith in our land. This book has been written with such in mind, and if it introduces the martyrs for the first time to even one new person I shall be content.

There have been many pamphlets and booklets and a few biographies of individuals among the Forty; for example, the *Life of Robert Southwell* by Father Christopher Devlin SJ; *Henry Morse* by Father Philip Caraman SJ, and Evelyn Waugh's *Edmund Campion*. But I have always felt the lack of a comprehensive, single volume that gives biographies of all Forty set within their historical context. Most of the publications on the martyrs appeared many years ago, pre-dating the 1970 canonization. Many were written in a high-flown style that is not appealing to a modern readership. In any event most of them are long out of print.

Preface

The sources for the lives and deaths of the martyrs are well established. Every writer on the subject inevitably draws on these same sources and subsequently upon each other. My work is no exception. There is no new, hitherto unpublished material and I make no claim to originality. By its very nature this is a compilation and I pay heartfelt tribute to all who have gone before me whose works I have culled. I gratefully acknowledge that without their efforts this book would not have been possible. I have utilised just about every previous author on the subject. It is fair to say that I have gleaned something, either consciously or subconsciously, from every one of them over many years of reading and in the course of writing this book. As the saying goes, no one is infallible, yet in the course of my research I have been surprised by the number of errors of fact and the self-contradictions that I have detected in the works of highly respected authors on the subject.

This is not a history book, but historical background has been included in order to elucidate the conditions under which the martyrs lived. This is not a book for academics and scholars: it is intended for a general readership. Thus it would be not only quite impractical, but also extremely tedious and distracting for the non-academic reader, if I was to specifically cite every reference either in the text or as notes. Appended is an extensive list which effectively credits my sources, none of whom must be held responsible for any mistakes in the text. If there are factual errors I accept full responsibility and plead, 'Mea culpa!' The opinions expressed and the interpretation of events and characters, however perverse, are entirely my own.

                                  Malcolm Pullan
                                  20 June 2005
                                  Feast of St Alban, protomartyr of Britain,
                                  who died for sheltering a priest

Introduction

Today the word martyr is frequently misused or, even worse, sacrilegiously misappropriated by terrorist suicide bombers. It is common to hear all manner of people described in the media as 'martyrs' to various causes. They may well have suffered for their consciences' sake but they are not martyrs in the recognised Christian sense. As St Augustine of Hippo (354–430) wrote, 'It is not the pain but the cause that makes the martyr'. The word 'martyr' comes from the Greek, meaning 'one who witnesses to the truth'.

The Forty Martyrs of England and Wales gave the ultimate witness to the truth of their Faith. They laid down their lives with astounding fortitude without any bitterness or anger towards those who sought to kill them. They were motivated entirely by love for their Lord Jesus Christ and His Church. The Forty came from many different backgrounds in terms of education, social status, age and temperament. They comprise thirteen secular priests, three Benedictines, three Carthusians, one Bridgettine, two Franciscans, one Augustinian, ten Jesuits and seven laymen and women.

Compared with our Continental cousins, or in recent times the Church in Asia and Latin America, England and Wales has been slothful in promoting the causes of its saints and martyrs. When Thomas More and John Fisher were canonized in 1935, after the most intense lobbying by Catholics in England and Wales, it had been 534 years since a native Englishman had been raised to the altars. (For the record, that was St John of Bridlington; all too little known today.)[1] From the start, those put to death for the Faith were regarded as martyrs by their co-religionists. Pope Gregory XIII Buoncompagni (1572–85) acknowledged this by allowing relics of the English and Welsh martyrs to be used in altars and their pictures to be venerated. This took the form of a group of frescoes painted by Nicholas Circiniani on the walls of the church of St Thomas of Canterbury at the English College in Rome, depicting the martyrs between

Introduction

1535 and 1583. The cost of the paintings was met by George Gilbert, a wealthy Englishman in exile for his faith. The Pope also authorised public Te Deums to be sung when news of martyrs was received.

Because the victims were so widely venerated, the first moves to promote the canonization of the English and Welsh martyrs were instituted by Pope Urban VIII Barberini (1623–44) as early as 1642 at the request of the exiled English Benedictines. Owing to the ongoing persecution, together with the Civil War, the investigation process was severely hampered by the difficulty of collecting convincing evidence to prove martyrdom, a process wilfully hindered by the obstruction of the government in this country. The most important and valuable work of Dr Richard Smith, Bishop of Chalcedon (1587–1655), was his meticulous catalogue of the English and Welsh martyrs which he submitted to Rome in 1628.

Another individual to whom an incalculable debt is owed was Father Christopher Grene SJ. He was born in Ireland of English parents in 1629. Ordained in Rome in 1653, he came to England in 1658, where he joined the Society of Jesus. By 1664 he was back in Italy and became the English penitentiary (priest appointed to administer penance) at the Holy House, Loreto, and then at St Peter's, Rome. He died in retirement at the English College in 1697. He collected, preserved, transcribed and catalogued reams of letters and other documents relating to the martyrs; information that is only available to us now because of his labours, as many of the originals have long been lost. In the eighteenth century, the work of Bishop Smith was updated, amplified and published by a saint whose cause we English have been neglectful of promoting: the Venerable Bishop Richard Challoner, Vicar Apostolic of the London District (1691–1781).[2] Challoner's *Memoirs of Missionary Priests* became the basis of the records of the martyrs whose cause was not revived until 1855, when following the restoration of the Catholic hierarchy the indefatigable Father John Morris SJ took it up in earnest.

The Synod of Westminster, held in 1859, unsuccessfully petitioned the Holy See in the hope of obtaining a papal decree officially approving the cult of the martyrs. It was not until 1874

Introduction

that a formal process was opened for 361 martyrs. The process proved difficult and time-consuming, not least because of the sheer number of martyrs involved. Tribute must be paid to the priests of the London Oratory for their commitment and devotion in collecting evidence in a form acceptable to Rome. In December 1886 Pope Leo XIII Pecci (1878–1903) introduced the Cause of 254 martyrs, and fifty-four were beatified, followed by nine others in May 1895. These sixty-three corresponded with those honoured by Pope Gregory XIII. In 1923 Cardinal Francis Bourne OP, Archbishop of Westminster (1903–1935), resumed the process, and in 1929 Pope Pius XI Ratti (1922–39) beatified a further 136 martyrs, although 241 had been submitted, entitling them to the epithet 'Venerable'. With the exception of the special case of More and Fisher, it took a further ninety-six years before any other martyrs were canonized.

The English and Welsh hierarchy decided once more to resume the martyrs' cause, but with just a small group. The names of the Forty Martyrs were submitted in December 1960 to the Holy See, which accepted the group as forming one Cause. Before that date, reports of many favours and cures attributed to the intercession of the Blessed Martyrs of England and Wales had been brought to the attention of the hierarchy and the authorities in Rome. Once the group of forty names were known there was an official and intense nationwide campaign of prayer. As a result, data on over twenty 'miracles' was presented to Cardinal William Godfrey, Archbishop of Westminster (1956–1963), who passed on the information to the Sacred Congregation in Rome. These claims were examined by medical experts of international repute and two particularly noteworthy cases were submitted to the Holy See. One of these, the cure of a malignant tumour in a young mother, was judged by the medical team to be perfect, constant and inexplicable by any natural means.

Pope Paul VI Montini (1963–78) confirmed the miraculous nature of the cure through the intercession of the Forty Martyrs. The Pope signified that he was prepared to go ahead with their canonization on the basis of this one miracle, bearing in mind that in the exceptional case of Fisher and More a dispensation had been given to proceed without a miracle. So, amidst great

Introduction

rejoicing, the canonization ceremony took place in St Peter's Basilica on 25 October 1970, with Pope Paul trying valiantly to cope with the pronunciation of the forty English and Welsh names as he read them out in chronological order.

The canonization of the Forty Martyrs must be set in the wider context of the multitude of martyrs and confessors who gave their lives for the Catholic Faith. The Forty are to be seen as representatives of those Catholics who suffered for their faith in various parts of England and Wales between 1534 and 1729. Some may be surprised that I include this late date when the 'accepted' date is usually taken as 1681, but the fact is that there were priests who continued to be imprisoned in the reign of William III (1689–1702) and under the Hanoverians. For example, there was the Franciscan Paul Atkinson of St Francis, a Yorkshireman who was condemned to perpetual imprisonment in 1699 after being betrayed by a servant in order to obtain the £100 reward on offer. He served thirty years in Hurst Castle on the Solent.

Why the decision was taken by the hierarchy to promote the Cause of only forty of the beatified martyrs, and exactly what motivated the choice of that particular forty in preference to others is not at all obvious. The explanation cannot be that the remainder were regarded as 'second-class' martyrs. And it was certainly not the case that there was more information in the form of the requisite documentary proof available about the forty selected than any other martyrs. Reasons advanced for the choice of those included in the Forty were the extent of devotion to each of them and how representative they were as regards place of origin and status. But I have to admit I never found this very convincing, given the equally strong and continuous devotion to many other martyrs such as Robert Ludlam, Nicholas Garlick, George Haydock and above all Nicholas Postgate. I suspect an underlying element of timidity on the part of those in Britain promoting the martyrs' Cause. Providing proof to Rome was certainly a daunting task, so was there fear of the potential costs and the time factor? Or was there overanxiety about upsetting ecumenical relations, particularly with the Anglican Church? Whatever the reservations of the Protestant Establishment, it should not have affected the judgement of the Church as to the

Introduction

sanctity of the Forty Martyrs. It was charitably courteous to wish to avoid distressing our Anglican friends by reminding them of the uncomfortable fact that their Church had been established by persecution, but the lengths to which the Catholic Church went to avoid that possibility seemed to me excessive. The monitoring of newspaper and magazine articles and general media reactions to assess the 'opportuneness' of the Cause, holding apologetic press conferences and seeking reassurances from the British Council of Churches, all looks rather 'over the top' and immature with hindsight. What need had the Church to apologise for honouring its martyred members? It served only to demonstrate how insecure and unsure of themselves Catholics still were about their place in British society.

I have no wish to be critical of the dedicated efforts of those admirable promoters involved at the time. But whatever the sincere motivation of those responsible, it can be cogently argued that the very process of selection has resulted, albeit unintentionally, in a grave injustice being done to hundreds of other martyrs equally worthy of veneration and the honour of being 'raised to the altars'. This applies above all to the inexplicable omission of those who were the actual *companions* in martyrdom of those numbered among the Forty. Even 'secular' authors such as Professor J P Kenyon, in his masterly and definitive study, *The Popish Plot* (1972), are baffled by the apparent inconsistency of the Catholic Church in its canonization policy with regard to the English martyrs. To quote Kenyon, 'This distinction cannot be explained by reference to historical sources', and he cites the specific case of Nicholas Postgate to illustrate his point.

Sufficient evidence having been amassed, a further group of eighty-four English and Welsh martyrs, plus the Scotsman George Douglas, who was executed at York, was beatified on 22 November 1987 by Pope John Paul II Wojtyla (1979–2005). There remain another thirty Venerable martyrs whose beatification cause was deferred in 1929; these too were regarded by their contemporaries, and ever afterwards, as genuine martyrs; but obtaining corroborative evidence now seems highly unlikely. The Church is, quite rightly, wary of treating as martyrs any

Introduction

whose deaths may have had 'political' connotations. Yet there are among the beatified martyrs some whose actions which led to their deaths may be construed as 'political', e.g. John Felton, 1570, Thomas Plumtree, 1570, Thomas Percy, 1572, or Edward Coleman, 1678.

In addition there is a supplementary list of 242 *praetermissi*, including twenty-four women, who died in prison. Many of these Venerable and 'passed over' martyrs were products of the seminaries, undertook the same dangerous work and suffered the same penalties, but their lives were spent in such obscurity that little is known about them. A great many others, religious and laymen and women, died in prison, confessors for the Faith. The problem is trying to prove that they died as a direct result of their imprisonment. At this distance in time it is difficult to see how such evidence will ever be forthcoming. But by the same token how can one differentiate between them and the case of St Philip Howard? It is to be fervently hoped that one day at least all the beatified martyrs of England and Wales will be formally enrolled by the Church among the saints.

Finally a word about nomenclature. Until relatively recent times only priests who were religious (i.e. belonging to a religious order) were called 'Father'; secular priests were called 'Mr', and that is how it would have been throughout the period covered by this book. However, for modern readership unfamiliar with these niceties it might prove confusing, therefore for the sake of clarity I have opted for the anachronism of referring to all priests as 'Father'.

Notes to the Introduction

[1] St John of Bridlington was born in East Yorkshire and studied at Oxford before becoming an Augustinian Canon at Bridlington. He held a number of offices in the monastery before being elected prior in 1362. A real man of prayer he was an outstanding and greatly loved and revered leader of his community. He died in 1379 and many miracles took place at his tomb. He was canonized in 1401.

[2] Bishop Richard Challoner was born at Lewes, Sussex in 1691. He was ordained at Douai in 1716 and spent the next fourteen years at the College as a professor and Vice-President. In 1730 he returned to England and ten years later was appointed a bishop and coadjutor to the Vicar Apostolic of the London District, Benjamin Petre, whom he succeeded in 1758. He was Vicar Apostolic until his death in 1781. Challoner's 'Memoirs of Missionary Priests' consists of biographies of around 300 Catholics who suffered for their faith between 1577 and 1684. It is an invaluable source of information as he made use of material that is no longer extant. He compiled one of the most popular and enduring prayer books for private devotions amongst English Catholics: the 'Garden of the Soul'. In 1749–50 he also published his revision of the Douai-Rheims Bible. His remains rest in Westminster Cathedral. The cause for the beatification of this wise and holy bishop was introduced many years ago but now sadly seems to have been abandoned.

Chapter One

The Henrician Martyrs

> No man is justified in doing evil on the ground of expediency.
>
> Theodore Roosevelt, 1858–1919

The martyrs' story begins in the reign of that abominable Tudor autocrat King Henry VIII (1509–47). Henry's enthusiastic profession of ultra-orthodox Catholicism in 1521 had earned him the title 'Defender of the Faith' from Pope Leo X Medici (1513–21) for his best-selling book in defence of the Seven Sacraments against Luther. Henry was so obsequious in expressing his devotion to the Holy See that Sir Thomas More counselled him to be more circumspect. However, when it came to the crunch and the teaching of the Church clashed with Henry's personal desires, his egoism carried the day.

Pared down to its simplest elements, the story ran as follows. In order to marry his mistress, Anne Boleyn, Henry was determined to divorce his lawful wife, Catherine of Aragon (1485–1536), to whom he had been married for twenty years. She had borne him three sons and two daughters, but only Princess Mary had survived. The self-righteous Henry was so egocentric that it never seems to have occurred to him that the Church would do any other than eventually give him what he desired just because he, the King, desired it. His case for marrying Anne was not helped by the fact that her elder sister, Mary, had already been Henry's mistress and in Canon Law this constituted a serious impediment.

Queen Catherine was much loved and undoubtedly enjoyed the support not only of a great many of the nobility and clergy, but also of the majority of the English people. Assailed on all sides, and believing it impossible to obtain a fair hearing in England, Catherine referred her case to Rome. In spite of all the

The Henrician Martyrs

bullying pressure exerted on him by Henry, Pope Clement VII Medici (1523–34) for various reasons – by no means all of them edifying or spiritual – vacillated about granting Henry's wish to have his marriage nullified. If Clement had had the courage to refuse an annulment immediately and not let the matter drag on, engendering greater resentment from Henry with each passing year, it is possible that the situation could have been salvaged and England saved from schism. Yet there has to be some sneaking sympathy for Clement. Following the Sack of Rome in 1527, Clement was the captive of the Emperor Charles V, and as the Emperor was uncle to Queen Catherine the Pope dared not offend him by giving in to Henry.

Amongst Catherine's supporters were Bishop John Fisher of Rochester and Sir Thomas More. William Warham, the devout and learned humanist Archbishop of Canterbury (1503–32), had at first been lukewarm in Catherine's cause but when he realised the direction in which ecclesiastical matters were going he woke up to the gravity of the situation and opposed the divorce in Parliament and all Acts derogatory to the Pope's authority. He died in August 1532, aged eighty-two. Henry was beside himself with rage and frustration at the delay in getting a papal decision. If the Pope could not, or would not, give him what he wanted then he would repudiate the Pope and find someone else who would accede to his wishes.

In March 1533, Archdeacon Thomas Cranmer (1489–1556), a former chaplain to the Boleyn family, was appointed Archbishop of Canterbury. In spite of being warned of Cranmer's unsuitability for the primacy, Pope Clement, anxious to mollify Henry, gave his approval of the appointment to the See of Canterbury. Cranmer, of course, hypocritically went along with his charade of loyalty to Rome just long enough to secure his installation as archbishop. A man of Protestant sympathies, Cranmer had defied the Church's discipline by secretly marrying a German Lutheran. He kept his marriage such a closely guarded secret that it is doubtful if Henry ever knew about it.

The King's compliant archbishop conveniently annulled his master's marriage to Catherine on 23 May. Cranmer did so in order to ensure that the child Anne was carrying would be legitimate, Anne and Henry having already been secretly married

The Henrician Martyrs

at Whitehall Palace four months earlier on 25 January. On 1 June, the obviously pregnant Anne was crowned queen by Cranmer. On 11 July, Pope Clement ineffectually retaliated to the news from London by excommunicating Henry and Cranmer, and declaring the purported annulment of the King's marriage to Catherine and his marriage to Anne Boleyn null and void.

In March 1534 the Act of Succession declared Princess Mary, the King's daughter by Catherine, a bastard, and made it an offence punishable by death to deny the validity of the King's new marriage. The first victims of the Act were Elizabeth Barton, the visionary 'Holy Maid of Kent', and some of her supporters.[1] After seven years of vacillation, on 23 March 1534 Pope Clement finally declared the King's first marriage to be valid and his marriage to Anne unlawful. In the end the papal judgment was morally right, but had political circumstances been different it is difficult to resist the conclusion that Clement would have felt it pragmatically expedient to sacrifice Queen Catherine in the wider political interest. However the papal procrastination only served to seriously damage even further the diminished respect in which the papacy was held in England.

Henry had first declared himself Supreme Head of the Church in England in 1531. On 11 February the majority of the Convocations of Clergy of Canterbury and York had tamely accepted the title adding the proviso, 'so far as the law of God allows' – a meaningless quibble. Bishop John Fisher of Rochester was the only dissenting voice. In 1532 the Church had surrendered its independence and canon law to the King. On 18 November 1534 Parliament subserviently ratified the de facto situation by passing the Act of Supremacy, in which, without any qualification, the King was declared to be 'the only supreme head on earth of the Church in England' with full powers, including spiritual, over clergy and laity. In a sense the Act only legalised what, in reality, had already been achieved. Papal jurisdiction had been formally severed, thereby putting England and Wales into schism from Rome.

With the exception of John Fisher, the bishops, who should have been the chief shepherds of their flock, lamentably failed in their responsibility. Why? The only explanation can be the quality of the bishops, their lukewarm faith, and the general malaise infecting parts of the Church. Everything that was wrong with the

The Henrician Martyrs

Church was epitomised by the career of Thomas Wolsey, by whom many of the bishops had been appointed. Those he elevated had been required to pay him for their bishoprics. They were men who could be counted on primarily to be loyal to him in order to secure his continued patronage and maintain him in power rather than for their outstanding spiritual attributes. From humble beginnings, Wolsey rose by intelligence, talent, industry and driving ambition to become Lord Chancellor and a Cardinal. But alongside these qualities he loved power, wealth and ostentation, his style of living rivalling that of the King for its lavishness and splendour. An absentee pluralist, in 1514 he was made Archbishop of York, and during the same period he held the bishoprics of Durham and Winchester. For a priest, his personal life was immoral. He had two children by his mistress. When Wolsey failed to deliver the annulment of the King's marriage, he bore the brunt of the Henry's anger and plummeted from power. Facing charges of treason he died in 1530, remorsefully wishing that he had served his God as diligently as he had served his King. Against this background, it is little wonder then that the bishops in a weakened Church without a strong leader had neither the faith nor courage to offer any resistance to the King.

The new Treason Act of 1534 (26 Henry VIII, c. 13), the culmination of anti-papal legislation, rendered it an offence punishable by death to deny the King his title. Henceforth it was high treason to deny in any way the King's supremacy. The Act introduced an entirely new principle into English law: treason could now be committed simply by words or opinion, and even Parliament's caveat by inserting 'maliciously' into the Act did nothing to lighten its oppressive impact. It was this Act that led to the martyrdoms of Henry's reign. The martyrs wished to continue as loyal subjects of the Crown but conscientiously refused to accept the King's spiritual supremacy, knowing that to do so rendered them guilty under the regime's newly invented notion of treason.

The first martyrs under the Act of Supremacy came from an unlikely source: the quiet cloisters of the Carthusian Order, eighteen of whose members were to suffer for their opposition. The chief source for our information about them comes from the

The Henrician Martyrs

contemporary account, *Historia aliquot nostri saeculi martyrum*, by Dom Maurice Chauncy, which exists in several versions. Chauncy was born at Sawbridgeworth, Hertfordshire, in 1509 and studied law at Gray's Inn before joining the London Charterhouse at around the time of John Houghton's election as prior. As a monk of the Charterhouse during the last few years of its existence, Chauncy was intimately acquainted with the martyrs and the life of the monastery. Although inclined to hagiographical hyperbole, as an eyewitness of many of the events he describes his trustworthiness is unimpeachable.

John Houghton, Robert Lawrence and Augustine Webster

That little spark of celestial fire called conscience

George Washington, 1732–99

What was to develop into the Carthusian Order was established in 1084 by St Bruno at Chartreuse near Grenoble; hence the Anglicisation to Charterhouse. By the reign of Henry VIII there were nine Charterhouses in England. The first English houses were both in Somerset: Witham, founded in 1178 by Henry II, followed by Hinton in 1227. Beauvale in Nottinghamshire was founded in 1343 by Sir Nicholas de Cantilupe. The Charterhouse of the Salutation of the Mother of God had been founded at Smithfield in 1371 by Sir Walter Manny, one of the knights of Edward III, and endowed by Bishop Northburgh of London. Eventually the monastery occupied about thirty acres, which included not only the monastic buildings but also an orchard and vegetable garden. It had an advanced piped water supply, drawn from a spring a mile or so away at Islington, fed into the monastery by underground lead pipes. The monastery was more than a century in construction. The remnant that exists today dates from the early Tudor period. It is just possible that the initials 'I. H.' that can be discerned in dark brick on a wall of the court are those of John Houghton. The church, as prescribed by the rules of the Order, was plain and austere. The cells, as in all

The Henrician Martyrs

Charterhouses, consisted of a two-storey house which stood in its own garden. Each had a workroom, oratory, bedroom and living room. In probably the most austere of all religious orders, the white-robed monks keep silence and live alone, usually eating alone except on Sundays and feast days, when they congregate in the refectory. They live on a vegetarian diet: Carthusians eat fish but never eat meat. They talk to each other on Sundays after refectory, when it is the custom to go for a walk outside the monastery.

Between 1499 and 1503, while still a law student, Thomas More frequently stayed at the monastery, joining in the offices and testing his vocation. Contemporaries said that if you wanted to hear the liturgy beautifully celebrated, the Charterhouse was the place to go. No religious house had a finer reputation. The monks were deeply respected for their strict observance of the rule and the number of applicants of quality wishing to join the community was so great that there was a waiting list.

In the period covered by this narrative there were three priors at the Charterhouse. Firstly there was William Tynbygh 1500–29, a man of conspicuous holiness, to whom must be attributed the high standards that distinguished his community; secondly came John Batmanson 1529–31; and thirdly John Houghton.

John Houghton was born in Essex in 1486 or '87. He studied Civil and Canon Law at Cambridge University and can most probably be identified with the student of that name who took his degree in Civil Law in 1506. Having returned to his parents' home in Essex, he found that they expected him to make a good marriage. But John had other ideas: he wanted to be a priest. We are told that he left home in secret to train for the priesthood. He went back home after his ordination and for about four years served as a parish priest before entering the London Charterhouse in 1515. In 1522 he became Sacrist and in 1527 was dismayed when appointed Procurator. The reason for his distress was that this office required him to travel outside the monastery on matters of business which interrupted his observance of solitude and silence.

In 1531, John – whom Chauncy tells us was 'of short stature, of dignified appearance; modest and gracious in speech' – was

The Henrician Martyrs

elected Prior of Beauvale, Nottinghamshire. Later that same year he returned to London, having been unanimously elected Prior of the London Charterhouse. There were thirty priest choir monks and eighteen lay brothers, most of them relatively young men. During his tenure of office the reputation of the house increased to an even higher level, under the guidance of a man whose combined qualities of holiness and leadership skills were an inspiration to his monks. Chauncy was of the opinion that even had Houghton not died a martyr he would have been worthy of sainthood. In 1532, the General Chapter of the Order appointed John as Provincial Visitor for England. This meant that he was required to make inspections every two years and report on the condition of all the Carthusian houses in the country.

Robert Lawrence, a monk of the London Charterhouse, succeeded John Houghton as Prior of Beauvale. Little is known of his early life. It has been suggested that he came from Dorset, and he may be the Robert Lawrence who took a degree in Civil Law at Cambridge in 1508. It is also possible that he may have served for a time as a chaplain to the Duke of Norfolk.

Augustine Webster was born about 1480. He was a monk of the Charterhouse of Jesus of Bethlehem at Sheen, Surrey; the largest of the English Charterhouses, it had been founded by Henry V (1413–22). Augustine too had studied at Cambridge, and is most likely the student of that name who is recorded as having taken the degrees of Bachelor and Master of Arts. In 1531 he became Prior of the Charterhouse of the Visitation of Our Lady, in the Isle of Axholme, Lincolnshire, which had been founded around 1395 by Thomas Mowbray, Earl Marshal of England.

Henry VIII was determined that the validity of his marriage to Anne Boleyn should be recognised and thereby secure the succession to the throne of their children, so the Carthusians, along with everyone else, were required to swear to the Act of Succession. On 4 May 1534, royal commissioners visited the London Charterhouse requiring the monks to take an oath to that effect. Prior Houghton told them that monks did not meddle in the King's affairs, but also gave the opinion that he did not see how a marriage of such long duration as the King's to Catherine could be invalid. Along with Father Humphrey Middlemore, the

The Henrician Martyrs

Procurator, John was imprisoned in the Tower. They were released after being persuaded to take the oath conditionally, i.e. so far as it was lawful; but the rest of the community were reluctant to swear even on those terms. Archdeacon Thomas Bedyll and Bishop Lee of Lichfield, the royal commissioners, again visited the Charterhouse on 29 May 1534, but without success. Only when Bishop Lee brought one of the sheriffs of London with an armed band of men on 6 June did they manage to secure the reluctant acceptance of all the community to the conditional oath.

When the Act of Supremacy without any qualification came into force, backed up by the Treason Act, Houghton was under no illusion that he and his community would face further trials. In April 1535 the royal commissioners were due to descend upon the Charterhouse to obtain the sworn acceptance of the monks to the Act of Supremacy, or risk being charged with high treason should they refuse. John asked for three days of special preparation to be held. The first was devoted to prayers and Prior Houghton's homily was a meditation on Psalm 59: 'Save me from my enemies, my God; protect me from those who attack me…' He concluded by saying, 'It is better for us to bear some brief punishment for our faults than to be preserved for eternal torments.' The second day was given over to confession and reconciliation with each other, and the third to a votive Mass of the Holy Spirit. It was a most moving experience for all the community. While this triduum was taking place, apparently quite by coincidence, Priors Lawrence and Webster came to London to consult with John Houghton and their brethren.

The three priors sought an interview with Thomas Cromwell (1485–1540),[2] Henry VIII's chief secretary and since 1535 Ecclesiastical Vicar General. Cromwell, along with his protégé, Richard Rich (*c*.1496–1567),[3] was responsible for the visitation and eventual suppression of the monasteries, euphemistically referred to as the 'dissolution'. This was the man the three monks naively hoped to persuade to give them exemption, or at least to agree a form of the oath that would be acceptable to their communities. Cromwell treated them discourteously and refused to listen. He committed all three of them to the Tower and on 20

April they were brought before Cromwell, Rich, Bedyll and others. They remained steadfast in their refusal to take the oath and consistent in the reasons they adduced for doing so. The priors declared themselves willing to take the oath if, once again, they could add, 'as far as the law of God allows'. But Cromwell would permit no such condition, and insisted that the oath be taken without reservation, which the three priors refused to do.

Richard Reynolds

> Integer vitae scelerisque purus
> *A man of upright life and free from guilt*
>
> Horace, *Odes* I, 22 (65–8 BC)

Joining the Carthusians in their stand was Richard Reynolds, a monk of the Bridgettine Order from Syon Abbey, Middlesex. Probably born in Devon about 1490, he had joined the Bridgettines after an exceptionally distinguished career at Cambridge. He took his BA in 1506 and his MA in 1509, becoming a fellow of Corpus Christi College where he attained the degree of Bachelor of Divinity in 1513, the same year in which he was appointed University Preacher.

The Bridgettine Order had been founded in 1346 by St Bridget (Birgitta) of Sweden (1303–73) and developed by her daughter St Catherine (Katrin) of Sweden (1331–81). The monastery of St Saviour and St Bridget, known as Syon Abbey, was the only Bridgettine house in England. Situated by the River Thames near Isleworth, it had been endowed by Henry V in 1415. It was a double monastery, consisting of separate enclosures for men and women with an abbess in overall charge of all temporal affairs. Each community had separate choirs in a common monastery church. An enclosed order, the Bridgettines were noted for their austerity as well as for their strictness in accepting new members. A contemporary chronicler called Syon 'the most virtuous house of religion in the land'.

It was well known to Queen Catherine and her daughter Mary, who often paid visits when staying at the nearby Richmond

Palace. Syon was also in the vanguard of what we would call evangelisation, taking advantage of the opportunities offered by the invention of printing. The many spiritual volumes that they produced were intended not only for religious but also for the growing lay reading public. These included an English translation of Thomas à Kempis's *Imitation of Christ* by Richard Whytford,[4] probably the best known member of the Bridgettine community at Syon.

The Bridgettine way of life, study and prayer, was eminently suitable for someone of Reynolds's temperament. When he was professed at Syon in 1513, he presented his great collection of books to its library. A friend of Sir Thomas More, he was a famous spiritual counsellor and preacher; one of the most respected, wise and learned priests of his time, he was familiar with Latin, Greek and Hebrew. Many people consulted him, particularly when the question of the King's divorce arose. These included Bishop John Fisher, who was Queen Catherine's chief supporter. But apart from his learning, Richard was also renowned for the holiness of his life. Chauncy was not the only contemporary to describe Richard as a man of angelic countenance and angelic life.

It was inevitable that Syon would attract the attention of the government, and that the 'King's great matter' would soon penetrate its hallowed precincts. In 1534 royal officials had visited the monastery in an effort to secure the signatures of the community acknowledging the validity of the King's second marriage. A draft was signed but the wording was too ambiguous to satisfy the King. A second, more explicit draft was submitted, which the brothers refused to sign, urging the nuns to follow suit. Queen Anne Boleyn made a personal visit to Syon in September 1534, presumably to see if that might persuade the community. Evidently it did not. By November 1534 the government had made the Oath of Succession obligatory, quickly to be followed by the Act of Supremacy.

Cromwell had to crush the opposition coming from the Carthusians and the Bridgettines, who enjoyed such high reputations. Cromwell clearly thought that if he could induce a man of such intellectual brilliance and holiness as Richard

Reynolds to take the Oath of Supremacy it would persuade others to follow. It cannot be without significance that Richard was the only one of the Syon community who was apprehended at this time. His arrest came in the spring of 1535 and he was sent to the Tower a few days after the Carthusian priors. On 25 April Cromwell and the royal commissioners came to see all four prisoners in the Tower, demanding that they should renounce the authority of the Pope and acknowledge that the King was supreme head of the Church in England. The answers they gave to the interrogations they underwent can still be read in the Public Records Office.

> John Houghton says he cannot take the King, our Sovereign Lord to be supreme head of the Church of England afore the apostles of Christ's Church.
>
> Robert Lawrence says that there is one Catholic Church of which the Bishop of Rome is the head; therefore he cannot believe that the King is supreme head of the Church.
>
> Augustine Webster says that he cannot take the King to be supreme head of the Church, but him that is by the doctors of the Church taken as head of the Church, that is the Bishop of Rome, as Ambrose, Jerome and Augustine affirm and is made at the Council of Basle.

Speaking for all the prisoners, Richard fearlessly replied that they could only accept the proposition 'so far as the law of Christ allows'. Following this encounter, Cromwell and the King agreed that the priests should be charged with high treason and sent for trial, knowing that the outcome of any trial would be a foregone conclusion. On 28 April 1535 the three Priors and Reynolds were taken for trial at Westminster Hall. The original indictment is still extant in the Public Records Office, leaving no doubt as to the reason they were convicted for 'Treacherously machinating and desiring to deprive the King of his title as Supreme Head of the Church and at the Tower of London on 26th April openly declaring "The King our Sovereign Lord is not Supreme Head on earth of the Church of England"'. They were joined by an elderly secular priest, John Haile, Vicar of Isleworth.[5]

A special commission was appointed to hear the case. Its

The Henrician Martyrs

members included Sir Thomas Audley, the Lord Chancellor; the Duke of Norfolk; the Marquis of Exeter; the Earl of Cumberland; the Earl of Wiltshire, who was Anne Boleyn's father; and Viscount Rochford, who was her brother, together with Thomas Cromwell, Sir Anthony Fitzherbert and other lawyers. All the accused pleaded 'not guilty' and a jury was sworn. Evidence was presented to show that Richard had encouraged others to oppose the divorce and the royal supremacy.

The prisoners were sent back to the Tower while the jury deliberated at length late into the evening. When Cromwell sent to ask why they had not yet reached a verdict, they responded that they could not find such holy men guilty, especially as they did not find it proved that they had – as was required by the Act – 'maliciously' denied the supremacy. Cromwell was furious and personally threatened the jurors with imprisonment and death. Only after this overnight intimidation did they bring in the required guilty verdict. Reynolds, Haile and the three priors were summoned back to Westminster the following day and urged to recant before sentence was passed. Richard seems to have acted as spokesman for all the accused.

In response to questions from the Lord Chancellor, he started by saying that it had been his intention to follow the example of Our Lord and keep silent before his accusers, but now felt that his conscience required him to speak out. He appealed to the rest of European Christendom and to the continuous history of the Church in England, which had owed allegiance to Rome for a thousand years.

Richard declared, 'I say that our belief is of greater weight and has far more abundant testimony in its behalf than yours. For instead of the few whom you bring forward out of the parliament of this kingdom I have the whole of Christendom in my favour. I can even say I have all this kingdom in my favour, although the smaller part holds with you, for I am sure the larger part is at heart of my opinion, although outwardly, partly from fear and partly from hope, they profess to be of yours in the hope of retaining royal favour. As to dead witnesses, I have on my side all the General Councils, all historians, the holy doctors of the Church for the last fifteen hundred years.'

The Henrician Martyrs

When warned only to answer to the charge that he had maliciously and against the King's authority tried to persuade many from submitting to the King's Majesty, he replied, 'If I were here arraigned before God's own tribunal, it would be made clear that never to a living man have I declared an opinion of my own maliciously against the King or anyone.' He said he had only spoken of the matter to clear his conscience or when asked about it in confession. 'I was indeed grieved to learn that His Majesty had fallen into so grave an error, but I said so to no one, except as I have declared. And had I not then declared what I believe I would say it openly now, seeing that I am bound by God and my conscience and in doing so neither my Sovereign nor anyone else may rightly take offence.'

At this point he was ordered to be silent. He replied, 'Since you will not let me say more, judge me according to your law.'

After the inevitable sentence had been pronounced, Richard asked if they could have two or three days in order to prepare for death. He was told this request was not in the judges' power to grant but rested with the King. The request was met, but the condemned were not left in a great deal of peace because Archbishop Cranmer and Cromwell did all in their power to get them to change their minds, sending various representatives to argue with them, but without any success.

On 4 May 1535 all five priests, wearing their religious habits, were dragged on hurdles through the streets of London from the Tower to Tyburn. Sir Thomas More was then a prisoner in the Tower awaiting trial. It so happened that on the day of the priests' execution his daughter Margaret Roper had been given permission to visit him. Through the narrow windows of his cell, father and daughter were able to see what was taking place.

'Lo, dost thou not see, Meg,' said More, 'that these blessed fathers be now as cheerfully going to their deaths as bridegrooms to their marriage? Whereas thy silly father, Meg… hath passed forth the whole course of his miserable life most sinfully, God, thinking him not worthy so soon to come to that eternal felicity, leaveth him here to be plagued with misery.'

Tyburn, to the west of London, had been the place for executions since the late twelfth century. The grisly ritual required the condemned to be tied onto hurdles, primitive frames that jolted along uncomfortably pulled by horses. The gallows consisted of a wooden upright against which a ladder was rested. The rope was placed around the neck and the condemned had to climb the ladder which, at the moment deemed appropriate, was pushed away, leaving the victim dangling.

A great crowd of spectators had gathered for the priests' execution. Eustace Chapuys, the Imperial Ambassador, who described the event, informs us that the leading nobility and most of the Court were present. Even on the scaffold, each one of the priests was offered a pardon if he would take the oath. Despite knowing the terrible consequences, each one refused. They faced the most barbarous of deaths. They were hanged by a rope around the neck, causing slow strangulation, but not long enough for them to die. While alive they were to be cut down, their genitals cut off, their insides ripped open with a knife, their heart and inner organs torn out and burned, and finally their bodies were to be cut into four sections and beheaded. As if that was not enough, there was the stomach-churning stench as the severed quarters were parboiled to help preserve them for public display.

John Houghton was the first to die. He embraced the executioner and forgave him for what he was about to do. He spoke up. 'I call Almighty God to witness, and I beseech all here present to attest for me on the dreadful day of judgement, that being about to die in public, I declare that I have refused to comply with the will of His Majesty the King, not from obstinacy, malice or a rebellious spirit, but solely for fear of offending the supreme Majesty of God. Our holy mother the Church has decreed and enjoined otherwise than the King and Parliament have decreed. I am therefore bound in conscience, and am ready and willing to suffer every kind of torture rather than deny a doctrine of the Church. Pray for me and have pity on me, my brethren, of whom I have been the unworthy prior. In Thee, O Lord, have I hoped; let me never be confounded.'

After he had been hanging for a while the rope was cut. John's habit was torn off revealing his hair shirt, and as the horrific butchery began while he was fully conscious, he cried out, 'Jesus, have mercy on me in this hour!' As the executioner groped for his heart, John was heard to say, 'Good Jesu, what will you do with my heart?'

His companions, who had to watch this ghastly spectacle taking place, showed no sign of human weakness, but rather called upon the crowd to live good lives and to serve the King faithfully in everything that was not contrary to the law of God and His Church. Reynolds, being the last to die, stood encouraging his brothers, calling on them to think of the heavenly banquet they would all soon be sharing together after 'their sharp breakfast, taken patiently for their Master's sake'. Eyewitnesses commented that Richard did not appear in the least upset or fearful, but submitted courageously to his torments.

The dismembered parts of the martyrs' bodies were displayed around the city of London as a warning to others, and Prior Houghton's left arm was hung up over the Charterhouse gate.

On 4 May, the same day as the priors' execution, Archdeacon Thomas Bedyll, the royal commissioner who had achieved some measure of success in persuading the Carthusians at Sheen, arrived at the monastery. Cromwell installed resident agents to report on the remaining monks. All their books were confiscated and they were forced to endure violent anti-papal harangues in an effort to break their resolve. We learn from Chauncy that the monks were deprived of food and drink and were constantly harassed so that they could not perform the daily monastic offices, being detained by diatribes from the commissioners.

These tactics went on for about three weeks and when they had no effect, Father Humphrey Middlemore,[6] whom Houghton had appointed Vicar and was now in charge of the monastery, and Father William Exmew,[7] the Procurator, along with Father Sebastian Newdigate,[8] were arrested. They were first sent to Cromwell at his house in Stepney before being committed to the Tower. They were treated with inhuman cruelty, being tied upright to posts with iron collars and chains around their necks and legs. Unable to move they were left in this state for two weeks enduring the stench of their own excrement. They were tried by a special commission presided over by Audley and defended themselves with arguments from Scripture and Tradition in favour of the papal primacy as to why the King could

The Henrician Martyrs

not be the head of the Church. Having been refused permission to receive Holy Communion on Saturday, 19 June 1535, they were hanged, drawn and quartered in their religious habits at Tyburn. This was quickly followed on 22 June by the execution of John Fisher,[9] Cardinal Bishop of Rochester on Tower Hill. On 6 July, Sir Thomas More met the same fate.[10]

Cromwell continued to bring every pressure to bear to wear down the resolve of the monks now deprived of leadership. In 1536 he appointed the subservient William Trafford, a member of the Sheen community and a former Procurator at Beauvale, as Prior of the London Charterhouse. Twenty choir monks and eighteen brothers remained: of the 'refuseniks' two of the most obdurate priests, John Rochester[11] and James Walworth, were sent to the Charterhouse at Hull. This monastery had been founded in 1378 but had been one of the houses already suppressed. A small group of monks had begged to be allowed to return and did so, only to find the place stripped bare. There John and James were left as virtual prisoners until March 1537 when they were placed in custody at St Mary's Monastery, York. The Duke of Norfolk, then in residence in the city, was reminded about them. He described John Rochester as a malign spirit who still believed in the primacy of the Pope and who might influence the opinions of others in that direction. On 15 May 1537, refusing to submit, the two monks were hanged in chains at York by order of the Duke, their bodies being left hanging on the walls of the city.

On 10 June, half of the monks, in the hope of saving the Charterhouse, capitulated by accepting the Royal Supremacy. Although Chauncy's signature does not appear amongst those who signed the oath he nonetheless admitted to having taken it, albeit against his conscience. His cowardice on this occasion seems to have haunted him for the rest of his life. Ten members of the community[12], three priests, a deacon and six brothers, refused to submit and were sent to Newgate, where they were chained to posts upright and left without food. Margaret Clement née Giggs,[13] the foster-daughter of Thomas More, bribed the jailer to let her visit the prisoners disguised as a milkmaid. She smuggled food in and fed them and tried to clean them of their filth, but when queries were raised as to why the prisoners were not already dead the jailer was too afraid to let her into the prison again. Nine of them were deliberately starved to death. The survivor, Blessed William Horne, was kept in the Tower for three years and finally hanged, drawn and quartered at Tyburn on 4 August 1540. Executed with him were Lawrence Cook, Carmelite Prior of Doncaster, Thomas Epson, a Benedictine, William Bird, Vicar of Bradford-on-Avon, and a layman, Giles Heron, the former ward and then son-in-law of Thomas More. Heron was hanged for high treason, although the official records offer no explanation as to what he was alleged to have done.

In the meantime, in exchange for a paltry pension, on 15 November 1539 Prior William Trafford had surrendered the remnant of the Charterhouse to the King under the most abject terms. The twelve surviving monks and six lay brothers were expelled, and Archdeacon Bedyll asked that the Charterhouse might be put to some 'better use'. Henry granted the property for use as a store for his hunting tents. In 1555 the buildings were granted to Sir Edward North, who turned them into a stately home for himself. He demolished the cloister and converted the chapel into a dining hall. In 1565 the property was sold to the Duke of Norfolk. It was destined to eventually become the famous public school.

John Stone

'Nothing in his life became him like the leaving of it.'

Macbeth, William Shakespeare, 1564–1616

He was an Augustinian friar and a doctor of theology about whose early life we know nothing. The Austin Friars had a number of houses in England. John Stone belonged to the Augustinian Priory at Canterbury, which had been founded in 1318. John had already come to the notice of the authorities when he publicly denounced from the pulpit the attempts of the King to divorce Queen Catherine. The final suppression of the monasteries began in 1538. On 14 December of that year, the King's agent, Richard

The Henrician Martyrs

Ingworth, schismatic Suffragan Bishop of Dover and former Dominican Prior of Kings Langley, arrived to suppress the priory. He demanded that all the friars acknowledge the King as head of the Church and sign a document surrendering the friary. John boldly refused to sign the Oath of Supremacy and upbraided Ingworth for doing the King's dirty work. On no account would he acknowledge the King as supreme head of the Church. As he endeavoured to persuade his fellow friars to also refuse, he was immediately detained. Ingworth sent a report of his visit to Cromwell.

> Being in the Austin Friars there the 14th day of December one friar there very rudely and traitorously used himself before all the company as by a bill enclosed you shall perceive part. To write half of his words and order there it were too long to write. I perceiving his demeanour straight away sequestered him so that none spoke with him. I sent for the mayor [of Canterbury]… I examined him before the mayor… and at all times he still held and willed to die for it, that the King may not be the head of the Church in England, but it must be a spiritual father appointed by God.

John was taken to London to be examined by Cromwell. He spent the next year in prison. On 27 October 1539 the Mayor of Canterbury was given a commission for John to be tried under the Treason Act, and for this purpose he was sent back to Canterbury; most likely imprisoned in the castle. John prayed and fasted for three days and while praying in his cell he heard a heavenly voice, although he saw no one. The voice addressed him by name, telling him to be of good heart, and encouraged him to remain constant unto death. He drew great spiritual courage and strength from the experience.

Exactly when his trial took place at Canterbury Guildhall is now unknown but it was just before Christmas. The importance attached to the trial may be gauged from the fact that the prosecution was in the hands of Sir Christopher Hales, former Attorney General and currently Master of the Rolls, who also prosecuted at the trials of John Fisher, Thomas More and Anne Boleyn. No doubt the whole affair was a formality and John was convicted of treason. John was removed to Westgate Tower in readiness for his execution, which was to be very public as a warning to others. He was hanged, drawn and quartered on a hill by the city walls known as Dane John, from where he would have been able to see his old, now empty, friary: the date was most probably 27 December 1539. Early authorities claim that on the scaffold John declared, 'I close my apostolate in my blood. In my death I shall find life, for I die for a holy cause, the defence of the Church of God.'

His head and quarters were displayed at the gates of the city. The bill for his execution is still extant in the account books of the City of Canterbury, which lists wood for the scaffold and other items purchased for the purpose. The total cost came to sixteen shillings and one penny.

Despite his relative obscurity, John's martyrdom must have been well known to his contemporaries, and his memory must have been revered. When Pope Gregory XIII, a great patron of the new Venerable English College at Rome, authorised the wall paintings of sixty-three English martyrs at the college in 1583, he thereby also recognised and sanctioned veneration of them. Forty-four years after his death, John Stone was among those depicted in the frescoes. It was John's name that headed the list of English martyrs first submitted to Rome for beatification.

The Aftermath

Henry VIII's paranoia, leading to the schism from Rome, was the direct precursor of what is now called the English Protestant Reformation. Of course everything in the garden was far from rosy. In the Church simony and nepotism were widespread; the selling of indulgences was a scandal and the ill-instructed laity was susceptible to superstition. The nature of men and women being what it is, laxity and complacency had inevitably crept into religious observances in monastic institutions, and many fell short of the high ideals they should have professed. This stricture also applied to the clergy in general; and there was much that needed to be reformed and renewed, as men like John Colet, Thomas More, Desiderius Erasmus and Thomas Linacre recognised. In addition to magnificent prelates like Cardinal Wolsey, unfortunately it was not difficult to find many other examples of unworthy churchmen more noted for their pride and worldliness than for their spirituality. To give credit where it is due, as well as seeking to control every aspect of the Church, Wolsey did try and defend the Church. Half-hearted attempts at reform had been tried by Wolsey under the authority of Pope Leo X, but how could such a degenerate churchman be taken seriously as a reformer when he condemned others for indulging in the same corrupt practices? With the Church under threat from Lutheran ideas, Wolsey, too occupied with matters of state during the fourteen years he held power, failed to take the necessary steps for counteracting Protestant heresy. Thomas More severely criticised Wolsey for his lack of resistance and wholly inadequate response to the danger.

The dissolution of religious houses was no new phenomenon. With permission from Pope Clement VII, Wolsey had at least thirty religious houses dissolved, including St Frideswide's Priory, Oxford, for being either too small or allegedly because the religious fell far short of their vocations. He used the proceeds to found educational establishments, most notably the Oxford college now known as Christ Church. In this he was not alone: other bishops acted in a similar manner, including John Fisher, who dissolved nunneries in order to maintain St John's College, Cambridge. But the depredations under Thomas Cromwell were of a totally different order to previous closures. This onslaught was aimed at nothing less than the wholesale root and branch destruction of religious life.

In 1535 Cromwell designated lay commissioners to make a systematic visitation of the religious houses, to report on their spiritual and moral condition and most importantly to assess their monetary worth. The value of the church plate and vestments, the goods and chattels of the community and even the amount of lead on the roof and its melted down value were all calculated for their likely worth to the King.

The whole process was a pretext to give some semblance of justice for what was planned because, as is clear from contemporary documentation, the closures had all been predetermined. Regardless of the content of the commissioners'

The Henrician Martyrs

reports, the monasteries were doomed. The commissioners' role was to denigrate the reputations of the monks and nuns. It is significant that the stories of corruption their reports contain are virtually the only sources for information on the state of the monasteries at this period. The truthfulness of the reports therefore rests entirely upon the credibility and trustworthiness or otherwise of the commissioners. As minions of Cromwell, their veracity is, at least, open to doubt. In support of the work of the commissioners, preachers were sent out to stir up public opinion against the monks, accusing them, among other things, of sorcery and idleness. Cromwell of course painted the blackest picture possible and was carefully selective in highlighting only those aspects of his agents' reports that recounted the immorality and misdeeds of some monks and nuns. Cases of drunkenness, debauchery and financial misdemeanours, sadly, undoubtedly existed; but the stories of widespread dissipation, concupiscence and corruption being rife in religious communities – in short that they were dens of iniquity – were largely false.

When the first measure for suppressing the monasteries came before Parliament, it appears that none of the 'evidence' gathered by Cromwell was presented. This may be surmised from the fact that in the preamble to the first Act of Dissolution the members of Parliament hedged their bets by stating that they accepted as true the accusations against the smaller monasteries purely because the King had declared them to be true. Yet in the same preamble it reads 'in the great and solemn monasteries of the realm' religion was well observed and God well served; perhaps a truer reflection of their real opinions. The fact is that the motivation for the religious changes from those in power was venal and base. It was not only to crush a major source of opposition to his royal supremacy that the King sought to abolish the religious houses, but also to swell his coffers. Thus the English Reformation was built upon wholesale sacrilege and pillage. In 1536 there were over 800 religious houses containing about 8,000 monks and nuns of various orders; by 1540 there were none. The last to go was the Augustinian Abbey of the Holy Cross at Waltham, near London, founded in 1060 by Harold II, the last Saxon king of England. The organist at Waltham Abbey at the time of the suppression was the great composer Thomas Tallis.

Henry quickly disposed of Anne Boleyn, the woman for whom he had been prepared to take his kingdom into schism. Cranmer obligingly declared the King's marriage to Anne null and void and she was beheaded on 19 May 1536. Just eleven days later Henry was already celebrating his marriage to Jane Seymour. In 1536, through Thomas Cromwell, Henry had 376 monasteries and convents dissolved whose annual revenue did not amount to more than £200. The religious innovations were not without a great deal of opposition, and soon there took place what was probably the largest civil rebellion in English history, known as the 'Pilgrimage of Grace'.

In Lincolnshire, the Midlands and the North unrest was fomenting. The first rebellion began at St James's Church, Louth, Lincolnshire, on 1 October 1536. The locals were angry at the closure of Louth Abbey and the actions of the royal commissioners, and the unrest quickly spread to nearby towns. Supported by the local gentry, up to 40,000 people occupied Lincoln and took over the cathedral, demanding that the religious changes should be halted. The protest was short-lived. When threatened with military action from the forces of the Duke of Suffolk, most of the people dispersed. However, within days Henry had to contend with a far more serious insurrection. Nominally led by Robert Aske, thousands occupied York, the expelled monks and nuns were invited to return to their houses and the full Catholic liturgy was reintroduced.

Aske, the son of Sir Robert Aske of Aughton near Selby, was a devout and charismatic figure, a well-connected Yorkshire gentleman and a barrister of Gray's Inn. By the end of October, the 'Pilgrimage of Grace', supported by the local nobility and clergy and with perhaps as many as 30,000 adherents on the march southwards, had grown into a full-scale revolt and posed a real threat to Henry. Aske forbade any use of force, so while maintaining their loyalty to the King the 'pilgrims' drew up a set of demands. These included halting any further religious changes, stopping the suppression of the monasteries and healing the breach with Rome, dismissing the King's heretical counsellors

The Henrician Martyrs

and holding a parliament in the North to address their religious and economic grievances. The Duke of Norfolk met the 'pilgrims' at Doncaster. Outnumbered three to one, Norfolk had been authorised by the thoroughly alarmed Henry to offer a free general pardon and assurances that a parliament would be held at York. Trusting in Henry's false promises, the insurgent leaders and their followers all dispersed.

Needless to say none of Henry's promises were kept, and in January 1537 a new rebellion began although Aske did all he could to prevent it. The rebellion was finally crushed with incredible savagery, Henry ordering 'such dreadful executions… as shall be a fearful warning'. In spite of a pardon promised to him personally by the King, in July 1537 Aske was hung in chains at York for high treason. Along with him died all the other pilgrimage leaders, including Sir John Bulmer, whose wife Margaret was sent to Smithfield and burnt at the stake. But vengeance was also visited upon hundreds of ordinary folk, including women and children. Among the victims were William Wood, Prior of Bridlington; William Thirsk, OCist, Prior of Fountains Abbey; Adam Sedbar, Abbot of Jervaulx; John Paslew, Abbot of Whalley; John Pickering OSD, Prior of York; James Cockerel, Prior of Guisborough; Richard Harrison, Abbot of Kirkstead; William Trafford, Abbot of Sawley; and Robert Hobbes, Abbot of Woburn. Henry made it abundantly clear that he would brook no opposition and woe betide anyone who attempted it.

The Observant Franciscan Friary adjoining the royal palace at Greenwich had been suppressed in August 1534 as punishment for the outspoken refusal of the friars to accept the validity of Henry's divorce and remarriage. The ascetic friars remained stalwart in their support for Queen Catherine who had always been their friend and admirer, as Henry had. In his rage Henry ordered the closure of all Observant houses and imprisoned or expelled the friars, of whom at least thirty-two died in prison, mostly in London. Three of the friars[14] whose names are known died in Newgate in 1537. They have been recognised by the Church.

After the failure of the 'Pilgrimage of Grace', the efforts to stamp out all dissent relentlessly continued. With this object in mind, Henry re-established the Council of the North at York with sweeping powers. In May 1538 the Observant Franciscan priest of Greenwich, John Forest,[15] was burned to death at Smithfield. He was hung from a chain over a fire while schismatic Bishop Hugh Latimer preached – at great length!

The pace of the destruction of images and relics gathered momentum along with the suppression of the religious houses. Throughout 1539 and 1540 Cromwell pursued his vendetta against the monasteries by suppressing the greater houses for the financial benefit of the Crown. Cromwell promised to make Henry the richest king that ever reigned in England.

When Westminster Abbey was surrendered in January 1540 the monks removed the body of St Edward the Confessor from its shrine and concealed it. Canterbury was not so fortunate. The internationally celebrated shrine of St Thomas Becket was one of the wonders of the religious world. It was covered in gold and precious stones donated by the faithful over centuries. Its treasures, which filled twenty-six carts, were plundered when the shrine was demolished. The great ruby that had been given by Louis VII of France was used to make a ring for Henry. The shrine of Our Lady at Walsingham, once so revered by the young Henry, was dismantled. All over the country the shrines of saints were being desecrated, while statues and roods were being torn down and burned. Along with the monasteries, the hospitals of St John of Jerusalem with their lands were confiscated for the Crown.

The suppression of the religious houses caused enormous social upheaval, involving not only the loss of the monastic hospitals but also their charitable work in providing help and shelter for the poor. The monasteries were the chief sources of learning, education and patronage of the arts. Furthermore, it also resulted in unemployment for those who worked for the monasteries. Some monasteries were bought and converted into palatial dwellings whose names even today, with their suffix 'abbey' or 'priory', are a reminder of their former purpose. The tenants of these new owners soon found what harsh landlords and taskmasters they turned out to be when compared with the

The Henrician Martyrs

monks. Some monastery churches were used as parish churches; many others were simply left to decay, the stones being recycled for new buildings. The metal from the bells that had once called the inhabitants to prayer was used to make guns.

It was not only the glorious religious edifices that were lost. One of the greatest losses, not just to England but to European culture, was the destruction of the monastic libraries. Instead of being preserved, the often irreplaceable books were wantonly broken up, their precious bindings ripped off and sold. The scale of the destruction was immense. For example, the Augustinian library at York had 650 volumes, and Worcester Priory over 600. John Bale, the former Carmelite Prior of Ipswich turned aggressive Protestant, who was made a bishop in Ireland in the reign of Edward VI, lamented in 1549 that the books had not been saved for the sake of learning and the good of posterity. Their destruction without consideration, he said, 'will be unto England for ever a most horrible infamy'. The libraries contained priceless treasures of early Anglo-Saxon manuscripts. Bale spoke of manuscripts and pages of books being used to clean boots, wrap soap or as toilet paper.

The rampant greed knew no bounds. None of the wealth accumulated was used for the good of the realm, let alone for any charitable purpose. It was used primarily to fill the avaricious King's emptying coffers, the religious properties being sold on for cash to those who could afford to buy them and aggrandise themselves even further. It was also a means of ensuring that these nouveau riche gentry were, in their own economic interests, allied to the new Protestant ascendancy.

A hypocritical charade was maintained that the religious willingly surrendered their houses to the King. The royal instruction was that if any of the heads of the houses that had already been 'appointed to be dissolved' (nota bene) obstinately refused to surrender, the property was to be seized by force. For such resistance on 15 November 1539 were hanged, drawn and quartered: Blessed Richard Whiting, Benedictine Abbot of Glastonbury since 1525, with two of his priest monks; Blessed John Thorne, the abbey treasurer, and Blessed Roger James, the sacristan; Blessed Hugh Faringdon, so called after his birthplace, but his real name was Cook, Benedictine Abbot of Reading since 1520, with Blessed John Eynon, priest at St Giles church, Reading; and Blessed John Rugg, a prebendary of Chichester Cathedral in retirement at Reading; Blessed John Beche, real name probably Marshall, since 1533 Benedictine Abbot of St John's, Colchester. Also in 1539 Venerable John Griffith, Vicar of Wandsworth and Venerable John Waire, a Franciscan priest, were executed at Southwark.

The following year three priests (Thomas Abel, Edward Powell and Richard Fetherston)[16] were executed at Smithfield, while Venerable Edmund Brindholme, parish priest of Our Lady, Calais, and a layman, Venerable Clement Philpot, suffered the same fate at Tyburn. In 1541 Margaret Pole, Countess of Salisbury, was beheaded.[17] On 7 March 1544, two priests and a layman suffered together at Tyburn: John Larke, John Ireland and German Gardiner.[18] Later that month, the layman Venerable Thomas Ashby joined them. In all, fifty-two Catholic martyrs suffered death in the last twelve years of Henry's reign, not counting the hundreds executed after the 'Pilgrimage of Grace'.

As his death approached, the King can have been under no illusions that Protestants were in the ascendancy at Court. The repellent ogre, who in his final speech to Parliament described himself as 'I whom God has appointed His Vicar', maintained the self-deception that he remained a Catholic to the end of his life. Believing personally in the Real Presence of Christ in the Eucharist, he did not hesitate to have Protestant heretics burned for denying the doctrine. In his will Henry commended himself to the prayers of the Blessed Virgin Mary and the saints and asked – surely greatly more in hope than expectation! – that Requiem Masses be said for his soul. Yet he appointed leading Protestants as the guardians and regents for his son, Edward.

The Henrician Martyrs

Notes to Chapter One

[1] Elizabeth Barton was a nun at St Sepulchre's Benedictine Convent at Canterbury. She was known for her exemplary holy life and she claimed to have experienced visions. She became known to Archbishop Warham, the Bridgettines at Syon, the Franciscans at Greenwich and the Carthusians at Sheen. She met Bishop Fisher three times and Thomas More once. She and everyone connected with her were in trouble when her prophecies spilled over into the political sphere and she began to speak ill of the King, predicting his doom because of his divorce and remarriage. Elizabeth was sent to the Tower but the government wanted to use her to ensnare as many others as possible who were opposed to the divorce. She was executed in April 1534 with four companions: John Dering OSB, Edward Bocking OSB, and two secular priests, Henry Gold and Richard Masters. A fifth priest, the Franciscan Hugh Rich OSF, had cheated the gallows by dying in prison.

[2] Thomas Cromwell was born at Putney, the son of a tradesman. After studying law he entered the service of Cardinal Wolsey. He became a Member of Parliament in 1523. During the King's divorce crisis, Cromwell made himself invaluable to Henry and by 1533 he was Secretary of State. It was most probably Cromwell who first suggested to Henry that he should make himself head of the Church, and he steered the necessary legislation through Parliament. He presided over the suppression of the monasteries and was created Earl of Essex in 1540. His downfall came when he arranged for Henry to marry Anne of Cleves, and this was the underlying reason why he was charged with treason and executed at the Tower in July 1540.

[3] Richard Rich was born in London into a wealthy mercer's family. He studied law at the Middle Temple, where he met Thomas More, who had no great opinion of Rich's moral qualities and deplored his ambitious streak. In 1533 Rich was knighted and appointed Solicitor General. He played an odious role in the trial of Thomas More, when he perjured himself in giving evidence. By 1536, the year he served as Speaker of the Commons, he was responsible for disposing of the monastic revenues, acquiring for himself Leighs Priory and around one hundred manors in Essex. In 1540 his evidence helped convict

The Henrician Martyrs

Thomas Cromwell. He was an executor of Henry VIII's will and became Lord Chancellor during the reign of Edward VI. He was made a baron in 1548. In spite of Rich's support for the Protestant reforms, when Mary I succeeded to the throne she retained his services in the Privy Council. Notwithstanding his self-serving career, he seems to have remained a Catholic at heart and played his part in actively persecuting heretics in Essex. He died in 1567.

[4] Richard Whytford came from a well-to-do family in Flintshire. A Fellow of Queen's College, Cambridge, he was a secular priest before joining the Bridgettines at Syon. He was closely connected with Queen Catherine and her circle, as he was for a time chaplain to Lord Mountjoy, her chamberlain. One of the great humanist scholars of his day, he was, like Thomas More, a close friend of Erasmus. He produced a stream of devotional works intended to help the laity lead a more prayerful life, but modestly never put his name to them. His wonderful translation of the *Imitation of Christ* has stood the test of time. There is no evidence that Whytford ever subscribed to the royal supremacy when, along with the remainder of his community, he was expelled with a small pension when Syon was suppressed in 1539.

[5] Blessed John Haile (or Hale) was perhaps a native of Worcestershire. He was a secular priest and Bachelor of Law from Cambridge, where he was a Fellow of King's Hall. In 1505 he was appointed Rector of St Dunstan's, Cranford, Middlesex, and in 1521 he became Vicar of Isleworth. In 1531 he was appointed a Canon of Wrigham, Kent, by Archbishop Warham. He originally came to the attention of the authorities for his forthright and somewhat intemperate condemnation of Henry's repudiation of Queen Catherine and his marriage to Anne Boleyn. A friend of the Bridgettines of Syon, he was an elderly man in poor health and greatly afraid of execution; but he remained stalwart in condemning Henry's marriage, his immoral life, his oppression of the Church and his heretical claim to be supreme head of the Church. Robert Feron, a priest from Teddington, was also tried and found guilty with Haile. He was pardoned after turning King's evidence by betraying the conversations that had taken place between him and Haile. John was beatified in 1886.

[6] Blessed Humphrey Middlemore, a priest, was almost certainly a member of the family of that name originating from Edgbaston,

The Henrician Martyrs

Warwickshire. Firstly Procurator then Vicar of the London Charterhouse. Beatified in 1886.

[7] Blessed William Exmew, priest. He was possibly related to a former Lord Mayor of London and educated at Cambridge. He was proficient in Latin and Greek. He joined the London Charterhouse *c.*1518 and became Vicar and then Procurator, where he enjoyed a reputation for holiness. His sister was a Dominican nun. He was no more than thirty years old at the time of his execution. Beatified in 1886.

[8] Blessed Sebastian Newdigate, a priest, came from an ancient family, being one of the many children of the Lord of the Manor of Harefield, Middlesex, where he was born on 7 September 1500. He was educated at Cambridge. He went to Court and became a member of the Privy Chamber. He married Katherine, co-heiress of Sir John Hampden and widow of Henry Ferrers of Baddesley Clinton. By her he had two daughters. After his wife's death he became a priest. At his trial, the judge reminded Sebastian not only that he belonged to the nobility but also how he had enjoyed the King's favour. Beatified in 1886.

[9] St John Fisher was born at Beverley, East Yorkshire, in 1469. Educated at Cambridge. In 1504 he was elected Chancellor of Cambridge University, which he reformed. Chaplain to Henry VII's mother, he was then appointed Bishop of Rochester, where he enjoyed a great reputation for erudition, austerity and holiness. Henry VIII declared that no other sovereign had such a brilliant prelate. He became confessor to Catherine of Aragon and opposed the King's divorce. He was the only one of the bishops to remain steadfast in opposing the royal supremacy of the Church. In 1534 he was sent to the Tower for refusing the oath. In May 1535 he was created a cardinal by Pope Paul III. After ten months in prison, on 22 June 1535, he was martyred by beheading on Tower Hill. Canonized in 1935.

[10] St Thomas More was born in London in 1477 or 1478, the son of a judge. He studied at Oxford and at Lincoln's Inn, being called to the Bar in 1501. In 1504 he became a Member of Parliament and was appointed Speaker in 1523. He married firstly Jane Colt, by whom he had four children, and secondly Alice Middleton. In 1529 he was appointed Lord Chancellor. He enjoyed a European-wide reputation as a humanist, wit and man of letters. He was sent to the Tower for refusing the Oath of

Supremacy. Like Bishop Fisher he was willing to swear to the succession to the Crown, that being a matter of civil law, but to the royal supremacy he 'could not swear without the jeopardising of my soul'. After fifteen months in prison he was martyred on Tower Hill by beheading on 6 July 1535: 'the King's good servant, but God's first'. Canonized in 1935, he is the patron saint of politicians.

[11] Blessed John Rochester, a priest, from an ancient family of Terling, Essex. He was the younger brother of Sir Robert Rochester who subsequently became Comptroller of Queen Mary Tudor's household and a Knight of the Garter. John was educated at Cambridge. During the period of oppression in the Charterhouse, John Rochester was summoned to see Archbishop Cranmer but the monk remained immune to his blandishments. His splendid letter defending his beliefs, written in York to the Duke of Norfolk, is extant in the Public Records Office.

[12] Of these ten members of the community seven starved to death in Newgate between 6 and 16 June 1537. They were: Brother William Greenwood, Deacon John Davy, Brother Robert Salt, Brother Walter Pierson, priest Thomas Green, Brother Thomas Scryven and Brother Thomas Reding. Two priests, Richard Bere and Thomas Johnson, were given food and water with the aim of saving them for execution, but this plan was abandoned. Oxford-educated Bere was a nephew of the Abbot of Glastonbury. He became a Carthusian *c.*1521 and was ordained priest in 1524. Bere survived until 9 August and Johnson until 20 September. Brother William Horne was kept alive only to face execution three years later. All ten have been beatified.

[13] Margaret Clement, née Giggs, born *c.*1508, was the foster-daughter of Thomas More. She was brought up as part of the family and appears with them in the famous Holbein painting. In 1526 she married the physician Dr John Clement, also an intimate of the More household. They had four children: a son and three daughters. Margaret died in exile at Mechlin in July 1570. Two of her daughters became nuns. Margaret became an Augustinian Canoness and one of the founding English sisters of St Monica's, Louvain. She served as the much loved prioress of St Ursula's in the same city for thirty-eight years. Her sister Dorothy was a Poor Clare.

The Henrician Martyrs

[14] These three friars were Anthony Brookby DD, Thomas Covert and Thomas Belchiam. Covert and Belchiam starved to death in Newgate in July/August 1537 and Brookby was strangled in the prison. All of them were declared 'venerable'.

[15] Blessed John Forest, an Oxford graduate and priest of the Observant Franciscan Order at Greenwich Friary. Confessor and strong supporter of Queen Catherine, he was imprisoned in 1534, accepted the supremacy and was released. The Greenwich Friary having been suppressed, he entered the Grey Friars in London. Rearrested and imprisoned in Newgate in 1538, he was condemned and burned to death at Smithfield on 22 May. Beatified in 1886.

[16] Blessed Thomas Abel DD, secular priest, chaplain to Queen Catherine. Blessed Edward Powell DD was a Welshman; fellow of Oriel College, Oxford; headmaster of Eton; vicar of St Mary Redcliffe, Bristol. Blessed Richard Fetherston DD, secular priest, tutor to Princess Mary, archdeacon of Brecknock. All of them were friends and supporters of Queen Catherine and sent to the Tower in 1534. All were hanged, drawn and quartered at Smithfield on 30 July 1540. Beatified in 1886.

[17] Blessed Margaret Pole, Countess of Salisbury. Born in 1473, she was the last of the Plantagenets, being the niece of Edward IV and Richard III and mother of Cardinal Reginald Pole. She was appointed godmother and governess to Princess Mary. She was forced to retire from Court after Henry's marriage to Anne Boleyn and her protests about declaring Princess Mary illegitimate. In 1538 she was arrested and kept in custody. The following year, partly in revenge for her son's publishing his *Defence of Church Unity* opposing the royal supremacy, she was attainted and sent to the Tower, but never brought to trial. She was beheaded on Tower Hill on 28 May 1541 aged sixty-eight. Beatified in 1886.

[18] Blessed John Larke, secular priest; rector of St Ethelburga's, Bishopsgate, London for twenty-six years then of Chelsea, Thomas More's parish church. Blessed John Ireland, secular priest; chaplain to the Roper Chantry, St Dunstan's, Canterbury. Blessed German Gardiner, layman; Cambridge educated; secretary to his uncle, Stephen Gardiner, Bishop of Winchester. All hanged, drawn and quartered at Tyburn on 7 March 1544. Beatified in 1886.

Chapter Two

Edward VI and Mary Tudor

> By education most have been misled; so they believe, because they were so bred.
>
> *The Hind and the Panther*, John Dryden, 1631–1700

On 28 January 1547 a delicate, sickly nine-year-old boy not only became King but also Supreme Head of the Church of England, which was now a hereditary office along with the Crown. The obstinate, bookish Edward shared the Lutheran beliefs of those who were now his masters, most notably the Lord Protector, his uncle, Edward Seymour, Duke of Somerset,[1] and the Regent, John Dudley, later Duke of Northumberland.[2] Together with Archbishop Cranmer they immediately set about turning England into a Protestant nation on the model of the Continental Reformation, knowing full well that their power base hinged upon their success in achieving this aim. Doctrines and practices were introduced for which adherents would have been burned as heretics in the previous reign.

Protestantism on any scale was still mainly confined to London and other larger towns and cities in the south of England. In rural areas the people carried on as before, attending Mass in their parish churches until new doctrines and liturgical innovations were forced on them by legislation. Royal commissioners were sent around the country with the task of removing every vestige of Catholic piety. All remaining shrines, chapels and chantries were dismantled, and then came the despoiling of the parish churches. Their altars were destroyed; sacred vessels and vestments were sold off for the personal profit of the ruling elite. Wall paintings were whitewashed over, stained glass windows were smashed and crucifixes were thrown out. Church feasts such as Palm Sunday were abolished. Disturbances

Edward VI and Mary Tudor

broke out in the disaffected West Country, protesting about the changes in worship and the abolition of holy water, rosaries, votive candles, making the sign of the Cross and saying prayers for the departed. The people of Devon, Cornwall and Somerset were in ferment, which led to bloodshed in a number of places. At Helston, while destroying the statues in the parish church, William Body, the royal commissioner, had been attacked and killed in April 1548. Retribution was swift, and dozens of Cornishmen who resisted the commissioners were executed, including the parish priest of St Keverne, who was hanged, drawn and quartered in London, his severed head being displayed on London Bridge.

The 1549 Act of Uniformity which came into effect on Whit Sunday, abolished the Mass and substituted a Protestant communion service in English in accordance with the first *Book of Common Prayer*. The King's half-sister, Princess Mary, had to petition for special permission for Mass to be celebrated in her household. In Devon and Cornwall many parishes refused to allow their priests to read the new service and magistrates were sent out to enforce the changes. The West Country disturbances, referred to as the Prayer Book Rebellion, became a widespread revolt, attracting the support of thousands of ordinary citizens on the march.

Thoroughly alarmed, the government of Somerset, the Lord Protector, mobilised an army of mostly German and other foreign mercenaries, and by August the uprising was swiftly and mercilessly quashed, with heavy loss of life. Around a thousand defenceless, bound, captured prisoners had their throats cut at Clyst near Exeter. Determined to exact the last ounce of revenge on those who had dared to rebel, Archbishop Cranmer issued orders that everyone involved should be hunted down. As a result the bloodshed continued, with many public executions of those who had been involved. At Exeter the parish priest of St Thomas's Church was hanged in chains from the church tower while in his vestments. The gentry, along with many of the rebels, were sent to London for execution.

The Protestants were divided into many opposing sects, all hating each other's guts, and the only factor that they had in

Edward VI and Mary Tudor

common was their even more virulent hatred of the Catholic Church. While the zealous Protestants said the newly imposed services were too Catholic, the Catholics did not believe them to be Catholic in any way, shape or form. What of the Catholics during this period? At least those who voiced their objections to all the Protestantising were spared execution; but many, including the more conservative bishops, were deprived of their sees and replaced by Protestants under letters patent from the King. Others were imprisoned without trial, some for the entire duration of Edward's reign. To replace the Catholic rite with a ceremony more compatible with Protestantism, a new ordinal was introduced in 1550. In 1552 the *Second Book of Common Prayer* was issued by the authority of Parliament; a most significant innovation, as hitherto religious doctrine had been considered the province of the Church. The Real Presence in the Eucharist was explicitly denied as 'idolatry'. Cranmer then produced the *Forty-two Articles of Religion*, in which only two Sacraments were acknowledged.

Dying of tuberculosis, in 1553 Edward was persuaded by the Regent Northumberland to remove his half-sisters, Mary and Elizabeth, from the succession. He willed the crown to Northumberland's daughter-in-law, Lady Jane Grey,[3] the granddaughter of Henry VIII's sister, Mary. The fact that Jane's mother was still alive and thereby had a better claim to the throne was immaterial.

Edward died at Greenwich in July 1553, and two days later Northumberland declared sixteen-year-old Jane Grey Queen. Poor Jane! Forced into marriage with Northumberland's son when it was clear that Edward was dying, she was the victim of a plot to usurp the throne. The only leading Anglican prelates who supported her were Cranmer and Nicholas Ridley, the Bishop of London. Lacking any real support, her 'reign' lasted just nine days. She subsequently paid for it with her life. London and the south-east, the fleet – even many of the Protestant zealots – rallied to Princess Mary, the lawful heir, and she was proclaimed Queen amid a spontaneous outburst of tremendous rejoicing. The citizens of London poured into the streets, singing and dancing, and the church bells rang incessantly.

Edward VI and Mary Tudor

Mary Tudor and the Reunion with Rome

And some there be which have no memorial.

Sirach/Ecclesiasticus 44:9

Few sovereigns can ever have come to the throne on such a tide of popular support as Mary Tudor (1516–58), the first Queen Regnant of England. Yet over the next five years she lost most of that goodwill, not least by her ill-advised marriage to Philip II of Spain. Mary believed it was her divinely given destiny to restore Catholicism. In a hurry to achieve this goal, she tragically misunderstood the public mood, especially in London, and was only too willing to listen to the misguided counsel of some of the more embittered Catholic prelates who had suffered so much at Protestant hands.

At first Mary had to accept the anti-Catholic legislation until Parliament should see fit to repeal it, and she had to proceed with caution, resisting pressure from Rome that she should restore communion with the Holy See without delay. At the outset of her reign she declared that while conscientious Protestants would not be compelled to go to Mass, Catholics must not be denied that opportunity; nor was it her desire to punish 'ignorant people who had been misled'. Mary restored the monastic lands and buildings in the possession of the Crown, including Westminster Abbey, which was reoccupied when John Feckenham was installed as Abbot, with fourteen monks. It was the only major abbey to be restored; Mary's example was not followed by any of the nobles. The Abbey church was in a shocking state with its whitewashed walls, denuded of all its beauty. The body of St Edward the Confessor was retrieved and replaced in the broken shrine. In tears, Mary gave her jewels to cover the cost of its repair.

In November 1554 Parliament repealed the Act of Supremacy and formally agreed to restore links with the papacy. The bill passed with only two votes against. Cardinal Reginald Pole,[4] son of the martyred Countess of Salisbury, and Mary's cousin, absolved England from schism, and reunion was accomplished. Dom Maurice Chauncy, the chronicler of the martyrdom of his brother monks, had fled overseas and joined the Carthusians of Sheen at Bruges. As the

Edward VI and Mary Tudor

old Charterhouse at Sheen had reverted to the Queen, she invited the Carthusians to return. In November 1556 a group of nineteen monks belonging to various houses reoccupied the derelict monastery and Chauncy was elected prior. It was to be a short-lived restoration, for Chauncy and his monks were again in exile at Bruges by 1559. There they lived with their Flemish brothers until 1569, when they obtained a house of their own with Chauncy still their prior. He died at the old Charterhouse in Bruges in July 1581. The English Carthusian community of Sheen survived abroad until the late eighteenth century.

Parliament repealed all the anti-Catholic legislation dating back to 1529 and also unanimously passed an act restoring punishments for heretics. This paved the way for the burning of heretics to begin. The burnings commenced in 1555 and continued for the next four years, earning Mary the soubriquet by which she is known to history: 'Bloody Mary'. The burning of heretics was very much in keeping with the spirit of the time. Heretics were regarded as moral outcasts who threatened the fabric of society. It must not be thought that the feelings of horror the burnings arouse in us would necessarily have had the same effect on our sixteenth-century forebears. Every year thousands were publicly executed for all sorts of offences and people were largely inured to it. Catholics and Protestants alike accepted that burning was the punishment prescribed for heresy. The fact is that given half a chance many of the Protestant victims would have been quite happy to see their fellow Protestants with whom they disagreed burned. In the reign of Mary's father, heretics had been burned by the score almost as a matter of routine. Few questioned that it was the legitimate and appropriate application of the law of the land. Even under Northumberland's Protectorship, extreme Protestants had been burned and later Elizabeth I had no qualms about burning Anabaptists and others. They were still burning Arian heretics at Smithfield by order of Archbishop George Abbot under James I. So why was there such a different reaction during Mary's reign? And why has such a different historical judgement been made about Mary, as distinct from her bloodthirsty father and her half-sister?

To answer the first question, it was not so much that the

Edward VI and Mary Tudor

heretics were being burned before a public accustomed to violence and executions, rather it was the *scale* of the burnings that was of significance. There were some 280 over a short period of time, concentrated mainly in and around London. Apart from a few prominent figures such as Bishops Cranmer, Latimer and Ridley, the fact that the majority of the condemned were ordinary, good-living, upright citizens, most of whom went to their terrible deaths with great courage, caused revulsion. As a result those who were burned became martyrs in the eyes of their neighbours. Towards the end of the reign, Mary ordered that only the most extreme heretics should suffer, but this had little impact on public opinion. The burnings inevitably became firmly associated in the minds of many people as the consequence of the official return of Catholicism and the reunion with Rome. What is more, the policy was a failure. Most Protestants, however insincerely, recanted and attended Mass; so instead of curing the ills of heresy, which Mary abhorred, it only served to strengthen the resolve of the more convinced Protestants.

The answer to the second question can be summed up in one word: prejudice. As the adage has it, the winners write history; and as the winners were the Protestants it was they who determined the perceptions of future generations, perceptions so deeply inculcated that even today they largely hold popular sway. Every schoolboy knew about 'bloody' Mary Tudor, the persecutor, and all suggestions that her sister was an even worse oppressor were laughed at scornfully. These stereotypes passed into the national consciousness, even though the 'Good Queen Bess' presiding over an 'Elizabethan golden age' of school history books was a myth. Dr Augustus Jessop, a nineteenth-century Anglican clergyman and former headmaster of King Edward's School, Norwich, spent many years carrying out important research into original sources for his fascinating book about the Walpole family, *One Generation of a Norfolk House* (1879). He wrote:

> As my book has proceeded the England of Queen Elizabeth's days has become to me an altogether different land from the England I had formerly imagined it to be: the conflict with Rome had gradually unfolded itself as a problem which must remain

unintelligible to the merely political historian... The real value of the [Walpole] story lies rather in this, that it is one which, mutatis mutandis, might be told of fifty families in England which were rich and prosperous in the first half of the 16th century and were simply reduced to beggary for conscience' sake.

Yet even Mary's most diehard opponents never questioned her sincerity, the depth of her religious beliefs or the strong moral principles that motivated her actions. She believed she was actually trying to save the souls of those in error from damnation. There can be many mitigating factors pleaded on Mary's behalf. Her precarious upbringing, with its daily insecurities, together with the privations and humiliations she and her mother suffered, all played a part in the formation of her personality. As a monarch she was impressively dignified and hard-working. On a personal level she led a simple life and was a very kind, charitable woman, especially to the poor and sick, possessing a sensitivity devoid of the overweening selfishness that characterised Henry VIII. She was certainly greatly loved by her Court, and her servants were devoted to her. But even when all this is taken into consideration, the undeniable fact remains that whoever initiated the policy towards heretics, Mary bore ultimate responsibility.

It was not that she lacked advice to pursue a different course. John Feckenham,[5] Abbot of the restored Westminster, had endured imprisonment in the Tower under Edward VI. He was no friend to Protestantism and opposed Cranmer, Latimer and Ridley, but he disliked the bigotry and the brutal measures being employed. He used all his influence with the Queen to procure pardons or mitigation of the punishment being meted out to poor Protestants. As Queen, Mary had the authority to change the disastrous policy and halt the burnings; she did not do so, therefore she must be held culpable for this heinous persecution, whose tragic legacy was persecution for Catholics and incalculable damage to the Catholic cause in England for generations to come.

Edward VI and Mary Tudor

Notes to Chapter Two

[1] Edward Seymour, Duke of Somerset. Born in 1506, he was the brother of Jane Seymour who became the third wife of Henry VIII. The marriage led to his rapid advancement in royal favour, being created Earl of Hertford. He was appointed Lord Protector of his nephew Edward VI, who made him a duke. Seymour exercised tremendous influence over the boy and was the real ruler of the country. His collaborator, John Dudley, turned against him. Seymour was sent to the Tower in 1549 and executed for treason in 1552.

[2] John Dudley, Duke of Northumberland. Born about 1502, he was one of the executors of Henry VIII's will. He collaborated with Lord Protector Somerset in governing the country during the reign of Edward VI. He appears to have been devoid of any real religious convictions, but being ambitious for power he hedged his bets both politically and in religious matters. He pursued a strongly Protestant agenda, promoting the Reformation when he saw it would suit his aims and increase his power base and influence over the boy King. Having disposed of his rival Somerset, he made himself a duke in 1551. In order to perpetuate his own rule he sought to place his daughter-in-law, Jane Grey, on the throne. His hypocritical attempt to evade execution by pretending to embrace Catholicism did not save him. He was executed for treason just a month after Mary came to the throne in 1553.

[3] Lady Jane Grey, born in 1537, was the daughter of Henry Grey, Marquess of Dorset, and Lady Frances Brandon, who was the daughter of Henry VIII's younger sister Mary. Attractive and intelligent, Jane had no desire to be Queen, but with the connivance of her parents she became the pawn of Dudley and the Protestant faction. Dudley and his self-serving hypocrisy disgusted Jane. She and her husband were sent to the Tower when Mary was proclaimed Queen but they were not executed until after Wyatt's rebellion had been crushed, when they were beheaded for treason in 1554.

[4] Cardinal Reginald Pole was born in Staffordshire in 1500, the grandson of George, Duke of Clarence, the brother of Edward IV. A BA of Oxford and Fellow of Corpus Christi College, in 1523 he left to study on the Continent where he came into contact with all the

leading Renaissance humanists of the day. He returned to England in 1526 and was eventually offered the Archbishopric of York, if he would promote Henry's divorce from Catherine. Rather than do so, Pole went into exile to continue his studies acquiring an international reputation. Although not a priest, he was made a cardinal in 1536 and was one of the three papal legates who presided over the Council of Trent. In 1549 Pole was almost elected Pope, falling short by only one or two votes. When Mary succeeded to the throne, Pole returned from exile as Papal Legate. He was ordained priest in 1557 and appointed Archbishop of Canterbury. He was to be the last Catholic to occupy the Primatial See. He died within hours of Mary in November 1558.

[5] John Feckenham (1515–84) was born at Feckenham in Worcestershire into a well-to-do yeoman family called Howman. When he entered religion he was known by the name of his birthplace. As a boy he was sent to the school at Evesham Abbey, and from there went to Oxford where he gained an Arts degree. He returned to Evesham and took monastic vows, afterwards completing his education at Oxford, where he became Bachelor of Divinity in 1539. He was a monk of Evesham when the monastery was suppressed in 1540. He was awarded a pension of £10 per annum. He became chaplain firstly to the Bishop of Worcester and secondly to Bishop Bonner of London from 1543 to 1549. He soon established a reputation both as an intellectual and as a preacher, as well as a man of great charity. In 1549 Feckenham was sent to the Tower by Cranmer, but released on Mary's accession to become her chaplain and confessor and Dean of St Paul's. His intervention with the Queen on behalf of the imprisoned Princess Elizabeth was not appreciated. In 1556 Oxford made him a Doctor of Divinity, and in November of that year he became Abbot of the restored Westminster. When Westminster was again suppressed in 1559, Feckenham was sent to the Tower by Archbishop Parker for refusing to conform. He spent virtually the rest of his life in confinement. Moved to the Marshalsea in 1574, although still a prisoner, for the good of his health he was allowed to sleep at a house in Holborn, where his charity to the poor was legendary. He set up a public aqueduct and a hospice; he took care of orphans and encouraged the youth to take up sports pastimes. In 1577 he was once more confined in the charge of

Edward VI and Mary Tudor

the Bishop of Winchester. In 1579 he was sent to Wisbech Castle – the first of many Catholics to be incarcerated in that place – where he was revered as a moderating influence. Having suffered for twenty-four years for his beliefs, he died in the prison in 1584 and was buried in an unknown grave at Wisbech parish church.

Chapter Three

The Elizabethan Persecution

> What a rocky-hearted perfidious Succubus was that Queen Elizabeth! Judas Iscariot was a sad dog to be sure, but still his demerits sink to insignifance, compared with the doings of the infernal Bess Tudor.
>
> *Letters to Dr John Moore*, Robert Burns, 1759–96

Elizabeth I (1533–1603) seems to have held no strong religious convictions whatever, but no one doubted, including her late half-sister, where her sympathies lay. She ignored the provisions of Mary's will but gave her a Catholic funeral in Westminster Abbey in December 1558, which was followed by the house arrest of Bishop John White of Winchester, who had delivered the eulogy, as it contained remarks considered to be critical of the new monarch. It was a portent of things to come. The Calvinists returned from their self-imposed exile in Geneva and Germany, and in the first few weeks of the reign William Cecil,[1] the newly appointed Secretary of State, made a written submission to the Queen in which he set out the pros and cons of either a Catholic or Protestant future for England. Cecil concluded that it would be politically expedient to opt for Protestantism. Although she gave instructions that nothing was to be changed immediately, it was a judgement that Elizabeth was happy to accept; after all, she was hardly likely to favour the religion of those who regarded her as Anne Boleyn's bastard daughter.

The Queen's behaviour at Mass on Christmas Day presaged what was in store when she left the royal chapel after the Gospel. Elizabeth's first major problem was finding someone to perform her Coronation. The death of Cardinal Pole on the same day as Queen Mary had left the See of Canterbury vacant. Several other deaths had occurred, so at the beginning of 1559 the hierarchy consisted of just

The Elizabethan Persecution

sixteen bishops. They were asked, in order of seniority, if they would perform the ceremony; they declined to do so. The duty therefore fell to Bishop Owen Oglethorpe of Carlisle, who somewhat naively agreed – providing it was a Catholic ceremony. He lived to bitterly regret his action. So the usually parsimonious Elizabeth spared no expense for her lavish Coronation, in which she was crowned and anointed as a Catholic and reluctantly took the oath to defend the Catholic Church. But during the celebration of Mass she absented herself. A few days later she began the task of bringing about a permanent religious settlement designed to end the upheavals of the last twenty-five years, an object that could only be achieved by enforcing religious uniformity and conformity.

As the majority of the population remained Catholic at heart, especially in the rural areas, they were not simply going to change their religion overnight. It is only through relatively recent scholarly research that some of the old 'received' history has been revised and assumptions discounted. Notable examples of this can be found not only in the work of Catholic historians such as Professors Eamon Duffy and JJ Scarisbrick, but also that of objective Protestants, e.g. Christopher Haigh and Diarmuid MacCulloch, an expert on Cranmer. The attachment to the old religion was far more tenacious than we had been led to believe from our school history lessons. In fact, all the evidence now available leads to the conclusion that the survival of Catholic piety has been greatly underestimated. For example, Professor Duffy maintains:

> … Late mediaeval Catholicism exerted an enormously strong, diverse and vigorous hold over the imagination and the loyalty of the people up to the very moment of the Reformation. Traditional religion had about it no particular marks of exhaustion or decay and indeed in a whole host of ways, from the multiplication of vernacular books to adaptations within the national and regional cult of the saints was showing itself well able to meet new needs and new conditions.
>
> From *The Stripping of the Altars* by Eamon Duffy[1]

---

[1] Copyright © 1992 by Yale University Press. Reproduced by permission of Professor Eamon Duffy and Yale University Press, London.

The Elizabethan Persecution

How was it then that the change of religion was apparently assented to by so many? Piety may well be the keyword. People were attached to the old, traditional devotional ways – but how deep or shallow was their understanding of real Catholic beliefs? There is much truth in the assertion that clergy and laity had become detached. The Mass was celebrated by the priest mostly sotto voce, without much participation by the congregation; indeed the more devout worshippers were probably saying their rosaries or reading some spiritual tract, only taking any notice at the Elevation when the sacring bell caught their attention!

Having said all that, the only way the new religion could be imposed on unwilling people was by force. Elizabeth could count upon the support of the nouveau riche who had profited from the spoliation of the Church and the religious houses. They now had a vested interest in maintaining the Anglican settlement.

In 1559, in the teeth of opposition from the bishops – Thomas Thirlby, Bishop of Ely declaring that he would rather die than consent to a change of religion – a new Act of Supremacy (1 Eliz. I, c. 1) was passed, making it high treason to acknowledge the Pope's authority in England and bestowing upon Elizabeth the title 'Supreme Governor as well in all spiritual or ecclesiastical things as temporal' of the Church. This was presumably felt to be less emotive than 'Head' of the Church, but for all practical purposes it meant exactly the same. To their eternal credit, unlike their timorous counterparts at the time of Henry VIII, all the bishops except Kitchin of Llandaff remained true. Within months of her accession Elizabeth had deprived them all of their sees. They were imprisoned, placed under house arrest or exiled. Twelve of them eventually died in confinement.[2] A large part of the higher clergy – deans, archdeacons, etc. – followed their bishops' lead and were deprived. Without any bishops, the Catholics were left without leaders and Elizabeth had to appoint a new Protestant hierarchy, men for whom she barely bothered to disguise her disdain. It was widely rumoured that Elizabeth in a private interview first offered the See of Canterbury to Abbot John Feckenham of Westminster, if he conformed. If that was the case, he certainly refused. He was the last abbot to sit in the House of Lords, where he opposed all the religious changes and was imprisoned by Matthew Parker, the new Protestant Archbishop of

Canterbury.[3] In July 1559 Westminster Abbey was once more dissolved and Feckenham spent virtually the rest of his life in confinement.

Later in 1559 came the Act of Uniformity (1 Eliz. I, c. 2), abolishing Mass and restoring the 1549 Second Protestant Prayer Book as the only permissible, indeed compulsory, form of worship. To quote David Starkey, a contemporary historian, Elizabeth 'created a kind of hybrid church'. Thus, a national State church, the Church of England as by law established, was invented and was imposed by intimidation. The compromise settlement was unacceptable to both Catholics and Protestants. As Father Godfrey Anstruther OP, in *Vaux of Harrowden*, (1953) put it so aptly, 'The religion of nobody imposed upon everybody'.

At first only higher ecclesiastics and those holding public office were obliged to take the Oath of Supremacy, but in 1562 this was extended to include all those in holy orders, members of Parliament, university graduates, lawyers and schoolmasters – in practice all Catholics.

To quote Dr Jessop again in his *One Generation of a Norfolk House*:

> At the accession of Elizabeth there were not wanting many men of conscientious convictions who would have boldly faced the scaffold rather than acknowledge the claim of the spiritual supremacy of the sovereign... The oath in its new form became the cause of deep and widespread offence. A large proportion of the English gentry refused to swear allegiance in the terms prescribed. But the Act of Uniformity was one which touched Catholics in a different way. The re-establishment of the Mass in Queen Mary's reign had caused immense joy throughout the land, now it was enacted that the *Book of Common Prayer* alone should be used and to 'sing or say any common or open prayer, or to administer any sacrament otherwise... than is mentioned in the said book... in any cathedral, parish church or chapel, or in any other place' subjected the offender to forfeiture of his goods and on repetition of his offence, to imprisonment for life. The Mass... was known to be the one great and precious mystery which every devout Catholic clung to with unspeakable awe and fervour and to rob him of that was to rob him of the one thing on which his religious life depended; that gone, it was imagined that all else would go with it.

The consequences of the new Anglican Church on the Catholic community were dire. Catholic Faith and worship was now illegal. Attendance at Protestant services was compulsory.

Penalties for both priests and laity who did not conform to the new services ranged from fines to life imprisonment. Unlike their bishops, the majority of the clergy, however reluctantly, docilely conformed, and their congregations mostly followed their example even though many were 'church papists' – that is, they conformed outwardly while secretly continuing to celebrate Mass. This compromise with conscience gradually led to a religious indifference as many sought to justify their conduct. After all, if the Anglican Communion service offered only bread, where was the harm in receiving it? Under the new religious settlement parishes were required to destroy all remaining remnants of Catholic piety, although many items such as vestments and images were hidden. As the parishes were denuded of their beauty it seems that the indifference this bred led to a diminished respect for the desecrated church buildings themselves. What incentive did congregations have to maintain desolate churches built to celebrate the Mass that had become whitewashed meeting halls, where they were expected to sit and listen to interminable sermons?

By the 1570s reports on the neglected and dilapidated state of the fabric of the nation's churches make sorry reading. The lead had been stripped from the roofs for profit; birds flew in freely through the smashed windows. Nonetheless the royal commissioners continued to report on the 'inveterate obstinacy that was found among the priests' in still practising the old Catholic ways. Protestant Bishop Aylmer of London complained in 1577 that 'the papists do marvellously increase both in number and in obstinate withdrawing of themselves from the church'.

We know that hundreds of priests resigned or were deprived of their parishes, were imprisoned or exiled rather than conform to the accommodating worldliness of the Established Church. From the records of the royal visitation to the Province of York in 1559, we see that ninety priests were summoned to take the oath at York: only twenty-one of them did so. Many others, deprived of their means of livelihood, wandered in disguise around the

The Elizabethan Persecution

country, ministering secretly to Catholics, particularly in the North. Yorkshire and Lancashire remained strongly Catholic; many areas ignored the new arrangements and continued to celebrate Mass in the parish churches. The vital part played by these faithful Marian priests in sustaining the Catholic community until priestly help arrived from overseas has never received the recognition it deserves. Many of those who remained were the time-servers, like the proverbial Vicar of Bray. Large numbers of parishes were left without pastors, and in the first years of Elizabeth's reign we are told that the Established Church was desperately short of clergy and had to resort to co-opting laymen who could barely read through the new services. Oxford University virtually ceased to function because most of the best and brightest tutors, fellows and students in the various colleges were Catholics who were expelled on Elizabeth's orders.

In the first few years the laws against Catholics were not always rigorously enforced, especially as it tended to be the extreme Protestants who caused more problems for the government: Elizabeth particularly hated the Puritans. A sea change came about in 1563. A more active and vigorous persecution was launched, in which the penalties for refusing to conform were made more stringent. To refuse to take the Oath of Supremacy from henceforward entailed not only fines and imprisonment but also disbarment from all office or employment. A second refusal carried with it the death penalty.

In the autumn of 1569 came the Northern Rising. Instigated by two North Yorkshire gentlemen, and under the leadership of the Earls of Northumberland and Westmorland, the people of Yorkshire and Durham rose up in their thousands in protest at the change in religion and to demand the release from captivity of Mary, Queen of Scots, the heir to the throne. The Queen's representative in Yorkshire, the trusted Sir Ralph Sadler, wrote to Secretary Cecil, 'There are not ten gentlemen in all this county who favour the new proceedings in religion'. Under a banner depicting the Five Wounds of Christ, the people's army marched southwards. Mass was sung again in the cathedrals of Durham, Ripon and York. Two hundred years later, William Wordsworth commemorated the event in his poem, *The White Doe of Rylstone*:

The Elizabethan Persecution

> It was the time when England's Queen
> Twelve years had reigned, a sovereign dread;
> Nor yet the restless crown had been
> Disturbed upon her virgin head;
> But now the inly-working North
> Was ripe to send its thousands forth,
> A potent vassalage to fight
> In Percy's and Neville's right…
> And boldly urged a general plea,
> The rites of ancient piety
> To be triumphantly restored.

Badly organised and ill-equipped, the rising was doomed to failure. It was crushed without mercy, Elizabeth insisting not only that its leaders be punished but also many hundreds of ordinary working men should be executed as a warning to others. A consequence of the rising was that the Oath of Uniformity was made obligatory on everyone in any official position.

In February 1570, Pope St Pius V Ghislieri (1566–72) issued the bull *Regnans in excelsis*, not only excommunicating Elizabeth but also purporting to depose her and release her subjects from their allegiance. Pius sincerely hoped that publishing the bull would assist the oppressed English Catholics, and from his viewpoint Elizabeth's conduct justified his action. But Rome had misjudged the situation and in reality it was a futile gesture, one which was deeply regretted by some of Pius's successors. In spite of the opposition of the great majority of English Catholics to the powers of deposition claimed in the bull, not surprisingly the repercussions from this papal action greatly reinforced antagonism towards Catholics who, because of their allegiance to Rome, were now seen as potential traitors. It played directly into the hands of Secretary Cecil, and presented him with the ammunition he needed. All recusants – those refusing to attend Church of England services – were forbidden to leave the country, and any who were abroad had to return and conform or forfeit their property.

The executions began in 1570, shortly after the Papal Bull. Thomas Plumtree[4] was executed at Durham for acting as a chaplain to the Northern Rising, and John Felton[5] was executed at St Paul's churchyard, London, for publishing the bull. An Act was passed (13 Eliz. I, c. 2, 1571) making it treason to bring papal bulls into England. Felton's execution was followed by that of John Storey[6] in 1571, and in 1573 Thomas Woodhouse,[7] a Marian priest who had served twelve years in prison.

Increasingly ferocious penal laws were introduced against those who refused to conform to the Established Church. In his ten-volume history, *The History of England from the First Invasion of the Romans to the Accession of William and Mary in 1688*, originally published in the first half of the nineteenth century, the Catholic John Lingard, writing of the reign of Elizabeth, commented:

> All her subjects were required to submit to the superior judgement of their sovereign and to practise that religious worship which she practised. Every other form of service... was strictly forbidden; and both the Catholic and the Puritan were subject to the severest penalties if they presumed to worship God according to the dictates of their conscience. It must appear singular that so intolerant a system should be enforced by men who loudly condemned the proceedings of the last reign, but in its defence they alleged... the Queen 'would not delve into consciences'. Internally her subjects might believe... what they pleased. All that she required was external conformity to the law. That she had a right to exact. If any man refused, the fault was his own; he suffered not for conscience sake, but for his obstinacy and his disobedience. That this miserable sophism should have satisfied the judgement of those who employed it can hardly be credited.

As the reign progressed, a succession of Acts of Parliament ever more firmly established state persecution of those who adhered to the Old Faith. Arnold Pritchard writes about the conclusions of some other authors:

> Others, much taken with Elizabeth's alleged desire not to open windows into men's souls, write as if Elizabeth's government was entirely uninterested in the religious beliefs of her subjects unless they became active traitors... The persecution was very real and

its long-range goal was the suppression of Catholicism per se, regardless of the political loyalty of any particular Catholic.

From *Catholic Loyalism in Elizabethan England* by Arnold Pritchard[2]

It became treason under the 1581 Act of Persuasion (23 Eliz. I, c. 1) to be reconciled to Catholicism or to shelter a reconciled Catholic. Both 'crimes' carried the death penalty. In March 1585 a retrospective Act was passed (27 Eliz. I, c. 2) against 'Jesuits and seminary priests and such like disobedient persons'. There was no other proof of any crime required; under the act it became treason simply to have been ordained priest overseas from the time of Elizabeth's accession. While the bill was being debated in Parliament, a group of prominent Catholics, believing or wanting to believe that the policy did not have the Queen's full approbation, drafted a supplication to Elizabeth pleading to be allowed some freedom of conscience.

Perusing the text today it is heart-rending to read the lamentations of the petitioners describing how they were persecuted. But the (no doubt obligatory) terms of grovelling, obsequious self-abasement in which it is couched make very uncomfortable reading. A gentleman by the name of Richard Shelley of Michelgrove, Sussex, undertook to deliver the petition personally to the Queen as she walked in her park at Greenwich. Shelley came from a family whose various branches had suffered greatly for their Faith. They gave priests to the Church as well as confessors who died in prison. Richard's brother, Edward, whom we shall meet again later, was martyred. After presenting the petition, Richard Shelley was arrested on the orders of Sir Francis Walsingham[8] and incarcerated in the Marshalsea on 15 March 1585. As he was unable to pay to provide for himself (prisoners were expected to pay for their food, drink, bedding, etc. or go without) he endured a miserable winter and soon became ill. He died in the Marshalsea early in 1586. His son, William, became a priest. It is perhaps superfluous to add that Elizabeth and her ministers completely ignored the petition, not deigning to respond. This notorious statute, 27. Eliz. I c.2, claimed the lives of

---

[2] Copyright © 1979 by the University of North Carolina Press. Used by the permission of the publisher.

The Elizabethan Persecution

over 150 innocent priests and their helpers.

The imprisoned Mary, Queen of Scots, continued to be a thorn in Elizabeth's side and a magnet for opposition. This led some Catholics to contemplate wildly unrealistic plots to depose Elizabeth, rescue Mary and place her on the throne. Such was the so-called Babington Plot of 1586. To what extent there ever was a genuine plot is a matter for conjecture. Babington and his cronies were dilettantes and the affair began as youthful posturing on their part. The serious content was provided by the government infiltrators and spies. Father Anthony Tyrell alleged at the behest of Lord Burghley that the idea originated with the priest John Ballard, whom he first met in the Gatehouse prison. They had struck up a friendship, which, as Tyrell confessed, he repaid with the most monstrous lies. Ballard is alleged to have played upon the romantic fancies of the vain Anthony Babington for rescuing the Queen of Scots from imprisonment. In truth the plot seems to have been an invention existing more in the fevered imagination of Anthony Tyrell than in reality.

Burghley supplied Tyrell with a list of names of 'divers gentlemen' and required Tyrell to supply him with incriminating evidence against them. Tyrell accordingly obliged, only later to recant and declare that not only were they all innocent of everything he had accused them but also that he had never even met some of them. Tyrell[9] was a priest whom we shall unfortunately encounter several times in our narrative. As in any totalitarian state with an efficient spy network, the government was well informed as to what was happening from an early stage. Sir Francis Walsingham instituted a system for 'secret' messages to be passed to Mary, all of which he could monitor as part of his objective to bring about the ruin of the Queen of Scots.

The conspirators' every move was closely observed by spies. One of these, Gilbert Gifford,[10] already ordained deacon, acted as a double agent, purportedly serving Mary's interests by smuggling letters to and from her while spying for Walsingham. It is clear that Walsingham nurtured, manipulated, fabricated and forged 'evidence' to make it appear that the plot included the assassination of Elizabeth, then chose the most propitious moment to pounce. Walsingham was aware of everything that was going on and the plot never posed any real threat to Elizabeth. Nonetheless, everyone deemed to be connected to the plot was executed in a particularly bloodthirsty fashion, including Father Ballard. Ordained in 1581, he seems to have been a somewhat shady character who worked under the alias 'Captain Fortescue' and liked to pretend he was influential. He appeared for his execution at Tyburn on 20 September 1586 accompanied by a servant and flamboyantly dressed 'in a grey cloak laid with gold lace, in velvet hose, a cut satin doublet, a fair hat of the newest fashion, the band being set with silver buttons'.

Justice Richard Young enlisted the help of Tyrell to send other Catholics to their deaths. Tyrell once again obliged by providing him with the false information he required, and within days of the executions of Ballard and his companions, three more victims of the lies of Anthony Tyrell were martyred on 8 October: Blessed John Adams, twenty-eight-year-old Blessed Robert Dibdale, and Blessed John Low. Adams came from Dorset. Ordained in 1580, he was described as being 'of average height with a dark beard, a sprightly look and black eyes. He was a good conversationalist, very straightforward, very pious and pre-eminently a man of hard work'. He had been captured at Winchester and banished in 1585. He must have returned immediately because he was in the Clink by December 1585. Dibdale was born at Shottery, Stratford-upon-Avon, and was sent to be educated at Louvain as a boy. He returned to England and served a term in the Gatehouse. He completed his studies at Rheims and was ordained there in the cathedral in 1584. In 1586 he was arrested in a London street. Low was born in London in 1553, the son of a merchant tailor. His family too were Catholics, for he was educated at Douai. He entered the English College, Rome, and was ordained in 1582. He was arrested near London Bridge in May 1586.

Tyrell had been moved to the Clink to preserve the pretence that he was a prisoner, while facilitating his spying activities. There he met Low, whom he calls 'a most blessed man and godly priest'. He admitted that he went to 'confession hypocritically' to Father Low in order to deceive him with his lies. He committed the further sacrilege of saying Mass in the prison the next day. Low's widowed mother lived on London Bridge, and one shudders to think that, following the usual custom, her son's severed head may have been impaled there after his execution, following which Tyrell was full of remorse. He later confessed his wickedness, declaring the priests 'three glorious and worthy martyrs' innocent of any offence, and he asked for the prayers of these and other martyrs for whose deaths he was responsible. Tyrell informs us that he was 'continually sending letters to my Lord Treasurer (Lord Burghley) and to Justice Young, 'heaping up most horrible and shameful lies' about fellow priests in custody in the Clink.

One reply from Burghley to Tyrell is illuminating. It tells him that his 'dissimulation is to a good end and therefore both tolerable and commendable'. He gave Tyrell the authority to continue acting as a Catholic priest, going to confession and celebrating Mass all in the cause of obtaining information with which to ruin his fellow Catholics. Burghley signs the letter 'Your loving friend'. Tyrell believed that the wily Burghley knew that most of the time he was lying but it suited the Lord Treasurer's purposes to treat the information Tyrell supplied as true. Shortly afterwards, Justice Young wrote to Tyrell confirming that Burghley was acting upon the authority of the Queen. Having had a meeting with Elizabeth, Young declared that Her Majesty's pleasure was to 'employ you in finding out those traitors and would have you keep your credit with them to the end that you may better decipher them'.

Walsingham, having contrived to bring about the downfall of the Queen of Scots, suggested on behalf of Elizabeth to Amias Paulet, Queen Mary's jailer, that he find some way of murdering his royal prisoner. Paulet honourably declined. So Elizabeth, always paranoid about the question of the succession, signed the death warrant and Mary was beheaded at Fotheringhay Castle in February 1587. By that stroke of the axe – or several, as it happened – Elizabeth had disposed of the rival for her throne and deprived the Catholics of a focus for conspiracies.

In spite of the way they were treated, the vast majority of the Catholics in England were very loyal and opposed any projected invasion by Spain. In spite of that, when the government got wind of the Spanish naval preparations it rounded up all prominent

Catholics, who were then imprisoned or placed under house arrest and made to pay huge fines. The fact that Catholics had demonstrated their loyalty by offering their services to the armed forces and by donating funds to the defence efforts was ignored. The failed Spanish Armada of July/August 1588 brought even greater misery and repression to Catholics, who were now suspected of being in league with foreign powers to destroy the Elizabethan regime. It resulted in the executions of over thirty priests and laypeople, all of whom have been beatified.

By this time the number of Catholics in jail was so great that new prisons had to be opened, utilising buildings such as castles. There were several such detention centres around the country, most notably the fifteenth-century Wisbech Castle in the Fens, which was used specifically for priests. Surrounded by a forty-feet-wide moat, the only access being via a drawbridge, it was in a ruinous condition by the time priests were sent there. Wisbech continued to be used as a clergy prison until 1615. Others prisons were reserved especially for the gentry. In this latter category can be cited the apparently mindless treatment meted out to John Towneley, from a prominent Lancashire family. Arrested and imprisoned at Chester Castle, he was then sent to the Marshalsea in London. From there he was sent to York Castle, then to a camp near Hull; then back to London to the Gatehouse; then to a camp at Ely. Aged seventy-three, blind and disabled, he was finally released on condition he never travelled more than five miles from his home and continued to pay the extortionate monthly fines.

It is easy to blame families who conformed, but the fines imposed for non-attendance at the Protestant services were so crippling that it meant absolute beggary for all except the wealthiest. Even keeping a known Catholic servant was an offence for which a fine had to be paid. By the end of the reign only sixteen Catholics were left still able to pay the full, annual £260 in fines for recusancy. The rest had forfeited most of their estates. Their goods – even their homes – were confiscated and sold to pay the fines. As the reign progressed, many Catholics who had Protestant relatives or friends arranged to transfer property to them in trust to protect it from the predations of the government.

The Elizabethan Persecution

I would like to give an illustration by telling the story of the Fitzherbert family because it is a classic example of the tragedy that engulfed so many recusant families.

The Preface has already alluded to the ruination of the Catholic Pulleyns of Yorkshire in penal times. The Fitzherberts were a prominent and ancient family whose estates were spread over Derbyshire and Staffordshire. Sir Anthony Fitzherbert (1470–1538), a famous lawyer and high court judge, was obliged to assist in the trial of the Carthusian priors and Richard Reynolds, and the tribunals that tried John Fisher and Thomas More. Three sons, Thomas, John and Richard, survived him. Sir Thomas, the eldest, succeeded his father as fifteenth Lord of Norbury. He was Sheriff of Staffordshire under Queen Mary. He inherited the manor of Padley through his marriage and handed over the tenancy to his younger brother, John. Under the Elizabethan penal laws he was made to pay a huge £260 a year for recusancy, which was more than his yearly rents. He had already been imprisoned many times for his refusal to conform. In 1561, when he was in the Fleet, among his fellow captives were the last Catholic Bishop of Chester and the last Catholic Dean of St Paul's. In 1568, while still in the Fleet, he witnessed the will of Dr Poole, the last Catholic Bishop of Peterborough.

In 1588 a special search of the Peak District was undertaken for papists. Sir Thomas's brother, John Fitzherbert, who had also served many terms of imprisonment, was caught hiding two priests – Blessed Robert Ludlam and Blessed Nicholas Garlick[11] – at Padley Hall. The Earl of Shrewsbury, Lord Lieutenant of Derbyshire, seized the house and all its contents on 12 July, together with many acres of surrounding land occupied by rent-paying tenants. John Fitzherbert's sons, John and Anthony, and his three married daughters, Matilda, Mary and Jane, together with their servants, were arrested.

John Fitzherbert was sent first to Sheffield and then to Derby jail, along with his son Anthony and ten servants. John and the priests Ludlam and Garlick were condemned to death, but John's life was saved by his son-in-law, who sold his manor and with the help of friends raised the huge sum of £10,000 to purchase a reprieve. However, John was kept in Derby prison for two years before being transferred to the Fleet, where he died of jail fever on 8 November 1590. Sir Anthony Fitzherbert's third son, Richard, had escaped to the Continent and later returned to Norbury, where he was arrested by order of the Privy Council in 1590. Despite falling ill in prison, he was transferred to London with his brother John, and there he too died.

Meanwhile their elder brother, Sir Thomas Fitzherbert, languished in the Tower, where he was tortured by the infamous Richard Topcliffe.[12] The shackles they placed on him were so heavy and tight that he lost the use of his legs. He was left in close confinement for three years and died in the Tower on 2 October 1591 aged seventy-four, having spent over thirty years of his life in various prisons. With the connivance of Sir Thomas's wicked nephew, Topcliffe managed to get his hands on the Padley estate for himself after the deaths of Sir Thomas and John Fitzherbert but had to forfeit it in 1603.

Of John Fitzherbert's two sons, the younger, Anthony, who had been arrested at Padley with his father, endured three years' imprisonment in Derby followed by a spell in a London jail. He continued to be harassed and convicted for recusancy for the rest of his life. The elder, Nicholas, having been attainted for treason in 1589, went into exile and became secretary to Cardinal William Allen in Rome. We shall meet his first cousin, Thomas Fitzherbert, elsewhere in our narrative.

Writing in the 1590s, Father Henry Garnet, Jesuit Superior in England, relates the following story to illustrate how desperate the persecution had become. A recusant nobleman and his eight-months pregnant wife, hiding from the authorities, lived for six weeks in an underground shelter that they had constructed under a large oak tree in their own park. They dared emerge from the narrow entrance, concealed by grass sods, only at night, when food was secretly brought to them from the house. When it rained and snowed the whole edifice collapsed in on them. Garnet also mentions groups of Catholics who banded together in comradeship, living in the ruins of old buildings to escape the pursuivants and avoid being forced to attend church or pay heavy fines.

It was not only the gentry who were caught in the clutches of the police state, which examined and recorded every minute detail of recusants' lives. Ordinary labourers were made destitute by crippling fines. Bear in mind that the fine for non-attendance at church was equivalent to two days' wages. Those recusants who could not pay were whipped in the market places, were put in the pillory, had their ears cut off, or were imprisoned until they yielded. Many spent years perpetually in and out of prison for being unable to pay the fines or endured life imprisonment rather than take the oath.

Yorkshire was recognised as the greatest centre of resistance to the Elizabethan settlement. From 1573 to the very end of the reign in 1602, there was a whole series of letters sent in the Queen's name to the mayor and aldermen of York, issuing detailed instructions on how the rigours of the law should be applied against recusants. The authorities responded by sending amazingly detailed reports back to London about known Catholics, their opinions and activities. These include tradesmen such as weavers, millers, locksmiths, tailors, butchers, carpenters, innkeepers and braziers. The names have been recorded of scores of Catholic women who suffered years of imprisonment in the most dreadful conditions in the York prisons, particularly the ghastly, disease-ridden Kidcote on Ousebridge. The dreaded lower Kidcote was regularly inundated by the river, so the inmates were in permanent damp and mud.

The long lists of those who died in the prisons of York and Hull make pitiful reading. No mercy was shown – not even to pregnant women such as Isabella Foster who was the married daughter of Blessed Richard Langley, martyred at York on 1 December 1586 for harbouring priests. Mrs Foster was in the habit of visiting the Catholic prisoners to take them food and alms and was arrested for her charity. She died a victim of disease as a close prisoner in York Castle on 3 December 1587.

Another prisoner was Isabel Whitehead, who had been a nun at Arthington Priory, Yorkshire, until her convent was closed. Arthington had been founded in 1241 and was one of only two Cluniac nunneries in England. The priory had been surrendered in November 1540 and the property given to Thomas Cranmer. The report made at the time of the suppression states that the

The Elizabethan Persecution

prioress and her nine nuns, aged between twenty-five and seventy-two, 'be of good religious living' and wished to continue in their vows. Sister Isabel seems to have spent the rest of her life in charitable work, especially visiting Catholic prisoners. Violently taken into custody while lying on her sickbed, she refused to reveal the names of priests or their whereabouts and was imprisoned and treated cruelly at York. Sister Isabel died a very old woman in March 1587 and was buried under the castle walls. She was perhaps one of the last surviving members of the suppressed religious orders.

Mrs Dorothy Brown, a widow with five children, was arraigned time after time at the assizes for refusing to attend church and each time committed to Ousebridge and other prisons. To get her released, her friends rallied round to pay her fines, she being too poor to be able to do so. She eked out a living by brewing in a small way, but in an act of petty revenge was forbidden by the Lord Mayor to carry on the trade and had her children taken from her unless she agreed to go to church. Cases such as these can be multiplied many thousands of times over year upon year.

The conspicuous part played by women in maintaining the Faith deserves deep study on its own, notwithstanding Father Roland Connelly's most valuable 1997 book on the subject, *Women of the Catholic Resistance: 1540–1680*. The records show that in the prisons it was the women who were in the majority for refusing to pay the fines. The authorities frequently adopted a policy of threatening punishment for husbands whose wives refused to conform. And completely ignoring the Pauline injunction that they should obey their husbands and submit to them, there are innumerable instances where husbands pleaded in mitigation that their obstinate wives persisted in their recusancy and they could do nothing about it.

Everyone over the age of sixteen who did not attend the Established Church was fined £20 per month, and in addition if the 'crime' persisted for a year a further fine of £200 was imposed. The statute expressly states that illness was not acceptable as an excuse for non-attendance. Those who could not pay were imprisoned without bail until they either paid or conformed.

The Elizabethan Persecution

Even young children were incarcerated to force them to incriminate their parents. A particularly cruel and wicked piece of legislation was that of 1593, which provided for the statutory removal of children from recusant parents. From the age of seven the children of such stubborn Catholics could be forcibly removed and given into the care of Protestant families. Not surprisingly, it caused significant numbers of the gentry to conform rather than lose their children. Those who had their children baptised by priests rather than in the local church were heavily fined – or worse. In Yorkshire, William Reynold was committed to York Castle for not having his child baptised in the Protestant church. He was then sent to Hull Castle, transferred to Hull Blockhouse and then sent back to York. Having spent years in jail he died there in February 1587.

Marriages were invalid unless conducted by a Protestant minister. Catholics who married secretly before a priest were punished by huge fines or imprisonment. They were regarded as 'living in sin' and their children as illegitimate. Under the Statute of Confinement, Catholics were not permitted to travel more than five miles from their homes without obtaining a licence from two magistrates and the bishop of the diocese to certify that their journey was bona fide. Failure to observe this requirement meant forfeiture of property for life.

Priests who had conformed to the Anglican services were punished for continuing to say the *Ave Maria*. The cult of the Blessed Virgin Mary, the *Mater Gloriosa*, was to be replaced with the nauseating cult of Gloriana, the 'Virgin Queen'.

Catholic books were proscribed, confiscated and burned. Smuggling Catholic literature was a very dangerous task. There was a well-organised network for supplying books, but those who printed or distributed them were severely punished. In 1577 a bookseller in Oxford was sentenced to having his ears nailed to the pillory; the only way for him to be released was for him to cut off his own ears. Others were executed, such as Blessed William Carter,[13] a printer who was hanged, drawn and quartered at Tyburn in 1584. William Roper, son-in-law of Sir Thomas More and like him a famous lawyer, got into trouble with the Council for sending money abroad for printing books. Later in the narrative we shall meet the Jesuit lay brother, Ralph Emerson, companion of Edmund Campion. Ralph was long occupied in book smuggling and when finally caught served twenty years in prison.

Dr Charles Cox, a late nineteenth-century Anglican clergyman and historian wrote in his *Three Centuries of Derbyshire Annals* (1890):

> A policy of outrageous and long-continued oppression, before which the short-lived Marian persecution absolutely pales in comparison... This page of our national history has been generally slurred over, through wilful suppression of the truth, by most of our historians. The facts are beyond dispute... every persecution was resorted to immediately after Elizabeth's accession.

The use of torture was shockingly widespread and was sanctioned by the Anglican establishment. The Calvinistic John Whitgift, Archbishop of Canterbury from 1588 to 1604, rigorously enforced the penal laws and defended the use of the rack against Catholics.

Even in death, Catholics continued to be persecuted. As recusants were excommunicated by the Established Church – the fact that they may never have belonged to that Church was a nicety that could be ignored – they were not permitted church funerals but were usually interred in common ground, often at night without any rites or ceremonies. Richard Bancroft, Protestant Archbishop of Canterbury from 1604 to 1610, complained that it was a secret practice of Catholics to wrap their dead in two winding sheets, the first containing soil blessed by a priest and placed around the corpse so that they would lie in consecrated earth. In later penal times, it was common for the relatives of dead Catholics to 'buy' an absolution in retrospect for their loved ones in order to procure for them a dignified funeral and interment close to past generations of the family. As the practice was widespread, presumably it was sufficiently lucrative to compensate the ecclesiastical authorities for their hypocritical connivance. In those rare instances where, through the influence and charity of a local landowner, a Catholic cemetery was established, the graves were usually desecrated.

The Catholic decline was a slow and gradual process, but by

The Elizabethan Persecution

the end of Elizabeth's reign of over forty-four years those attached to the Old Faith were in a minority, albeit still a substantial minority. In addition to the hundreds who suffered imprisonment and penury in the reign of 'Good Queen Bess', 128 priests and sixty-three laypeople were executed for their Catholic faith, not including those who were executed after the Northern Rising. The persecution continued to the bitter end of the reign: the last martyr, the Yorkshire priest Blessed William Richardson,[14] was executed at Tyburn just a month before the Queen's death.

The Elizabethan government anticipated that as the older priests who had been ordained in the reigns of Henry VIII and Queen Mary died out, the Catholic Church in England and Wales would simply cease to exist. It was against this background that seminaries were set up on the Continent to train devoted, courageous new priests prepared to undertake the dangerous task of ministering to the remaining faithful. The first of these seminaries was established in a hired house in 1568 by William Allen[15] at Douai in Flanders. Located on the River Scarpe, about twenty miles south of Lille, since 1677 Douai has been part of northern France, but in Allen's time it was in the territory of the Spanish Netherlands under the rule of Philip II.

Douai was a new university opened in 1562 with the aim of combating Protestantism. It was modelled on Louvain University, from which most of its early teaching staff was drawn; but there was a strong English presence and Englishmen held some of the chief posts in the early years. The first chancellor was Richard Smith, formerly Fellow of Merton College and regius professor of divinity at Oxford. Dr Owen Lewis was regius professor of canon law, having held the same post at Oxford, so many of the old Oxford traditions were maintained at Douai. It was thus a most congenial place for the Fellow of Oriel and former Principal of St Mary's Hall, William Allen, to set up his new college.

It attracted many students of the highest calibre and published a stream of polemical works and Catholic literature. First among them was the English translation of the Bible – 'Douai-Rheims' – so named because, following the unstable political situation in Flanders, the English College resided at Rheims in France from 1578 to 1593. The project to translate the Latin Vulgate into

English was of long gestation until undertaken by Gregory Martin[16] at the behest of William Allen. The New Testament was published in 1582 and the Old Testament in 1609. The debt owed by the translators of the later Authorised Version under James I to the Douai-Rheims Bible has never received the recognition it deserves. Douai College was suppressed in 1792 during the French Revolution and re-founded at Ware, Hertfordshire, in 1793 and Ushaw, Durham, in 1808.

The lasting work of Douai on which rests its fame was the training of seminary priests for the English mission: the only means by which Catholicism in England could be saved from extinction. The first Douai seminary priest to return to England in 1574 was the Welshman, Lewis Barlow,[17] who worked mainly in Suffolk. He was the precursor of hundreds of Douai-trained priests, nearly 170 of whom were executed and a great many more suffered imprisonment and torture. Allen was also instrumental, together with Pope Gregory XIII Buoncompagni (1572–85) as patron, in converting the old English hospice in Rome into a seminary in 1580, named the Venerable English College. It continued to be administered by the Jesuits until 1773. In 1589 Allen cooperated with the Jesuits in establishing an English College at Valladolid, Spain, which they continued to administer until 1767. Other colleges under the Jesuits were later set up in Seville in 1592 and Lisbon in 1628, a college that survived until 1971.

The Elizabethan government employed spies who entered the seminaries only to return to England to inform on their brethren. It is the case that by no means were all the seminary priests as faithful or courageous as our martyrs. Sad to relate, many priests apostatised and saved themselves by agreeing Judas-like to become government spies, some being planted in the prisons. From these renegades the government was able to obtain authentic information about the seminaries and who frequented them. Because they were able to identify priests, the traitors were responsible for causing the imprisonment or death of a great many colleagues and imperilled the Catholics who had risked their lives to shelter them. Some apostate priests were rewarded with parishes or positions in the Established Church. A couple are

The Elizabethan Persecution

known to have died on the gallows as common criminals.

With the benefit of charitable hindsight, these priests should be pitied for their weakness rather than condemned for their treachery. They knew only too well, particularly in the later years of Elizabeth's reign, that they could expect no mercy if captured. Take the case of Yorkshireman Thomas Bell as an instance of the kind of treatment to which they were subjected. Bell was ordained in 1580 and at one time he had boldly infiltrated York Castle and for fourteen days remained undetected while saying Mass and hearing confessions. He then moved to Lancashire and served diligently, often in great danger. Back in York, he was captured and committed to Ousebridge, where he remained several years. We are told that one exceptionally freezing cold winter he was kept in the stocks day after day while being harangued by Protestant ministers. By 1592, obviously unable to withstand the pressures, he had conformed, apostatised and become a spy. Other prisoners might be treated more humanely, but not priests. For example, the records show that in the three-year period between 1592 and 1594 there were sixty-one pardons issued for murderers, burglars and highway robbers; there is not one pardon for a priest or anyone who sheltered him.

The seminary priests lived lonely, hunted lives, rarely daring to relax their vigilance, placing their trust in those brave enough to offer them shelter, and in perpetual anxiety that they and their hosts, who were constantly under surveillance, may be captured at any time. The pursuivants who hunted them were nothing but bandits plying their vile government-sanctioned trade for profit and sadistic satisfaction. They behaved with impunity, raiding and ransacking houses without warning at any time, night or day, smashing up the property, plundering possessions and livestock and physically mistreating the occupants in their lucrative search for priests or evidence of a Catholic presence.

In urban areas, most priests lived shut away in attics or cellars, afraid to have a light that might attract attention and unable to move around too much for fear of making a noise that would alert the servants. They might spend weeks in oppressive isolation, venturing out only in the dead of night to perform some priestly function or meet up with a fellow priest. In rural areas they were able to travel around either on foot or, if lucky, on horseback. They were constantly on the move from place to place, reliant upon a farm, a cottage or a secluded country house which they would stealthily enter to spend a restless night before heading off again before dawn. Failing that they would spend their nights in barns or under the hedgerows. The fortunate ones – if such a term may be used in the context – were those who obtained rare, semi-permanent places in the houses of the nobility or gentry. Here they would enjoy greater liberty and be able to carry on a fruitful ministry within the household and to the neighbourhood. Father John Gerard SJ[18] described the houses of the Catholic country gentry as the churches of the time. In all but a few of the larger towns and cities, Catholicism depended upon them for its survival.

Since necessity required that they lived in secrecy, disguised and under false names, all too little is recorded about the hundreds of seminary priests who lived and died in obscurity. There are some seminary priests whose real names have never been discovered. They are known to us only by the aliases they adopted. Father Gerard tells us that when a priest died it was imperative that his identity be kept secret, as he was in the country illegally. Those who died in towns had to be buried on the properties they occupied, sometimes in gardens or even basements. Such was the fate of the Cornishman Father John Curry. Ordained in 1577, he joined the Jesuits in 1583. He was closely associated with many martyrs. He helped St Edmund Campion distribute his books and shared a room with St Ralph Sherwin. He moved to Dorset and became chaplain to Lady Arundell at Chideock, at whose house also lived Blessed John Cornelius SJ, martyred at Dorchester in 1594 along with three laymen who had sheltered him: Blessed Thomas Bosgrave, Blessed John Carey and Blessed Patrick Salmon.

Father Curry moved back to London and was described by a spy as being 'about forty years old, long, slender-faced, with black hair and a little black beard.' Father Gerard records that he died in the house kept by St Anne Line and was buried there secretly. All the information about Father Curry's movements comes from informers. It is an irony of history that so much information

The Elizabethan Persecution

about our martyrs, including their physical descriptions and the clothes they wore, comes via reports from the efficient network of spies and informers who infiltrated the Catholic community.

The lengths to which the informers went to ingratiate themselves with Catholics can be illustrated by the case of Nicholas Berden, one of the best – if one can use that adjective pejoratively – of Francis Walsingham's spies. In 1586, for sordid gain, Berden wrote to Thomas Phelippes, the government's forger-in-chief, asking him to intercede with his master, Walsingham, to procure the release of two priests: Ralph Bickley, the friend of St Ralph Sherwin, who had been in the Gatehouse for a year; and Richard Sherwood, alias Carleton, then in the Counter, Wood Street. (We shall meet Richard again in the story of St Edmund Gennings.) The mercenary Berden said the two priests were worth £20 and £30 to him respectively, as someone would go surety for their release. It would also make them more beholden to Berden. Phelippes passed on the request to Walsingham, but it was not granted, as Sherwood was banished later that year and Bickley was sent to Wisbech Castle, where he became a Jesuit and remained until 1618.

Undeterred, Berden soon tried again. He wrote directly to Walsingham, thanking him for sparing the life of Father Christopher Dryland (who we shall come across in our narrative) at Berden's request, because it had 'much increased my credit amongst the Papists' if they thought that it was by his endeavour that the priest's life had been saved. He declared how much he abhorred the priest but asked Walsingham the favour of releasing Dryland from prison, as that would further increase the trust the papists had in him. Berden clearly had great influence; one wonders just how many more like him there were.

The State Papers contain his comments to Walsingham on captured priests as to whether they should be executed or kept in prison. Were it not there in black and white as proof it would be unthinkable that the lives of priests might have depended upon the whim of such a squalid villain. He was instrumental in deciding to which prisons some priests were directed. Working in league with the prison keepers, from whom he received backhanders, he produced lists of the names of priests in various jails, arranging for the 'best priests', i.e. those who could afford to pay most for their custody, to be sent to them, enabling the keepers to make a bigger profit. When Anthony Tyrell's inventive fabrications had run their course he asked to be released from the Clink and was party to a similar subterfuge. In an attempt at allaying suspicion he asked Justice Young to also release Father Nicholas Gellebrand, a Marian priest.

George Orwell did not invent 'Big Brother' or the thought police in his novel *1984*. Nor did that dubious distinction belong to the Stalinist system Orwell was satirising: Elizabeth I and her merciless ministers had beaten Stalin to it 350 years earlier. The ruthless activities of the Elizabethan government against the Catholic community may be justifiably compared with the methods used by the totalitarian regimes of the twentieth century, and it is the only rationale that satisfactorily explains why the majority of the population became Protestant. But just as it survived under those totalitarian regimes, the Faith in England and Wales was not extinguished; sustained by the brave seminary priests, it survived its catacomb existence.

The Elizabethan Persecution

Notes to Chapter Three

[1] William Cecil, Baron Burghley, was born in 1520. He served in various capacities during the Lord Protectorship of Somerset, and under Northumberland he was made Secretary of State. He managed to avoid getting involved in Northumberland's attempt to usurp the throne and suffered no consequences during Mary's reign, when he sat in Parliament. He came to prominence under Elizabeth whom he served as secretary and Lord Treasurer and as her chief adviser for forty years. He was to all intents and purposes what today would be the Prime Minister. His personal religious views were Puritan but he recognised that he had to support the Anglican Establishment. He was uncompromisingly harsh towards Catholics, whose continuing presence he did all in his power to crush. Created a baron in 1571, he died in 1598.

[2] Edmund Bonner of London was deprived May 1559 and sent to the Marshalsea where he spent ten years, dying in September 1569; Ralph Bayne of Lichfield, deprived June, died November 1559; Owen Oglethorpe of Carlisle, deprived June, died December 1559; Henry Morgan of St David's, deprived June 1559, died December 1559; John White of Winchester, deprived June 1559, died January 1560; Cuthbert Scott of Chester, deprived June 1559, died 1565; Richard Pate of Worcester, deprived June 1559, died 1565; Thomas Watson of Lincoln, deprived June 1559, died in Wisbech Castle in September 1584 at the age of seventy-one having spent twenty-five years in prison. Thomas Thirlby of Ely, deprived July 1559, died 1570; Nicholas Heath of York, deprived July 1559, died 1579; Gilbert Bourne of Bath and Wells, deprived October 1559, died 1569; Cuthbert Tunstall of Durham, deprived September and died November 1559 aged eighty-five; David Poole of Peterborough, deprived November 1559, died 1568; James Turberville of Exeter, deprived November 1559, died 1570. The last survivor of the hierarchy, Thomas Goldwell of St Asaph, was deprived July 1559 and fled to Rome, where he spent most of the rest of his life. He died in Rome in 1585 at the age of eighty-five. As a footnote of history, it was he who ordained priest St Camillus de Lellis (1550–1614) who

became the founder of the Ministers of the Sick, the forerunner of the Red Cross.

[3] Matthew Parker, the first Anglican Archbishop of Canterbury, was born in Norwich 1504. After achieving a BA at Cambridge, he was ordained priest in 1527. He became the favourite chaplain of Queen Anne Boleyn before becoming Vice-Chancellor of Cambridge University on the nomination of Henry VIII. Within a short time of the accession of Edward VI, he 'jumped the gun' by taking a wife prior to the legalisation of clergy marriages. By this time he had aligned himself firmly in the Protestant camp, but in 1552 was made Dean of Lincoln. Under Mary, Parker was deprived of his appointments. When Elizabeth succeeded to the throne she chose Parker to be her Archbishop of Canterbury. He had to wait five months for his consecration because it proved difficult to find the four bishops required to ordain him to the episcopate. The reason why the depositions of the Catholic bishops was spread out over a number of months was in the hope that some of them would consent to consecrate Parker. None did so. Four Protestant bishops who had been deprived under Mary, two of whom had been excommunicated and had never been validly consecrated, performed the task, for which purpose the Edwardine Ordinal was used. This was not legal at the time as it had been abolished by Parliament under Mary, so Parker's claim to validity as archbishop rested entirely upon the will of Elizabeth as Supreme Governor of the Church of England. Contemporary Catholics derided the validity of Anglican orders and from the outset consistently referred to Church of England clerics as 'pretended bishops and false priests'. The Catholic Church has always maintained that Parker's consecration was invalid because it was defective both in form and intention, and therefore neither he nor any whom he subsequently ordained were in the Apostolic Succession. Parker was a moderate man who never involved himself in the government. He died in 1575.

[4] Blessed Thomas Plumtree was educated at Corpus Christi, Oxford. He was Rector of Stubton in his native Lincolnshire. He resigned his parish with the accession of Elizabeth and became a schoolmaster, only to have to give up his post because he would not conform. Having acted as a chaplain in the Northern Rising and celebrated

Mass in the cathedral, he was hanged, drawn and quartered at Durham on 4 January 1570.

[5] Blessed John Felton came from a Norfolk family but was born at Bermondsey in London. He was condemned for publishing the bull of Pope Pius V excommunicating Elizabeth by nailing it to the door of the Bishop of London. After being tortured in the Tower, he was hanged, drawn and quartered in St Paul's Churchyard, London on 8 August 1570.

[6] Blessed John Storey was born at Salisbury and educated at Oxford, becoming a Doctor of Law. He served as a Member of Parliament for Wiltshire, but being unable to accept the new religious settlement he went to live abroad. He was tricked into boarding a ship at Antwerp, forcibly taken to England and imprisoned in the Tower. He was falsely accused of treason and without any real evidence was condemned. Before he was hanged, drawn and quartered at Tyburn on 1 June 1571, he made a plea for his wife and four children to be taken care of.

[7] Blessed Thomas Woodhouse was ordained during the reign of Mary and served as a parish priest in Lincolnshire. He was arrested for continuing to say Mass and imprisoned in Newgate, where he remained for twelve years before being condemned to death for refusing to conform. He was hanged, drawn and quartered at Tyburn on 19 June 1573.

[8] Sir Francis Walsingham (c.1530–1590) was born at Chislehurst, Kent. He studied at Cambridge but did not take a degree. In 1552 he enrolled at Gray's Inn, but on Mary's accession he went abroad, returning when Elizabeth succeeded. A protégé of William Cecil, he was elected to Parliament in 1559. He became the chief spymaster of the Elizabethan government, organising one of the most efficient European-wide spy networks in history, indulging in deceptions and fabrications and plots against all those thought suspect in loyalty. His spies were skilled at forging documents and he was adept at concocting plots to entrap his victims, including Mary, Queen of Scots. The wily, cunning character of the man is well captured in his portrait.

[9] Anthony Tyrell is archetypical of the damage that an apostate priest could inflict on Catholics. Born in 1552, he came from an Essex

recusant family who fled abroad. He was one of the original band of students at the English College, Rome, and was ordained in 1580. Having returned to England he was captured in London in 1581 and sent to the Gatehouse, from where he escaped early in 1582. He spent two years abroad doing precisely no one knows what before returning to England with Father John Ballard in the autumn of 1584. At the time of the supposed discovery of the Babington Plot, Tyrell was arrested and imprisoned. He was examined by Walsingham, Topcliffe and Justice Young. The nature of the pressures that may have been exerted upon him is unclear, but by his own testimony they seem to have taken the form of subtle persuasion rather than physical threats. Nonetheless he proceeded to incriminate Father Ballard and many others. Among other outrageous accusations he claimed they had obtained the Pope's authority to assassinate Elizabeth. He then issued a long recantation, confessing that it was all lies. It did not save the fourteen who were executed for their supposed part in the Babington Plot. He also wrote to the relatives of those whom he had falsely accused asking their forgiveness, as well as sending a long missive to the Queen craving her pardon for all the lying information he had supplied, which he attributes to 'sin and the devil'. Tyrell apostatised and recanted at least three more times. A pathological liar, it is impossible to know which, if indeed any, of his statements are true. Later in life he wrote an excruciatingly long and exaggerated account of his 'lamentable fall' in which he listed forty-seven people, including the Pope, the Queen of Scots and St Philip Howard and his wife, all of whom he had maliciously accused with his abominable lies. He retracted everything he had said about them and begged their forgiveness. In 1589 Tyrell was granted a pardon for his services and made rector of Dengie, Essex. He was deprived of this living but became vicar of Southminster in 1591. Now married, he went through yet another reversion to Catholicism and was sent to the Marshalsea in 1593, from where he wrote a grovelling letter to Robert Cecil. He continued as a Protestant minister and gave anti-Catholic evidence before Archbishop Bancroft in 1602. What then happened to him is unsure but it appears he retired to Belgium, where his Catholic brother lived. As all bad pennies have a habit of doing, he finally turned up again in Naples, where he died in 1615 –

allegedly reconciled to the Church to which his treachery had done so much harm.

[10] Gilbert Gifford, born in 1560, came from a Staffordshire recusant family and was a second cousin of Father John Gerard. He went to Douai in 1577, later transferring to the English College, Rome. He was expelled but given a second chance by Cardinal Allen and was finally ordained deacon in 1585. Later that year he returned to England, where he was arrested and examined by Francis Walsingham. This resulted in Gifford agreeing to act as a double agent. His actions ensured the downfall of Anthony Babington and all associated with him. He left England after the executions and despite Allen's misgivings was inexplicably ordained priest in March 1587. In December of that year he was arrested in a Paris brothel. He continued sending information to the British government about his co-religionists until his death in 1590.

[11] Ludlam and Garlick: Robert Ludlam, born in Derbyshire c.1551, studied at St John's College, Oxford and at Rheims, where he was ordained in 1581. He returned to England in 1582 and worked on the English mission for about six years. Arrested at Padley Hall, he was sent to Derby jail, where he met Father Richard Simpson, who had already been tried and condemned but reprieved because he was wavering. Robert was hanged, drawn and quartered at St Mary's Bridge, Derby on 24 July 1588. Nicholas Garlick, born near Glossop, Derbyshire c.1555, studied at Gloucester Hall, Oxford, but did not take a degree. He became a schoolmaster at Tideswell Grammar School. One of his pupils was Christopher Buxton, who became a priest and was martyred at Canterbury in 1588. Nicholas was ordained at Rheims in 1582 and returned to work on the English mission. He was arrested and banished in 1585 but soon returned and was captured and executed, with Ludlam and Simpson. The latter was born near Ripon, went to Douai and was ordained in 1577. The company of Ludlam and Garlick strengthened his resolve and he was martyred with them. All three were beatified in 1987.

[12] Richard Topcliffe (1532–1604) came from a landed Lincolnshire family. He was orphaned at a young age and studied law at Gray's Inn. He was a Member of Parliament in the service of William Cecil and worked closely with Francis Walsingham. His precise official status remains a mystery but he was known as 'Her Majesty's Servant'

The Elizabethan Persecution

and held a commission to hunt down priests and had permission to torture them in the private torture chamber installed at his home. In a letter to Queen Elizabeth he boasted that he had been responsible for sending more priests to Tyburn than anyone else. There are no words adequate to convey the depraved nature of this cruel, vicious, evil, sadistic monster, who today would be classed as a psychopath.

[13] Blessed William Carter, born in London *c.*1550, was a printer and because of his trade he was constantly under surveillance. He was married but his wife died in 1582. He was arrested in 1578 and spent time in prison. Committed to the Gatehouse in 1579 for recusancy, he was released in 1581. He was discovered printing Catholic books, in particular Father Gregory Martin's *A Treatise of Schism*, and also storing vestments and sacred vessels. Arrested again in 1582 by Topcliffe, he was sent to the Tower and tortured but he refused to reveal information about his fellow Catholics. His trial, presided over by John Aylmer, Bishop of London, was a travesty. He was violently insulted and abused by the prosecution and the judges joined in urging his guilt. He was hanged, drawn and quartered at Tyburn on 1 January 1584.

[14] Blessed William Richardson was born near Sheffield in 1572. Educated at Valladolid, he was ordained at Seville. Betrayed by a false Catholic, he was captured at one of the Inns of Court and sent to Newgate in February 1603. He was tried before Lord Chief Justice Popham, condemned to death for his priesthood, and hanged, drawn and quartered at Tyburn the next day, accompanied by a throng of Catholics who crowded around him until the end.

[15] William Allen was born in the parish of Poulton-le-Fylde, Lancashire in 1522, the son of John Allen and Jane Lister. A BA and MA of Oriel College, Oxford, he became principal of St Mary's Hall. He left England permanently in 1565 and was ordained at Malines. Convinced that the future of Catholicism depended upon a supply of well-trained priests in tune with the Counter-Reformation spirit of the Council of Trent, he established the college at Douai to send clergy to the English mission. He was president of Douai for seventeen years. Called to serve in Rome in 1585 he was created Cardinal in 1587. He published many works in defence of Catholicism. He became involved in political intrigues with Spain, which was not at all in accordance with the views of most Catholics

in England. Nonetheless Allen deserved the gratitude of English Catholics for his lifelong labours in preserving the Faith in their country. He died in Rome in 1594 and was buried in the chapel of the English College. Two of his nieces, Helen and Catherine Allen, became nuns at St Monica's, Louvain, under Mother Margaret Clement.

[16] Gregory Martin was born in Sussex. He spent thirteen years at Oxford and acquired a reputation as a brilliant scholar and linguist. He was ordained deacon in the Anglican Church, but being Catholic at heart he left the university and for a time was tutor to Philip Howard, Earl of Arundel, the future martyr. He went to Douai and was ordained priest in 1573. He devoted the remainder of his life to teaching and to the work on which rests his lasting fame: the translation of the Bible into English from the Vulgate. Although the translation lacks the harmonious cadences of the later Authorised Version, its value lies in its accuracy, a fact recognised by all modern translations. Worn out by his labours, Gregory died of consumption at Rheims in 1582.

[17] Lewis Barlow, born in Pembrokeshire, entered the Middle Temple in 1567, followed by an exile in Flanders in 1571. Ordained in 1574, he returned to England and worked mainly in Suffolk. Arrested in 1587, thanks to the treachery of Anthony Tyrell, he was imprisoned in the Counter, Wood Street, London. He was moved to the Marshalsea, where he sent for Tyrell to admonish him very lovingly for his anti-Catholic activities, urging him to repentance. Barlow was moved to Wisbech Castle in 1588 before being banished in 1603. He returned to England later that same year and died in Oxfordshire in 1610.

[18] John Gerard SJ was born in 1564, the son of Sir Thomas Gerard. He is one of the most fascinating of all the priests who worked in England. His two books, the *Narrative of the Gunpowder Plot* and his *Autobiography*, provide a vivid insight into the lives of the English Catholic community. The books are invaluable sources of contemporary information. Ordained in 1588, he joined the Jesuits and returned to England. He avoided capture on many occasions but at the time of the Gunpowder Plot he also suffered imprisonment and torture, primarily in an attempt to make him reveal the whereabouts of Father Henry Garnet. In spite of his weakness from

torture while awaiting trial, with the aid of friends outside, by means of a rope attached to a tower and stretched across the moat he made a daredevil escape from the Tower of London in 1597. He carried on his ministry, a wanted man, until 3 May 1606, when he crossed the Channel disguised in the livery of an ambassador on the very day that his Superior, Father Henry Garnet, was executed. He died at the English College, Rome, in 1637 aged seventy-three. To quote the nineteenth-century Anglican, Dr Jessop, writing in 1881:

> The extent of Gerard's influence was nothing less than marvellous. His powers of endurance of fatigue and pain were almost superhuman... his autobiography... recent research has proved to be absolutely correct. As a literary effort merely the autobiography is marvellous.

Chapter Four

The Elizabethan Martyrs, 1577–1601

Cuthbert Mayne

Tyrants seldom want pretexts.

Edmund Burke 1729–97

The first martyr of the seminaries was the son of William Mayne of Youlston in the parish of Sherwell near Barnstaple, Devon. He was baptised on St Cuthbert's Day, 20 March 1544. His uncle was a priest who had conformed to the Established Church in order to keep his benefice. Hoping that his nephew would succeed him in his comfortable living, he had Cuthbert educated at Barnstaple Grammar School. In December 1561, at the age of seventeen, Cuthbert was inducted as rector of the village of Huntshaw, south of Barnstaple. He soon went to Oxford to prepare for ordination, firstly to St Alban's Hall (since renamed Merton College) and then to St John's College. He took the oath and orders in the Anglican Church and became chaplain of St John's College. He graduated BA in 1566 and MA in 1570.

At Oxford University he found that there was still a strong attachment to Catholicism and he became friends with several staunch Catholics. He also met the two men who were to influence the whole direction of his life: the convinced Catholic Gregory Martin and the wavering Edmund Campion. Cuthbert gradually became uneasy about his own religious position, watching as one after another men were forced to resign or were deprived of their teaching posts because of their Catholic sympathies. Francis Walsingham, Elizabeth's spymaster in chief, wrote, 'Those who are seminary priests learnt not their papistry abroad but carried it with them from their Oxford colleges.'

The Elizabethan Martyrs, 1577-1601

Martin and Campion wrote frequently to Mayne to persuade him to join them at Douai. In 1570 a letter to him from Gregory Martin on matters of faith was intercepted by the Protestant Bishop of London who deduced from it that Mayne was a suspect papist and sent a pursuivant to Oxford to arrest him. Warned of his imminent arrest by a fellow Devonian student, Thomas Ford,[1] Cuthbert had already left Oxford for Devon. Here he made contact with Catholics, including old Marian priests, as he made his way into Cornwall. After three years of spiritual struggle his mind was at last made up. He took ship, probably from Padstow, directly to France and made his way to Douai, where he was received into the Catholic Church. In 1575 he was ordained priest and in February 1576 he graduated from Douai University.

On 24 April 1576, at his own request, he set out for England in the company of another future martyr, John Paine. Strictly enjoined not to engage in any political activity, they were equipped with the bare necessities to carry out their priestly functions: a Mass kit, a small crucifix, a stole suitable for all seasons, vestments and copies of the scriptures. Cuthbert also carried with him a printed copy of an outdated papal bull announcing the Jubilee year in 1575, which he had bought in Douai probably as a souvenir. After a stormy crossing, the two priests landed in England and were detained on suspicion and examined. Their baggage was searched and their papers scrutinised by port officers. In spite of the religious contents of their luggage they were allowed to proceed. Cuthbert made his way to London, where he is believed to have stayed at the house of the Arundells in Clerkenwell; it was they no doubt who arranged for him to go to the Tregians in Cornwall. Cuthbert was taken in by the long-suffering Francis Tregian at his home, Golden Manor, at Probus near Tregony, a few miles east of Truro. Here Cuthbert acted as steward on the extensive Tregian estates.

Almost nothing is known of Cuthbert's year-long apostolate but it is not difficult to imagine the form it took: saying Mass for the family and neighbours, administering the Sacraments and reconciling those who had conformed. He would have ridden about the country lanes visiting Catholic families while ostensibly

The Elizabethan Martyrs, 1577-1601

keeping an eye on the widespread Tregian farms and properties. He made friends with a number of families who were later to suffer for their loyalty. It is known that he visited Sir John Arundell's house, Lanherne, at St Mawgan on a number of occasions. The Arundells were among the leading West Country families, and were connected to the royal family by marriage. Despite enduring many vicissitudes they had remained faithful Catholics. Francis Tregian's mother being an Arundell, they were closely allied to the Tregians by marriage. In this lay the seeds of the downfall of Cuthbert and his protectors.

The subsequently famous Richard Grenville had been made Sheriff of Cornwall in 1576. He was a member of an old Cornish seafaring family whose father had lost his life in the sinking of the *Mary Rose* in 1545. He had twice been a Member of Parliament but, currently out of favour at Court, Grenville was anxious to ingratiate himself once more. We can still read in the State Papers a contemporary assessment of his character. He was a man of 'intolerable pride and insatiable ambition, unquiet in his mind… of nature very severe, so that his own people hated him for his fierceness and spoke hardly of him'.

Grenville was envious of the wealth and influence of the Arundells and Tregians. A fanatical anti-Catholic, in 1570 he had made a declaration of his acceptance of the Act of Uniformity. He harboured a personal hatred for Francis Tregian and Sir John Arundell. He must have been made aware for some time that a priest was operating from Golden Manor, but he bided his time. From the evidence now available, it appears that the government was watching Tregian and intended to make an example of him. The Queen authorised her Boleyn cousin, Sir George Carey, to proceed against Tregian, applying the statute of praemunire, under which it was a felony to recognise the authority of the Pope in England. If found guilty the penalty was forfeiture of all goods and perpetual imprisonment. Carey's prize for a successful outcome would be the possession of Tregian's estates. Carey, later Lord Hunsdon, enlisted the help of Richard Grenville.

On 8 June 1577, which happened to be Corpus Christi that year, came the pretext he needed to act. A prisoner had escaped and efforts were being made to recapture him. There was never any suggestion that he might have found his way onto the Tregian estates, but as the Protestant Bishop of Exeter was on a visitation to Truro at the time he was persuaded by Grenville to agree to a search of Golden Manor. The legality of the proposed raid was extremely doubtful; nonetheless Grenville assembled a formidable armed posse of over one hundred for the purpose, which descended en masse upon Golden Manor. The house was surrounded as Tregian met Grenville in the courtyard, protesting at the unwarranted intrusion and denying any knowledge of the escaped convict. Grenville forced his way in. Cuthbert had been in the garden, but hearing the commotion had re-entered his chamber from outside. Grenville, presumably having been tipped off, made his way straight to the room and hammered on the door. He must have been nonplussed when Cuthbert himself opened it. Seizing Cuthbert, he shouted, 'What have we here? Who are you?' To which Mayne simply, if somewhat ironically, replied, 'A man, sir.'

While Cuthbert was securely held, Grenville ripped off the priest's doublet revealing a thin cord from which was suspended a little wax Agnus Dei medallion. He snatched the image from Mayne's neck. Cuthbert's room was then thoroughly ransacked and all his books, papers and his 'massing stuff' seized as evidence. Grenville ordered the arrest of Cuthbert and Tregian along with eight others. Their hands tied behind their backs, they were carried off to Truro.

The elderly Bishop Broadbridge, not feeling up to interrogating a popish priest, was given the uncomfortable task of examining Francis Tregian, one of the wealthiest leaders of Cornish society. He found that Tregian, rock solid in his Faith, had no patience with theological niceties and appeared rather unconcerned with the affairs of the world, so the bishop threw in the towel. As a symbol of his power and authority, following an unprecedented ransacking of homes, in August Grenville had ordered the arrest of thirty-one other leading Cornish Catholics for recusancy, including Sir John Arundell. Grenville had been thorough; hardly any family among the Catholic gentry of Cornwall had been left untouched.

Tregian was sent to the Fleet prison and Arundell to the Tower of London in readiness for their trial before the Council.

Anthony Tyrell was called into service to provide 'evidence' against Arundell. He claimed to have visited him at his house and heard Sir John and his family indulge in 'treasonable' talk, when in truth he had never met Arundell. Cuthbert, loaded with iron chains, was dragged in stages the forty miles from Truro to Launceston Castle, where he was incarcerated in virtual solitary confinement in a dark and filthy dungeon to await trial.

On 23 September 1577, he and his eight companions were indicted for treason at the assizes. Cuthbert faced six indictments, including bringing in the papal bull and the Agnus Dei, for saying Mass and for upholding the authority of the Pope. Tregian was named as the procurer of the priest's services and Arundell was indicted for refusing to go to church. Of the eight others all were charged with aiding and abetting the priest. They had accompanied Cuthbert on some of his journeys and delivered messages for him. John Kempe, Richard Tremayne, Thomas Harris and Richard Hore were all persons of social standing in the county. Hore was cited as being in possession of a rosary. John Williams, a schoolmaster, had brought his child to Golden to be baptised. John Hodge was a tailor who supervised all the household sewing requirements, while John Philips and James Humphreys were yeomen farmers.

Prosecuting was Sir John Popham, soon to become Solicitor General and a future Attorney General and Lord Chief Justice. Hearing the case were Sir Roger Manwood, an ardent Protestant and a harsh and cruel judge, and Sir John Jeffreys. There was a flaw in the proceedings insofar as the laws that were to make the trial a mere formality had not yet been passed, but there was enough anti-Catholic legislation to make a charge stick: after all, it was treasonable to bring any papal bull into the country. Jeffreys was satisfied that the bull was no longer in force. But Manwood told the jury to ignore this fact, calling Cuthbert a 'traitor to the Queen's realm'. Jeffreys, who was clearly unhappy with the whole proceedings, also felt that the evidence for saying Mass was entirely circumstantial; but again he was overruled. Grenville, anxious to ensure that it was established that Mayne had said Mass at Golden, was allowed to harangue the jury. The jury was informed that 'where proof could not be procured, strong presumption might supply its place' (Lingard).

The Elizabethan Martyrs, 1577-1601

As the eminent historian, Lord Macaulay (1800–59) wrote in his *Essay on the History of the Reformation*:

> The trials of the accused Catholics were exactly like all state trials of those days; that is to say, as infamous as they could be. A state trial was merely a murder preceded by the uttering of certain gibberish and the performance of certain mummeries.

Thus it was with Mayne; thus it was with all those priests who suffered after him.

After such a blatantly sham propaganda trial, they were all found guilty on every point of their indictment. Cuthbert and Francis Tregian were sentenced to death. When passing sentence, Manwood agreed that 'Though the bull be out of date we never did nor do account any such thing to be of force or to be worth a straw. Yet the same is by the law of this realm treason and thou therefore have deserved to die.'

Cuthbert received his sentence with a happy countenance, raised his eyes and said '*Deo gratias.*'

John Jeffreys was uneasy that a man was to be executed just because of his religion. He thought it a poor advertisement for the justice system of a Queen who had declared she would not 'open windows into men's souls'. He successfully had the case referred to the whole bench of judges in London. On balance, the majority shared Jeffreys' view, but the final decision rested with the Privy Council. As a result Mayne was made to wait three months before the sentence was carried out.

Grenville in the meantime had hurried off to London, fearful that the death sentence would not be upheld. He found the Council split in their opinions, while expressing approval of the measures he had taken against the Catholics in his jurisdiction. The Council finally upheld the sentence on the grounds that 'we need to make a terror for these papists'. Grenville visited the Queen at Windsor, where she bestowed a knighthood on him for his services in dealing with 'a matter of religion'. Having obtained confirmation of the sentence, Grenville, presumably enjoying his reinstatement at Court, surprisingly lingered on in London rather than hurrying back to Launceston for the execution.

Cuthbert was given three days' notice of his execution. He was

The Elizabethan Martyrs, 1577-1601

offered life and liberty if he would take the Oath of Supremacy but he refused. When the jailer told him the day on which he was to die, he replied, 'I wish I had something valuable to give you for the good news you bring me.'

The following day he was taken to the Assize Hall and made to stand for seven hours with fetters on his ankles and wrists while being questioned by a group of Protestant ministers and officials. Their threats and promises could not shake his resolve. Full details of his examination may still be read in the Public Records Office. While admitting his priesthood, he refused to disclose any information about his contacts or where he had said Mass. Calling for a Bible and kissing it, he stoutly maintained that 'the Queen neither ever was, nor is, nor ever shall be, head of the Church in England', and upheld the conscientious right of Catholics to refuse to attend the Established Church. He also asked for clemency to be shown to those convicted with him. The written statements of his replies bear Cuthbert's signature: 'These things affirmed by me Cuthbert Mayne I think to be trewe'.

On 30 November 1577 he was placed on a hurdle and led out to suffer the full agony of his sentence in Launceston market place. The deputy sheriff, George Grenville, presided over the execution. On the scaffold Cuthbert was pressed to incriminate Tregian and Arundell, but he defended their reputation saying only that he knew them to be 'good and godly gentlemen'. As a final indignity he was made to ascend the ladder backwards so that he faced the crowd of spectators. This he accomplished with great difficulty, his feet slipping off the rungs as the hangman supported him up to the platform from where he began a brief speech. He said that the law had judged him worthy of death but he asserted his innocence as God would shortly be his judge. He was interrupted by one of the magistrates, who called on the hangman to make haste and place the rope around his neck. As he was quickly turned off the ladder he was heard to exclaim, '*In manus tuas, Domine.*'

They had built an exceptionally high gallows and Cuthbert swung widely from the gibbet, his head violently striking the side of the scaffold, severely bruising his face and damaging his eye, while the executioner wildly slashed at the rope. As he fell to the

The Elizabethan Martyrs, 1577-1601

ground the executioner tore off his clothes, straddling his body as he carried out the bloody butchery. Cuthbert's head was hung on Launceston Castle and his quarters sent to Bodmin, Wadebridge, Tregony and to Barnstaple as a warning to all. Father Gregory Martin wrote to inform Edmund Campion of Cuthbert's martyrdom. 'The novice has outdistanced me,' was Edmund's reaction. 'May he be favourable to his old friend and tutor. I shall boast of these titles now more than ever.'

Cuthbert's martyrdom and the wholesale round-up of Catholics associated with him had far greater significance than the death of one priest. It was tantamount to an acknowledgment by the government that its policy had failed and that far more brutal measures would have to be employed if Catholicism was to be eradicated. This was especially so with the influx of zealous young priests now coming in from the Continent, who were strengthening the resolve of the Catholic community and instilling in them a renewed ardour for their faith.

Grenville obtained his revenge in full measure. After the execution the other weary prisoners were dragged to London and brought before the court, which ordered them to be returned to Cornwall. The evidence presented against them was proved to be perjured, but this was blatantly ignored by Justice Manwood. He pronounced them guilty under the statute of praemunire to lose land and goods and to endure perpetual imprisonment at the Queen's pleasure. Sir John Arundell was regularly in and out of prison. His home, Lanherne, was given in the eighteenth century to the nuns of the Carmelite Order and is the oldest Carmelite House in England. Fittingly, the nuns are the proud possessors of the chief relics of Cuthbert Mayne, including his skull.

Francis Tregian was reprieved but condemned to life imprisonment and forfeiture of all his goods. His lands were given to Lord Hunsdon, a Boleyn cousin of the Queen's, who travelled to Cornwall to evict Tregian's mother and family from Golden Manor. Tregian's wife, who had been allowed to join him in the Fleet, coming and going as she pleased, never ceased to petition Elizabeth on behalf of her husband, who endured twenty-seven years' imprisonment. While in prison, Francis managed to convert several of his fellow inmates. Released on

The Elizabethan Martyrs, 1577-1601

condition of going into exile on the accession of James I, he died at Lisbon in September 1608. He was buried in the church of São Roque, where there is an epitaph detailing his life and sufferings for the Faith.

Seventeen years later his grave was opened and his body was found to be incorrupt, in a remarkable state of preservation. The cause for Tregian's beatification is still actively pending. To his son, the younger Francis, we owe a special debt of gratitude. Douai educated, he was a fine scholar and musician who endured imprisonment for the Faith and died in the Fleet. Without his efforts in collecting Elizabethan music, including one of England's greatest composers, the Catholic William Byrd, much of our musical heritage would have been lost.

Edmund Campion

Always to be best and distinguished above others.

Homer, *Iliad*, *c.*1000 BC

He was born in London on 25 January 1540 and named after his father, a bookseller, who later conformed to the Established Church under Queen Elizabeth. It was intended that Edmund would follow his father's trade, but he was obviously such a gifted child that from the age of ten his education at Christ's Hospital was sponsored by the Grocers' Company, one of the City of London Livery Companies. As a 'bluecoat boy' he was so precocious that he was chosen to deliver a speech of welcome when Queen Mary entered London in 1553.

The Lord Mayor of London, Sir Thomas White, had established St John's College, Oxford, to which Edmund won a scholarship. In 1557, at seventeen years old he became a Junior Fellow of St John's. Edmund completed his degree and became a tutor and junior proctor. As the centre of an admiring group, his mannerisms were imitated by his fellows and his exceptional brilliance, eloquence and great popularity made him a person of outstanding importance; one of the most notable men of his time. It won him the patronage of the Queen's favourite, Robert

The Elizabethan Martyrs, 1577-1601

Dudley, Earl of Leicester, who was chancellor of the university, as well as attracting the notice of William Cecil. Edmund was chosen to deliver the orations at the funerals of Leicester's wife, Amy Robsart, who had died in unexplained circumstances, and Sir Thomas White. When the Queen, amidst scenes of incredible pomp, visited Oxford University in 1566, Campion was the natural choice to deliver the speech of welcome. Elizabeth was greatly impressed: a golden future clearly lay ahead.

Having already taken the Oath of Supremacy, he was ordained a deacon in the Anglican Church in 1568/69 by Bishop Richard Cheney of Gloucester, but remained uncertain of his religious position. His studies made him increasingly uneasy, as he realised that the doctrine of the Established Church could not be identified or reconciled with that of the Fathers of the Church. Nor could he accept the premise inherent in the Protestant position that for over 1500 years God had allowed his Church to promulgate false teaching, until suddenly men had appeared on the scene to enlighten mankind as to the iniquitous error of their ways. He began to openly show signs of sympathy with the Catholic cause, and this cost him the support of the Grocers' Company, which insisted that he come to London to publicly express his confidence in the Established Church. When Edmund declined, they withdrew their financial support from him. He was compensated for this loss by being presented with a benefice, the vicarage of Sherborne, by his friend Bishop Cheney. The much maligned Cheney was eventually to be excommunicated by the Anglican Church for his Catholic beliefs, although there is no conclusive evidence that he was ever reconciled to the Catholic Church before he died.

Full of remorse for having accepted Anglican Orders, at the invitation of the Stanihurst family in 1569 Edmund travelled to Ireland to act as tutor to their children. Sir James Stanihurst was Speaker of the Irish House of Commons. It was hoped that Edmund would play a part in trying to revive a university in Dublin. He attracted favourable attention from Sir Philip Sidney, the Lord Deputy, in the process. But in Ireland his religious views brought him under suspicion, especially in the wake of Pius V's excommunication of Elizabeth. He had to go into hiding in friendly houses to avoid the pursuivants. While in Ireland he began writing *A History of Ireland*, which he graciously dedicated to the Earl of Leicester in gratitude for his patronage.

Urged on by Gregory Martin, who had already gone to Douai in 1570, Edmund finally gave in and acknowledged that he was a Catholic. Still he delayed joining Martin at Douai. He returned to England in disguise and under an assumed name in May 1571. The executions in retaliation for the papal bull had already begun, and while in London Edmund witnessed the trial and condemnation of Blessed John Storey in Westminster Hall. Despite his powerful friends and scholarly reputation, Edmund realised that he had no choice but to respond to the sacrifice that was being asked of him. Acting upon his convictions he left all behind him and in June secretly took a boat to cross to Douai. The vessel was stopped in the Channel and he was put aboard an English frigate and taken to Dover. It seems Edmund bribed the captain by handing over his purse and he was let go. Edmund raised money from friends in Kent and once more took ship to Calais. He made his way to Douai and was reconciled to the Catholic Church. When his departure became known – which would not have taken long, given the efficient spy system – William Cecil, now Baron Burghley, expressed his regret at the loss of 'one of the diamonds of England'.

Edmund studied theology at Douai and was ordained subdeacon. In April 1573 he set out for Rome on foot in order to join the Society of Jesus. As there was no English province of the Jesuits, he was assigned to the province of Bohemia and was sent to the novitiate at Brno, the capital of Moravia. He spent six years in Prague, where he taught rhetoric in the Jesuit school, and in 1578 was ordained priest. The following year the Pope agreed to William Allen's request to send Jesuits to the English mission and Edmund and Father Robert Persons[2] were chosen as the vanguard, setting off in 1580 via Rome and Milan.

Disguised as a soldier, Father Persons arrived at Dover in June 1581 and reached London without encountering any problems. Accompanied by the Jesuit lay brother Ralph Emerson, Edmund landed at Dover on 25 June, posing as a merchant in precious stones. He was detained by the authorities on suspicion but released. Making his way to London, he made contact with a secret network of young Catholic gentlemen dedicated to assisting priests. Edmund was kitted out by them as a gentleman with clothes, a horse and money. At first his reception by his co-religionists was by no means universally welcoming. The beleaguered Catholics were fearful that the arrival of the Jesuits would only bring further troubles upon them, especially as it unfortunately coincided with another piece of papal politicking when Gregory XIII funded an unsuccessful Spanish expeditionary force to Ireland. But through his forceful personality, his holiness and cheerfulness, Edmund won them over and put new heart and hope into the disconsolate Catholics.

In a letter to the General of the Society of Jesus, Campion wrote:

> I came to London and my good angel guided me into the same house that had harboured Father Robert before, whither young gentlemen came to me on every hand... they reapparel me, furnish me, weapon me and convey me out of the city. I ride about some piece of the country every day. The harvest is wonderful great. On horseback I meditate my sermon; when I come to the house I polish it. Then I talk with such as come to speak with me, or hear their confessions. In the morning, after Mass, I preach; they hear with exceeding greediness and very often receive the Sacrament... I dare scarcely touch the exceeding reverence all Catholics do unto us... we are ever well assisted by the priests, whom we find in every place... I cannot long escape the hands of the heretics; the enemies have so many eyes, so many tongues, so many spies... I am in apparel to myself very ridiculous; I often change it and my name also... My soul is in my own hands ever... There will never want in England men that will have a care of their own salvation, nor such as shall advance other men's. Neither shall this Church here ever fail; so long as priests and pastors shall be found to their sheep, rage man or devil never so much.

It may have been while staying at Hoxton near London that Edmund wrote his open letter to 'The Lords of Her Majestie's Privy Council', subsequently known as 'Campion's Brag'. It set out the purpose of his mission 'of free cost to preach the Gospel, to minister the Sacraments, to instruct the simple, to reform sinners' and generally reclaim Catholics from error. The letter set out a challenge to the government.

> Touching the Society, be it known that we have made a league... cheerfully to carry the cross you lay upon us, and never to despair your recovery, while we have a man left to enjoy your Tyburn, or be racked with your torments, or consumed with your prisons. The expense is reckoned, the enterprise is begun; it is of God, it cannot be withstood. So the faith was planted: so it must be restored.

The letter was not intended for publication but was to be held in readiness should he be captured. When it was prematurely published, Edmund became the object of an intensive manhunt, so he left London for Berkshire. During the course of a year he worked secretly in various parts of the country, incessantly travelling, rarely stopping more than one night at any house in order to keep one step ahead of the spies who relentlessly pursued him. He found many of his recusant hosts greatly impoverished and had many hair's breadth escapes from the priest hunters. 'Everyone talks of death, prison, fines or the ruin of friends', he wrote.

As well as covering much of the Home Counties he visited Oxfordshire, Northamptonshire, Derbyshire, Nottinghamshire, Lancashire and Yorkshire. It was in North Yorkshire early in 1581 while staying with the Harrington family at Mount St John, Felixkirk, that over a period of twelve days Edmund wrote his famous book, *Decem Rationes*. *Ten Reasons* succinctly set out the arguments for Catholicism and challenged the Protestants to debate with him.

Campion made such an impression on fifteen-year-old William Harrington that the following year he entered the English College at Rheims. Because of ill-health and other vicissitudes he had to return home. An apostate Catholic spy reported him as lodging at the White Horse in Holborn and being at Mass with eighteen others at the home of Lord Vaux at Hackney. William was not ordained until 1591. He ministered partly in the West Country for a year before being captured in London. Sent to

The Elizabethan Martyrs, 1577-1601

Newgate, he was condemned and martyred at Tyburn on 18 February 1594 aged twenty-seven.

Another of Edmund's hosts in Yorkshire was Blessed Ralph Grimston, a married man with a family from Nidd. He regularly harboured priests and suffered imprisonment. In 1594 he was convicted on the evidence of the apostate Yorkshire priest William Hardesty, whom he had sheltered. The ingrate had been given a pardon in exchange for becoming a government spy. In 1598 Grimston was caught with Blessed Peter Snow from Ripon, who had been ordained in 1591. Ralph tried to thwart the priest's arrest. They were martyred together at York on 15 June.

In the spring of 1581 Edmund was at Stonor Park, Oxfordshire, the guest of Dame Cecily Stonor. Here a rather primitive, but effective, secret printing press had been set up to print *Decem Rationes*. If evidence were needed to demonstrate Edmund's outstanding scholarship, one need look no further than this extraordinary little book. It is remarkable for its myriad quotations from scripture, the Fathers and saints of the Church, all of which was done from memory, as Campion did not have access to any library. The proof was sent to Father Persons, the Jesuit Superior, who was amazed by it. His prudence would not allow him to authorise its publication without first having all the quotations checked. Thomas Fitzherbert, the future priest, undertook that task, scouring various libraries. He was able to verify the accuracy of all the references and copies of the book were accordingly printed. The future Tyburn martyr William Hartley[3] secretly distributed 400 copies of the book around Oxford University in June 1581. This caused quite a stir, galvanising the government to redouble its efforts to capture Edmund.

In July, Campion and Persons enjoyed a brief reunion. Edmund planned to return to Lancashire to collect some of his papers and then move into Norfolk. Before embarking upon the journey he received an invitation to visit the home of Mr Yates at Lyford Grange near Wantage, Berkshire. As a recusant, Mr Yates was in prison at the time, but his mother lived at Lyford, which also housed a small group of Bridgettine nuns and two priests, Fathers John Colleton and Thomas Ford. Because Lyford Grange was such a well-known refuge for Catholics, Father Persons only very reluctantly gave his consent to Edmund's visit, placing him under obedience to the presumably more cautious Brother Ralph Emerson,[4] who was to accompany him to Norfolk. Edmund duly went to Lyford and stayed overnight, saying Mass the following morning. Afterwards he and Father Colleton quietly departed.

Those 'in the know' about Campion's visit could not resist telling their fellow Catholics about it, who were upset at not having had the opportunity of meeting the famous Jesuit. Father Ford was asked to go after Edmund and persuade him and Colleton to return. He caught up with them at an inn near Oxford and entreated them to come back to Lyford. Brother Ralph was unhappy with the idea, but finally gave in when Edmund promised he would stay just over the weekend. It was agreed that Ralph would ride into Lancashire, collect the missing papers and then meet up with Edmund at the arranged rendezvous in Norfolk. It was not to be.

Campion spent two happy days in the company of the group of Catholics. On Sunday morning, 17 July, after Mass he would depart for Norfolk. Father Ford planned to say Mass first for the sizeable gathering of over forty people, consisting of the members of the household and neighbours. While Father Ford was still at the altar, it was reported by the watchman that two visitors had arrived at the gates. They were George Eliot and David Jenkins. Both were priest hunters in the pay of the government. Eliot was a low-lifer who had ingratiated himself by claiming to be a Catholic, being formerly employed as a servant with the Roper family in Kent and Lady Petre at Ingatestone. He was arrested for embezzlement, rape and murder and to save his skin had written from prison to offer his services to the government informing on Catholics. Secretary Cecil and spymaster Walsingham were very interested, and Eliot was offered his freedom in return for a government commission to find and arrest as many priests as he could.

Eliot was unaware that Campion was at Lyford and had no idea what a prize catch was awaiting him. He was sure that the house was an important recusant centre and had called in expectation of finding a Mass that Sunday morning. As it happened, Eliot was acquainted with one of the servants, Cooper, who was the cook at Lyford Grange. He had also been employed by the Ropers and Eliot asked to speak to him. The wary watchman made them wait at the gate while he went in to fetch Cooper, who came out, recognised Eliot and invited him to stay for dinner. Leaving Jenkins down in the kitchen, Eliot was taken to the room where Campion was about to say Mass. Feigning piety, Eliot joined with the congregation. After Mass Edmund distributed blessed bread and water to all present, including Eliot, before sitting down to give a sermon lasting about an hour. Immediately afterwards, excusing himself from dinner, Eliot rejoined Jenkins, and the two of them rode off post-haste to alert the local authorities.

A number of Catholics had stayed for dinner and it was around one o'clock that the watchman raised the alarm that the house was surrounded by armed men. Eliot and Jenkins, with the local magistrate and a posse of soldiers, demanded admission. The nuns quickly put on lay dress while Mrs Yates insisted that the three priests take something to eat and drink and get into one of the hiding places which they managed to do, having just enough room to lie side by side when the panelling was closed. When all the incriminating religious evidence had also been hidden away, the magistrate was admitted. Accused of hearing Mass that morning, the whole company denied it and the magistrate seemed prepared to take the word of Mrs Yates and her gentlemen guests. However, Eliot insisted that the house be searched; but nothing was found. The magistrate and his men left the house and those inside breathed a sigh of relief – but not for long. Persuaded by Eliot, making great play with his royal commission, the party returned and conducted a thorough search, smashing through walls and panelling in the process. Eliot sent for reinforcements in the person of a second magistrate, who arrived with a gang of his own servants. Still no sign of the priests was found. So a guard of around sixty men was ranged about the house overnight.

Campion, Colleton and Ford were still squashed together in a secret chamber at the top of the house. Early in the morning the search was renewed, as Eliot was convinced that the priests had to be hidden somewhere on the premises. Just when he was beginning to think they might have escaped after all, a beam of light was spotted coming from a narrow gap in the stairwell. Jenkins broke it open and called out, 'I've found the traitors!' They then discovered the secret compartment, revealing the priests, who quietly surrendered themselves.

The High Sheriff was summoned and, giving orders that the prisoners be treated courteously, he sent a messenger to the Court to ask for instructions. But Eliot had rushed to London to claim the credit and armed with authority he returned to Lyford Grange to escort the priests to London under guard. A fourth priest, William Filby[5] had the ill luck to choose that fateful day to call at Lyford Grange, knowing he could expect a warm welcome. The welcome he got was from those now in control of the house and he was promptly arrested.

The journey to London took two full days, during which Campion managed to charm his guards, who clearly despised and ignored the exultant Eliot. Finally he said to Edmund, 'Mr Campion, you look cheerfully on everyone but me. I know you are angry with me for this work.'

Edmund replied, 'God forgive thee, Eliot, for so judging me. I forgive thee,' and raising his cup he drank to the health of his captor, whom he begged to repent.

Strongly bound to their horses, on 22 July Campion and his companions arrived in London and were ignominiously paraded through the streets. Attached to Edmund's hat was a label reading 'Campion the seditious Jesuit'. The four priests were all committed to the Tower. Edmund was shut in a cell which can still be seen today, known as 'Little Ease' because it is too small for a man to either lie or stand in it.

The government was willing to go to any lengths to get him to conform. After four days crouching in his dark cell, he was taken upriver to the Earl of Leicester's house, where he also found Queen Elizabeth waiting for him. Closely questioned by the politicians present about his motives and his loyalty to the Queen, Edmund acknowledged Elizabeth as his lawful sovereign in all temporal matters, but quoted Christ: 'Render to Caesar the things that are Caesar's, and to God the things that are God's.'

It is fair to say that Elizabeth and her ministers probably had no particular desire to see Edmund executed, but he could not be allowed to defy them. He was promised that he could expect an Anglican bishopric if he would publicly abjure his Catholicism and conform. Campion refused the offer and was sent back to the Tower.

As no useful information could be extracted from him, five days later Burghley issued the order that he be tortured. The register of the Tower of London in a most revealing slip of the pen contains the instruction, 'In case he continues to wilfully tell the truth, then to deal with him by the rack'. After being racked a third time, Edmund was asked how he felt. 'Not ill,' he replied, 'because not at all.'

He lost most of his fingernails by having iron spikes thrust down them. In order to disgrace Edmund in the eyes of the Catholic community, the government repeatedly claimed that under torture he had revealed the names of some of the people who had sheltered him, yet no written evidence was ever produced to substantiate the allegation. That he betrayed those who had been his friends is highly unlikely. The State Papers show that Burghley was already in possession of many details about people and places where Edmund had stayed; information no doubt supplied by spies. If there is any shred of truth in the government propaganda, it is that confronted with the evidence Edmund perhaps admitted that it was correct. There was little point in denying it at that stage, as those identified were already in deep trouble. When it was clear they had obtained all the information they were likely to get from him, Edmund was kept in the Tower in solitary confinement for the next four months, during which the government fostered many lying statements about him.

On the orders of the Privy Council, anxious to discredit him in any way they could, he was brought from his cell on four occasions to face public disputations with different groups and academics. At one of these sessions Edmund explicitly denied that he had betrayed anyone. Refuting the claim that he had been tortured for matters of state, rather than for religion, he was reported as saying his punishment was because 'he would not betray the places and persons with whom he had conversed and

The Elizabethan Martyrs, 1577-1601

dealt with concerning the Catholic cause'. He cited the example of the early Christians who had suffered martyrdom rather than yield up the sacred books and vessels to the pagan authorities.

'Much more I ought to suffer anything rather than to betray the bodies of those who ministered necessaries to supply my lack.'

His opponents, deciding they were on shaky ground chose not to pursue the matter, but were especially eager to respond to his *Ten Reasons*.

Stands had been erected for members of the Court to enjoy the spectacle. Weak from torture, given no prior warning and therefore unable to prepare for the confrontations, without notes Campion endeavoured to rebut the arguments put to him, despite the obvious unfairness and inequality of the proceedings. He was constantly interrupted, insulted and refused access to books. Catholic witnesses reported that Edmund looked deathly pale, exhibiting signs of confusion at times by getting his quotations mixed up. Nonetheless it was generally conceded that he emerged from the ordeals with integrity. As they could not demonstrably get the better of him, the Council put an end to the farce and left Edmund alone in his cell to await trial.

For propaganda purposes the government had to destroy the perception that Campion was being indicted purely for spiritual reasons: they had to impugn his motives, calling into question his loyalty. Having interrogated dozens of witnesses under duress, they failed to establish that Edmund had been involved in any treasonable activity. So in the absence of evidence they fabricated a fictitious conspiracy to assassinate the Queen, in which he and several priests had been allegedly involved at Rheims and Rome. Planning to kill many birds with one stone, the government took the opportunity of adding to the charge the names of every priest they held in custody in London.

On 14 November 1581 Campion was arraigned in Westminster Hall with fellow priests Ralph Sherwin, Luke Kirby, Thomas Cottam[6] and Robert Johnson,[7] all of whom were also destined for martyrdom. Edmund's hands were tucked into the sleeves of his gown but were so crippled by torture that he was unable to hold a Bible or raise his right arm to take the oath. One of his companions pulled back the sleeve, kissed his hand and raised his arm for him.

The Elizabethan Martyrs, 1577-1601

'I protest before God and his holy angels, before heaven and earth, before the world and this bar whereat I stand... that I am not guilty of any part of the treason contained in the indictment or of any other treason whatever.'

When the trial was fixed for 20 November, Edmund asked incredulously if it would be possible to find twelve men so wicked and lacking in conscience that they would find the priests guilty. No fair trial was possible; the verdict had been pre-determined by the Privy Council. The jury was rigged; the foreman was a Calvinist and a government informer. Three men refused to serve and were replaced by others more likely to produce the required guilty verdict. False witnesses were suborned (and paid) to testify against the priests, most of whom were unknown to each other. Among the unsavoury bunch of witnesses, in addition to Eliot, were Charles Sledd, a notorious spy, and Anthony Munday, a government informer who had once been at the English College, Rome, and ingratiated himself with the Catholics in order to spy on them. It was he who perjured himself by claiming to know of the pretended plot to assassinate the Queen.

A large group of priests, nineteen in all, were sent for trial with Campion before Sir Christopher Wray, the Lord Chief Justice. They included Alexander Briant, Thomas Cottam, William Filby, John Hart,[8] Robert Johnson, Luke Kirby, Lawrence Richardson (real name Johnson),[9] Edward Rishton,[10] Ralph Sherwin, John Shert,[11] John Colleton,[12] James Bosgrave[13] and Thomas Ford. Prosecuting were the Attorney General, John Popham, Solicitor General, Thomas Egerton, and Mr Anderson, QC. Prisoners were allowed no defence counsel so they had to defend themselves. Campion inevitably became the spokesman for all the accused. He asked that they all be given individual trials but the request was refused on the grounds that time did not permit it.

Campion put up an impressive defence, ably refuting the accusations and allegations, although on the principal charge of treasonably plotting to kill the Queen no evidence against him was actually offered. The dates on which he was supposed to have been in Rheims or Rome are demonstrably impossible, but that seems to have been irrelevant. Some of the accusations made by Eliot and Munday against his co-defendants were ludicrous. For example, Munday told the court that Father Rishton planned to use fireworks to burn the Queen, and Father Cottam was accused of possessing an objectionable book.

Edmund was allowed to address the jury before they retired. He asked them what truth might be expected from the likes of Eliot, a murderer, and Munday, a professed atheist; men devoid of any honesty who had betrayed both God and man. How could such men be believed? And he made a somewhat forlorn final appeal to their consciences, as they were to 'render at the dreadful Day of Judgement'.

The jury was not long in returning the expected verdict and Edmund was given the chance of addressing the court before sentence was passed.

'It was not our death that we ever feared. But we knew we were not lords of our own lives and therefore for want of an answer would not be guilty of our deaths. The only thing that we now have to say is, that if our religion do make us traitors, we are worthy to be condemned; but otherwise are, and have been, as good subjects as ever the Queen had. In condemning us,' he said, 'you condemn all your own ancestors – all the ancient priests, bishops and kings – all that was once the glory of England, the island of saints and the most devoted child of the See of Peter. For what have we taught, however you may qualify it with the odious name of treason, that they did not uniformly teach? To be condemned with these lights – not of England only, but of the world – by their degenerate descendants, is both gladness and glory to us. God lives: posterity will live: their judgement is not so liable to corruption as that of those who are now going to sentence us to death.'

When the dreadful sentence was pronounced, the priests spontaneously sang the Te Deum. The next day a further seven priests were condemned, including Fathers Colleton and Ford, neither of whom had ever set foot in either Rheims or Rome. Both of them produced alibis that they were elsewhere on the dates when they were alleged to have been plotting at Rheims. Ford's alibi was rejected, but as Father Colleton could bring a witness to prove he was in London he was acquitted of the treason charge but still kept in prison.

For a further eleven days Edmund lay in chains in the Tower. Even at this late stage attempts were still made to persuade him to conform, making him promises of rewards. For the first time we hear of him having a sister who was allowed to visit him, offering a lucrative benefice in the Established Church on behalf of the government. One of his visitors was none other than George Eliot, claiming that when he had betrayed him he had not thought it would lead to his execution, only imprisonment. It seems that Eliot was motivated by fear of reprisals, as he had already been called 'Judas' by passers-by in the street. Campion gave him the benefit of the doubt, treated him courteously and begged him to confess his crime and repent. Sadly the counsel fell on deaf ears; Eliot continued his spying career. But Edmund made one last convert: his jailer who, much moved and impressed by his prisoner, became a Catholic.

On 1 December 1581 Campion was strapped to a hurdle, while Alexander Briant and Ralph Sherwin were bound together on a second hurdle. 'God bless you and make you all good Catholics!' Edmund called out to the bystanders. They were dragged through the muddy streets to be hanged, drawn and quartered at Tyburn. All along the route people called out asking for a blessing. In spite of the awful weather, there was a huge crowd which included many of the leading members of the Court. The eyewitnesses noted that the mud-spattered Edmund and his companions were laughing together and did not seem to care at all that they were about to die.

Standing in the cart, the rope around his neck, Edmund tried to make himself heard above the noise. 'As to the treasons which have been laid to my charge, and for which I come here to suffer, I desire you all to bear witness with me that I am thereto altogether innocent. I am a Catholic man and a priest; in that Faith I have lived and in that Faith do I intend to die. If you esteem my religion treason, then I am guilty; as for the other treason, I never committed any, God is my judge.'

All the while he had to endure taunts and heckling from the dignitaries present. He forgave his persecutors and asked pardon of any he might have harmed. The courtiers demanded that he ask the Queen's forgiveness and pray for her. 'Wherein have I offended her?' he asked, 'In this I am innocent. I do pray for her... Elizabeth your Queen and my Queen, unto whom I wish a long quiet reign with all prosperity.'

These were his last audible words as the cart was pulled from under him and he was left hanging from the gibbet. Thankfully he appears to have been unconscious before the dismembering began. His quarters were displayed on each of the four city gates.

All shades of religious and political opinion have never been in any doubt that the trial of Campion and his companions was an appalling travesty – judicial murder at its worst. There is likewise unanimous concurrence that with Campion this country lost a brilliant thinker and writer, a man of genius, not just a great Elizabethan but a great Englishman. Let Evelyn Waugh have the last word:

> He was one of a host of martyrs... some performed more sensational feats of adventure... many suffered crueller tortures, but to his own and to each succeeding generation, Campion's fame has burned with unique warmth and brilliance; it was his genius to express, in sentences that have resounded across the centuries, the spirit of chivalry in which they suffered, to typify in his zeal, his innocence, his inflexible purpose, the pattern which they followed.
>
> From *Edmund Campion* by Evelyn Waugh[1]

Ralph Sherwin

Must they fall? The young... the brave, to swell one bloated chief's unwholesome reign.

Childe Harold's Pilgrimage, Lord Byron, 1788–1824

He was born at Rodsley, near Ashbourne, Derbyshire in 1549/50. Raised as a Protestant, he was educated at Exeter College, Oxford. The College had been founded in 1314 by Walter de Stapeldon, Bishop of Exeter, under the patronage of the Virgin Mary,

---

[1] Copyright © The Estate of Evelyn Waugh, reproduced by permission of PFD on behalf of the Estate of Evelyn Waugh

St Peter and St Thomas of Canterbury. In the sixteenth century it was transformed and expanded with generous donations by a graduate of the College, Sir William Petre of Ingatestone, Essex, and became one of the leading colleges of the university. Sir William, who held public office in the royal service for many years, had got rich by profiting from the suppression of the religious houses. He was probably a secret Catholic. Certainly his wife was a Catholic and priests were sheltered at Ingatestone Hall. The Petres were to become one of the staunchest Catholic families of England, giving many priests and two bishops to the Church.

Ralph's uncle was a Marian priest, Father John Woodward, who acted as chaplain to the Petres at Ingatestone. It was through his influence that Sir William nominated Ralph for an Exeter fellowship in 1568. The College was notable for its Catholic sympathies. In the 1570s the royal commissioners paid visits to the College to purge it of papists and as result the Rector, the Sub-Rector and the Dean had to leave. Ralph took his MA with honours in 1574, and became noted as a Greek and Hebrew scholar as well as a philosopher. He had a great zest for life and adventure; vivacious and impulsive, he accumulated a large circle of good friends. He pursued his highly successful academic career, and a public disputation brought him to the favourable notice of the Earl of Leicester.

He seems to have been close to his priest uncle and what role Father Woodward may have played in his conversion and subsequent vocation is unknown, but in 1574/75 Ralph became a Catholic. In that latter year he was given leave to study abroad. He gave up the prospect of a brilliant career and travelled to Douai. He was ordained priest at Cateau-Cambresis on 23 March 1577 together with the future martyr, Lawrence Johnson. In August of that year, in the company of Father Edward Rishton, he was transferred to Rome to continue his theological studies at the newly established English College in the Eternal City. Of the fifty students who took the College oath on 23 April 1579, his name stands first in the register. The fourteenth name in the list was that of the future apostate Anthony Tyrell. The College students were required to swear an oath that they were prepared to serve

The Elizabethan Martyrs, 1577-1601

on the English mission. When it was Ralph's turn to swear it is recorded that he added, 'Rather today than tomorrow.' Thus Ralph became the protomartyr of the English College, Rome.

All was not well at the Roman College. There was discord between the Welsh and English students, the latter claiming with some justification that the Welsh received preferential treatment from their superiors who were also Welsh. However, the dispute went much deeper than national rivalries. There was a fundamental difference of approach to their studies and objectives between many of the students from Douai and the older, more conservative priests who had been placed in charge of the College. The latter still seemed to think of it as a place of genteel higher education, whereas the students were fired with zeal for the English mission which was their goal. The dispute turned into a full-scale revolt, in which Ralph appears to have been one of the vociferous leaders, making full use of his oratorial skills. Sherwin was somewhat uncharitably forthright in referring to the Welsh as barbarous savages. He composed a petition to the Cardinal Protector of the College explaining that the only reason for their being there was to acquire sufficient knowledge to better equip them to return to England.

Dr Clynogg, the Rector, resigned and the students made it clear that they wished to have the College under the direction of the Jesuits, but not even appeals to the Pope had any effect. The students were threatened with expulsion unless they agreed to obey the reappointed Rector. Instead of waiting, with typical student defiance, all thirty-three of the students, including the Welsh, walked out and were offered accommodation elsewhere in Rome. There is no doubt that the students had the sympathy of the Romans on their side and recognising that the intolerable situation was causing scandal Pope Gregory XIII gave in to their demands and placed the Jesuits in charge of the College.

Ralph spent a further year in Rome studying hard and when he left the *Annals* of the English College had nothing but praise for him. On 18 April 1580, he set off on foot from Rome to begin the journey to England in the company of Edmund Campion, Robert Persons, Luke Kirby, Edward Rishton, four old Marian priests and two laymen, Thomas Briscoe and John Paschal, the

The Elizabethan Martyrs, 1577-1601

latter being a pupil and friend of Ralph's from his Exeter College days. Also in the party was the Jesuit brother, Ralph Emerson, who was carrying Catholic books. Before leaving Rome the group had called on St Philip Neri, who gave them his blessing. Describing their journey in a letter to a friend, Campion wrote, 'I see them all so prodigal of blood and life that I am ashamed of my backwardness.'

They travelled by way of Bologna and Milan, where they stayed for several days with the Archbishop, St Charles Borromeo, and Ralph was asked to preach. From there they reached Turin but instead of crossing directly into France, because of political problems they opted for continuing their journey via Switzerland. They entered Geneva in disguise, Campion pretending to be an Irish servant. During their stay they sought out the famous Theodore Beza, the successor of Calvin and one of the leading figures of Protestantism. Sherwin does not seem to have been impressed with Beza, judging by his less than complimentary comments about him. Before leaving they also had some reckless fun, arguing in the street with one of the nine Calvinist leaders of the city. Ralph wrote to his friend Ralph Bickley, studying for the priesthood back in Rome, that they had sparred with the minister so long 'we almost made the fellow mad'.

On 31 May the group arrived at Rheims, where Douai College was then located. The Pope had agreed that a bishop was needed for England and the octogenarian Thomas Goldwell, Bishop of St Asaph, the only surviving member of the old Catholic hierarchy, had volunteered to return. The Bishop had arrived at Rheims from Rome a few days before and Ralph and John Paschal were chosen to accompany him to England. Although the Bishop attempted the journey to Paris, ill health forced his return to Rheims – which was just as well because spies had reported his intentions to the English Government, whose agents were waiting to arrest him should he try to set foot in England.

In a letter written from Rheims to the English College in Rome, Ralph remarked:

The Elizabethan Martyrs, 1577-1601

> They say here that our names are betrayed to the enemy; but let them say and plot what they like, we shall take our lives in our hands and break through the ranks of our foes. The nearer we get to the labours and perils of England, the more eagerly we advance upon the country commended to our zeal.

Ralph's presumption was only too true. Before he had even left Rome a spy's report was on its way to London in which Sherwin was described as being aged about thirty, 'tall of stature and slender, his face lean, his beard of a flaxen colour cut short'.

Bidding farewell to Bishop Goldwell, Sherwin and Paschal set out on the final leg of their journey home. In his letter to Ralph Bickley written from Paris on 11 June 1580, Sherwin wrote self-mockingly of how foppish he looked in his French garb, disguised as a man about town in silk doublet and hose.

'You'll never be handsome,' Paschal told him, 'not even in that colourful attire,' to which Sherwin replied, 'There was never a priest handsome in this attire. Thus for Christ we put ourselves in colours.'

By 3 July, Rouen was reached and Ralph was able to visit his priest uncle, then living in retirement, to say goodbye. Paschal was taken ill at Rouen, which delayed their journey. In a letter to Father Alfonso Agazzari, Rector of the English College, Rome, Ralph mentions that he left Rouen on the Feast of St Peter's Chains, which would have been 1 August. He asks his correspondent to 'say his beads' for him 'so that in humility and constancy, with perseverance to the end, I may know God in this vocation whereunto though unworthy I am called'.

From where the two travellers embarked or at what place they landed in England is unknown, but they must have arrived in late August. Ralph made an immediate impression. In a letter to Father Agazzari, Robert Persons wrote in praise of Ralph's 'ardour of spirit' when preaching. Sherwin's apostolate lasted barely three months. In November Ralph visited Father Persons and told him that the spies were so close on his heels that he expected to be captured at any time; later that day he was taken while preaching at the house of his old university friend, Nicholas Roscarrock, in London. The Roscarrocks were a Cornish family, allied by marriage to the Arundells, and had been closely associated with

Cuthbert Mayne, for which they were made to suffer. Ralph was imprisoned in the Marshalsea in heavy chains that rattled loudly whenever he moved. This greatly amused Ralph, to the consternation of his fellow prisoners. Writing to Father Persons to thank him for the money he had sent him to buy food, he remarked,

> I have on my feet some little bells that remind me, when I walk, who I am and to whom I belong. I have never heard sweeter harmony than this. Pray for me that I may finish my course with courage.

He added that when the money was spent he would

> ...go down to my brothers the thieves in the pit and subsist on the common basket of alms; and I shall go to it with more alacrity than ever to a banquet; for that bread of charity, for my Lord's sake, will be sweeter to me than honey or all kinds of dainties.

By this he literally meant that he was prepared to subsist on the charitable offerings put into the 'beggar's basket' of the prison, the only means by which prisoners unable to pay would get something to eat.

Shortly afterwards, his friend Paschal was sent to join him in prison. John had always been full of zealous speeches which Ralph often reproved him for, telling him that it was one thing to be brave now, but what would he do when put to the test? It was almost prophetic, for, unlike Ralph, Paschal did not have the inner steel to withstand the threats of torture; out of fear, a few months later he conformed. In later life he returned to the Church and remained a much persecuted recusant. During the month Ralph spent in the Marshalsea, he made converts among the prisoners. In December he was sent to the Tower along with Luke Kirby, Robert Johnson, Thomas Cottam and Nicholas Roscarrock. On two successive days Ralph was cruelly tortured on the rack while undergoing intensive interrogation to make him reveal the names of his converts and to incriminate Campion, but he did not utter a word. He was put into solitary confinement and starved for five days and nights, and then left chained in the snow to make him divulge information. Roscarrock, who was also

The Elizabethan Martyrs, 1577-1601

racked, could hear him groaning. Sherwin's brother, John, managed to get in to visit him and reported on his condition. It is from him that we learn of the offer made to Ralph – whether seriously or not – that he would be offered an Anglican bishopric if he would conform.

Three times in the new year Ralph, Roscarrock and the others were forcibly taken to a Protestant church to listen to a sermon, but they protested so much that the farce was not repeated. Roscarrock was sent to the Fleet to join his fellow Cornishman, Francis Tregian. In June 1581 Sherwin, Kirby and Cottam were asked if they would voluntarily go to the Protestant church. When they refused they were told that they would be charged under the new recusancy law. This is significant because it proves that the later allegations of treasonable plotting against the Queen, under which they were brought to trial, had not yet been invented by the government.

Ralph spent a whole weary year suffering in prison. He knew that his execution was inevitable and wished it would come soon, and he prepared himself with much prayer and meditation, especially upon Christ's Passion. A letter he wrote to a friend is quoted in Cardinal Allen's *Briefe History of the Glorious Martyrdom of Twelve Reverend Priests*:

> My sins are great I confess but I flee to God's mercy... I have no boldness but in his blood; His bitter passion is my only consolation... Our Lord perfect us to that end whereunto we were created, that leaving this world, we may live in Him and of Him. World without end... God grant us humility, that we following His footsteps may obtain the victory.

Arraigned and tried with Campion in November 1581, Ralph declared boldly, 'The plain reason for our standing here is religion and not treason.' To show that this was true, Campion pointed out that Ralph's friend, John Paschal, had been given his freedom because he had agreed to conform. Sherwin was specifically accused by the prosecution of unlawfully persuading the Queen's subjects to the Catholic Faith, against her injunctions as to what they ought to believe and profess. His answer was to appeal to the Apostles and Fathers of the early Church in whose footsteps he was following.

He regarded his death sentence as a victory achieved. Returning to the Tower, Ralph pointed to the shining sun and said, 'Father Campion, I shall soon be above yonder fellow.' From his cell he wrote a final, loving letter to his uncle, Father Woodward:

> After many conflicts… mixed with spiritual consolations and Christian comforts, it hath pleased God of his unspeakable mercy to call me out of this vale of misery. To him therefore… be all praise and glory. Your tender care always had over me and cost bestowed on me I trust in heaven shall be rewarded. Was advertised by superior authority that tomorrow I was to end the course of this life… Innocence is my only comfort against all the forged villainy which is fathered on my fellow priests and me… When by the High Judge, God himself, this false visage of treason shall be removed from true Catholic men's faces, then shall it appear who they be that carry a well meaning and who an evil murdering mind. In the meantime God forgive all injustice; and if it be His blessed will to convert our persecutors, that they may become professors of the truth.

He asked for his uncle's prayers and said he was never quieter in mind nor less troubled.

> I bid you farewell once again to the lovingest uncle that ever kinsman had in this world. God grant us both His grace and blessing until the end that living in His fear and dying in His favour we may enjoy one another for ever.

Taken to Tyburn the thirty-one-year-old Ralph watched his fellow priest die. 'Come, Sherwin, take thy wages,' said the hangman. Ralph then kissed the hands of the executioner covered in Campion's blood before climbing into the cart. Ralph tried to speak but was interrupted by the officials. He insisted that he was innocent of any treasonable crime.

'I have no occasion to lie,' he insisted, 'for so doing I should condemn my own soul; and although in this short time of mortal life I am to undergo the infamy and punishment of a traitor, I make no doubt of my future happiness, through Jesus Christ, in whose death, passion and blood I only trust.'

One of the courtiers urged him to confess his treason, to

which he replied, 'If to be a Catholic only... be to be a traitor, then I am a traitor.'

As they placed the noose around his neck and drew away the cart, he kept on repeating the name of Jesus. Someone in the crowd called out, 'Good Mr Sherwin, God receive your soul.'

A postscript may be added concerning Ralph's parents. Six years after his death they were both indicted for persistent recusancy. His mother, Constance, was committed to jail. She begged to be released, promising to attend church, in order to look after her blind, incontinent, bedridden husband, John; the only reason, so the official report states, that he too was not sent to prison, was in case he died.

Alexander Briant

White as an angel is the English child.

The Little Black Boy, William Blake, 1757–1827

Alexander was born into a yeoman family in Somerset in 1556 and may well have been raised a Catholic. While a teenager, he was sent to Oxford where, because of his purity and handsome face, he was known as 'the beautiful youth'. He studied at Hart Hall, where he matriculated in 1574, the year he was reconciled to the Catholic Church. He moved to Balliol College, where Robert Persons was his tutor. Although Persons left Oxford just a few months later, his influence on Alexander was profound. Persons was later to describe Briant as his disciple and pupil. Another tutor was Richard Holtby, who left the University for Douai, arriving there on 3 August 1577. Eight days later he was joined at the college by Briant. They were ordained priests in the same ceremony at Cambrai on Holy Saturday, 29 March 1578. Alexander set out to return to England on 3 August 1579.

He went home to Somerset and visited his mother. He reconciled many to the Church, including Robert Persons' father. Persons wrote that Briant never willingly left his side. It was this attachment that caused his capture. Two years later, Alexander was living in London close to Father Persons' secret lodgings near

St Bride's Church in the Strand. Father Persons rented the house from a Protestant bookseller and used it for meetings and to store religious artefacts. A servant had unwisely been allowed to see the stock of rosaries, crosses and pictures, and he reported his find to the authorities. On 28 April 1581 the priest hunters searching for Father Persons raided the house, but the Jesuit was out of London at the time. So the pursuivants decided to search the adjoining house, where they discovered Alexander. Finding him in possession of a silver chalice, among other things, they suspected he was a priest and took him into custody.

He was taken first to the Compter or Counter, one of the sheriff's prisons in Wood Street, off Cheapside. He was kept in solitary confinement and left without food or drink for forty-eight hours. He was so thirsty that he tried to catch the rainwater falling from the prison eaves in his hat. Someone showed pity by giving him a little piece of bread and cheese and some beer, and this is all he had for six days. As he refused to reveal the whereabouts of Father Persons and his fellow priests, by order of the Privy Council on 25 March he was taken to the Tower with instructions that he be tortured. He arrived in such a wretched weak state that he could barely stand. In spite of that, he was loaded with heavy chains. He was tortured for the first time on 27 March. The Public Records Office has a list of the questions he was persistently asked in order to extract information about Persons' and Briant's attitudes towards the Queen and her authority. The only answers that are recorded – which speak volumes – are that he was content to affirm Elizabeth as his sovereign lady, but he would not be drawn into the question of whether the Pope had authority to withdraw subjects from obedience to her.

They used the thumbscrews on him and resorted to the 'pricking' torture which involved thrusting needles or iron spikes under his fingernails and possibly his toenails. Through it all he recited the Miserere psalm. He was then racked, but throughout his excruciating ordeals he seemed to remain unmoved. Alexander later revealed that under torture he fixed his mind on the passion of Christ and became so absorbed that he felt no pain. Only when the torture was stopped did the agonising pain start. One of his

The Elizabethan Martyrs, 1577-1601

tormentors raged that they were unable to make Alexander give them any information. He was later reported as saying, 'This is an evident miracle, but it is a miracle of indomitable pertinacity in the popish priest; otherwise from the very pain of the torture he was bound to confess not only facts but cognizance of them, nay even his inmost thoughts.' And he expressed the opinion that it was just as well that only convinced Protestants were present, otherwise the priest's fortitude might well convert them.

On 6 April Alexander was cast into the Pit, a subterranean dungeon some twenty feet deep. He was kept in the dark in this vermin-ridden hole for eight days, only to be brought out to face more torture on the rack. This was a large wooden frame on which the prisoner was laid. Cords were tied around his ankles and wrists, and the cords were attached to wooden rollers at either end of the frame. As the levers were pulled, rotating the rollers, the prisoner's body was stretched; the more turns of the rollers the harder the stretching. Prolonged racking caused permanent dislocation of the limbs as well as internal damage. In spite of the pains that affected his whole body, and his congealed blood – an effect of racking – the following day Alexander was racked yet again. He thought he was going to die but was resolved to make no answer that might betray anyone. Repeatedly asked whether the Queen was head of the Church in England, Alexander responded, 'I am a Catholic and I believe as a Catholic should do.'

Thomas Norton,[14] the barbaric rack-master, countered, 'And they say the Pope is,' to which came the reply, 'And so say I.'

Each time he lost consciousness cold water was thrown on his face to revive him and he was stretched even harder. His body became so disjointed that Norton boasted he had made him a foot longer than God intended. Hopton, the Lieutenant of the Tower, behaved appallingly to him, reviling him and slapping him in the face.

He was consigned to an underground chamber where, barely able to move as a result of the racking, he was left for days. Some reports claim that he was also subjected to the Scavenger's Daughter. When details of Briant's tortures became known, the public revulsion was so great that the government made Norton a scapegoat by going through the motions of having him confined to prison for a few days so as to appear not to have sanctioned the atrocities. Lord Burghley later felt obliged to issue a pamphlet seeking to exonerate the government, by placing all the blame for his sufferings on Alexander himself because of his 'extreme impudent obstinacy', including his refusal to write and ask his jailers for food and drink.

Alexander's importance to the government is revealed in the State Papers. In a letter written on 3 May 1581 from the Council to Hopton, Lieutenant of the Tower, more than a month after Alexander was first tortured, they graphically refer to subjecting him to 'torture, pain and terror' to 'wring from him the knowledge of things as shall appertain'. The letter candidly reveals that the government was not interested in the truth but only in making him confess to anything incriminating, however false. Throughout all these sufferings, he stalwartly revealed nothing. Bishop Richard Challoner in his *Memoirs* compares Alexander to the martyrs of the early Church. Briant very much wanted to join the Society of Jesus and he wrote a hasty letter asking to be admitted. In his letter he explained how he had resolved to join the Society while on the rack.

> In my afflictions and torments God himself of His infinite goodness mercifully and tenderly did stand by and assist me, comforting me... Whether this be miraculous or no, God knoweth. But it is true. Giving my mind up to prayer and commending myself to our Lord, I was replenished and filled with a kind of supernatural sweetness of spirit; and even while I was calling upon the holy name of Jesus and upon the Blessed Virgin Mary, my mind was cheerfully disposed, well comforted and readily prepared... to endure these torments. At length my former purpose to become a Jesuit came to my mind.

The letter was smuggled out of the Tower for him and safely reached its destination. Although his situation meant that he could not be formally inducted to the Order, he expressed his intentions so clearly that the Jesuits were proud to claim him as one of their own.

On 15 November Alexander was arraigned with six other priests. The trial took place on the 21st, the day after Campion and his companions. Alexander came into Court having roughly

The Elizabethan Martyrs, 1577-1601

tonsured his head to indicate he was a priest. In prison he had made a rough wooden cross on which he had drawn in charcoal a picture of the Crucified Christ. He clasped the cross in his hand and kept gazing at it during the trial. One of the Protestant ministers told him to throw the cross away, but he answered, 'Never. I am a soldier of the cross and this is my standard unto death.' When the cross was snatched from his hands he replied, 'You may tear this cross from my hands but not from my heart… until I shall shed my blood for him who for my sake poured out his upon the cross of Calvary'. The cross was later acquired by some Catholics and is now among the relics in the English College in Rome.

Few details of the trial are known. Alexander had never been to Rome and had left Rheims many months before the date when the alleged plot was supposed to have been concocted. It obviously made no difference to the proceedings which, no doubt, followed a similar pattern to those of Campion and Sherwin. Munday and Sledd once again gave 'evidence' for the prosecution. Despite going through the legal motions of questioning and cross-questioning, the verdict was in no doubt. When it was delivered Briant, his face radiant with peace and serenity, recited Psalm 42: 'Judge me, O God and distinguish my cause from the nation that is not holy… I will go unto the altar of God: to God who giveth joy to my youth.'

Briant was returned to the Tower and loaded with chains awaiting his execution. Early in the morning of 1 December, he and Sherwin stood by the Coldharbour Tower waiting for Campion to be brought to join them. When he arrived they all embraced. Dragged from the Tower to Tyburn with Campion and Sherwin, he had to watch while both of them were executed. Perhaps this was a deliberate ploy by the authorities to see if it would shake his resolve. If so, the stratagem failed. The crowd was greatly moved at the sight of Alexander's handsome young face. He was described as a man of angelic beauty, both of body and soul, and of obvious simplicity, which despite all his sufferings had not been dimmed. He did not say very much except to protest his innocence of any wrongdoing, not only in deed but also in thought. He professed his faith and greatly rejoiced that God had found him worthy to die in the company of Father Campion, whom he revered with all his heart. While he said the *Miserere* psalm the cart was pulled away. Due to either the malice or the carelessness of the executioner, the rope slipped, and instead of being rendered insensible Alexander was fully conscious when cut down to endure the disembowelling. He was just twenty-six years old.

John Paine

'Well done, good and faithful servant.'

Matthew 25:21

John Paine or Payne was born at Peterborough, Northamptonshire, perhaps as early as 1532, but nothing else is known of his early life. As he mentions his 'very earnest Protestant brother', it has been inferred that John was a convert, although there is no evidence for this, and when or where he became a Catholic is unknown. He entered the English College at Douai as a mature student in 1574 and served as the College bursar. The fact that he was ordained priest so soon afterwards, at Cambrai on 7 April 1576, suggests he was already advanced in his studies. He spent the two weeks after his ordination following the *Spiritual Exercises* of Ignatius Loyola before returning to England with Cuthbert Mayne.

Although John's apostolate ranged over a wide area, including visits to London, he made his headquarters at Ingatestone Hall, Essex, the home of Anne, Lady Petre, the second wife and widow of Sir William Petre, whom we have already briefly met in the life of Ralph Sherwin. John's name appears in a list of recusants at Ingatestone prepared for the Bishop of London in 1577.

As Secretary of State under Henry VIII, Sir William Petre had been responsible for visiting the religious houses in Southern England and trying to persuade them to surrender to the King. The nuns of Barking Abbey had a manor at Yenge-atte-Stone (hence Ingatestone), and Sir William purchased this property in 1539 when Barking Abbey was dissolved. Under Queen Mary,

The Elizabethan Martyrs, 1577-1601

Sir William obtained a papal bull exonerating him from wrongdoing in his acquisition and confirming him in possession. He then built the house which still stands today, and after his death his staunchly Catholic widow, Anne, daughter of a former Lord Mayor of London, continued to live there. The Hall possessed a tiny secret chapel accessible through the back of a cupboard in an alcove, and a priests' hiding place some fourteen feet long by two feet wide and ten feet high. The entrance to it was beneath the flooring.

Paine acted the part of estate steward while ministering to the scattered Catholic community. Details of his movements are sketchy, but he was clearly a very active missionary. He was first arrested at Ingatestone around June 1576 but had certainly been released before March 1577. He was at Douai in November 1577 but the reason for his visit or its duration are unknown. He was back at Ingatestone by June 1578 because he was one of the witnesses to Lady Petre's will. In January 1579 he was lodging with a Catholic woman in London for a time. If the evidence of George 'Judas' Eliot, capturer of Campion, is to be believed, John was at Ingatestone for Christmas, which is where he claimed to have met him for the first time. Eliot, who pretended to be a good Catholic, was employed for a time as a servant at Ingatestone.

We next hear of John at Haddon in Oxfordshire, where he stayed at the house of William Moore, together with Father George Godsalf. Here, Eliot alleged, he celebrated Mass on 2 July 1581. Godsalf had been ordained deacon during the reign of Queen Mary but had then developed Protestant sympathies. He was befriended by John who, three months after his arrival in Essex, reconciled him to the Church and recommended him to Douai in 1576. Godsalf took with him a letter from Paine in which he wrote:

> On all sides, in daily increasing numbers, a great many are reconciled to the Catholic Faith, to the amazement of many of the heretics. And when any of them as does happen fall into the hands of the raging heretics, with such fortitude, with such courage and constancy do they publicly confess the Catholic Faith... that the heretics are dumbfounded with astonishment and already begin to give up hope of putting them down by violence. Greatly also are they troubled by the very name of the

The Elizabethan Martyrs, 1577-1601

> Douai priests... which on the other hand fills all Catholics with consolation and the greatest hope of the recovery of the Catholic religion. They lay snares therefore for all priests, but especially and most eagerly for those sent from thence.

Priests were urgently needed and he begged that more be sent. He beseeches that he and his priestly colleagues be daily remembered in the prayers of Douai that they may persevere in their work.

Godsalf was ordained at Cambrai on 22 December 1576 and returned to England the following June. He and John were betrayed by Eliot and captured in Warwickshire in July 1581. After being examined by Sir Francis Walsingham at Greenwich, they were both sent to the Tower on 14 July. Although no one was in any doubt that John was a Douai priest, the law making this fact treason was not yet on the statute book, so a new charge had to be devised. Here Eliot proved his usefulness. He alleged that Paine had conspired to kill the Queen and tried to involve him in the plan. Walsingham felt that the accusation was too general and could not be sustained. Eliot accordingly obliged by supplying much greater detail elaborating the alleged conspiracy. Fifty armed men were involved, to be paid for by the Pope. For good measure the plan now also included assassinating the Earl of Leicester, Walsingham and Burghley, as well as Elizabeth, whom Paine would personally stab to death.

Imprisoned in the Tower for nine months, John was repeatedly tortured by order of the Privy Council. The Tower diary for August 31 records that 'John Paine, priest was most violently tormented on the rack'. The Lieutenant of the Tower, Sir Owen Hopton, told him to write a confession revealing those who had sheltered him and what he had plotted against the Queen and State. If he failed to do so he would answer at his utmost peril. Unable to use his hands after being racked, John dictated his response:

> Right Worshipful, My duty remembered, being not able to write without better hands, I have by your appointment used the help of your servant. For answer to your interrogations I have already said sufficient for a man that regardeth his own salvation, and that with such advised assentations uttered, as amongst Christian men ought to be believed. Yet once again briefly for obedience sake.

The Elizabethan Martyrs, 1577-1601

> First, touching Her Majesty, I pray God to preserve her Highness to His honour and her heart's desire; unto whom I always have and during life will wish no worse than to my own soul. If her pleasure be not that I shall live and serve her as my Sovereign Prince, then will I willingly die her faithful subject, and I trust God's true servant.
>
> Touching the State, I protest that I am and ever have been free from the knowledge of any practice whatever, either within or without the realm, intended against the same. For the verity whereof, as I have often before you and the rest of her Grace's commissioners called God to witness, so do I now again; and one day before His Majesty the truth, now not credited, will then be revealed.
>
> For Eliot I forgive his monstrous wickedness and defy his malicious inventions; wishing that his former behaviour towards others, being well known, as hereafter it will be, were not a sufficient proof of these devised slanders.
>
> For host or other person living, in London or elsewhere, unless they be by subornation of my bloody enemy corrupted, I know they can neither for word, deed nor any disloyalty, justly touch me. And so before the seat of God, as also before the sight of men, I will answer at my utmost peril.

At the same time Campion, Sherwin, Briant and others were held in the Tower, tried and condemned on similarly perjured 'evidence'. Why Paine was not included with them remains a mystery.

During the night of 20 March 1582, John was abruptly roused by the Lieutenant of the Tower. Denied the opportunity to dress, gather his belongings or retrieve his purse, he was handed over to officers and hurried away to Chelmsford to be tried at the assizes. In spite of the nine months' delay affording the government the opportunity to gather further evidence, none was forthcoming, so John was charged solely on the testimony of Eliot; he was the only perjured witness. At the trial on 23 March the prosecuting counsel told the jury that they should presume the truth of Eliot's accusation because John had committed the crime of 'going beyond the seas' to be ordained priest. Despite knowing the hopelessness of his situation, John vigorously defended himself, vehemently denying the charges and protesting his innocence. He pointed out that it was totally unjust and against all

The Elizabethan Martyrs, 1577-1601

natural law that he should be condemned on the uncorroborated evidence of one man, especially such a notoriously infamous character as Eliot.

When the jury delivered the verdict expected of them John excused them for being 'poor, simple men, nothing at all understanding what treason is'. He accepted his sentence calmly, and his comment, 'If it please the Queen and her Council that I shall die, I refer my case to God,' revealed that he was under no illusions that his condemnation had been engineered, and by whom. In the days before his execution he had to endure the unwanted attentions of two Puritan ministers, who greatly vexed and troubled him 'by their foolish babbling'. He was offered a pardon if he agreed to conform, leaving no one, then or since, in any doubt that he was to die purely for his religion.

Paine was a meek and gentle man, greatly loved by all who knew him. An anonymous contemporary account, probably by a fellow priest, published in the *Brief History of Twelve Reverend Priests*, states:

> All the town loved him exceedingly and so did the keepers. No man seemed to dislike him, but much sorrowed and lamented his death. I, amongst many, coming to him about ten of the clock with the officers, he most comfortably and meekly uttered words of constancy to me and with a loving kiss took leave of me.

He was lodged in a dungeon at Colchester Castle to await execution, which took place on 2 April 1582 at Chelmsford. On the scaffold he was offered a pardon if he would conform, but he courteously refused. He asked forgiveness of anyone he had wronged, forgiving everyone who had harmed him, including Eliot, whom he named and prayed for. Despite being harangued by the ministers who insisted he pray in English, not Latin, he knelt in prayer and then ascended the ladder with a smile on his face. He kissed the gallows and was allowed to speak to the crowd. He protested his innocence.

'My feet never did tread, my hands never did write, nor my wit ever invent any treason against her Majesty,' he declared. But Lord Rich, who was in the crowd, called out to him to confess his guilt. Paine replied that to confess a lie was to condemn his own soul. 'Sweet my Lord,' he said, 'certify her Majesty thereof, that she suffer not hereafter innocent blood to be cast away which is a great sin.' When one of the ministers claimed that John's brother had confirmed the charge of conspiracy, he temporarily lost his composure. '*Bone Deus*! My brother is, and always has been, a very earnest Protestant; yet I know he will not say so falsely of me.'

His brother, whose name may have been Jerome, was not present to speak for himself; and if the statement were true, why did the government not summon him to give evidence to that effect? In fact, when he heard about the matter, the brother completely denied it, saying it was all a fabrication.

The Spanish ambassador wrote that Paine died with the greatest fortitude. When John was turned off the ladder, he hung without moving hand or foot, repeating the name of Jesus. He was so well liked in the neighbourhood that some men in the crowd 'courteously' hung onto his feet and made sure that he was dead before he was cut down to suffer the subsequent barbarities, much to the annoyance of Simon Bull, the hangman of Newgate, who had been specially brought to Essex for the execution.

Father Godsalf remained in the Tower until the end of 1583. In February 1584 he was transferred to the Marshalsea, where he was kept until banished in September 1585. He died in Paris about six years later.

There remains in existence an interesting reminder of an episode in John Paine's life: the 'Bosworth Burse'. The burse has an embroidered image of Christ appearing from the Chalice, an image well known in iconography; but in this instance it commemorates a vision claimed to have been seen by John while at Douai.

Luke Kirby

We step from days of sour division into the grandeur of our fate.

The Fourth of August, Laurence Binyon, 1869–1943

According to Bishop Challoner, Luke was born at Bedale, North Yorkshire, in 1548. Other sources claim Richmond, a little further north, as his birthplace. It is believed he was a graduate of

Cambridge University, yet the records of Louvain University, Belgium, show that Kirby matriculated there in August 1566 having, one assumes, taken his MA. It is said he was a convert; if that is so his attendance at Louvain suggests that he became a Catholic there or as a teenager rather than later. Luke is said to have arrived at Douai in 1576. What he was doing or where he lived in the intervening ten years is unknown. While at Douai we are told he suffered from 'the stone' – whether kidney or bladder is not disclosed – but it was extremely painful. Luke submitted to the gruesome surgery for its removal, but afterwards his health was always rather frail.

He was ordained at Cambrai on 21 September 1577, choosing to wait to say his first Mass until 18 October, the feast day of his patron, St Luke. On 3 May 1578 he was sent to England but was back in Douai by July, when it was decided to send him to Rome for further study. He left Douai for the English College, Rome, on 17 August and spent the next two years there, taking the missionary oath on 23 April 1579, the same day as Ralph Sherwin. An observant English spy mentions him in a report as being thirty-two years of age, of reasonable stature and well built, his beard cut short, of a brown colour, having prominent teeth and a little stutter. In Rome he was noted for his charity towards all, ever ready to empty his purse, and once literally gave the shirt off his back to a beggar. He spent Lent of 1580 preparing himself with great fervour for his return to England. In April, in company with Robert Persons, Edmund Campion and Ralph Sherwin, he set off for home. He particularly enjoyed the encounter they had with Beza in Geneva. Making his way to Dunkirk, it is believed he may have crossed over to Dover in June 1580.

Wherever it was he landed, he was arrested immediately on arrival. He was sent to the Gatehouse Prison in London where he found many other Catholics. On 4 December he was moved to the Tower where six days later he was cruelly tortured with the Scavenger's Daughter. The name was a corruption of that of its inventor, Sir William Skevington, Lieutenant of the Tower under Henry VIII. The instrument was a hinged hoop of iron in which the victim's whole body was rolled into a ball and compressed into the hoop which was placed under his legs and over his back.

The Elizabethan Martyrs, 1577-1601

It caused nosebleeds and blood to flow from under the finger and toenails. Luke was left in this agonising state for hours.

He was arraigned with Campion and his companions on 14 November and tried and condemned with them on 20 November. One of the suborned witnesses, Sledd, gave evidence against him, alleging that Kirby had talked of the great day when there would be an invasion of England by the King of Spain and the Pope. Luke's answer was, 'As I hope to be saved at the last doom, there is not one word of this that... is either true or credible. Neither at any time made I the least mention of that alleged day... I always bore as true and faithful a heart to her Majesty as any subject whatsoever did in England... I defended her cause and always spoke the best of her highness.'

Luke was not executed with Campion; his execution was delayed until 1582. While in prison in January of that year he wrote a long letter to friends from which the following extracts are taken. The John Nichols to whom he refers was a well-known Calvinist minister who had converted to Catholicism while living in France but had reverted to Protestantism on his return to England. He made an uncharitable habit of haranguing and annoying Catholic prisoners. On the day after Alexander Briant's arrest, the apostate Nichols had spotted Anthony Tyrell in the street and had him arrested. Tyrell was sent to the Gatehouse, from which he soon contrived to escape. Richardson, Filby and Hart were, of course, Luke's fellow priest prisoners.

> My most hearty commendations to you and the rest of my dearest friends. If you send anything to me you must make haste because we look to suffer death very shortly, as already it is signified to us. John Nichols came to my chamber window with humble submission, to crave mercy and pardon for all his wickedness and treacheries committed against us and to acknowledge his books, sermons and infamous speeches to our infamy and discredit, to be wicked, false and most execrable before God and man which he had indulged in for favour and hope of promotion.
>
> He knoweth in conscience our accusations and the evidence brought against us to be false and to have no colour of truth, but only out of malice forged by our enemies. As for Sledd and Munday, he is himself to accuse them of this wicked treachery and falsehood and of their naughty and abominable life... for

which cause he hath forsaken his ministry and is minded to teach a school... in Norfolk. I wished him to make amends for his sins and go to a place of penance... He offered to go to... Mr Secretary Walsingham and declare how injuriously I and the rest were condemned, that he might be free from shedding innocent blood. He was afraid to show himself in London where already he had declared our innocent behaviour... To give my censure and judgement of him, certain I think he will within a short time fall into infidelity, except God of His goodness in the meantime be merciful to him... yet it would seem he hath not lost all good gifts of nature, when as in conscience he was pricked to open the truth in our defence... I am minded to signify to Sir Francis Walsingham this his submission to us, except in the meantime I shall learn that he has, as he promised faithfully to me, already opened the same. Mr Richardson and Mr Filby have now obtained some bedding, who since their condemnation have laid upon the boards. Mr Hart hath had many great conflicts with his adversaries. This morning... he was committed to the dungeon where he now remaineth. God comfort him; he taketh it very quietly and patiently... Thus beseeching you to assist us with your good prayers whereof now especially we stand in need, as we by God's grace shall not be unmindful of you.

John Nichols did honour his promise. He confessed to the Lieutenant of the Tower, who ignored him. He later confessed to Burghley, who admitted that they all knew Nichols was a liar but it made no difference. Nichols later returned to France.

On 30 May 1582 Luke suffered with three other priests, William Filby, Laurence Richardson and Thomas Cottam. Even on the scaffold, on behalf of the Queen, the sheriff offered them their lives and liberty; but Luke and his companions refused to deny their faith. Standing in the cart Luke declared his innocence and the fact that he was to die for his religion. A group of ministers constantly importuned him so that he had to struggle to prepare himself amidst the harassment. Finally they offered to pray with him, suggesting that they say the words and if he did not find them objectionable he could repeat them. Luke told them he preferred to pray on his own and, saying the Pater Noster and Ave Maria, he was turned off the ladder.

Unusually, the quartered bodies of the four priests were not

The Elizabethan Martyrs, 1577-1601

displayed but were buried in the common grave by the Tyburn gallows and relics of Luke were obtained. While in prison materials were smuggled in to him to enable him to say Mass. The linen corporal that he used was given by him to another priest prisoner who was later exiled. It has survived and along with the other relics it now rests at Stonyhurst College.

Richard Gwyn

> He that hath left life's vain joys and vain care… hath got an house where many mansions are and keeps his soul unto eternal mirth.
>
> *The Timber*, Henry Vaughan, 1622–95

Wales had long remained a bastion of Catholicism, but Richard, who it is believed was raised as a Protestant, was the first Welshman to die for the Faith under Elizabeth. He was born about 1537 at Llanidloes, then in Montgomeryshire, but now in Powys. At the age of twenty he went to Oxford, where he studied for a time before moving to St John's College, Cambridge, where he lived largely on the charity of Dr George Bullock, the Master.

Dr Bullock had left England during Edward VI's reign but returned at the accession of Queen Mary. When Elizabeth came to the throne he had to resign his Mastership for refusing the Oath of Supremacy and went to spend the rest of his life abroad. The loss of his benefactor made life very difficult for Richard, and to earn money he took pupils. After leaving the university he returned to Wales in 1562 and became a schoolmaster, teaching at Overton and Gresford, both close to Wrexham, while continuing his own studies in theology and history. It must have been sometime during this period that he became a Catholic, presumably reconciled by a seminary priest. He was fascinated by the rich folklore of his country, and being fluent in Welsh wrote songs and poetry in the language. He married a girl from Overton called Catherine and they had six children, three of whom survived.

As a recusant in a small community, Richard's absence from church was very noticeable. He tried by all possible means,

The Elizabethan Martyrs, 1577-1601

frequently moving around, to avoid taking the Oath of Supremacy and was threatened with fines or imprisonment if he did not conform. What is more, he was not one to keep his opinions to himself, exhorting his neighbours to return to the Catholic Church. The Anglican bishops were told to be more vigilant against recusants, especially schoolmasters, who exercised great influence. William Downham, Bishop of Chester, took action and within a month Richard had been arrested by the Bishop's officers. Threatened with imprisonment, Richard was concerned about the welfare of his family and after much bullying he very reluctantly agreed to go to church at Overton the following Sunday. As he left church a strange thing happened; a great flock of crows and kites swooped down and began to peck at his face and head. Richard took this as an omen and resolved never again to violate his conscience by attending the Protestant church.

Incensed at Richard's refusal, the Bishop made life so unbearable for him that he and his family packed up and left Overton on foot. Arriving at Erbistock, they found an old deserted barn where they made their home. He set up a secret school for the local Catholic children, but while visiting Wrexham cattle market he was recognised by the vicar, an apostate priest, who had him arrested and imprisoned. Told he was to appear before the magistrates the next day, he escaped during the night. Now he was really a marked man. He was at liberty for eighteen months.

Richard was stopped on the public highway by a fanatical Puritan cloth merchant called David Edwards, who without any legal authority had him dragged to his house and chained up while the magistrates were summoned. Richard was taken to Wrexham prison and locked in a horrible underground dungeon, known as the Black Chamber, for two days. Brought before the magistrate, he was sent back to prison on suspicion of treason. Within a month Richard had been moved to Ruthin Castle, where he was harshly treated. On his repeated refusal to conform he was put in heavy manacles. At the Michaelmas Assizes he was asked to betray the people whose children he had taught. This he refused to do; nor would he consent to go to church so he was returned to prison. About Christmas time he was sent back to Wrexham jail, his hands and legs heavily loaded with irons. Brought once more before the magistrates, he refused to conform.

At the May Assizes, the magistrates ordered that Richard be forcibly taken to church. He was carried into St Giles's Parish church by six of the sheriff's men and laid under the pulpit to hear the minister preach. Richard rattled his chains so loudly that no one could hear a word of the sermon. Furious, the magistrates ordered him to be put in the stocks from 10 a.m. until 8 p.m. – 'vexed all the time with a rabble of ministers'. Taken back to his cell, he was visited by some of the ministers. One of them, who had a very large purple nose, wanted to dispute with Richard about the keys of the Kingdom of Heaven, asserting that God had given those keys also to him and not only to St Peter.

'There is a difference,' said Richard. 'St Peter was entrusted with the keys of the Kingdom of Heaven, while the keys entrusted to you appear to be those of the beer cellar!'

Brought to court, the only new charge they could make against him was for causing a disturbance in church, for which he was heavily fined. In September 1581 he was moved from Wrexham to Denbigh Castle. Tried before Sir George Bromley, he was fined £140 for refusing to go to church. That was an absolutely enormous sum for the time. When asked how he was going to pay, he told the magistrate that he had something towards it.

'How much?' Sir George asked, to which Richard replied, 'Sixpence.'

Angrily, the judge ordered him to be sent back to prison in extra irons. He was soon joined by two other recusants, John Hughes and Robert Morris. In readiness for the Spring Assizes of 1582, they were moved to Wrexham. When brought to court they found that the judge had engaged a minister to come and preach to them. The three prisoners responded by haranguing the preacher, one in Welsh, one in English and one in Latin, until he gave up.

They next appeared at the Assize at Holt. David Edwards had tried to bribe two other prisoners, Wynne and Thomas, into giving evidence that Richard had been persuading them not to

The Elizabethan Martyrs, 1577-1601

attend church. The plan failed because when Wynne and Thomas were called they told the court it was a lie and that they had been bribed to give false witness. In May 1583 Richard was sent before the Council of the Marches in the company of three other recusants and a Welsh priest, Father John Bennet, who served the chapel at St Winefride's Well, Holywell. When sent to the Council, the prisoners were all brutally tortured at Bewdley and Ludlow to make them reveal the names and whereabouts of other Catholics. Richard was put in the manacles, that is, he was hung up by his wrists to a post while being interrogated.

Despite the agony he refused to reveal anything and only spoke in prayer for himself and his tormentors, which angered the judge. 'There is no more pity to be had on thee than on a mad dog,' he retorted. 'Wretches like you should all be hanged!'

Richard's answer was, 'I pray you put me to death... and therein you shall do me greater pleasure than to kill me continually with these tortures,' after which he continued to pray in silence.

When Father Bennet was eventually tried he was not condemned to death. He was later moved to London and sent into exile, where he joined the Society of Jesus. He returned to Wales and Holywell and ministered for many years before dying in London in 1625.

On 9 October 1584 Richard, Hughes and Morris were tried for high treason before Sir George Bromley, the Chief Justice of Chester, at Wrexham. No one wished to sit on the jury so a collection of the local anti-Catholic riff-raff had to be paid to do jury service. Richard was accused of reconciling a man called Gronow to the Church, of making up satirical verses against married priests, and for maintaining the papal supremacy. Richard denied ever having met Gronow. John Hughes called in a witness of his own who could testify that the prosecution evidence had been obtained by bribery. The jury were understandably disturbed by this revelation, but the trial continued. It was later shown that the witnesses had indeed been bribed at the instigation of the vicar of Wrexham. As Richard refused to go to church or acknowledge Elizabeth as head of the Church there were plenty of grounds on which to convict him of treason.

The Elizabethan Martyrs, 1577-1601

The jurymen were clearly unhappy with the evidence they had heard. Sir George threatened them with dire consequences if they did not bring in a guilty verdict and they retired for the night. Unable to reach a decision they sent a delegation to the judge to seek his advice. Whom, they asked, should we convict and whom acquit? So Bromley told them. Next morning the verdicts were announced: Richard and John Hughes were found guilty of treason and Robert Morris was discharged; poor Morris wept. Then the judge announced that Hughes was to be reprieved but Richard was to be hanged, drawn and quartered.

Seemingly unperturbed, Richard accepted his sentence calmly. 'What is all this? Is it any more than one death?' he asked.

Mrs Gwyn and Mrs Hughes were in court holding their babies. Richard and Hughes had been granted an unauthorised parole by the sympathetic jailer, Coytmore, the result of which was now all too obvious to the authorities who were not best pleased at this breach. The judge admonished the two wives not to follow the bad example of their husbands. Unfazed, Mrs Gwyn responded, 'If it is blood you want, you may take my life as well as my husband's. Fetch the witnesses and give them a little bribe and they will bear evidence against me as well as they did against him.' For thus speaking up the two women were sent to prison for a few days.

Two days before his execution Richard was visited by the sheriff with the offer that if he would accept the Queen as head of the Church he would even now go free. The offer was refused. Catherine was allowed to join her husband in jail and the next day he asked her to purchase for him two dozen silk ribbons. These he kissed and asked his wife to distribute to twelve priests. His personal belongings, including his signet ring, he also asked to be sent to close friends as keepsakes. Thursday was the day appointed for the execution and in the morning they caught sight of David Edwards. Catherine shouted after him, 'God be a righteous judge between thee and me.'

Richard gently rebuked her telling her that if they did not now freely forgive him all their sufferings would have been in vain. Shortly afterwards they heard loud weeping and discovered it was Mrs Coytmore, the jailer's wife. She and her husband had become fond of Richard and now – perhaps as a punishment for his earlier act of clemency – Coytmore had been designated as hangman. Richard sent Catherine to comfort her before going down into the part of the jail where common thieves were kept to say farewell to them.

As he left the jail a crowd of sympathisers greeted him, many of them in tears, including some of his former pupils. To one young man Richard said, 'Weep not for me, for I do but pay the rent before the rent day.' Someone had sent him five shillings in small pieces of silver, and this he distributed to the poor people. To Catherine, who was carrying their month-old baby son, he gave his rosary and his remaining money, then he kissed her and she knelt for his blessing, all the while being harassed by the sheriff. Richard was tied to the hurdle and dragged to the market place, all the time saying the rosary using his chains.

It was pouring with rain and when Richard reached the scaffold he remarked, 'God is merciful to us; even the elements shed tears for our sins.'

The hangman knelt down to ask his forgiveness, which Richard gladly gave him, saying, 'I do forgive thee before God and I wish thee no more harm than I wish my own heart.'

The sheriff asked him if he repented of his treason against the Queen. 'I have never committed any treason against her any more than your father or grandfather, unless it be treason to pray.' This was his way of signifying that although their forebears were all Catholics, it was now treason to be one. The vicar of Wrexham pressed him whether he acknowledged the Queen to be head of the Church. Richard indicated that he held her to be the lawful Queen, but not head of the Church.

Climbing the ladder, Richard spoke to the crowd. 'My dear countrymen, remember your souls and do not lose them for this vile transitory muck which Christ hath so dearly bought. This is but one hour's pain to me, and what is that in respect of the torments in hell which shall never have an end?'

The hangman was so overcome with emotion that Richard had to help him put the rope around his neck and a handkerchief was tied across his eyes. He asked forgiveness of any whom he had offended. As he was saying, 'God be merciful to me a sinner,' he was turned off the ladder. He hung from the rope some considerable time, beating his breast and crying, 'Jesus, have mercy on me!'

As the crowd called out that he should be allowed to die before dismemberment, the hangman hung onto his legs hoping to hasten the end. When Richard appeared to be insensible he was cut down, but revived as he was being disembowelled. He cried out in Welsh in his pain, 'Holy God, what is this?' His last words before his head was severed were, 'Jesus, have mercy on me.'

Margaret Clitherow

> No coward soul is mine... I see Heaven's glories shine and faith shines equal, arming me from fear.
>
> *Last Lines*, Emily Bronte, 1818–38

Popularly known as 'the Pearl of York', Margaret was born in Davygate, York in 1553, the year of Queen Mary's accession. She was the second daughter and the youngest child of four of Thomas and Jane Middleton née Turner. The father of Jane Turner was the successful landlord of the Angel inn and her brother Robert was a priest. The Middletons were a prominent and very prosperous York family. Thomas was a wax chandler and a churchwarden of St Martin's, Coney Street. He later served a term as Sheriff of York and was elected to its Privy Council.

For the early years of her life, Margaret would have experienced the Mass and Catholic liturgy, but the full impact of the Elizabethan settlement hit St Martin's in 1561. The high altar and side altars were dismantled and the statues destroyed. Thomas knew 'on which side his bread was buttered' and conformed, at least outwardly. In this he seems to have been following his parish priest, Thomas Grayson, who was also a close friend. In 1567 Grayson was summoned before the Ecclesiastical Commissioners for possessing Catholic books which should have been burned. Margaret, having been raised in the Established Church, was fourteen when her father Thomas died in May 1567. His true religious feelings may be gathered from his bequest of

The Elizabethan Martyrs, 1577-1601

money to the poor on condition that they prayed for the repose of his soul. He was buried in St Martin's, Coney Street, and his will clearly reveals his wealth, owning property and land not only in York but also Ripon. He left a silver goblet and six silver spoons to Margaret as well as his house in Davygate after his widow's death.

Barely four months later, Margaret's mother remarried. Her new husband, Henry May, who came from the South of England, was an ambitious but penniless social climber and a rich widow was just what he needed to help him achieve his ambitions. Jane would have been in her fifties at the time and Henry in his twenties! He succeeded insofar as he rose to be Lord Mayor, but proved no friend either to his stepdaughter or the Catholics of York. May soon converted the large house in Davygate into a flourishing inn and as a teenager Margaret was very much involved in its busy social life. His new-found connections soon began to pay off: within months of marrying May was elected a chamberlain of York and was granted trading privileges. He became a churchwarden at St Martin's, with the responsibility of eliminating any remaining traces of Catholicism. This included selling off the chalices and patens, removing the rood screen and loft and paying for an anti-Catholic pamphlet. In 1570 May became one of the two Sheriffs of York.

As well as being very attractive, Margaret was an intelligent and sharp-witted young woman. On 1 July 1571 at St Martin's, Coney Street, she was married to John Clitherow. Margaret was John's second wife, his first wife Maud Mudd having died, leaving him a widower with two young sons. John was a grazier and butcher by trade, a hard-nosed, ambitious businessman who became a chamberlain of York in 1574 and one of the richest citizens of the city. Their home in Christ's parish was in The Shambles, the meat market of York from where John conducted his trade, and they 'lived over the shop'. Margaret was invaluable, helping her husband run his business and we are told how he liked to show off his lovely young wife at York's social gatherings. Their reputed house at No. 36 in the well-preserved medieval street still stands and is a chapel shrine. John's family remained Catholic, although John, who does not appear to have had any deep religious beliefs, had conformed. His brother William became a seminary priest, being ordained at Soissons in 1582 and he ended his life as a Carthusian monk at Louvain, Belgium. John Clitherow in 1572 was asked to participate with his parish officials in enforcing newly issued orders from the Council of the North. These instructions required every person who was an upright citizen to spy upon and report all recusants to the authorities.

In 1574, apparently quite suddenly, Margaret decided to become reconciled to the Catholic Church. Margaret's spiritual director for the last two years of her life was Father John Mush,[15] who clearly admired and revered her for her holiness. 'This golden woman', he calls her in the emotional biography he wrote in the summer of 1586, *A True Report of the Life and Martyrdom of Mrs Margaret Clitherow*. Mush tells us that 'to her beautiful and gracious soul God gave her a body with comely face and beauty correspondent'. We can forgive him his irascibility, his verbosity and his antipathy towards the Jesuits for leaving us this priceless record of Margaret.

Mush writes that Margaret converted because

> she found no substance, truth nor Christian comfort in the ministers of the new church, nor in their doctrine itself, and hearing also many priests and lay people to suffer for the defence of the ancient Catholic Faith.

She knew she was playing with fire and can have been under no illusion about the dangerous step she had taken. She could see persecution all around her in York, where the prisons were constantly full of Catholics. Close to home in her street and parish there were prominent recusants such as Janet Geldard, another butcher's wife, and the physician Dr Thomas Vavasour and Dorothy his wife. Janet had converted her husband and she and Dorothy were among the first women of York to be imprisoned for recusancy. There were also cousins such as Anne Weddell and family friends suffering for their faith.

When Margaret's conversion became known her family was deeply displeased, to put it mildly. What engendered her conversion is unknown. Father Mush gives us no clue because writing so close in time to the events he described he had to be very circumspect; but there are a number of possibilities.

The Elizabethan Martyrs, 1577-1601

Margaret may have been taken to visit priests imprisoned in the Ousebridge Kidcote such as Father Henry Comberford. He had been a parish priest under Queen Mary but was deprived by Elizabeth and spent sixteen years in jail in York and Hull; or maybe her Catholic in-laws or recusant neighbours, such as Mrs Vavasour, introduced her to a seminary priest. We can only speculate; we will never know.

Margaret and Mrs Vavasour became good friends. The doctor's wife was an excellent midwife whose home, as well as being a refuge for priests, was a place where women could deliver their babies in safety. Often several women were summoned to help with a confinement, and this served as an excellent cover, when necessary, for Margaret and others to meet together to receive the Sacraments from a visiting priest without arousing suspicion.

Margaret possessed great tranquillity of soul and humility. 'In her own eyes she thought herself nobody but an unprofitable servant to God and man.' As became her social status, she had servants; but 'there was nothing to be done in the house so base that she would not be most ready to do or take in hand herself'. She would not disdain to make the fire or sweep the house or wash the dishes. 'God forbid,' she would say, 'that I should will any to do that in my house which I would not willingly do myself first.'

Margaret had a highly developed sensitive conscience, and Father Mush records that after hearing her confession of her small imperfections he was 'cast into some extraordinary sense of joy of mind' and always felt humbled and more conscious of his own sins and failings, hoping to emulate 'some little part of that virtue and purity' with which she was endowed.

John and Margaret seem to have had a happy marriage, despite the fact that over the next ten years she was in and out of jail many times. John once said that Margaret had only two faults: she fasted too much and would not accompany him to church. And Margaret declared that she loved her husband next only to God. In spite of her worldly responsibilities she found time to lead a very devout life. Every morning she would spend over an hour in prayer and meditation on her knees in her room, after which she would attend Mass in the secret chamber if a priest was in the house.

The priest's chamber was actually a room in her neighbour's house which she had hired, and it was connected to Margaret's attic. The concealed exit enabling the priest to escape without detection led through the neighbour's property. Who had the skill to carry out the work is unknown; it had to be constructed in great secrecy – presumably without the knowledge of John Clitherow. This may have been possible because the neighbours on one side were John's sister and her husband, Millicent and William Calvert; on the other side lived relatives of John's first wife, Michael Mudd and his wife, all of whom were Catholics. Margaret would again devote time to prayer after completing the day's household duties late in the evening. She was also much engaged in charitable work, frequently visiting the jails to bring material comfort to the poor prisoners.

Margaret's home became one of the chief secret Mass centres of York. Her easy-going husband seems to have turned a blind eye to her activities, although he must surely have been aware of what was going on in his own house. However, at no time in his life does he seem to have felt any desire to become a Catholic, although Margaret declared how much it grieved her heart that he would not convert. As well as being a good wife and a loving if rather strict mother, it was said of Margaret that 'everyone loved her and would run to her for help, comfort and counsel in distress'.

Margaret was always kind and charitable towards her neighbours who regarded her as a 'jewel' in their midst. It is a testament to her goodness and popularity that none of her Protestant neighbours, who were well aware of what was going on under their noses, ever betrayed her. Indeed, she enjoyed such goodwill amongst her neighbours that they would warn her of any likely danger. Margaret's prudence and 'discretion was marvellous', but the only criticism that Father Mush makes of her is that in her fervent desire to serve God and the Church she tended to 'adventure more than in these ungracious times' was wise. It greatly concerned him that she let her children and their schoolmates into the secrets of the house, including the location of the priest's chamber. Yet he declares he dare not condemn her for this indiscretion because her intention was sincere and good.

In 1576 a crackdown was ordered on the recusants of York. As an active Catholic, Margaret was soon in trouble, and by June of that year her name appears for the first time in the lists of recusants, where she was described as heavily pregnant. On 2 August 1577 Margaret and John were summoned before Archbishop Edwin Sandys and the Ecclesiastical Commissioners. This resulted in John being imprisoned in the Kidcote for three days for refusing to pay more fines, although he promised to try and persuade his wife to attend church.

Margaret, pregnant once more, refused to consider the idea and was sent to York Castle in the company of several other women, including Anne Weddell and Janet Geldard, who were judged to be particularly dangerous for the influence they might have on others. The great numbers of Catholics in York Castle formed a real community. The priest prisoners were sometimes able to hear confessions and say Mass and Margaret had many opportunities to nurture her spiritual life. 'The prison she accounted a most happy and profitable school,' and it was while in prison that she learned to read. As a result she came to know Thomas à Kempis's *Imitation of Christ* and later the Douai-Rheims New Testament which was her delight when she had leisure time for reading. She was released in February 1578 but ordered to present herself at the Castle on 8 April. She duly reported, and was sent home to be confined to her house except for attending church; for every non-appearance John was to be fined two shillings. Needless to say, Margaret had no intention of attending the Protestant church and appeared before the Ecclesiastical Commissioners on 3 October 1580. When she refused to take the oath she was committed a close prisoner to the Castle. She was freed on 24 April 1581 in order to give birth, on condition that six weeks later she returned to jail. She must have been bitterly disappointed to learn that while in prison she had missed the opportunity of meeting Father Edmund Campion, who had celebrated Mass at the home of the Vavasours.

Henry May became an alderman and Justice of the Peace in March 1581. He could have tried to protect Margaret but he did

The Elizabethan Martyrs, 1577-1601

just the opposite. His attitude to Catholics may be gauged from two events. Early in 1581 he had presented to the Ecclesiastical Commission a list of the names of twenty-five recusants. It must have been galling for Margaret to learn that on the Feast of the Assumption 1581 he took part in the raid on Dr Thomas Vavasour's house in Christ's parish and arrested him at Mass with his wife, the old Marian priest, Father Wilkinson, and eleven others including William Hutton, a draper, and his wife Mary. Father Wilkinson was dragged through the streets of York still wearing his vestments while being mocked and spat upon. The whole group was committed to prison.

There is a York Council record of February 1583 complaining that the children of the still imprisoned Huttons were free to carry messages between their parents and for other prisoners. As a result, the children were denied all access to their father and ordered to be locked up with their mother because there was nowhere else for them to go. Dr Vavasour died a prisoner at Hull Blockhouse in 1585. His wife Dorothy died in the New Counter, Ousebridge, on 26 October 1587, the day after the death of Mary Hutton.

In August 1582 Margaret was convicted of recusancy at the Quarter Sessions. Convicted again in early March 1583 she was sent to the Castle and was released on bond for two months in May 1584, but must have returned to prison because she was released on bond that autumn. On each occasion it was John who was summoned to pay the recently increased heavy fines and put up the large amounts demanded in bond money. The terms of these bonds meant that for long periods she was confined to her own house.

Some time in 1584 Margaret took a great risk by sending her eldest son Henry to Douai to be educated and hopefully train for the priesthood. What her husband thought of this when he found out is not recorded. In spite of his mercenary preoccupation with accumulating wealth and getting on in the world, he was an indulgent husband. Margaret, aware that she was being watched, had to be extra careful. In addition to Henry she had three other children: Anne, born in 1574; a second daughter whose name is unknown and a second son (John?), probably the child born in

1581. Out of the generous allowance given to her by her husband, Margaret committed the criminal offence of paying for a private Catholic schoolmaster for her own children and those of her neighbours. He was a former prisoner whom she had met in York Castle and when he managed to escape she hid him in her house. Priests were also constantly sheltered in her house; just how many priests we will never know. Margaret provided beautiful vestments for them, the finest altar linen and sacred vessels.

Father Mush informs us that many of the priests who suffered martyrdom at York had passed through Margaret's house. They included William Lacey,[16] Richard Kirkman,[17] James Thompson,[18] William Hart,[19] Richard Thirkeld[20] and Francis Ingleby.[21] Margaret would often recall with joy the conversations she had with these holy priests and the spiritual profit she had derived from them. We learn that when her husband was away on business it was her practice to visit the York Tyburn at the Knavesmire at night to pray. This was the hallowed place where the Catholic martyrs were executed; so many that it was only surpassed by the London Tyburn.

In March 1585 the Act was passed making it an offence punishable by death to receive a Catholic priest. Margaret's Catholic friends begged her not to offer priests hospitality anymore. She was rather shocked by this pusillanimous attitude. Her answer was, 'I will not be afraid to serve God and do well. If God's priests dare to venture to my house I will never refuse them.'

Following the death of her mother in June 1585 she inherited the inn at Davygate. Although Henry May now possessed property of his own, he must have been aggrieved at being deprived of the inn by his recalcitrant stepdaughter. She may well have used the property as a Catholic centre. In February 1586 Henry May remarried in a splendid ceremony, having by then achieved the summit of his ambitions by becoming Lord Mayor. Margaret did not attend the wedding. One can imagine the scandalous gossip in the city when the Lord Mayor's recusant stepdaughter was arrested.

The Council of the North set about implementing the 1585 Act in earnest and raids on the homes of recusants were carried

The Elizabethan Martyrs, 1577-1601

out. One of those arrested accused, under torture, a married layman, Blessed Marmaduke Bowes, of harbouring the recently ordained Durham-born priest, Blessed Hugh Taylor. Bowes and Taylor were quickly apprehended, tried and condemned to death. Father Taylor was hanged, drawn and quartered on 26 November, and the following day Mr Bowes was hanged: the first execution under the new Act for harbouring a priest.

In 1586 the Council of the North swooped on York and on 10 March John Clitherow was summoned for a second time before Lord Eure, the Vice-President, and others to explain his missing son's whereabouts. His explanations proving unsatisfactory, he was arrested and confined to York Castle. While he was absent his house was raided and thoroughly searched by the two sheriffs and their constables looking for Father Ingleby. Margaret was at home and although Mass had been celebrated that morning no priest was found. He had safely exited via the small door, an awkward task because it was only 'large enough for a boy', and made his escape through the house next door.

Mr Stapleton, the schoolmaster, knowing that he too was in danger, remained with his pupils locked in an attic room. When he was discovered the searcher, armed with a sword, assumed he was a priest, and while he was calling for reinforcements Stapleton managed to get away through the priest's chamber into the neighbour's house, which left only the children to face the interrogators. The searchers had still not discovered the secret entrance into the priest's chamber and despite the bullying tactics they were unable to extract anything incriminating from the servants or the children. Among them was a Flemish boy aged about ten years old who, stripped naked and threatened with a whipping, revealed to them the priest's chamber where vestments and altar utensils were discovered.

That was proof enough; Margaret was arrested and her servants and the children were sent to various prisons. She never saw her children again. Brought before Lord Eure and members of the Council of the North, she was questioned for hours but maintained her composure and conceded nothing. At about 7 p.m. she was imprisoned in York Castle. The poor Flemish boy had by then also named Father Ingleby and Father Mush, and supplied the names of those who attended Mass in the Shambles. Among them was Mrs Anne Tesh, who was also arrested and sent to the Castle where she and Margaret occupied the same chamber over the weekend. John Clitherow was still in detention and was brought to see Margaret in the hope that he would persuade her to recant. If that was the object it did not succeed. It was to be John and Margaret's last meeting.

On the afternoon of 14 March 1586 Margaret was arraigned at the Common Hall, charged specifically with sheltering Francis Ingleby, the charge being brought under the Act against 'Jesuits and Seminary priests'. John Clinch and Francis Rhodes, two Assize judges, presided, accompanied by members of the Council of the North, watched by Lord Mayor Henry May. When asked how she pleaded, guilty or not guilty, Margaret answered that she knew of no offence which she had committed requiring her to plead one way or the other. The judge insisted that she had maintained enemies of Her Majesty, to which Margaret forthrightly responded that she had never harboured traitors. Moving on, the judge then asked her, as required by law, how she would be tried, anticipating the stock answer, 'by a jury'. Instead, Margaret replied, 'Having made no offence, I need no trial,' and despite all the attempts of the judge she refused to plead. The most she would concede was, 'If you say I have offended and must be tried, I will be tried by none but God and your own consciences.'

Even by the standards of Elizabethan courts of law, what followed was deeply offensive. The vestments and chalices taken from Margaret's house were brought into court, two men dressed themselves in them and holding up the altar wafers lampooned the actions of the priest at Mass in a sacrilegious travesty. Asked how she liked the vestments, Margaret answered that she liked them well enough if they had been on the backs of those that were fit to use them in God's honour, as they were intended. Every means was used to persuade her to plead but she resolutely refused.

Father Mush relates that later Margaret privately explained her reasons for refusing. Her refusal to plead, and thereby avoid a trial, was to save the jurymen, several of whom were known to

The Elizabethan Martyrs, 1577-1601

her, from being complicit in her condemnation; her in-laws, friends, servants and neighbours from incriminating themselves; and she from incriminating them, and above all her children, from having to give evidence against her – or if they did so, from perjuring themselves in order to save her. She explained, 'If I had put myself to the country, evidence must needs have come against me which I know none could give but only my children and servants. It would have been more grievous to me than a thousand deaths if I should have seen any of them brought forth before me to give evidence against me.'

Losing patience, the judges reminded her that the law imposed a terrible penalty for refusing to plead. She said, 'God's will be done. I think I may suffer any death for this good cause.'

Yet it is doubtful if Margaret fully understood at this stage just what the penalty involved. The law demanded that such a person be crushed to death; the 'peine forte et dure'.

Accompanied by a troop of men with halberds, Margaret, smiling and serene, was taken from the Common Hall. The judges ordered that she be detained overnight at John Trewe's house, the New Counter Prison on Ousebridge. Here she was locked up in a close parlour with a Protestant couple, Mr and Mrs Yoward, who were in prison for debt. That evening Margaret was visited by Parson Wigginton, but she sent him away, having no wish to converse with him. To counteract the sympathy that the city had for Margaret, the Council spread vile slanders about her that she had adulterous relationships with the priests she sheltered.

At 8 a.m. the following morning she was taken back to court and asked yet again if she would plead and be tried, bearing in mind that the only real evidence against her was the word of one small boy.

'Indeed, I think you have no witness against me but children, which with an apple and a rod you can make to say what you will,' was her somewhat sardonic reply. Margaret then engaged in an argument with the judges about the true purpose of the seminary priests. 'I know no cause why I should refuse them as long as I live. They come only to do good to me and others,' she declared. 'I know them for virtuous men sent by God.'

Mr Justice Clinch again reminded her of the punishment that she faced. Mr Wigginton was present in the court and he shouted out, 'You sit here to do justice; this woman's case is a matter of life and death: you ought not, either by God's law or man's, judge her to die upon the slender witness of a boy, unless you have two or three men of good credit to also give evidence against her!'

Angry at the interruption, Clinch retorted, 'I may do it by law.' At which Mr Wigginton asked, 'By what law?'

'By the Queen's law,' came the answer, to which Wigginton responded, 'That may well be, but you cannot do it by God's law.'

Mr Justice Rhodes angrily asked why the court was wasting its time with such a wilful woman and demanded that sentence be passed. Clinch, who clearly was anxious to spare her, even now delayed and once again urged Margaret to plead; but to no avail, and in the end he was overruled by the members of the Council present and pronounced the dreadful sentence.

This came as a shock to Margaret, especially the knowledge that she would be stripped naked, but she retained her composure, saying, 'If this judgement be according to your conscience, I pray God send you a better judgement before Him. I thank God heartily for this.'

Even after pronouncing sentence, Clinch said it was still not too late for her to save her life by agreeing to plead. He asked her to think of her husband and children and not needlessly throw her life away.

'I would to God that my husband might suffer with me for such a good cause,' was her response. In spite of the judge's urging, Margaret remained resolute. 'Whatever God sends shall be welcome to me. I am not worthy of so good a death as this.'

So, with her arms bound and with a smiling countenance, she was escorted back to prison. When the news of Margaret's condemnation was broken to John Clitherow, he broke down and wept violently like a man out of his wits. 'Let them take all I have and save her, for she is the best wife in all England.'

As the judge had ordered a delay in carrying out the sentence, for the remaining ten days of her life Margaret was confined in the prison on the bridge. During this time Sir Thomas Fairfax and other members of the Council came to urge her to go to church with them. Protestant ministers were then sent to harangue and pester her incessantly in an effort to convert her. Margaret's answer to them was, 'I am fully resolved in all things touching my faith, which I ground upon Jesus Christ and by Him I steadfastly believe to be saved, which faith I acknowledge to be the same that He left to His Apostles and they to their successors… and is taught in the Catholic Church throughout Christendom, and promised to remain with her unto the world's end… and by God's assistance I mean to live and die in the same faith, for if an angel came from heaven and preached any other doctrine than we have received the Apostle biddeth us not to believe him. Therefore if I should follow your doctrine I would disobey the Apostle's commandment. Wherefore I pray you, take this for an answer and trouble me no more for my conscience.'

The only one she received kindly was Mr Wigginton, who visited her twice; they discussed their religious differences, but the parson went away regretting that he had been unable to persuade Margaret.

Some of her friends and relations tried to obtain a stay of execution by claiming that she was pregnant. Margaret herself was questioned on the subject, but she could only answer that it was possible but if so only in the very early stages. Mr Justice Clinch asked that the claim be investigated, as he was not prepared to sanction her execution and be responsible for the death of an unborn infant if it was true.

'You are too merciful, Brother Clinch,' said Mr Justice Rhodes, urging that Margaret had to be executed regardless. None of this cut much ice with the Council, whose members insisted to Clinch that even if she were pregnant she still had to die, if only to make of her an example to others who might be tempted to flout the law.

Margaret was also visited by her stepfather, Henry May, who with 'a great show of sorrow and affection' claimed he could use his influence to obtain a pardon for her if she would renounce her Catholicism. He then asked Margaret to give him custody of her daughter, Anne, which she refused. Having thus been rebuffed, Henry made his real, unsympathetic feelings plain, accusing her of immorality and courting suicide; later he tried to blacken her memory.

The Elizabethan Martyrs, 1577-1601

She was urged to confess that she had offended her husband. 'If I have offended my husband in anything but for my conscience, I ask God and him forgiveness,' she replied. 'I beseech you let me speak with him before I die,' she begged; but her request to met John having been refused, she knew she would never see him again.

Margaret realised that her execution would be soon when she learned that her husband had been released from prison and banished from York for five days until after her execution had taken place. From Father Mush's biography we know a great deal about her final days in prison. On Tuesday she was informed by the sheriffs that she was to die on Friday. After they had left she admitted, 'Now I feel the frailty of mine own flesh, which trembleth at these news, although my spirit greatly rejoiceth. Therefore for God's sake pray for me and desire all good folks to do the same.'

She then began a strict fast. She also got someone to obtain some white linen and with it she made a short, loose-fitting habit 'like to an alb' to wear for her execution. Father Mush's account of Margaret's last hours in prison was taken from the details given to him by Mrs Yoward, the Protestant lady imprisoned for debt, who befriended Margaret and spent the last night with her to keep her company. Margaret was clearly very disturbed and could not rest. She spent a long time kneeling in prayer, needing to summon up all her strength and courage to face her ordeal. At midnight she undressed and put on the linen habit and continued praying until 3 a.m. before finally going to bed. She left her hat for her husband as a sign of her loving duty to him as to her head. To her daughter, Anne, she sent her shoes hoping that she would serve God and follow in her mother's steps.

Margaret rose by 6 a.m. to prepare herself. At 8 a.m. on the morning of Friday, 25 March 1586, the Feast of the Annunciation, Roland Fawcet, the Sheriff of York, came to lead the thirty-three-year-old, barefooted, bareheaded Margaret from the Ousebridge Prison to the Tollbooth for her execution. Carrying her linen garment over her arm, she appeared smiling and cheerful and spoke of going to her marriage. It was only six or seven yards' distance to the Tollbooth and as she walked across the crowded

The Elizabethan Martyrs, 1577-1601

street she gave out alms. Entering the Tollbooth, she knelt and prayed for the Church, the Pope and the Queen 'that God turn her to the Catholic Faith and that after this life she may receive the joys of heaven. For I wish as much good to her majesty's soul as to mine own.'

The Protestant ministers continued to pester her and announced that they would pray with her. In common with other martyrs, Margaret replied, 'I will not pray with you, nor shall you pray with me: neither will I say amen to your prayers, nor you to mine.'

In our so-called more enlightened, ecumenical age on the face of it this sounds harsh; but in the circumstances of the time, when Catholics and their Church were literally fighting for survival amidst bloody persecution from the Protestant Establishment, it is not to be wondered at. William Gibson, the Undersheriff of York, was deeply distressed and stood weeping by the doorway. When the Sheriff himself remarked, 'Remember, Mrs Clitherow, you die for treason,' Margaret replied in a loud voice, 'No, Master Sheriff, I die for the love of my Lord Jesus.'

The sentence was that she be stripped naked, laid down with a large, sharp stone placed under her back and weights placed upon her until she was crushed to death. Margaret was very distressed about being stripped in front of everyone and begged on her knees that it be omitted. This request was refused, the Sheriff insisting that she must die naked, exactly as she had been sentenced. The four women friends accompanying her gathered around to shield her. When they had undressed her and put on her the linen garment she quickly lay down, her face covered by a handkerchief. A door was placed on top of her and in these last moments, with death imminent, Margaret experienced a very human fear. She firstly clasped her hands tightly in front of her face and then over the door but they were pulled apart and her arms were stretched out in the form of a cross and her wrists tied to stakes in the ground. Weights were then placed on the door. As she felt the weights pressing down on her she cried out, 'Jesu! Jesu! Jesu! Have mercy on me!'

These were her last words. The weights they piled on her were so great – about 800 pounds – that her ribs burst out through her skin. For a quarter of an hour she moaned in agony and then all was quiet. It was 9 a.m. in the morning and Margaret Clitherow's crushed body was left in the press until 3 p.m.

By order of the sheriffs, Margaret was buried in secrecy at night in 'a filthy place' as a contemporary chronicler describes it. It is reported that Father Mush was able to discover the place and six weeks later he and others exhumed the remains, which although broken and bruised showed no sign of corruption. Two weeks later he had the remains re-buried far away from York. Where that was is unknown but Margaret's right hand is preserved in a reliquary at the Bar Convent, York.

After Margaret's death John Clitherow married for a third time. Margaret's children remained faithful. Henry studied at the English Colleges at Rheims and Rome. He eventually joined the Dominican Order and died in Italy. There is no record of his ever being ordained. Anne was twelve years old at the time of her mother's martyrdom. After suffering imprisonment at Lancaster in 1593 for refusing to conform, she made her way to the Continent and became a nun of the order of Augustinian Canonesses at St Ursula's, Louvain. A contemporary of Mother Margaret Clement, she died there in August 1622, bequeathing to her order her copy of Father Mush's *True Report*.

Margaret must have had a lasting influence on her two stepsons, the children of John Clitherow and his first wife, Maude, who were also constant. Thomas the youngest suffered in York Castle and died a prisoner for religion at Hull in 1603. William, his brother, often mistakenly referred to as Margaret's son instead of stepson, visited his half-sister Anne at Louvain before entering Douai in 1604. Ordained and sent to England in 1608, William ministered in Yorkshire for many years, suffered several terms of imprisonment in York Castle, and died in 1636. There seems to be every reason to believe that the Brian Stapleton of York who arrived at Rheims in 1586 and was ordained priest in 1589 was none other than the schoolmaster engaged by Margaret. He returned to England and was ministering in the North in 1593.

Mrs Anne Tesh was constantly in and out of prison for recusancy and hearing Mass. In 1596, together with another of

The Elizabethan Martyrs, 1577-1601

Margaret's friends, Mrs Bridget Maskew, she was sentenced to be burned to death, the penalty for women convicted of treason. Condemned with them were three laymen, Blessed George Errington, Blessed William Knight and Blessed William Gibson. Anne and Bridget were reprieved, their sentence being commuted to life imprisonment. They remained in York Castle until the end of the reign, being brought out on occasions and taken forcibly to listen to Protestant sermons. Errington, Knight and Gibson[22] were martyred at York on 29 November.

Margaret Ward

> The martyr does not see the hooting throng. Their eyes are fixed on the eternities.
>
> Benjamin N Cardozo 1870–1938

Our second Margaret reputedly came from a gentleman's family at Congleton in Cheshire. Beyond that we know nothing of her early life. At an early age she went into service in London as maid/companion to a well-to-do Catholic lady, Mrs Whittle, who often sheltered priests. It was presumably this involvement that led to the exploit for which Margaret is principally known: her part in the escape of the priest William Watson from the Bridewell Prison. In retrospect it is to be regretted that Margaret forfeited her life helping a priest so unworthy of her as Watson. It was, perhaps, a blessing that she did not live to see his subsequent ignominious career, although charity requires us to accord him a measure of sympathy if he was suffering from some form of mental illness.

The Bridewell, situated by the Fleet River, had started life as one of Henry VIII's palaces. It was a rambling brick edifice built around three courtyards and was the scene of many famous historical occurrences. Under Edward VI it became a reception centre for vagrants and orphans. In 1556 the City of London took it over and turned it into a prison. Flogging was a regular feature of Bridewell's function, and public flogging sessions took place twice a week.

The Elizabethan Martyrs, 1577-1601

Father Watson unfortunately seems to have had few attractive characteristics. Born in Durham in 1558, he had a violent streak, manifested in his vituperative and vociferous calumnies against the Jesuits. Even the autobiography he wrote in 1598 is highly suspect, as it is so full of inconsistencies and lies. For example, he claimed to have studied at Oxford, when in truth he was there in the capacity of servant to a future martyr, John Boste. Ordained in April 1586, he returned to England that year. A few months later he was captured and served about five months in the Marshalsea. He obtained his freedom by agreeing to attend the Established Church. According to his account he had been released pending banishment but was retaken after abjuring his apostasy.

He was committed to the Bridewell, kept in terrible conditions and inhumanely treated by Richard Topcliffe; at least that part is not difficult to believe. He was later moved to a cell high up in the building but got no peace from wearisome, pestering Protestants anxious to get him to apostatise once more. As a result he was said to be suffering greatly, and in his mentally unstable condition was in need of help and support. Whether this was a naturally occurring deterioration or had been brought on by his treatment we cannot know.

Margaret, obviously a girl of spirit and courage, resolved to help him. By making friends with the jailer's wife she succeeded, after much difficulty, in obtaining permission to visit the priest. At first she was carefully watched and searched on entering and leaving the prison and was only allowed to speak to the priest in the jailer's presence. But in time the jailer's vigilance gradually relaxed and Margaret, in addition to comforting the priest, managed to smuggle in various items, one of them a rope concealed under a basket of food. In the meantime she had arranged with an Irish waterman, John Roche, alias Neale, to procure a boat and to wait below the prison wall in the early hours of the next morning. The priest was confined in a cell on the top floor of the prison. At the appointed time, Father Watson let himself down by the rope, but it was either not long enough or he had not tied it correctly because he had to jump the remaining distance, badly injuring himself in the fall. John Roche, waiting below, helped the priest get away and exchanged clothes with

The Elizabethan Martyrs, 1577-1601

him. As the rope was left hanging from the window the jailer immediately guessed that Margaret was responsible and the following morning she and John Roche were arrested.

There could not have been a more fateful time for a Catholic to fall into the hands of the authorities. The Spanish Armada had sailed in May 1588 and finally appeared off the Cornish coast in late July. A great many myths have been perpetuated by the British about the Armada. Its main purpose was to punish England for encouraging its privateers to attack Spanish treasure ships and Spain's colonies in the New World, as well as to cut off English support for the rebels in the Netherlands. As a by-product it was also hoped that the action would curtail or even reverse the Protestant ascendancy in England.

With the aim of achieving all these objectives, an army from the Spanish Netherlands was to affect a landing in south-east England. Pope Sixtus V Perretti (1585–1590) supported the Spanish expedition and promised a large papal subsidy if a landing was successful. As matters turned out, it was the atrocious weather as much as English and Dutch naval action that saved England from invasion. The English nonetheless hailed it as a great victory, claiming that it showed that God, who had blown His Protestant winds to scatter the Spanish fleet, was on their side. Aside from the sailors and soldiers who lost their lives, the people who suffered most horrendously as a consequence of His Catholic Majesty Philip II's projected invasion were the English Catholics.

The Armada was either still in the English Channel or seeking a way of escape by sailing around Scotland when Margaret Ward was arrested. She was treated with incredible brutality, kept in heavy irons for eight days and severely flogged. She was hung up by the wrists for hours, the tips of her toes barely touching the ground. As a result of this ill-treatment she was crippled and partially paralysed. She and John Roche were taken to the Old Bailey for trial on 26 August. She admitted that she had helped Father Watson escape, but in spite of threats of more torture she resolutely refused to disclose his whereabouts. Directed to ask the Queen's pardon she declined on the grounds that she had not committed any offence against her. In the face of such danger Margaret boldly told the court that never in her life had she done anything which she less regretted than rescuing Father Watson from the hands of bloodthirsty wolves. She declared that if the Queen was a woman of any compassion she would understand. Both she and John were promised their freedom if they would conform to the Established Church. They expressed their position very clearly: it was not lawful for them as Catholics to do so. Margaret said she was prepared to lay down many lives if she possessed them rather than go against her conscientious beliefs, thereby offending God and His Church. John declared he had done nothing to offend the Queen but it was against his conscience to attend a Protestant church. Margaret and John were sentenced to be hanged for rescuing Watson.

With the country in ferment following the threat of the Armada, Elizabeth and her government were determined to seek revenge by executing the priests held in custody; as a result, Catholics were martyred in greater numbers than ever. The first victim was Robert Sutton at Stafford in July.[23] On 28 August alone, eight were martyred[24] at different locations in and around London in order to make a wider impact by spreading the terror.

On 30 August 1588 Margaret was executed at Tyburn with her helper, Blessed John Roche, and four others: a twenty-seven-year-old priest, Blessed Richard Leigh,[25] who was another victim of Anthony Tyrell's betrayal, and three Blessed laymen. They were Edward Shelley, of the famous recusant family of that name from Sussex; Shropshire-born and Oxford-educated Richard Martin; and twenty-two-year-old Richard Flower or Floyd from Anglesey, all condemned for sheltering priests, the last named specifically for harbouring Father William Horner in the parish of St Dunstan, London. The holy sextet sang hymns as they were carted off to their execution. They had to suffer filthy abuse from Topcliffe as they waited to die. Except for Father Leigh, they were all forbidden to speak to the crowd from the scaffold, presumably because of the impact that the last words of a group of young people going courageously to their deaths might have on their hearers.

The Catholics in England could be forgiven for thinking that God had abandoned them as the vengeful executions continued throughout the summer and autumn of 1588. A simple glove-maker of Gloucester, Blessed William Lampley, was hanged, drawn and quartered for 'persuading to popery'. A further seven were martyred on 1 October,[26] followed by William Way[27] on 23 September, three more on 5 October,[28] and finally Edward Burden on 29 November.[29]

As for Father Watson, after his rescue he went to Belgium for about two years and returned to England in 1590. By May 1597 he was once more in the Bridewell but managed to escape. He turns up next in the Gatehouse, from which he escaped in 1599. Escapology seems to have been one talent for which he had an aptitude. He then served a term in the Clink, but was caught with other priests preparing to say Mass for the Catholic prisoners and confined to the King's Bench prison in 1602, being released on the accession of James I.

In 1603 he teamed up with another priest, William Clark, who had been suspended in 1601 by Archpriest George Blackwell, and they became involved with others in the so-called Bye Plot against the King. From what little evidence there is available, it is difficult to decide if the plot was real or if it only existed in the fevered imagination of Watson. The plan was to kidnap James, imprison him in the Tower, force him to dismiss his ministers and appoint Catholics in their place. In this coup Watson had allocated to himself the post of Lord Chancellor! Father Henry Garnet, the Jesuit Superior, got to hear of the scheme and, fearing the consequences to the Catholic community, tipped off the government. Watson and Clark were arrested. Committed to the Tower, they were both taken to Winchester for trial in November 1603 and hanged in the market place.

Edmund Gennings

> Dying has made us rarer gifts than gold... poured out the red sweet wine of youth.
>
> *The Dead*, Rupert Brooke, 1887–1915

Edmund was the son of John Gennings, an innkeeper at Lichfield, Staffordshire. He was born in 1567 and raised in the Established Church. He was always a boy of a serious frame of mind and he loved contemplating the night sky. He attended Lichfield

The Elizabethan Martyrs, 1577-1601

Grammar School and then at the age of sixteen was recommended as page in the Sherwood household, a family of London drapers who were staunch Catholics. Mr Sherwood senior died in prison and Elizabeth, his widow, also suffered a long prison term in the Marshalsea. There were three sons, John, Henry and Richard, who had also been imprisoned for recusancy and who all became seminary priests. Henry Sherwood arrived at Rheims in 1587, his health ruined by seven years' imprisonment. He was ordained three years later. John Sherwood was ordained in 1583. Having returned to England he became chaplain to Sir John Arundell at Isleworth and continued as chaplain to his widow at Chideock, Dorset, where he died in 1593. Under his employer's influence, Edmund became a Catholic. Richard Sherwood junior left England in 1583 and was ordained at Soissons in 1584. Using the alias Carleton, he ministered in London for about a year before being imprisoned in 1585 and banished in December 1586, never to return to England. Edmund followed his master's example and on 12 August 1583 entered the English College, then at Rheims.

His health was poor and he was found to be suffering from tuberculosis. After some time spent by the sea at Havre-de-Grâce, Normandy, he recovered sufficiently to resume his studies. On 18 March 1590, he was ordained at Soissons by special dispensation because he was under the canonical age. He greatly hoped he would be sent to England as a missionary and less than a month later his wish was granted. He set off from Rheims on 9 April 1590 in the company of two other newly ordained priests: Alexander Rawlins, with whom he had been ordained, and Polydore Plasden. En route they were waylaid by a party of Huguenots, robbed and kept in prison for three days. They were later joined by Father William Mush, the recently ordained younger brother of John Mush, and eventually embarked from Treport, Normandy, and landed secretly at night on the Yorkshire coast near Whitby. The following morning Gennings and Plasden were nearly caught at an inn near Whitby by a famous pursuivant called Ratcliffe. Managing to give him the slip, they made their way to a Catholic gentleman's house a few miles away, where they parted. (William Mush worked in Yorkshire for several years until

The Elizabethan Martyrs, 1577-1601

he was captured in 1608 and sentenced to death. With the help of the jailer he managed to escape from York Castle.)

After working for some months in the North, Edmund made his way to Lichfield to find his family. He was told that his parents had died but his younger brother, John, was in London. He spent a month searching for his brother until one day he met him quite by chance on Ludgate Hill. They had not seen one another for over eight years, but Edmund felt sure it was his brother and on speaking to him so it turned out. But Edmund was bitterly disappointed: his brother was rabidly anti-Catholic and urged Edmund to leave the country.

He left London for a time and worked in the countryside, but on his return to the capital he met up with his former companion, Polydore Plasden, and they arranged to say Mass at the house of Mr Swithun Wells in Gray's Inn Lane. The day appointed was 28 November 1591, the first Sunday of Advent. Early in the morning, Edmund was saying Mass in an upstairs room for a small group of ten Catholics when there was banging on the front door below. When the door was opened it revealed a posse of officers; leading them was Richard Topcliffe – 'This most sordid of men' – as Henry Garnet described him. They forced their way in, but some of the gentlemen drew their swords and forcibly kept Topcliffe from entering the room where Mass was in progress. He was seized and held by John Mason, and in the scuffle that ensued Topcliffe fell downstairs, injuring his head. After much argument and to avoid further force being used against him, Topcliffe agreed to let the Mass proceed to its conclusion, provided they all undertook to surrender themselves to him.

As soon as Mass was over Topcliffe rushed in and arrested Edmund, still in his vestments. He was dressed in a fool's coat to make him look ridiculous as he was led through the streets. He was committed to the Gatehouse prison, examined by Justice Young and committed for trial. The same day Topcliffe received a letter from the Council commissioning him to carry out an examination of Gennings and those apprehended with him.

On 4 December they were all tried at Newgate, the jury having been instructed in advance to find them guilty. Although the only evidence offered against them was the celebrating of

Mass, they were found guilty, the priests for treason and the laymen and women for the felony of assisting priests. They were all offered their liberty if they conformed, but refused. Edmund's response was, 'I will live and die in the true Roman Catholic Faith which... all antiquity had ever professed and would by no means go to the Protestant church or ever think that the Queen could be head of the Church in spiritual matters.'

On 10 December 1591 Edmund and Swithun Wells were taken back to Gray's Inn Lane, where a gallows had been erected outside Mr Wells's house. 'Confess your popish treason,' said Topcliffe.

Edmund replied, 'If to return to England a priest or to say Mass be popish treason, I here confess that I am a traitor; but I think not so and therefore I acknowledge myself guilty of those things, not with repentance, but with an open protestation of inward joy.'

Topcliffe was furious at the priest's attitude and in his rage he ordered the hangman to turn the ladder, and then immediately had the rope cut so that Edmund was totally conscious when he fell and was able to stand up. The hangman pushed him to the ground and began his butchery. Edmund screamed in agony while Swithun encouraged him to be brave. While Bull, the executioner, was groping for his heart, Edmund was heard to say, 'St Gregory, pray for me.' This elicited the hangman's callous riposte, 'See, his heart is in my hand, yet St Gregory is in his mouth.'

Edmund Gennings is the youngest of the Forty Martyrs. He was just twenty-four years of age. No wonder the judges sometimes spoke disparagingly of these 'Romish boy priests'. John Gennings at first 'rejoiced rather than bewailed the untimely and bloody end' of his brother, but ten days after Edmund's execution a change came over him. He began to dwell on the manner of his death and to compare his own worldly life with that of his martyred brother. Full of remorse, he prayed for guidance and concluded that he should become a Catholic. He went to the English College, Rome, and was ordained priest in 1600.

In 1601 he was sent to England where he ministered until 1611, when he was imprisoned for a time at Newgate. In 1614 he published a biography of his brother. Shortly afterwards he entered the Franciscan Order and became eager to restore the English Province of the Franciscan Observants. John obtained a house for English Franciscan sisters at Gravelines and then established St Bonaventure's Friary at Douai. In 1618 he was formally commissioned to re-establish the English Province. By 1625 the number of English friars had considerably grown and Rome was requested to canonically set up an English Province. John became the first Minister Provincial in 1629 and died at Douai in 1660.

Swithun Wells

We'll to the woods no more.

Last Poems, Alfred E Houseman, 1859–1936

Swithun or Swithin Wells, who came from a wealthy family, was born at Brambridge, near Winchester, Hampshire *c.*1536. Obviously named after the great Saxon bishop of Winchester, he was the youngest of the six sons of Thomas Wells and Mary Mompesson. We know that two of his brothers were called Gilbert and Henry. Gilbert suffered much for his faith and Henry, who studied at Winchester College and Oxford, also remained true. Swithun was a cultured, witty, well-educated man of many pursuits; a poet and musician as well as country sportsman. For a time he was a tutor in the household of the Earl of Southampton. He travelled widely, visiting Italy, and after spending some years in Rome could speak Italian well. Returning to England, he married Alice Morren or Morin, a Catholic lady. He outwardly conformed to the Established Church becoming a 'church papist' for a time, while living a peaceful country gentleman's life until middle age.

Around 1576 he set up his own school for young gentlemen at Monkton Farleigh in Wiltshire. One of the masters was the future priest and martyr, Nicholas Woodfen.[30] In May 1582 Swithun came under suspicion for his Catholic sympathies and the Privy Council ordered that he be investigated. As a result he had to give

The Elizabethan Martyrs, 1577-1601

up the school, but it was about this time that he was formally reconciled to the Church. He and his wife actively supported priests, organising their dangerous journeys from one safe house to another. When this work became too hazardous, Swithun, by now somewhat impoverished, with his wife and daughter, decided to move to London in 1585.

In 1586 Swithun moved to a little house in Gray's Inn Lane, London, which quickly became a place of hospitality for priests. In June he was arrested with Father Christopher Dryland[31] and the future priest and martyr, Alexander Rawlins, and imprisoned at Newgate. He was bailed by his nephew on 4 July. He was then arrested on 9 August and interrogated in the Fleet about his knowledge of the Babington Plot. He was released on 30 November. Shortly afterwards he undertook a mission about which we tantalisingly know little. It may have come about because of his Hampshire connections and/or the fact that he knew Rome and spoke Italian, but he travelled to Rome in the service of Henry Wriothesley, 3rd Earl of Southampton. The Earl was not only one of the richest and most fashionable young noblemen in England but also a Catholic. Southampton's father had known and helped Edmund Campion and his mother succoured priests at her homes in London and Sussex. Southampton himself was acquainted with Robert Southwell. Much of the Earl's fame rests upon the fact that he was Shakespeare's patron and the dedicatee of some of his works.

Swithun could not have been absent from England for long because from further questioning he underwent in the spring of 1587 we learn that his cousin was George Cotton, of the well-known recusant family at Warblington, Hampshire. In the summer of 1588 Swithun spent some months in Newgate following the capture of Thomas Holford[32] when leaving his house after saying Mass. Father Holford was 'on the run', having escaped from his captors almost a year earlier, and being a wanted man was recognised by a pursuivant in the street.

In November 1591, when Edmund Gennings and Polydore Plasden were arrested after saying Mass in Swithun's house, his wife, their servants and all those present were apprehended with the priests. Swithun was not in the house at the time, but when

The Elizabethan Martyrs, 1577-1601

he returned home he found the house ransacked and his wife arrested. He went straight to the authorities to demand the release of his wife, but was arrested and sent to Newgate in chains. When examined he declared that although he had not been present at the celebration of Mass he believed his house to have been greatly honoured that the divine sacrifice had been offered there. While in prison he wrote to his brother-in-law:

> I renounced the world before ever I tasted of imprisonment, even in my baptism; which promise and profession, however slenderly soever I have kept heretofore, I purpose for the time to come, God assisting me, to continue to my life's end.

The whole group was indicted at Westminster on 4 December, tried alongside the priests on the 5th and condemned to death. Taken from prison with her husband on the day of execution, to her great sorrow Mrs Alice Wells was told she had been reprieved and was not to die. She was returned to Newgate, sentenced to life imprisonment. She died in prison ten years later in 1602. Her daughter, Margaret, later became a nun.

As already related, on 10 December Swithun was executed with Edmund Gennings on a gallows specially erected outside his own house. Seeing an old friend in the crowd, Swithun cheerfully called out to him, 'Goodbye, dear friend. Farewell all hunting parties and old pastimes; I am now going a better way.'

He had to watch while the priest was butchered: 'Your pain is great, but it is almost past. Pray for me now, good saint, that mine may come.' It was a bitterly cold day, and when he was stripped he turned to Topcliffe and said jocularly, 'Hurry up, please, Mr Topcliffe. Are you not ashamed to make a poor old man stand in his shirt in this cold? God pardon you and make you of a Saul a Paul, of a bloody persecutor one of the Catholic Church's children; by your malice I am thus to be executed, but you have done me the greatest benefit that ever I could have had. I heartily forgive you.'

Topcliffe sneered at him, 'See what your priests have brought you to.'

Swithun replied, 'I am happy and thank God to have been so favoured to have so many and such saint-like priests under my roof.'

Polydore Plasden

The white flower of a blameless life.

The Idylls of the King, Alfred, Lord Tennyson, 1809–92

Polydore strikes us as a very unusual name but in the sixteenth century it was not so uncommon. There was at least one other priest of that name, the Welshman Polydore Morgan. (Ordained in 1579 he spent more than two years in the Gatehouse without the authorities realising he was a priest. On his release he went to France and ended his days as a Capuchin at Tours in 1616.) Polydore Plasden was born in 1563 by Fleet Bridge, one of the four bridges which then spanned the Fleet River. The bridge linked Fleet Street and Ludgate Hill, London. His father was a musical instrument maker, 'a horner' and retailer at Ludgate Circus. Polydore was educated at Rheims, where he is recorded under his alias of Oliver Palmer. Some sources would have us believe that Palmer was his real name and Polydore Plasden his alias, but it is a highly improbable choice of alias; far likelier that Palmer was his chosen alias. The extant examples of his signature read both Oliver Plasden and Polydore Plasden. He entered the English College, Rome, on 25 April 1585 and was among the group of students who signed the petition in August requesting that the Jesuits should be retained to run the College.

He was ordained priest at St John Lateran, the cathedral of Rome, on 7 December 1586. He returned to Rheims in April 1588. The College diary shows that he left again in September 1588, but where he spent the next eighteen months is uncertain. As there is a mention of him working in Sussex it is possible to speculate that he came to England in 1588 and then returned to Rheims. As this was the year of the Spanish Armada, it was an especially dangerous time for any priest to be in the country. In April 1590 he again left Rheims for England in company with Edmund Gennings, landing with him at night at Whitby, where they separated. For the next four years he ministered in and around Holborn, in the very area of London in which he had been born.

Polydore met Edmund Gennings again by chance one evening

The Elizabethan Martyrs, 1577-1601

in November 1591. They said matins together and arranged to say Mass the next day at Swithun Wells's house. When the house was raided by Topcliffe it was Polydore, concerned about the safety of the Blessed Sacrament, who promised him that they would surrender themselves if he let the Mass proceed. Arrested with Gennings and the Wells's household, he was tried and condemned with them at Westminster before the Lord Chief Justice and William Fleetwood, Recorder of London. After the guilty verdict was delivered, Plasden was asked if he had anything to say.

'These twelve simple men find us guilty of treason for exercising our priestly function. But you, learned in the law and in history, know very well that the priesthood was in all ages an honourable calling if yet you dare speak the truth.'

Mr Recorder Fleetwood made a tasteless joke at Polydore's expense. Alluding to his father's trade, he said, 'Plasden, dost thou talk so? Methinks thou wouldst better wind a horn, for I think thy father is a horner at Fleet Bridge' – which the court found highly amusing.

On 10 December he was taken to Tyburn with Father Eustace White and three Blessed laymen, all to die for relieving priests. They were John Mason and Sidney Hodgson, servants of the Wells, and Brian Lacey of Brockdish, Norfolk, who had been cruelly tortured by Topcliffe. As he stood on the scaffold, Polydore prayed aloud for the Queen. Sir Walter Raleigh was in the crowd and he asked Polydore if he sincerely meant his prayers. 'Yes,' answered Plasden, 'otherwise I could expect no salvation.' Raleigh questioned him further, asking if he acknowledged Elizabeth as his lawful Queen, and would he defend her against foreign enemies?

When Plasden replied in the affirmative, Raleigh declared he was no traitor and could see no cause why such an honest man should die. He offered to go immediately to the Court to plead with the Queen herself for a reprieve, if the sheriff would delay the execution. But Richard Topcliffe, who had dashed from the execution of Gennings and Wells at Gray's Inn Road, intervened. He asked Plasden if he thought the Queen had any right to impose her religion and forbid Catholicism, to which Polydore answered no. He then wanted to know, if the Pope came to establish Catholicism, would Plasden defend the Queen against the Pope?

'I would never fight nor counsel others to fight against my religion, for that were to deny my faith.'

Topcliffe demanded confirmation that Polydore was a Catholic priest and this he confessed, kissing the rope and saying he would rather forfeit a thousand lives than deny Christ. After this Raleigh allowed the execution to proceed, but he insisted that Polydore be allowed to hang until he was dead.

Eustace White

Truth put down by persecution.

On Liberty, John Stuart Mill, 1806–73

Eustace was born at Louth, Lincolnshire, in 1560, the son of William White and Anne Booth. They were a prominent Protestant family and William White was involved in the town corporation and the management of the grammar school. When Eustace became a Catholic in 1584 his father laid a curse on him. How much did Eustace know about the recent religious history of his native town? The forerunner of the 'Pilgrimage of Grace' in 1536, the Lincolnshire revolt started at Louth when, following the suppression of the nearby Cistercian monastery, the parish priest, Thomas Kendall, urged his congregation to resist the King's commissioners. In 1537 Kendall was hanged, drawn and quartered at Tyburn and many of the townsfolk were hanged in Louth market place.

Eustace arrived at Rheims on 31 October 1584 and transferred to the English College, Rome, on 24 October 1586. He was ordained deacon on 16 April 1588. It is presumed that he was ordained priest in Rome later in the same year as he was sent back to Rheims that autumn, leaving for England on 2 November.

On his return to England he ministered to the Catholics in the West Country for almost three years. One day when on a journey

The Elizabethan Martyrs, 1577-1601

he met a lawyer. They rode along together for some time and as his companion seemed friendly Eustace conversed about religion. It was 1 September 1591 when they reached Blandford in Dorset. The lawyer insisted that Eustace join him for breakfast at the inn. Suspecting that he was a priest, the lawyer betrayed him to the local authorities. When arrested and charged, Eustace admitted that he was a priest. A Protestant minister was sent for to make him see the error of his ways. During their disputation, Eustace, to support a Catholic doctrine, used a quotation from the Gospels which the minister insisted did not exist and accused him of lying.

'Bring me your own Bible,' said White, 'and I will show you that it exists in your own version. If you are right and the passage does not exist I will go with you to the Protestant church.'

The minister retorted, 'If you can show me that the text exists to support your view, I will become a papist.'

News of this spread all over the town and the next day a large crowd assembled to hear the continuation of the debate. When asked to show the disputed text, the minister refused and clutched his Bible tightly under his arm, trying to turn the debate on to other subjects. Eustace insisted that the Bible be given to him but the minister refused. White then turned to the crowd and explained what had happened. They demanded that the Bible be handed over to be checked to see if the disputed text existed. Despite all efforts, to the jeers of the crowd, the minister clung onto the Bible, refusing to relinquish it and refusing to admit that he was wrong. Eustace cautioned them to beware of the erroneous religious teaching they were being given, which included the falsification of the scriptures.

The townspeople were so impressed with Eustace – who was described as a fine gentleman-like man of good conversation – that they organised a petition for his release. He must have had musical abilities too, as a silver flute was listed amongst his possessions when he was arrested. He was sent to the Council at Basing before being taken to London and put in the Bridewell Prison on 18 September; the following month his torture was authorised in a letter dated 25 October to Topcliffe from the Privy Council. It stated that Eustace should 'be put to the manacles and such other tortures as are used in Bridewell'.

The sadistic Topcliffe tortured him with the greatest savagery. He was racked seven times and once was hung up by his wrists in manacles for eight hours while remorselessly interrogated to reveal in whose houses he had said Mass or who had helped him in his mission. Eyewitnesses testified that White poured so much with sweat from his ordeal that it ran from his clothes and lay in a pool on the ground beneath him. They could extract no information from him. 'Lord, more pain if you please and more patience,' was White's prayer. We have a vivid first-hand account of what this torture was like from Father John Gerard, who had to endure it twice a day. In his autobiography he tells us:

> They took me to a big upright pillar, one of the wooden posts which held the roof... Driven into the top of it were iron staples for supporting heavy weights. Then they put my wrists into iron gauntlets and ordered me to climb two or three wicker steps. My arms were then lifted up and an iron bar was passed through the rings of one gauntlet, then through the staple and rings of the second gauntlet. This done... removing the wicker steps... they left me hanging by my hands and arms fastened above my head... Such a gripping pain came over me. It was worst in my chest and belly, my hands and arms. All the blood in my body seemed to rush up into my arms and hands and I thought that blood was oozing out from the ends of my fingers and the pores of my skin. But it was only a sensation caused by my flesh swelling above the irons holding them. The pain was so intense that I thought I could not possibly endure it... the perspiration ran in drops continuously down my face and body... I fell into a faint... the men held my body up... until I came to... I fainted eight or nine times that day... they took me down... it was a great effort to stand upright.

The second day Gerard was hung up once again just as before, fainting and being revived before being taken back to his cell by the warder who had to feed him.

> For many days after I could not hold a knife in my hands – that day I could not even move my fingers or help myself in the smallest way. He had to do everything for me.

The Elizabethan Martyrs, 1577-1601

After undergoing similar torture, Eustace told Topcliffe, 'I am not angry with you for all this, but I shall pray to God for your salvation.' Topcliffe furiously replied that he did not want the prayers of a traitor who he would see hanged. 'Then,' said White, 'I shall pray for you even on the gallows, for you are in great need of prayers.'

On 23 November Eustace managed to smuggle out a letter to Father Henry Garnet by a good man who had been a servant of Sir Thomas Fitzherbert and who now tried to help Eustace. The letter, which reveals the appalling conditions in which he was kept reads:

> This bearer, late and last servant unto the good Sir Thomas Fitzherbert for he attended on him... his death in the Tower, can partly relate unto you mine estate... He hath spared from himself to relieve me with victuals as he could through a little hole and with other such necessaries as he could by that means do, whom truly I did never see in my life but through a hole. Nothing was too dear to him that he could convey unto me, for whom as I am bound so will I daily pray while I live. I have been a close prisoner [solitary confinement] since the 18th day of September, where for forty-six days together I lay upon a little straw in my boots, my hands continually manacled in irons for one month together never once taken off.

Tried with Gennings, Plasden, Wells and their companions, he was condemned. Moved to Newgate to await execution, on 10 December 1591 Eustace was taken to Tyburn, together with Plasden and the three blessed laymen arrested and tried with them. Not wanting to miss the culmination of his handiwork Topcliffe rushed from Gray's Inn Lane to be present.

Eustace spoke to the spectators. 'Christian people, I was condemned as a traitor for being a priest and coming into this country to reconcile and use other of my priestly functions, all which I confess I have done in sundry places of this realm for some years together. I thank God that it hath pleased Him to bless my labours with this happy end, when I now am to die for my faith and my priesthood. Other treasons I have not committed. If I had ever so many lives I would think them very few to bestow upon your Tyburns to defend my religion. I wish I had a great many more than one, you should have them all one after another.'

He was cut down while still alive and tried to rise to his feet. Two men held him down by standing on his arms while he suffered the butchery.

John Boste

> We wrestle against... the rulers of the darkness of this world, against spiritual wickedness in high places.
>
> St Paul's Letter to the Ephesians

John, the son of Nicholas Boste, was born *c.*1543 at Dufton, Westmorland, just north of Appleby. The religious affiliation of his family is unknown, but there are several pointers in his later life that at least his mother may have been a Catholic. As a boy he attended Appleby Grammar School. The school had long-established connections with Queen's College, Oxford, and John was given a scholarship to the college. He graduated BA and then Master of Arts in June 1572 and was elected a Fellow of the College. It must have been around this time that he was ordained in the Anglican Church. John's brother, Laurence, was also a minister of the Established Church. By 1574 John is recorded as being a schoolmaster at Appleby, probably on the recommendation of Queen's College.

By 1578 he was back at Oxford as master of the college junior school. He began to doubt the validity of his orders in the Established Church and before long he was expelled for being absent without leave. What brought about his conversion to the Catholic Faith is unknown. Perhaps it was the result of his reading or contacts with Catholics at the university. Some sources state he was converted as early as 1576. This is possible, but seems doubtful as it does not readily fit in with his known movements and career during that period.

He left England and is recorded as acting as schoolteacher to Gerard Clibburn, one of his former Oxford pupils, at Louvain. Together with Clibburn, John was admitted to the English College (then at Rheims) on 4 August 1580. He progressed rapidly through his studies and within a year was ordained priest at Chalons on 4 March 1581. His protégé, Clibburn, was ordained in 1587 and returned to England the following year. On 11 April 1581 John left for England, landing at Hartlepool after dark under the alias of John Harckley. Perhaps abiding by a prior arrangement, he made his way to Norfolk, where he stayed with an Anglican minister called Warcop who came from Appleby. Escorted by Warcop, John set off for London and then pushed on westwards along the Thames Valley, meeting up with a relative of his mother's, Andrew Hilton, who was to severely suffer for his faith. For a time John took on the role of servant to the Catholic Lord Montague. This cover enabled him to travel reasonably freely and John made his way northwards. A description of Boste's appearance at this time says he dressed in a brown cloak, a white wool jerkin laced with blue and a pair of leather breeches.

Because of the coal boats plying their trade between the Continent and Newcastle, that port was used for smuggling in not only priests but also Catholic literature. There is ample evidence that Boste was involved in the distribution of these contraband books, and we read in one of his letters how he regrets not having more time to engage in this work. Certainly some Catholic books were later found in his mother's house. He also appears to have supplied information about shipping to those charged with securing safe passages for priests or young men going abroad to be educated.

Boste spent nearly twelve years in a very active ministry, covering a wide area of the north of England and the Scottish borders. It is known that he visited Edinburgh more than once and that he stayed with George, 5th Lord Seton, near Jedburgh. He was so successful that he was the most wanted priest in the North.

Given the widespread survival of Catholicism in Yorkshire and the other northern counties, an effective organisation was needed to keep its adherents ruthlessly subdued. That role was undertaken by the York-based Council of the North, comprising several knights and landed gentry under the Presidency, since 1572, of the viciously anti-Catholic Henry Hastings, 3rd Earl of Huntingdon. Hastings was a great-grandson of the martyred

Blessed Margaret Pole and therefore he had Plantagenet royal blood. He ruthlessly presided over the Council of the North for over twenty years, during which 'the Tyrant', as they termed him, earned the hatred of the Catholics for his unrelenting treatment of them.

Huntingdon offered a special reward for John's capture. John must have been in Hull at some time because there is a letter from Huntingdon ordering a search for him in that town. It is a tribute to the brave people who sheltered him that he was able to evade capture for so long. Many of them paid a heavy penalty for their compassion, for example, John Carr, the postmaster of Newcastle, who was arrested and tried for sheltering Boste. It is also indicative of how closely Boste's whereabouts were monitored by the spies.

Another of those who gave him assistance was Blessed Robert Bickerdike, who came from Knaresborough and was an apprentice in York. Robert was maliciously accused of various offences and acquitted of the charges, but he was soon imprisoned again as a recusant. He was tried before Mr Justice Clinch and Mr Justice Rhodes, but once again the jury returned a 'Not guilty' verdict. Furious, the prosecuting attorney had him committed to York Castle, determined to convict him. At the time when Francis Ingleby was being drawn to his execution, Robert overhead a conversation between a minister's wife and her sister in which she had remarked that they should go and see the traitor coming over the Ousebridge on the hurdle. Robert had protested to her that the priest was no traitor but as true as she was.

The altercation was reported and used as the excuse to bring him to trial for a third time. He was accused of harbouring priests because he had been seen in the company of Father Boste, for whom he had bought a pot of ale. He was asked whose part he would take if the Pope made war against the Queen. He replied that he would react as God would put him in mind at the time. The judges demanded he be found guilty of treason, and this time the jury obliged. Robert was hanged, drawn and quartered at York in 1586.

Huntingdon was so desperate to capture John that he engaged a spy called Francis Ecclesfield specifically for the task. In

The Elizabethan Martyrs, 1577-1601

common with other priests in the area, John often said Mass at Waterhouse, the small thatched house of William Clapton who had endured long imprisonment for his religion. (Many sources – following Challoner – call him Claxton, but contemporary documents clearly name him Clapton.) Waterhouse was an isolated place among dense woodland. It stood near Brancepeth, not far from Durham, on what was formerly the estate of Charles Neville, 6th Earl of Westmorland, now in exile following the abortive Northern Rising of 1569.

Amongst those who frequently attended Mass at Waterhouse were Lady Margaret Neville and her married sister, Lady Catherine Gray, daughters of the disgraced Earl. Ecclesfield, pretending to be a Catholic, somehow ingratiated himself with this little recusant community and gained their trust. He was present at a Mass celebrated by Boste in August 1593 and learned that he was due to return in September. A former Marian priest, Anthony Atkinson, had also turned informer, and between him and Ecclesfield the Council was kept supplied with the names of those who either celebrated or attended Mass at Waterhouse.

On 10 September John returned to Waterhouse as planned. While Mass was in progress the house was surrounded. When Mass was over, John made ready to leave, but Ecclesfield knelt and asked for his blessing – no doubt the Judas-like pre-arranged signal to identify the priest for those watching. Perhaps having the intuition to read the man's true character, John immediately retreated into the house and climbed into the hiding place over the chimney breast. The pursuivants ransacked the house, smashing through walls and taking up the floorboards until they finally found Boste. At the time, William Clapton was once again in prison, but they arrested his wife Grace and his daughter along with John, together with Lady Margaret Neville. When the news was relayed to him, Huntingdon exclaimed that he had caught one of the biggest stags of the forest.

The prisoners were taken to Durham and detained in one of the city Gatehouses. John was put in chains and the next day was examined by Huntingdon and Dean Tobie Mathew,[33] future Protestant Bishop of Durham and Archbishop of York who had once debated with the imprisoned Edmund Campion.

Huntingdon could not conceal his delight that after so many years they had at last captured a notorious traitor. With a jocular pun on his own name, John said, 'After all this search, My Lord, at last you have got your Boast.'

John confessed to all that we know of his career and was said to be 'resolute, bold, joyful and pleasant'. He was sent under guard to York, where he was lodged in the former house of the abbots. A few days later a letter arrived conveying the Queen's congratulations and instructions to send Boste to London. Strapped to a horse and under strict guard, he was transferred to the Tower, where he was interrogated by Burghley. In a letter describing the event, Topcliffe, who was present, opined that they had never seen a more resolute traitor.

John was examined fifteen times and tortured on five occasions; four on the rack and once hung up by the manacles, which he said was the worst of all. We are told in a contemporary account that he was so badly crippled that he was never again able to stand upright but walked bent double, very slowly with the aid of a stick. The Council were only too well aware that with his long ministry John must be privy to most of the secrets of the Catholics in the North, and therefore in possession of invaluable information. Yet he disclosed nothing that was not already available to the government.

Once while being racked he spotted a familiar face watching the savagery: Anthony Major. London-born, he had been ordained in 1590 and returned to England. He was arrested in 1593 in imprisoned at York. After some months in prison, lacking the courage to resist, he apostatised and was taken into the household of the Earl of Huntingdon. He agreed to inform on his brethren, which cost the lives of several priests. Major was pardoned and rewarded with a benefice in the Established Church for his services. He named a number of places in the North where he had been with Boste and John admitted it was true, there being little point in denying it. The other apostate, Anthony Atkinson, asked Burghley to let him speak to John to try and obtain information from him by more subtle means than torture. At one point John was sent to Windsor to be examined by the Privy Council and to enable the Queen to have a look at him. The

The Elizabethan Martyrs, 1577-1601

warrant of payment for the guards who escorted him to and from Windsor is extant in the Exchequer Records.

As his ministry had been in the area, it was decided to send Boste back to Durham via York for trial. On the journey he was accompanied by Father John Ingram. This twenty-nine-year-old priest was a convert born in Herefordshire. He had been ordained at Rome in 1589 but had worked mainly in Scotland. In November 1593 some urgent business had brought him across the border into England. After only a few hours in England he was returning to Scotland at Norham when he was arrested on the River Tweed and taken to Berwick. Brought to York, he had been identified by the apostate Anthony Major, and like Boste had been sent to the Tower. Here he had endured torture at the hands of Topcliffe, who, furious that he could get nothing out of him, called him a monster of taciturnity. The two priests were tied to horses for the long journey north and kept apart so they could not confer.

The Durham Assizes began on Monday, 22 July, and to set the tone Matthew Hutton, thrice-married Bishop of Durham, future Archbishop of York and eventual successor of Huntingdon as Lord President of the Council of the North, preached an anti-Catholic tirade in which he urged the judges to use all the rigour of the law against seminary priests. The following day the trial of the two priests took place before Sir Francis Beaumont, Lord Huntingdon and Hutton. Beaumont, a judge of the Queen's Bench, York division, was an interesting representative of his times. He was raised as a Catholic by his devout mother who regularly sheltered priests. She was attended secretly in her last illness and death by Father Henry Garnet SJ, who called her 'saintly'. By her request, her son was not informed of her death until after a Requiem Mass had been celebrated for her. Beaumont's wife was also a Catholic. Garnet described Beaumont as a man of honour who did not want to be involved in religious cases, but his weakness was his ambition. His son, another Francis, became a leading poet and playwright of the Jacobean era. In one of his poems he wrote, 'The greatest attribute of Heaven is mercy.' One wonders how much the father may have shared his son's sentiment.

John was brought into court and the charges of his being a priest and having said Mass at Waterhouse were read out. John said, 'Woe be to them that have taught that true obedience to the Queen and true religion cannot stand together well. I do not mean that any of this inquest shall stand charged or be guilty of my blood. I had rather confess the whole indictment.' So to save the jury he declared that as a priest of the Catholic Church he had come to preach the Gospel and administer the Sacraments, and greatly rejoiced that he had done so.

No further proceedings were required; his confession was recorded and he was removed from court. He was followed on the stand by Father Ingram. He too confessed that he was a priest, but opted for a trial. He acknowledged that he had come into England for about ten hours but had not exercised any priestly function in the country. The evidence of yet another apostate priest turned spy, William Hardesty, was then produced identifying Ingram. After that, the bench gave Ingram short shrift, telling him that coming into England as a priest was treason, and sent him back to prison.

Then a former Protestant minister and schoolteacher, George Swallowell, who had converted, was indicted for being reconciled to the Church and for persuading others to popery. He was accused of extolling the virtues of four Blessed priests – twenty-seven-year-old Edmund Duke, and Richard Hill, John Hogg and Richard Holiday – who were all aged twenty-five. Ordained in September 1589, and having been back in England barely two months, they had been martyred at Durham on 27 May 1590.

Later that afternoon, Swallowell and Father Ingram were pronounced guilty of treason, Ingram strenuously protesting, 'There is no Christian law in all the world that can make the saying of Mass treason.' He was quickly silenced and returned to his cell.

The following morning, 24 July, John was called back into court with Ingram and Swallowell and the jury gave the expected guilty verdict. Asked if they had anything to say before sentencing, there followed a series of altercations with the bench, but Beaumont commanded John to be silent. Father

The Elizabethan Martyrs, 1577-1601

Ingram told them he forgave them and all his accusers with all his heart and asked God to give him strength to face what lay ahead. Mr Swallowell however, being very fearful, asked for mercy, even to the extent of indicating that he would take the oath to save his life. When the death sentence was pronounced, the two priests kissed and embraced one another, joyfully bursting into the Te Deum, much to the consternation of the court. Seeing the reaction of the priests put new heart into the wavering Swallowell, who called out that he was resolved to die a Catholic. He told the court that it had been made out the priests were to die for treason, whereas they were martyrs, 'yet in very truth they die for religion... and I am content to suffer with them.' The bench was nonplussed by this change of heart, but after a hurried consultation the death sentence was confirmed on Swallowell.

That same afternoon, John was put into a cart and, followed by a large crowd, was taken to his execution at Dryburn outside the city. He wore a nightcap on which was embroidered the name of Jesus and an Agnus Dei symbol. John was so popular that special precautions had to be taken to prevent a rescue attempt. After kneeling in prayer he was denied the chance to speak to the spectators. As he mounted the ladder to the scaffold, John made the sign of the Cross and began the Hail Mary, pausing on each step as he continued the prayer. Reaching the top of the ladder with the rope around his neck he again attempted to address the crowd but was silenced. He said, 'Will you not allow me to thank these ladies and gentlemen who have done me the honour and kindness to accompany me today?' He then asked if he might not 'speak to my own soul' in the words of the psalmist, and holding up his hands began Psalm 116: 'I love the Lord because he hears me; he listens to my prayers'; he interposed illuminating comments about the contemporary situation between the verses. The sheriff objected to this and told him if he wanted to continue the psalm it had to be in Latin.

When called upon to ask the Queen's pardon, he replied, 'I have never offended her. I take it upon my death, I never went about to hurt her. I wish to God that my blood may be in satisfaction for her sins.'

The Elizabethan Martyrs, 1577-1601

At this the sheriff ordered him turned off the ladder. The bystanders heard John say, 'Father, into your hands I commend my spirit.'

He was allowed to hang for a few minutes until he lost consciousness. After he had been cut down from the rope and was being butchered, he recovered consciousness. While he was being disembowelled, he cried, 'God forgive thee, go on, go on. Lay not this sin to their charge.'

His four quarters were set up on Durham Castle and his head on Framwellgate Bridge. The vivid account of John's trial and execution was written by Blessed Christopher Robinson,[34] a priest who was himself martyred in 1597.

On 26 July, two days after Boste's martyrdom, Blessed John Ingram was taken from Durham to Gateshead. He wore a cap embroidered in red with the name of Jesus. At 3 p.m. he was laid in a cart and taken to the place of his execution. As he ascended the ladder he declared, 'I take God and His holy angels to the record that I die only for the holy Catholic Faith and religion and I do rejoice and thank God with all my heart that hath made me worthy to testify my Faith by the spending of my blood in this manner.'

As he finished his prayers and made the sign of the Cross he was turned off the ladder. His head was sent to Newcastle and set up on the bridge beside those of two other martyred priests, Joseph Lambton[35] and Edward Waterson.[36] On the same day, Blessed George Swallowell suffered the same fate as Ingram at Darlington.

Of those taken with Boste at Waterhouse, Mrs Clapton and Lady Margaret Neville were tried before Lord Huntingdon on 1 February 1594. The court had a busy day, with over eighty recusants indicted, among them Blessed John Speed aged about twenty-two years, who was convicted of relieving priests. He was hanged on 4 February. Lady Margaret was reprieved when she humbly begged the Queen's mercy. She was put under house arrest with Bishop Hutton of Durham. When she was liberated she married and conformed to the Established Church.

The Elizabethan Martyrs, 1577-1601

Robert Southwell

God's gift am I and none but God shall have me.

The Nativity of Christ, Robert Southwell, 1561–94

Robert was the youngest of the eight children of Sir Richard Southwell (pronounced 'Suthell' as per the Nottinghamshire town) and Bridget Copley. He was born at what was once an old Benedictine priory at Horsham St Faith, Norfolk, in late 1561. His grandfather, Sir Richard, Sheriff of Norfolk, had been prominent at the Court of Henry VIII and had been called as a witness (a truthful one, as it happened!) at the trial of Thomas More. It was he who had acquired the old priory along with other monastic properties after their closure. Robert's father was a 'church papist', that is, he had outwardly conformed to the state religion in order to preserve his status and wealth. His mother, who had been a companion of Princess Elizabeth, remained loyal to the Old Faith and regularly sheltered priests. Her brother had gone into exile for his faith. As a small child Robert had been stolen by gypsies. In adulthood he often speculated what his life might have been like had his nurse not rescued him. Robert was brought up as a Catholic surrounded by recusant relations. At the age of fifteen he was sent to Douai to complete his education. He was a pupil of a Jesuit, Leonard Lessius, famous for the austerity of his life. He also studied for a short time in Paris with another Jesuit, Thomas Darbyshire, who had once been archdeacon of Essex under Queen Mary.

Robert had thought of becoming a Carthusian but abandoned that idea when at the age of seventeen he decided to join the Society of Jesus. He was refused on account of his youth. He was so determined that he walked all the way to Rome and was accepted by the Jesuits as a novice on 17 October 1578, taking simple vows in 1580. He spent his novitiate at Tournai returning to Rome to finish his studies. A brilliant student, his poetry was already beginning to attract attention. He was made Prefect of Studies at the English College and was ordained priest in 1584. He was much influenced by Father Robert Persons and was eager to return to England to help in the mission. In 1586 he wrote to

The Elizabethan Martyrs, 1577-1601

Claudio Aquaviva, the young, dynamic General of the Society of Jesus, expressing the hope that he would soon be sent home, even if that meant he was going to his death.

He did not have long to wait. At the age of twenty-five he was sent to England in the company of fellow Jesuit Father Henry Garnet, with whom he came to enjoy a close and loving friendship. Spies had alerted the government to their coming, so they secretly disembarked on a secluded stretch of the coast near Folkestone. It was not a propitious time – if there ever was such a time – because it coincided with the fallout from the so-called Babington Plot.

Fashionably dressed and using the alias of Cotton, Robert travelled to London. Here, he and Garnet made their way to one of the prisons, as this was one place they were sure to find Catholic contacts. As a result they were given temporary shelter with an innkeeper. On being told of their arrival, Father William Weston, the Jesuit Superior, went to the inn to welcome them. Weston was at the time the only Jesuit still at liberty and he managed to get them out of London in the nick of time. He escorted them to Hurleyford House in Buckinghamshire, the home of Richard Bold, where they found sanctuary and also met the great Catholic composer and musician, William Byrd.

They spent a whole week at the house and we know that they sang Mass. As there was a chapel with an organ it is not too fanciful to imagine that Southwell and his companions may have taken part in the singing of one of Byrd's three great Masses. Based upon information supplied to them by Father Weston, the opportunity was also taken to work out an organisational plan for the better future deployment of priests on the mission, as well as consolidating the network of safe houses for them.

Walsingham closed in after the Babington Plot had been revealed. His spies must have reported about the Hurleyford House gathering because William Byrd's house was one of those raided and twelve days after his return to London Father Weston was arrested. It was left to Garnet, who succeeded Weston as Superior, to put into effect the plans that had been agreed.

Garnet left London for the Midlands where he was sheltered by Eleanor and Anne, two daughters of Lord Vaux of Harrowden. Robert found refuge with Lord Vaux at his house in Hackney.

The Elizabethan Martyrs, 1577-1601

Few families suffered as much for their faith as did the Vauxes. A great deal of Southwell's correspondence has survived, so we have a good picture about his activities. He was lucky in managing to evade capture on several occasions. While staying at the Vaux house he had at least one narrow escape from the pursuivants when the house was raided on a tip-off from the apostate priest Anthony Tyrell. Robert describes how from behind a partition he heard the searchers smashing the woodwork and sounding all the walls but without finding him. For several nights afterwards he slept in his clothes in a very uncomfortable hiding place.

At first he moved about London fairly freely, often in disguise and one morning he came across a group of Catholics who were being dragged off to prison having been evicted from their homes. He was able to go about the countryside around the capital administering the Sacraments. It was the Jesuit custom for as many of their number as possible to meet up bi-annually to renew their vows and give an account to the Superior, Father Garnet. In a letter Robert described one such gathering held in 1589:

> We have all together with the greatest joy renewed our vows, according to our custom... It seemed to me that I saw the cradle of the Catholic religion which is now being born in England, the seeds of which we now sow in tears that others may come and bear the sheaves in gladness.

On one occasion, Robert was at Baddesley Clinton in Warwickshire for one of these meetings with the Jesuits Henry Garnet, John Gerard, Edward Oldcorne and Thomas Stanney, when the moated manor house was raided by armed pursuivants at 5 a.m. just as he was preparing to say Mass. Hearing the uproar, Robert pulled off his vestments and hid all the altar furniture. Even the mattresses were turned in case any warmth on them betrayed that the beds had been slept in. While the servants tried to hold off the invaders, the priests scrambled into an underground tunnel hiding place where they had to stand in water up to their ankles for over four hours. Father Gerard tells us how he taught Robert the country sporting terms that would enable him to converse in gentlemanly company and so maintain his disguise.

The Elizabethan Martyrs, 1577-1601

Robert was of a sweet and gentle disposition and always kept aloof from politics and controversy, but in the aftermath of the Armada scare in 1588 he had to find new secure lodgings in London. This was provided at Arundel House, in all but name a palace. Situated in the Strand, with a River Thames frontage, it was the home of Anne Dacre, Countess of Arundel, whose husband, Philip Howard, was in the Tower. Robert was able to secretly correspond with Philip and offer him some measure of comfort. With Somerset House and Leicester House for neighbours, Southwell stayed in a secret room of the house by day, going out in disguise at night to minister to Catholics, especially those in the prisons. But his ministry was by no means confined to London. In the dark days following the Armada he travelled widely in Sussex, the Midlands and East Anglia, encouraging the beleaguered Catholics to remain steadfast.

In this way he laboured with great zeal for the next six years. It was at this time that he wrote his many well-known works of poetry and prose, which he managed to publish on a private printing press which he and Garnet had funded in order to publish books of devotion and counterblasts to the anti-Catholic polemical pamphlets. His admired poetry was immediately popular and went through many editions throughout the sixteenth and seventeenth centuries and is said to have influenced Shakespeare. He wrote a 'Humble Supplication' to the Queen, in which he writes as if Elizabeth were unaware of what was going on; far removed from the truth, of course. He described what Catholics had to endure and the tortures employed in the prisons and appealed to her 'merciful hand' to alleviate their sufferings. To the General of the Jesuits in Rome, he wrote:

> It seems to me that I see the beginning of a religious life set on foot in England, of which we now sow the seeds in tears that others may hereafter with joy carry in the sheaves to the heavenly granaries. We look for the time (if we are not unworthy of so great a glory) when our time shall come.

Robert often visited the manor house of the Catholic Bellamy family at Uxendon, Harrow. The family was notorious for sheltering priests including Edmund Campion and Father Robert

The Elizabethan Martyrs, 1577-1601

Persons. At the time the house was occupied by Catherine Bellamy, a widow since 1581. She and her son Richard had been indicted for recusancy in 1583, and his brother Robert had been imprisoned. Coinciding with the Babington Plot in 1586, for harbouring priests Catherine was imprisoned in the Fleet, later being removed to the Tower. She was a member of the Page family of Harrow, who gave two priest martyrs to the Church. There is an extant, handwritten note of Walsingham's ordering her condemnation before any trial had taken place. Elderly and sickly Mrs Bellamy never emerged from the Tower; she died there, as did her third son, Bartholomew, who died under torture. Her fifth son, Jerome, was executed for giving food to Babington and some of the escaping alleged plotters who had hidden near Harrow. Her fourth son, Robert, suffered greatly for his religion. Early in 1585 he was committed to Newgate for hearing Mass celebrated by William Thomson, who was martyred on 20 April 1586. Arrested with the priest, he was imprisoned for fifteen months without trial. He was still there in June 1586 and was a prisoner in the Clink in December of that year. He was in the Marshalsea in 1593, having been in jail for the past seven years.

The eldest son, Richard Bellamy and his wife, another Catherine, who were Southwell's hosts, moved into Uxendon when his mother was imprisoned. They had five children, the youngest of whom was Anne. On one of his raids, as well as taking away a great number of Catholic books, Topcliffe had carried Anne off to the Gatehouse prison. The evidence clearly shows that she was terrorised and seduced by Topcliffe and became pregnant. She was compelled to marry Nicholas Jones, a former servant of Topcliffe's, who worked as an under-keeper at the Gatehouse. After Anne had given birth, Topcliffe, seeking to add insult to injury by profiting from his misdeeds, asked her father for a marriage portion and for Preston manor house! Richard angrily refused the request. Having been closely confined for months, Anne seems to have been promised that she could obtain a pardon for all her family if she betrayed Southwell, so she sent a message asking him to meet her at Uxendon once more. Unsuspecting, Robert agreed, and also arranged to meet fellow Jesuit Father Richard Blount at Harrow. Fortunately for Blount he was delayed and was thus spared the same fate as Southwell.

On 20 June 1592 Robert said Mass for the Bellamys and remained overnight. Having been tipped off by Nicholas Jones, Topcliffe arrived in the middle of the night with his search party and started to ransack the house. In an effort to save the family from worse trouble, Robert came out of his hiding place and surrendered. Anne was not only the ruin of Robert but also of her whole family. Her parents and her two brothers and two sisters were arrested. On Topcliffe's personal instructions, Mr and Mrs Bellamy – whom he described as 'the old hen that hatched those chicks (the worst that ever was)' – were sent to the Gatehouse, their daughters to the Clink and their sons to St Catharine's. (Richard Bellamy remained a prisoner for ten years in harsh conditions. He sold Uxendon and went to live abroad, dying in poverty in Belgium. His wife and sons eventually conformed to the extent of attending the Anglican Church but not receiving communion. The two daughters were made of sterner stuff; Audrey and Mary declared that their consciences would not allow them to go to church.)

Topcliffe was jubilant at capturing Robert and wrote triumphantly to the Queen in his idiosyncratic spelling assuring her that he would extract from the Jesuit all his secrets. 'I never did take such a weighty man… I have him here within my strong chamber in Westminster churchyard.' 'Her Majesty's Servant' was sure he could break Southwell, describing to the Queen what torture he intended to apply and asking her what she would like to know from him and he would force him to divulge it. Father Gerard described Topcliffe as 'the cruellest tyrant of all England… a man most infamous and hateful to all the realm'.

Her Majesty's pleasure being to allow Topcliffe to do whatever he liked with his captive, Robert was sadistically tortured with unimaginable severity. He underwent the so-called 'wall torture' ten times. He was hung from the wall by his wrists, a sharp circle of iron around each wrist. His legs were bent backwards, his feet tied to his thighs. He was left hanging like this for hours at a time while undergoing questioning. Each time he appeared to be on the point of death he was taken down, revived and hung up again, despite coughing up large amounts of blood.

The Elizabethan Martyrs, 1577-1601

This barbarity left Robert with permanent injuries. Afterwards he was to admit that the pain was so bad death would have been preferable. Lord Burghley's son, Sir Robert Cecil, Secretary of State,[37] who was a relative of Southwell's, witnessed one of these interrogations. Afterwards he wrote,

> We have a new torture thought impossible for a man to bear. And yet I have seen Robert Southwell hanging by it, still as a tree trunk and no one able to drag one word from his mouth.

His torturers, having failed to extract anything from him, imprisoned him in the Gatehouse in a filthy cell where his keepers were Nicholas Jones and his wife, Anne Bellamy. Robert's father was allowed to visit him, and seeing him covered with filth and lice petitioned the Queen that his son should either be brought to trial or at least, as he was a gentleman, that she should order he be treated like one, even though he was a Jesuit. As a result Robert was moved to the Tower and his father was allowed to send clean clothes and bedding. He was left in close confinement in the Tower for nearly three years. Although he found the solitary existence hard to bear it was here that many of his most well-known poems were written. They are very much in the popular style of his day as well as reflecting the nature and character of their author: ascetic, compact, emotional, intense and lyrical; redolent of the sense that he was destined for the path of martyrdom.

In all that time he was allowed only one visit, from his sister Mary. Through the complicity of the warders, he and Philip Howard were occasionally able to smuggle notes to one another. Robert begged Cecil to bring him to trial. 'If he is in so much hurry to be hanged,' he replied, 'he should quickly have his desire.'

In readiness for his trial he was moved to Newgate and placed in the underground dungeon known as 'Limbo', where he was kept for three or four days and the Catholics sent in food, drink and candles for him.

Robert was eventually tried at Westminster Hall on 20 February 1595 under Lord Chief Justice Popham, who had come a long way since the trial of Cuthbert Mayne. Henry Garnet was in the street to witness Robert being taken by road from Newgate to Westminster.

The Elizabethan Martyrs, 1577-1601

Popham opened the proceedings with the usual invective against seminary priests and Jesuits in particular. Robert's voice had been badly affected and he could only speak in a hoarse whisper. He complained that his memory had been affected by the years of confinement and the tortures he had undergone, and expressed the wish that torturers would stop when it was clear that the victim was not going to reveal anything instead of cruelly carrying on. With quiet dignity he described his tortures to the court – much to the discomfort of Topcliffe, who tried to shout him down. When Topcliffe claimed that he had the permission of the Council to act as he did, Southwell told him, 'You are a bad man.' The court seemed genuinely shocked at the revelations.

Having been taken at Harrow, Robert said there was no point in denying the charges and confessed that he was a priest and thanked God for it. But he insisted that he was no traitor; his only crime had been to administer the Sacraments to those willing to receive them. Sad to relate, Anne Jones, née Bellamy, gave evidence against Robert. The jury returned the only verdict they were allowed to deliver and the death sentence was pronounced. Robert responded, 'I pray God to forgive all of those who are in any way accessories to my death.' Popham offered him the services of an Anglican minister but he courteously declined, saying that he would rely upon the grace of God. He was then returned to Newgate and incarcerated in Limbo.

The very next morning the keeper of Newgate came to conduct the thirty-three-year-old Robert to Tyburn for execution. He thanked the keeper, telling him that no one had ever brought him such good news before. The words that Robert penned on the execution of Mary, Queen of Scots in 1587 were just as apt when applied to himself.

> Rue not my death, rejoice at my repose,
> It was not death to me but to my woe;
> The bud was opened to let out the rose,
> The chain was loosed to let the captive go.

On reaching the scaffold, Southwell's face radiated happiness. Father Garnet wrote that Robert's courage, nobility and

The Elizabethan Martyrs, 1577-1601

gentleness won the hearts of all. There was an enormous crowd and Robert asked if he may speak. When he was refused, the crowd, not wanting to be deprived of the full drama of the event, shouted out that this should be allowed. He began by trying to make the sign of the Cross with his pinioned hands. He spoke on the text from Paul's letter to the Romans, chapter 14: 'If we live, it is for the Lord that we live, and if we die, it is for the Lord that we die. So whether we live or die, we belong to the Lord.'

He prayed for the country and the Queen and for her salvation, denying that he had ever wished her harm. He asked pardon for his sins, professed his faith, acknowledged his priesthood and begged his friends to pray for him, hoping that his death, 'though seeming disgraceful, yet I hope in time to come it will be to my eternal glory.' As the hangman placed the noose around his neck, Robert prayed, 'Blessed Mary, ever virgin and all you saints and angels, assist me. Into thy hands, O Lord, I commend my spirit.' The cart was pulled away, and Robert attained the desire he had expressed in his poem 'Life is but Loss': 'Free would my soul from mortal body fly.'

Lord Mountjoy was present along with other nobles from the Court. He insisted that Robert be left hanging until he was dead. When his head was severed from his body and held up for the crowd to see, instead of the usual shouts there was an eerie silence. It is very unlikely that Lord Mountjoy knew Robert's poetic sentiment, 'when he taketh leave of life, then love begins his joys'; but as he left Tyburn, Mountjoy was heard to say, 'I cannot answer for Southwell's religion, but I pray my soul may be with his.' He was, no doubt, echoing a sentiment shared by many: what was the country coming to when it subjected talented, gentle poets with a mystical turn of mind like Southwell to such barbarity for their religion?

Henry Walpole

One crowded hour of glorious life.

The Bee, Thomas Mordaunt, 1730–1809

Henry was born at Docking Hall, Norfolk, in October 1558. He was the eldest of the six sons of Christopher Walpole and Margery Beckham, who married at Docking in 1557. The Walpoles could trace their ancestry at Docking and Houghton in North West Norfolk back to at least the early twelfth century. At the time of Henry's birth they were a wealthy, property-owning family with interests in sheep farming. It was the Houghton branch of this same family who, in the eighteenth century, produced Sir Robert Walpole, England's first Prime Minister, and today they are still prominent amongst the aristocracy and landed gentry of East Anglia. Having been born just weeks before the death of Queen Mary, Henry was baptised a Catholic and brought up in the Faith.

A clever boy, Henry was sent to Norwich Grammar School and received the classical education of the period. He was expected to attend the Anglican services but he seems to have remained Catholic at heart, even if he did not exhibit any strong religious convictions. He went to Peterhouse, Cambridge, in 1575, where he showed great ability as a budding poet. Assenting to the Oath of Supremacy was a pre-requisite of obtaining a university degree. As Henry left Cambridge in 1579 without taking a degree, the obvious conclusion may be drawn. He decided to study law and took chambers at Gray's Inn, London, whose members had a reputation for their Catholic sympathies. Henry attended one of the public disputations in the Tower between Edmund Campion and the Protestant ministers and also witnessed the trial of the famous Jesuit and his companions in Westminster Hall. He was present at the execution of Campion, and while standing near the Tyburn gallows some of Campion's blood splashed his clothes; it changed his life. The event made such an impact that he wrote a long narrative poem, entitled *An Epitaph of the Life and Death of the most Famous and Virtuous Priest*

The Elizabethan Martyrs, 1577-1601

Edmund Campion. He had the poem privately printed and distributed. It begins:

> Why do I use my paper, ink and pen?
> or call my wits to counsel what to say?
> Such memories were made for mortal men,
> I speak of saints whose names cannot decay.
> An angel's trumpet were meeter far to sound
> Their glorious deaths, if such on earth were found.

The government ordered that all copies of the poem be confiscated and burned. When the printer was discovered, he was heavily fined and had his ears cut off in the pillory.

Having made his sympathies plain, it appears that Henry was under suspicion, and for a time he returned to his family in Norfolk and kept a low profile. But his mind was made up that he wanted to be a priest. He travelled all the way to Newcastle and from there crossed to France. In July 1582 he arrived at the English College, then resident at Rheims, and on 28 April the following year he was sent to the English College, Rome. In 1584 he joined the Society of Jesus but during his novitiate his health deteriorated and he returned to France to continue his studies at Pont à Mousson. Despite his poor health, which no doubt accounted for the delay, he was ordained deacon at Metz, and then priest at Paris on 17 December 1588.

A cultured man with a captivating personality as well as being a skilful linguist, fluent in French, Italian and Spanish, Henry was sent to Brussels to become a chaplain to the British soldiers fighting in the Spanish army in the Netherlands, then still part of the Spanish Empire. In 1589 Henry was captured by the English forces fighting on the side of the rebellious Dutch and sent to Flushing prison. Having nothing but the clothes he stood up in he was soon experiencing great privation. He managed to send a message of his situation to his family and his brother Michael secretly made his way to Flushing. There, by paying a ransom, Michael secured Henry's release early in 1590.

Henry's younger brother, Richard, born in October 1564, seems to have followed closely in his footsteps. Also educated at

Peterhouse, he arrived at Rheims in 1584 and in 1585 was sent to Rome, where he was ordained in 1589. He died at Valladolid in 1607. Henry was soon joined by two more brothers: Michael, born in September 1570, and Christopher, born in October 1568; and their Houghton cousin, Edward, born in January 1560. Richard, Michael, Christopher and Edward all became Jesuits. Christopher had been received into the Church by Father Gerard, who provided him with finance to make the journey to Rome to study. After ordination he joined the Society of Jesus in 1592 but died at Valladolid in 1606. For a time Michael was personal servant to Father Gerard before joining the Jesuits in 1593. He was twice imprisoned and exiled, rose to be Jesuit Superior and acquired a position of influence in England. He died in Spain in 1624. Edward died in London in 1637 after forty years on the mission.

In spite of his experience, Henry continued as a military chaplain for a further two years, after which he made his final vows in the Society of Jesus at Tournai. He longed to join the English mission but was sent instead to Spain to teach in the English Colleges at Seville and Valladolid, where he was appointed Vice-Rector. In Madrid he had an audience at the Escorial with Philip II, from whom approval was obtained for the foundation of the college at Saint-Omer. At last Henry got his heart's desire and in 1593 he was asked to go to England. To the rector of the English College at Seville, Henry wrote from Madrid:

> Being on the point of departing to that perilous country whence come our young men, I could not forbear commending myself to you and all those of the Society who are with you, asking their prayers that God may grant me strength to carry out this voyage of mine successfully and to the glory of Our Lord.

Henry left Madrid in August and arrived at Douai in September. He tried to arrange passage from Calais but there was another outbreak of plague in England and no ship would take the risk of landing at Dover. Henry finally set sail from Dunkirk in November, having paid for his passage on a privateer. He had hoped to disembark on the Essex or Norfolk coast but the

The Elizabethan Martyrs, 1577-1601

weather was atrocious and the ship was carried ever further northwards. By the evening of 4 December they were off Flamborough Head on the Yorkshire coast. Henry, 'for very weariness of the sea', asked to be put ashore at Bridlington. Unknown to Henry, a spy on board an accompanying ship had already managed to get ashore and report the priest's arrival to the authorities. Henry hid in woodland overnight and then made his way a few miles inland to Kilham village, arriving at the inn there the following morning wet and hungry. Arousing the suspicion of the locals, he was arrested and imprisoned at York Castle, where he confessed to being a Jesuit priest.

At the end of January 1594 the dreaded Richard Topcliffe arrived in York to interrogate Henry, but he provided no useful information. Father Richard Holtby contrived to get in and out of York Castle frequently, and although the two Jesuits never had any personal contact they managed to keep up a smuggled correspondence, which greatly encouraged Henry. In a letter written by Henry to Father Holtby at this time he says:

> When Topcliffe threatened that he would make me answer when he had me in Bridewell or the Tower, I told him, Our Lord I hoped would never permit me, for fear of any torments… to go against my own conscience.

He spent the winter in prison and plans were discussed by friends on the outside to organise his escape. However, Father Holtby advised against such a risky undertaking. In February Henry was transferred to the Tower of London. Among a great many inscriptions, Walpole's name, carved by himself along with the names of Jesus and Mary, can still be seen in the middle cell of the Salt Tower. The same cell was later occupied by another famous Jesuit, Father John Gerard.

Henry was held a 'close prisoner' for over two months, unable to communicate with the outside world. Such prisoners were brutally treated by the jailers, with scarcely anything to eat and only the ground to lie on without any covering. Father Henry Garnet, the Jesuit Superior, later wrote:

> Father Walpole met in the Tower of London with the greatest misery and poverty, so that the Lieutenant himself, though

otherwise a hard-hearted man, was moved to inquire after some of the Father's relations and told them that he was in great and extraordinary want – without bed, without clothes, without anything to cover him... when the cold was most sharp and piercing.

Robert Southwell was a fellow prisoner but it seems most unlikely that he and Henry ever met, though circumstantial evidence suggests they found some means to communicate. Some of the information Henry later disclosed under torture was probably obtained from Southwell. Kept in the Tower for over a year, he was horrendously tortured by Topcliffe with the rack, thumbscrews, the Scavenger's Daughter, and hung up in the manacles. Henry Walpole has the dubious distinction of having been subjected to the most atrocious forms of torture more than any other martyr – no less than fourteen times – in an attempt to break him. As a result his hands were so crippled he could no longer properly sign his name.

Under such torture and relentless questioning some information was obtained from Henry but he never betrayed anyone. For example, he admitted he knew that Father Henry Garnet had stayed at Braddocks, the Essex home of the Wiseman family. In the nineteenth century, documents were discovered in the Public Records Office purporting to be confessions made by Henry under torture. The confessions, allegedly bearing Henry's signature, abjectly beg the Queen's pardon and mercy and agree to join the Protestant Church. Scholars who have subsequently examined these confessions are convinced that they are forgeries. Briefly, there are a number of reasons for this conclusion. The first and most overwhelming reason remains that if the confessions were genuine, why were they not produced in evidence at Henry's trial? What an unprecedented coup it would have been for the government to have such confessions read out in court; but they were never even mentioned.

The second reason is that every piece of contemporary information we have indicates that Henry was unable to write legibly after being tortured. Father John Gerard tells us,

The Elizabethan Martyrs, 1577-1601

> He lost through it the proper use of his fingers. This I can vouch for from the following circumstances. He had a discussion with some ministers which he wrote out with his own hand. A part of this writing was given to me… these writings, however, I could scarcely read at all… because the hand of the writer could not form the letters. It seemed more like the first attempts of a child, than the handwriting of a scholar and gentleman such as he was.

Yet the signatures on the confessions are perfectly formed and may be compared with those on letters prior to his torture. It is likely that the counterfeiting was carried out by Thomas Phellips, who was in the pay of Walsingham and had been responsible for the forgeries to the letters of Mary, Queen of Scots for the benefit of the government.

In spring 1595 Henry, physically a broken man, was sent back to York for trial at the Mid-Lent Assizes under Judges Francis Beaumont, who had presided at the trial of John Boste; Matthew Ewens; William Hillyard, Recorder of York; and the Earl of Huntingdon. Serjeant Saville prosecuted. Although at first denied by Hillyard any right to be heard in his own defence, Henry successfully appealed against this objection. As a trained lawyer, Henry was able to make a good defence. Pleading 'not guilty', he argued that the priesthood had been instituted by Christ and given by Him to the Apostles and their successors down to the present. The Gospel had been brought to England by priests, therefore being a priest could not ipso facto constitute treason. He denied any harmful intent towards the Queen or country, but only wished to exercise his functions as a priest.

The judges were forced to concede the point but countered that a priest returning to England was illegal. Beaumont pointed out that the law required any priest entering the country to present himself to a justice within three days and make his submission to the Queen in matters of religion; otherwise he would be deemed a traitor. Henry then made the valid defence plea that he had been in the country less than twenty-four hours before he was apprehended. The period of time allowed under the Statute had not thereby elapsed, so his arrest was not strictly in accordance with the law and he should not have a case to answer.

The court ignored such niceties, and he was asked if he would now renounce his Catholicism and submit to the Queen in religion. Walpole protested that he prayed for the Queen that God would bless her and fill her with His Holy Spirit. He would most willingly submit to the Queen's authority in all things except his religion, on the conscientious grounds that the submission he owed to the Queen was subordinate to that he owed to the King of Heaven. He said, 'May His divine Majesty never suffer me to consent to the least thing by which He might be dishonoured, nor you desire it of me, and God is my witness, that all here present and particularly to my accusers, I wish as to myself the salvation of their souls and to this end they may live in the True Catholic Faith, the only way to eternal happiness.'

After the prosecution had denounced Henry as a traitor, the jury was directed to find him guilty. As they left to consider their verdict, Henry addressed them. 'Gentlemen of the jury, I confess most willingly that I am a priest and that I am of the Company of Jesus... that I came over in order to convert my country to the Catholic Faith and to invite sinners to repentance. All this I will never deny; this is the duty of my calling. If you find anything else in me that is not agreeable to my profession, show me no favour. In the meantime act according to your consciences and remember you must give an account to God.'

The outcome was a foregone conclusion and Henry was returned to York Castle to await execution.

In his last letter written to Father Holtby, he said:

> I am to be executed tomorrow. I commend myself to your prayers and those of our fathers and brethren... I tell you nothing of all that passed during my year's detention in the Tower of London. You will know it in heaven when we shall see each other again.

On 7 April 1595, together with Blessed Alexander Rawlins,[38] Henry was taken to the Knavesmire. Father Rawlins had refused to lie on the right side of the hurdle, which honour should go to Henry. They were laid head to toe, Henry with his head behind the horses. On the scaffold, Father Rawlins asked Henry for his blessing. Henry then had to watch his companion being hanged and butchered. They showed the mangled remains of Father

The Elizabethan Martyrs, 1577-1601

Rawlins to Henry and even at that stage he was offered his life if he would conform. When asked to join in prayer with the Protestant ministers for his own peaceful death, he replied that by the grace of God he was in peace with all the world and prayed God for all, particularly those who were the cause of his death. They kept him standing on the ladder for a long time as they harangued him. He said the Pater Noster and was just beginning the Ave Maria when he was turned off. Mercifully they allowed him to hang until he was dead. Afterwards, his head was stuck on one of the gates of York. The fact that Henry Walpole, having been immediately captured, was never able to work as a priest in England may be thought to be a waste of a life. Not so: his witness unto death for the Faith was just as valuable and powerful as any other martyr.

Philip Howard

His trust was with the eternal... the sum of earthly bliss

Paradise Lost, John Milton, 1608–74

Most of our information for the details of the life of Philip Howard comes from a contemporary biography written by an anonymous Jesuit priest who served as chaplain to his widow. Philip, the son and heir of Thomas Howard, 4th Duke of Norfolk, was born in London on 28 June 1557. He was heir not only to the premier dukedom and earldom of England but also five baronies. He was baptised in the gold font hitherto reserved for royal babies in the Chapel Royal at Whitehall by Nicholas Heath, Archbishop of York. His godparents were Queen Mary and King Philip of Spain, after whom he was named. His talented sixteen-year-old mother, Mary Fitzalan, daughter and heiress of the Earl of Arundel, died only a few weeks after Philip's birth.

The Duke quickly married again, and when his second wife died he took a third, Lady Elizabeth Dacre, a wealthy Catholic widow with four children. Although supporting the Catholic cause under Mary, the Duke was content to conform to the state religion under Elizabeth. John Foxe, who gained fame as the

The Elizabethan Martyrs, 1577-1601

somewhat unreliable – and untruthful – chronicler of the Protestants burned under Queen Mary, was appointed Philip's tutor and enjoyed the Duke's lifelong patronage. As the son and heir of the richest and most eminent nobleman in the land, Philip was destined for the greatest position after the throne itself. Descended from the royal Plantagenets, the Howards were also related to the Queen through the Boleyn family.

The Duke had bought the former London Charterhouse, converted it into his London residence and renamed it Howard House. It was here that Philip and his brothers and sisters grew up. By all accounts the Duke was a good father. With the aim of keeping their wealth and titles in the family, at the age of twelve Philip was married to Anne Dacre, his late stepmother's daughter. His brothers, William and Thomas, were married respectively to Anne's sisters, Elizabeth and Marie. Despite the Duke's avowed Protestantism, for a time Philip's tutor was Dr Gregory Martin of St John's College, Oxford, the English translator of the Douai-Rheims Bible.

The Duke's ambition got the better of him and he became involved in secret negotiations with the imprisoned Mary, Queen of Scots, with a view to a possible marriage with her as his fourth wife. It was his ruin. When his plans were discovered he was sent to the Tower. He was deprived of his dukedom, found guilty of high treason and executed in 1572. Philip was only fourteen, but in his will his father had selected Lord Burghley to be his guardian. Martin was dismissed as Philip's tutor and he was sent to Cambridge to complete his education, being awarded his degree in 1576. A handsome and gifted young man, Philip went to Court at the age of eighteen and became a favourite of the Queen's whom he showered with gifts. He entertained her lavishly at several of his houses and led a worldly and extravagant life of pleasure for six years. Elizabeth did not like the wives of courtiers to be around, so Philip left Anne behind at Arundel Castle, not only cruelly neglecting her while spending her inheritance but also being unfaithful.

The Norfolk dukedom had been forfeited by his father, but in 1580 Philip inherited his maternal Fitzalan grandfather's earldom of Arundel. He took his place in Parliament as the premier earl of

The Elizabethan Martyrs, 1577-1601

England and began to show signs of taking his responsibilities more seriously. These included his wife who, after her grandfather's death, had come to live with him in London. At first he was rude and resentful towards her, but gradually reconciliation was effected largely because of Anne's loving sweetness towards her husband. A clever and studious young woman, Anne was convinced of the truth of the Catholic Faith in which she had been brought up. She eventually took the step of asking a Marian priest to secretly reconcile her to the Church, in spite of the risks this entailed. To her surprise, when Philip was informed he did not seem to mind.

The reason for this was that Philip was in turmoil about his own religious position. In 1581 he had gone out of curiosity to hear a disputation in the Tower between Edmund Campion and the Deans of St Paul's and Windsor. The dirty, dishevelled Campion's sincere and solitary defence of the Catholic Faith made a deep impression on him, in contrast to the superficial mockery of his detractors. Philip was also present at Campion's trial. Much to the Queen's annoyance, he afterwards attended Court less frequently, spending more time with his wife, whom he came to love dearly. Anne was expecting a child and when it became known that she was a reconciled Catholic she was presented as a recusant. The vindictive and jealous Elizabeth, to show her new hostility to Philip, ordered Anne's arrest. She was placed in the custody of a courtier in Sussex with strict instructions that she was not to be allowed visitors. As a lonely prisoner, Anne gave birth to a daughter who, perhaps as a gesture towards the Queen, was named Elizabeth.

For two years Philip had agonised over his future until he finally made up his mind to become a Catholic. In September 1584 he asked one of his Catholic servants to recommend a priest. The choice fell upon a saintly Jesuit, recently arrived in England, Father William Weston, alias Edmonds.[39] Weston was brought to Philip at night, and he reconciled him and his brother William to the Church. Henceforward Philip kept a priest at Howard House and often served Mass. It was a torment to Philip that he now had to dissemble about his religion, feigning sickness or other excuses to avoid attending the Protestant services at Court. But the change

The Elizabethan Martyrs, 1577-1601

that had come over him could not be concealed from the Queen. Meanwhile, united in faith, Philip and Anne drew even closer together.

They found it frustrating not to be able to practise their religion and Philip wrote to Cardinal William Allen for advice. Under the efficient spy system his letter was intercepted and a plan for the Earl's entrapment was laid. Using the alias of Bridges, Father Edward Grately had become chaplain to Philip at Arundel House. He had formerly been with Henry, the son of Lord Vaux, but was now working for spymaster Francis Walsingham and was to play a role in the Babington Plot the following year. Grately was designated to deliver Allen's fake answer, the gist of which was that Philip and Anne should flee to the Continent. Philip sought the advice of Father Weston, who tried to dissuade him from such action, urging him to stay in England where he would be an encouragement to his fellow Catholics.

Philip should have listened to this wise advice. Instead he began arranging his escape, and all the while his plans were being betrayed to the government by Grately. Anne was pregnant again, so it was decided that Philip would go alone and she would follow later with the children. Philip wrote a very long letter to the Queen in which he explained the reasons for his conduct… 'in which he must consent either to the certain destruction of his body or the manifest endangering of his soul'. He wanted to be able to practise his religion in peace and bring up his children as Catholics, none of which he could legally do in England. The letter was left in the keeping of Grately, to be passed to the Queen once Philip was safely across the Channel.

Some sources state that Philip embarked at Littlehampton, Sussex, while others claim it was Lymington, Hampshire. The former seems the more likely, but whichever place it was he left on 24 April 1585 with two servants and in the company of Father Jonas Meredith.[40] As soon as the boat reached open sea, it was boarded by government agents led by Captain Kelloway. He showed Philip his letter of authority from the Council to arrest him, which he proceeded to do, having first stolen all the valuables Philip had with him.

They spent the night at Guildford en route for London, and

The Elizabethan Martyrs, 1577-1601

on arrival there Philip was sent to the Tower, where so many members of his family had been before him. His letter to the Queen had already been handed over to the government by Grately and was made public, so that when Philip appeared before the Star Chamber he was accused of libelling the court and disparaging the Queen. His situation was made worse by the totally unfounded lies of Anthony Tyrell, who accused the Earl of supplying Father John Ballard with money for subversive purposes. Tyrell also dragged the Countess into his slanders.

Philip was charged with being reconciled to the Catholic Church, attempting to flee the country and corresponding with Cardinal Allen. He was fined £10,000 and sentenced to imprisonment at the Queen's pleasure, i.e. indefinitely. William, his half-brother, and his half-sister, Margaret Sackville, Countess of Dorset, whom he greatly loved, both of them reconciled Catholics, were also arrested and committed to prison. Writing to his wife, Philip said the imprisonment of his sister caused him more grief than his own incarceration. Elizabeth's malice against the Howards had got to be sated. Edward Grately openly apostatised and was last heard of in the prison of the Inquisition in Rome.

Philip was kept in solitary confinement in the Beauchamp Tower. The Lieutenant of the Tower treated him with great discourtesy but Philip accepted all the petty insults with humility. Elizabeth thought that the spoiled young courtier she had known would soon break down under such treatment. But she had reckoned without the grace of God that was at work in Philip's soul, which enabled him not only to face his weary ordeal but also to grow in holiness. He became devoted to a life of prayer, meditation and mortification. His greatest distress was to be deprived of his wife and family, and he suffered greatly from remorse about the way he had treated her in the past – the sin he most grievously regretted in all his life. His pitiful requests to the Queen for Anne to be allowed to visit him were consistently refused. Even the news of the safe delivery of his son, Thomas, was kept from him. Meanwhile the Queen continued to find every opportunity to spitefully insult the Countess. Philip's health soon began to suffer from the fasting and privation and he was constantly watched, but he was not devoid of spiritual comfort. Father Robert Southwell, who had taken up residence at Arundel House, wrote to Philip, and the letters reached him through bribing the warders. The beautiful letters were later collected and secretly published under the title *An Epistle of Comfort*.

In 1587, for whatever reasons, Philip's conditions of imprisonment were relaxed a little and he was moved to the Lanthorn Tower. Here he was able to have contact with other Catholic prisoners, including an old priest, Father William Bennett who, with the connivance of the daughter of the Lieutenant of the Tower, managed to say Mass. The renewed persecution that followed the failure of the Spanish Armada in 1588 presented a perfect excuse for attacking Philip. He was accused of having prayed for the success of the invasion, whereas he maintained he had prayed only for the safety of the Catholics, who it was feared would be massacred by the government if the Spaniards landed.

He was charged with treason and brought to trial before his peers in Westminster Hall on 14 April 1589. The trial, not surprisingly, attracted a great deal of public interest, but legally it was a farce. Prosecuting was the Attorney General, John Popham, whose anti-Catholic credentials were impeccable, as we have already encountered. There was no real evidence to substantiate the charges against Philip, but that did not stop the prosecution from indulging in the usual tirade, throwing in every bit of gossip and slanderous allegation it could muster. The extant State Papers contain a letter from Popham in which he acknowledges that he was well aware that the evidence was fraudulent.

The principal witness was Father William Bennett, who repeated his earlier sworn statement which had been extorted under threat of torture. He claimed that Philip had asked him to pray for the success of the Spanish fleet, requesting a votive Mass of the Holy Ghost for that purpose. Philip told the court that this was an obvious lie because as a recent convert he was unaware of such Masses. He also informed the court that Bennett had written him a letter asking his pardon for falsely accusing him. The priest denied having done so, but to great consternation Philip produced the letter in which Father Bennett admitted to saying anything that his interrogators wished to hear and craving God's and the Earl's forgiveness.

With the exposure of the fabricated and perjured evidence, Philip's acquittal seemed assured. The issue revolved around whether or not private prayers could be legally interpreted as treasonable. The peers debated the question and called in the judges for advice. The lawyers' opinion was that prayer could not constitute treason, but Lord Burghley assured the peers that only a guilty verdict was sought; the Queen did not intend to execute the Earl. As a result the required guilty verdict was pronounced and Philip was sentenced to death. Asked if he had anything to say, Philip replied, 'Let it be done unto me as the Lord wills.' He then asked to see his wife and son and was promised that the request would be forwarded to the Queen.

There was widespread disbelief and indignation when the sentence became known. The general unpopularity of the verdict may have contributed to the endless postponement in carrying out the sentence. On the other hand, the Queen may indeed never have intended that Philip should be executed. Perhaps she wanted to prolong his misery, and certainly the fact that he was never told she had not signed his death warrant was an added piece of callousness. Returned to the Tower, he was constantly spied upon and his treatment worsened. Soon he became an emaciated shadow of his former self. He lived in daily expectation of death showing great fortitude and resignation to a heroic degree. As Father Henry Garnet expressed it, 'Each night as he lay upon his pillow, he was uncertain whether the morning might not summon him to another world.'

In a declaration he had prepared pending his anticipated execution, he wrote:

> The Catholic Faith which I hold is the only cause why either I have been thus long imprisoned or why I am now ready to be executed.

With his correspondent Robert Southwell, he could equally say, 'I live but such a life as ever dies.' Philip and Southwell wrote to one another frequently, even after Southwell was himself imprisoned in the Tower. Philip was inexpressibly grateful to Southwell, but sadly they were never allowed to meet. Philip was permitted to keep for company a dog that had belonged to his wife, and one

The Elizabethan Martyrs, 1577-1601

day it followed a warder into Southwell's cell, whereupon Philip remarked that he now loved his dog even more. Philip spent increasingly longer hours in prayer and when not engaged in his devotions he filled his time reading the Fathers of the Church and translating religious works from Latin. He also wrote meditations and poetry.

By the time Southwell was executed in 1595, Philip was gravely ill, unable to rise from his bed. He seems to have had some dysentery-like disease brought on by so many years of unhealthy incarceration, although the possibility of poison cannot be ruled out. He wrote to the Queen asking to be allowed to see his wife and children, especially the son whom he had never seen. Elizabeth's answer was that if Philip would conform he would not only be allowed to see his family but also be restored to liberty with all his rank and honours.

It was to be her last vengeful act against him. Sorrowfully, he sent back the message that he could not accept the offer. 'I am sorry that I have but one life to lose for this cause,' he said. Doctors were brought to him but he was now beyond their help. The Lieutenant of the Tower who had treated him so harshly came to ask his forgiveness. Taking the Lieutenant by the hand, Philip said, 'I forgive you in the same sort as I desire myself to be forgiven at the hands of God,' adding the advice that in future he should not be so severe with prisoners. They already had enough to bear and he should not add to their sorrows.

About midday on 19 October 1595, lying with his hands across his breast, whispering the names of Jesus and Mary, without any sign of grief or pain, he turned his face aside and quietly died with the words, 'Lord, you are my hope.' He was thirty-eight years old. Suspicions that he had been poisoned were voiced, but no proof of this has ever been discovered. Philip bequeathed to Father Weston his breviary, which he passed on to Father Henry Garnet.

For two days after his death his body was left wrapped in a sheet before being taken to the Tower chapel, where a Protestant minister who conducted the service preached a heartless and vindictive sermon against him, declaring, 'We are not come to honour this man…'

The Elizabethan Martyrs, 1577-1601

The cost of the funeral was a paltry four pounds thirteen shillings. Philip was buried in the Tower chapel of St Peter ad Vincula and there he remained until 1624, when his widow had the body removed, eventually to rest in the Howard chapel at Arundel.

Anne Howard, a remarkable lady of courage and generosity, became an exceptionally good and holy woman who had to suffer many hardships. Cardinal Basil Hume OSB, Archbishop of Westminster, in a homily given at Arundel Cathedral in 1995, said of her, 'I believe that Anne herself achieved the highest degree of sanctity.' The Countess, who died in 1630 at the age of seventy-three, spent her life in charitable work for the sick and orphans as well as sheltering many priests, including Father Gerard for a time, and when she died she was laid to rest in the vault beside her husband.

In 1971, following his canonization, Philip's remains were removed from the Howard chapel to a shrine in Arundel Cathedral. In 1973 the dedication of the cathedral was changed to that of Our Lady and St Philip Howard. Philip's daughter, Elizabeth, died at the age of sixteen in 1599. His son, Thomas, succeeded him as 24th Earl of Arundel. He died a Catholic and his son, Blessed William Howard, Viscount Stafford, was to follow in his grandfather's footsteps by dying on the scaffold in 1680, a martyr to the Catholic cause. Philip's great-grandson was Cardinal Philip Howard.

If you visit the Tower of London, climb the narrow stairs to the middle cell of the thirteenth-century Beauchamp Tower, where you will find among a great many other carvings three inscriptions, now protected under glass, incised by Philip Howard's own hand on the walls. Over the fireplace is a Latin quotation from St Paul's Letter to the Romans; it reads:

> *Quanto plus afflictionis pro Christo in hoc saeculo, tanto plus gloriae cum Christo in futuro: Arundell June 22 1587.*

This translates as, 'The more suffering endured for Christ in this world, the greater will be the glory with Him in the life to come'. Beneath this inscription you will see another added by the hand of

Anthony Tuchiner,[41] who occupied the cell after Philip. Tuchiner, who later became a priest on the English mission, carved a quotation conflated from Psalms 8 and 111: '*Gloria et honore eum coronasti domine in memoria aeterna erit justus.*' ('You have crowned him with glory and honour, Lord; the just man shall be in everlasting remembrance.')

John Jones

A rendezvous with death.

'I Have a Rendezvous with Death', Alan Seeger, 1888–1916

John Jones was born into a Catholic family at Clynog Fawr, Caernarvonshire, North Wales. In what year we do not know because nothing is recorded of his early life and nowhere do there seem to be any useful clues as to his age. The older sources, followed by Bishop Challoner, claim that in his youth he became a Franciscan at the Observant convent in Greenwich during the short time it had been reconstituted under Queen Mary. When the convent was again suppressed in 1559 under Elizabeth, John left for northern France where he entered the convent at Pontoise, was professed and ordained priest. Other authorities make the claim that John did not join the Franciscan convent at Pontoise until about 1590 when he was already a priest. If the Greenwich story is correct, it fills in the whole of the early period of John's life. If it is untrue then, assuming he was actually alive, we have to ask where he was and what was he was doing until 1590 when, according to the alternative version, he suddenly turned up at Pontoise.

Following the 'Greenwich tradition', John remained at Pontoise for many years before travelling to Rome in 1591 to enter the famous ancient convent of Santa Maria in Aracoeli (St Mary of the Altar of Heaven) located on the summit of the Capitoline Hill. Later that same year, having become drawn to their ideals, he left the Conventuals and joined the Stricter Observance of the Roman Province. Perhaps in Rome he came in contact with the students of the English College preparing for the English mission. Whatever it was that motivated him, he begged his superiors to send him to England and the request was granted. Before leaving Rome he had an audience with Pope Clement VIII Aldobrandini (1592–1605), from whom he received a special blessing.

He arrived in London in late 1592 and, according to Father John Gerard, with whom he developed a close friendship, Jones went to stay with him.

> I was particularly glad to give him the hospitality of my house in order to foster good relations between his Order and ours. But after a few months he found friends of his own and went to stay with them.

His fellow Franciscans elected him as their Provincial. John ministered in different parts of the country under the alias of Buckley and was recorded as working among the Catholic prisoners in the Marshalsea.

Through Father Gerard, John may have come to hear about the 'wonderfully good' Mrs Jane Wiseman, née Vaughan. Her husband had died in 1585 leaving her a wealthy widow with eight children and an estate and 'fine mansion' called Broadoak or Braddocks near Saffron Walden, Essex, which Father Gerard used as his base for a considerable time. Mrs Wiseman used her wealth to help poor Catholics, especially those in prison. She was 'a holy soul' who regularly sheltered priests and kept her own chaplain, Father Richard Jackson, an old Marian priest. Her whole family were devoted to the Faith. All of her daughters became nuns: Anne and Barbara joined the Bridgettines in Portugal; Bridget was professed at St Monica's, Louvain in 1595, in the same ceremony as Margaret Garnet, sister of Father Henry Garnet SJ. Two of her sons, John and Thomas, became Jesuits. Her eldest son, the deeply devout William, married Jane Huddlestone, the eldest daughter of another famous recusant family, and they had two daughters.

Life at Braddocks was becoming too dangerous, and at the suggestion of Father Gerard, Mrs Wiseman moved to another of her houses, Bullocks near Great Dunmow, leaving William and Jane at Braddocks. In December 1593, Bullocks was raided and although the resident priest escaped detection, Mrs Wiseman was

The Elizabethan Martyrs, 1577-1601

thereafter closely watched and it was noted that she visited Wisbech Castle to relieve the many priests imprisoned there, taking with her a rich vestment she had made. During her visit she went to confession to Father Weston, as did her son William. Father Gerard had returned to Braddocks and stayed to celebrate Holy Week. On Easter Monday, 1 April 1594, a raid took place and Father Gerard was hidden in one of Nicholas Owen's constructions where, unable to stand up or lie down for several days, he survived on a few biscuits and a little quince jelly supplied by the distraught younger Jane, whose husband William was then a prisoner in London. Anthony Tyrell had been on hand to ensnare the Wisemans in his web of deceit for the benefit of his masters, only to later confess that he did not know them.

For her activities in sheltering and relieving priests, Mrs Jane Wiseman was arrested and imprisoned in the Gatehouse, but no direct evidence could be found that would convict her. While in prison she spent her time in prayer and embroidering vestments. Half of the income she received was sent to Father Gerard, while she used much of the remainder in helping poor Catholic prisoners.

Richard Topcliffe suspected that John Jones was a priest and set out to trap both him and Mrs Wiseman. She was well known as a nurse and one of Topcliffe's agents at the Gatehouse, Nicholas Blackwall, persuaded her to allow Jones, who was suffering from an ulcer on his leg, to visit her in prison so that she could apply a poultice. John was brought in and Mrs Wiseman attended to his leg, but Blackwall spied on them; something in their conversation confirmed that Jones was a priest and he was arrested, while Mrs Wiseman was accused of comforting and relieving priests.

She was eventually indicted on 30 June 1598 in the Queen's Bench Court, Westminster, with the usual false witnesses produced to testify against her. Indicted with her was Robert Barnes, who lived at Mapledurham House on the banks of the Thames in Oxfordshire. He was also accused of sheltering priests, in particular John Jones. Barnes was sentenced to death but had his sentence commuted to imprisonment. Like Margaret Clitherow before her, Jane Wiseman refused to plead and was sentenced to be taken to the Marshalsea prison and crushed to death. The Queen and Privy Council got cold feet, afraid of public reaction; and so she was reprieved, to spend the next five years in a filthy prison cell – 'deprived of all she possessed', Gerard informs us.

After her release in 1603 she returned to Bullocks and continued to offer priests hospitality. Her son William, who was complicit in the escape of Father Gerard from the Tower in 1597, also spent years in prison, as did several of his family's faithful servants, in Colchester jail. The magistrates complained to the Council that none of them would inform on their master. William and his wife never ceased to assist priests. The elder Mrs Wiseman went to live in Louvain, where her daughters were Augustinian nuns, and she died there in 1610.

After his arrest John Jones was stripped and whipped; he was put in the manacles and tortured in Topcliffe's house. He was also subjected to unspeakable physical degradation at the hands of this degenerate. He was kept in prison for nearly two years before being brought to trial on 3 July 1598 on a charge of treason. The treason, according to the indictment, consisted of his having gone overseas during the first year of Her Majesty's reign (i.e. 1558/9) and been made priest by the authority of Rome and then returning to England contrary to 27 Eliz. I, c. 2. This accords with Challoner's account and conclusively settles the argument in favour of the 'Greenwich tradition' as being accurate and the alternative history as mistaken.

John protested his innocence. He had never plotted against the Queen and he refused to allow the case to go before a jury in order, he said, to save twelve simple men from complicity in his unjust condemnation. He appealed to the judges to hear his case according to their consciences. Mr Justice Clinch, presiding, told Jones that it was clear he had never contrived anything against the Queen, but as a priest of the Roman Church by his own admission, that constituted treason under Statute 27. John replied, 'If this be a crime I must own myself guilty; for I am a priest and came over into England to gain as many souls as I could to Christ.' He was condemned, and when sentence was passed John fell on his knees and gave thanks to God.

Perhaps because the populace was growing weary of the public butchery, John's execution had been ordered for 7 a.m. on 12 July 1598. He was taken to St Thomas Waterings, then a marsh two miles from London near the present Old Kent Road, where common criminals were hanged. The place got its name because it was where pilgrims to the shrine of St Thomas Becket made their first halt to water their horses, and is mentioned by Chaucer in his Prologue to the *Canterbury Tales*. Despite the early hour, a crowd had gathered. It was discovered that the hangman had forgotten the rope, so John was kept standing in the cart waiting until a rope was brought.

He spent the time in prayer and speaking to the crowd. He declared his innocence of all political wrongdoing, saying, 'I have never spoken a word or entertained a thought in my whole life against the Queen or my country, but have daily prayed for their welfare.' He told them his only crime was his religion and his priesthood and the crowd showed their sympathy. He specifically exonerated Mrs Wiseman of any offence, denying he had ever said Mass for her.

After an hour a horseman was seen galloping up pell-mell. The crowd excitedly thought it signalled a last minute reprieve, but it was the man bringing the rope. John was allowed to hang until he was dead. His head was set up on a pole in South London and his four quarters stuck up on trees in St George's Fields, Southwark, and by the roadside to Lambeth and Newington. Two young men were caught trying to remove one of the quarters and received long prison sentences. It is good to record that a relic of John Jones did eventually reach the Franciscans at his old convent at Pontoise, where he was professed.

John Rigby

What serves this life... except a thousand deaths to give?

St John of the Cross, 1542–91

John was born *c.*1570 at Harrock Hall, Eccleston, near Wigan. He was either the fifth or sixth son of Nicholas Rigby, an impoverished Catholic gentleman, by Mary Breres. Because of his

The Elizabethan Martyrs, 1577-1601

family's straitened circumstances he had to enter domestic service to earn his living with a Protestant family, with whom he occasionally attended church. Regretting this he sought out Father John Gerard, then a prisoner in the Clink, made his confession and was reconciled to the Church. Contrary to what is asserted by numerous sources, he was not reconciled by Father John Jones. In his autobiography Father Gerard is absolutely clear on the matter. He tells us that when John Rigby was questioned about his reconciliation he was asked the name of the priest who had done this and (quote), 'He did not want to implicate me, so he mentioned the name of a priest who had been martyred a short time before.' That priest was John Jones, but Rigby himself also specifically referred to Father Gerard as the priest who brought him back to the Church.

Shortly afterwards Rigby went into service with the staunchly Catholic Sir Edmund Huddlestone at Sawston Hall, some five miles south of Cambridge. Two years later on 13 February 1600 he was sent to the Sessions House at the Old Bailey to plead illness as the excuse for the non-appearance of Mrs Fortescue, one of Sir Edmund's daughters and the sister of the younger Mrs Jane Wiseman. Mrs Fortescue had been summoned to the sessions at Newgate on a charge of failing to attend the Protestant church. After he had delivered his testimony, one of the magistrates began questioning Rigby about his own religion. As Father Gerard tells us in his autobiography, John, being a straightforward chap, probably did not see the trap being laid for him and honestly admitted to being a reconciled Catholic – a treasonous offence. John was immediately committed to Newgate prison. He was required to sign a confession of his religious beliefs. When the jailer was putting the chains on him, John quipped that he would not exchange his chain for the Lord Mayor's great chain and gave the jailer sixpence.

John wrote a detailed account of his arrest and trials, which was saved by a friend and published by Douai College in 1601. Augmented by the narrative of Bishop Challoner, a booklet version was published in 1928 by Father C Newdigate. Some years ago the trial account was dramatised and presented in London by members of the Catholic Stage Guild.

The Elizabethan Martyrs, 1577-1601

Brought to trial on 4 March, John was repeatedly asked if he would recognise the Queen as head of the Church and conform, but declined. One of the judges, Mr Justice Gaudy, was very unhappy with the proceedings and did his best to help Rigby. During the afternoon the judge asked to see John privately and told him that if he was willing to become a good subject of the Queen's and would consent to go to church he would get the case dismissed.

'No, My Lord,' answered John, 'I assure you I am a true subject and obedient to her Majesty and her laws in anything which may not hurt my conscience; but to say that I will go to church, that I never will. Take my first answer as it is; there is my hand, here is my whole body and most ready and willing I am to seal it with my blood.'

Next day John was brought before the sessions at St Margaret's Hill. Once more Judge Gaudy almost begged him just to say in front of the jury that he would go to church and he would proceed no further. John's response was, 'If that be all the offence I have committed, as I know it is, and if there be no other way but going to church to help it, I would not wish your lordship to think I have (as I hope) risen this many steps towards Heaven, only to let my foot slip now and fall into the bottomless pit of hell. I hope in Jesus. He will strengthen me rather to suffer a thousand deaths if I had so many lives to lose. Let your law take its course.'

When the judge asked the jury what was their verdict, the foreman was so inaudible that Rigby called out to him, 'Speak up, man, do not be afraid!' When the guilty sentence was announced John responded, 'Praise be to thee, O Lord, King of Eternal Glory.'

To their credit, the judges remained reluctant to condemn him and only after much discussion was it agreed that there was no alternative. When the sentence was passed, John said, 'That is a fleabite in comparison of what it pleased my sweet Saviour Jesus to suffer for my salvation. I freely forgive your Lordship and the poor jury and all other persecutors.'

Moved and impressed by John, Mr Justice Gaudy obtained for him a reprieve of three months in the hope that in time he might change his mind and conform. After that period had elapsed, Rigby was again brought to court before new judges on 19 June. In spite of being offered life and liberty if he would conform, he remained resolute in his refusal to attend a Protestant church. He stood in the dock heavily shackled and at that moment the chains that had bound his legs inexplicably fell off. He was sentenced to death for the second time.

Awaiting execution, John sent a letter of thanks to Father Gerard for making him a Catholic and enclosed his purse as a keepsake. Father Gerard ever afterwards used the purse in which to carry his reliquary. On 21 June 1600, when told he was to die that same day, he answered, '*Deo gratias*. This is the best tidings that was ever brought to me since I was born.' As he was tied to the hurdle to take him to the gallows at St Thomas Waterings, he said, 'Bear witness with me, all good people, that I am now forthwith to give my life only for the Catholic cause.'

Father Gerard informs us that the Earl of Rutland, with a Captain Whitlock and a group of noblemen, happened to be in the street where John was being dragged along on the hurdle. The Earl asked what was his offence and John himself answered that he was guilty of no offence whatever but died for his Catholic Faith. John was urged by the Earl to conform. Such a handsome young man, he said, was made for a wife and children, not to die for his faith.

'As for a wife,' John responded, 'I have never in my life had intercourse with a woman.' At this Captain Whitlock asked for his prayers. Father Gerard confirmed that John had indeed kept his virginal purity.

Arrived at the scaffold, John gave the hangman a gold coin, saying, 'Take this in token that I freely forgive thee and all others who have been accessory to my death.'

All the eyewitnesses of his execution remarked how handsome he was and upon his fine physique, his outstanding cheerfulness and courage.

'I am a poor gentleman of the House of Harrock in Lancashire,' he said. 'My age thirty years and my judgement and condemnation to this death is only for that I answered the judge that I was reconciled and for that I refused to go to church.'

He was treated with exceptional barbarity. After he had been cut down by the hangman he was able to stand upright and was thrown to the ground while one of the officials pressed his foot on John's throat and others grasped his arms and legs to hold him down as he was butchered while still conscious. As they disembowelled him his last words were, 'May God forgive you. Lord Jesus receive my soul.'

Bishop Challoner in his *Memoirs of Missionary Priests* records that the people complained bitterly of the barbarity and bewailed John's death.

Anne Line

A ministering angel shall my sister be.

Hamlet, William Shakespeare, 1564–1616

Anne was the second daughter of William Heigham by Anne Allen. She was born *c*.1565 at Dunmow in Essex. Her father was a strict Calvinist who owned property that had once belonged to the religious houses. When Anne and her younger brother, William, who was the Heighams' only son, became Catholics as teenagers, their father disinherited them both and used every means of vindictiveness against his own children. Anne married Roger Line when she was nineteen. Roger came from a wealthy, long-established recusant family at Ringwood in the New Forest and was heir to an estate in Hampshire.

Anne's brother, William, had a priest who lodged at his house in London. This was Father William Thomson, who is also mentioned as having been chaplain to Anne. Could it be that after their marriage Anne and Roger were living with her brother? In February 1585, not long after his marriage, Roger and his brother-in-law William were arrested while at Mass with Father Thomson at a house 'without Bishopsgate'. Roger was committed to the Compter or Counter in Wood Street, along with the priest, and was examined by the vicious Mr Justice Young. While in prison Roger received a message from his uncle that unless he conformed he would be disinherited by his family. Roger sent back the reply, 'If I must desert either the world or God then I desert the world.'

As a result, the inheritance from his father and uncle went to Richard, his younger brother. William Heigham was transferred to the Bridewell and Father John Gerard tells us how he saw him being forced to work the treadmill in the prison while being lashed. He had to pay a heavy fine for his release. Father Gerard also witnessed twenty-six-year-old Blessed William Thomson's martyrdom at Tyburn on 20 April 1586.[42] William Heigham, whom we are told played the harp skilfully, firstly became a tutor to a Catholic family and then went abroad where he became a Jesuit brother.

Roger Line was sentenced to perpetual imprisonment, but as an alternative he was banished on pain of death and sent into exile in Flanders, where he received a small allowance from the King of Spain, some of which he sent to Anne. Roger died in Flanders in 1594 and Anne was left destitute and homeless. Father Gerard introduced her to Mrs Jane Wiseman, who offered her free board and lodging, while he provided her with whatever else she might need; so for a time she stayed with the Wisemans at Braddocks in Essex. Father Gerard had established a safe house in London as a refuge for priests and he could think of no better person than Anne to supervise this for him, so he asked her if she was prepared to become his housekeeper. Although frail in health, Anne managed the house very capably. She looked after all the household affairs, kept the accounts, answered inquiries, taught catechism and embroidered vestments. The priests who found shelter under her roof called her 'Mrs Martha'. Father Gerard, who always refers to her as 'saintly', tells us that Anne was 'full of kindness and possessed her soul in great peace'. It is clear that Anne played a vital role in the underground network of sheltering priests. We are told by Father Gerard that she was a chronic invalid. This is confirmed in an account by another contemporary, Dr Anthony Champney, in his manuscript *History of the Reign of Queen Elizabeth*, where it was stated that Anne was always suffering from various ailments, in particular continual headaches. Bishop Challoner, citing this manuscript as his source, records that Anne told her confessor of a vision she had of Christ

The Elizabethan Martyrs, 1577-1601

in the Blessed Sacrament carrying His Cross. She also confided to her confessor that she hoped one day to be found worthy of martyrdom.

When Father Gerard, after years of imprisonment and torture, made his hair-raising escape from the Tower in October 1597, he visited Anne at night. She was well known to so many people that she was under suspicion and it was unsafe for Father Gerard to visit any house she occupied. They agreed she had to move house so she rented apartments. At her new location she continued to shelter priests. In order to make her dedication more complete she took vows of poverty, chastity and obedience. In July 1599 the new safe house was raided while Father Gerard and his companion, John Lillie, were in residence. The searchers came to the room where they were and as the door had no lock the two inside held down the latch as tightly as they could. Anne, keeping her cool, calmly said that the servant whose room it was must have gone off with the key and volunteered to go and find him. The pursuivants were having none of that and said they would accompany her… and off they went without ever noticing that there was no lock on the door! This gave Gerard an opportunity to sneak out and get into hiding, leaving John Lillie behind to face arrest by the searchers when they returned.

On Candlemas Day, 2 February 1601, Anne allowed an unusually large number of Catholics to come to the house for Mass. The neighbours noticed people arriving at an early hour and informed the constables. Everything was ready for Mass when the priest hunters arrived. The priest, Francis Page,[43] managed to pull off his vestments and mingle with the congregation. Rushing upstairs, the constables found a room full of people and an altar, but no one would admit that a priest was actually in the house, although they could not deny they were waiting for Mass. In all the confusion Father Page managed to slip out of the room and hide before making his escape. Anne and most of those present were arrested.

On 26 February 1601, Anne was tried at the Old Bailey on a charge of sheltering Francis Page; a treasonous act under Elizabeth Statute 27. She was so weak and ill that she had to be carried into court on a chair. She was tried before Lord Chief

The Elizabethan Martyrs, 1577-1601

Justice Popham. On trial with her was Lady Gage, who had been sentenced to death once before for sheltering priests. The prosecution failed to make a case. It produced only one witness who gave the slender testimony that he had seen a man dressed all in white in Anne's house, but as the priest allegedly in question was not in custody he could not be produced. Nonetheless Popham, who seems to have harboured a venomous, personal hatred against Catholics, instructed the jury to return a guilty verdict. Anne received her sentence with thankfulness. Lady Gage was again reprieved. Three of her four sons became priests.

While awaiting execution in Newgate, Anne wrote a letter to Father Page in which she disposed of her possessions. To Father Gerard she left a gold cross which had belonged to her husband. She also gave verbal instructions that she bequeathed her bed to the priest. Sadly, after her execution the jailers had so ransacked her cell that when Father Gerard went to buy the bed back from them all that was left was the coverlet. Gerard informs us that he always slept under the coverlet whenever he stayed in London and felt protected by it.

Early next morning Anne was told she was to die that day but showed no sign of fear. It also happened to be the day fixed for the execution of Robert Devereux, Earl of Essex, for treason and as his condemnation was unpopular it was thought that butchering a batch of Catholics would provide a diversion. In a freezing snowstorm, Anne was taken to Tyburn to be executed along with two young priests who had been lifelong friends, Roger Filcock,[44] who had often been her confessor, and Mark Barkworth.[45] The priests loudly sang, 'This is the day the Lord has made, we rejoice and are glad in it.'

On the scaffold Anne was pestered by the Protestant ministers. 'Away with you, I have nothing in common with any of you,' she told them. Speaking boldly to the crowd, Anne said, 'I am sentenced to die for harbouring a Catholic priest and so far am I from repenting of what I have done that I wish with all my soul that where I have entertained one I could have entertained a thousand.'

A contemporary manuscript account of her execution, now belonging to the family of the Duke of Rutland, tells that after

The Elizabethan Martyrs, 1577-1601

kneeling to pray, 'She behaved herself most meekly, patiently and virtuously to her last breath. She kissed the gallows and then made the sign of the Cross'.

She continued praying as she was hanged but never moved. While Anne hung from the gallows, Father Barkworth, who was the second to die, reverently kissed the hem of her robe, saying, 'Sister, you've got ahead of us but we'll follow you to bliss as quickly as we can.' He told the crowd, 'I come here to die being a Catholic priest... belonging to the Order of St Benedict; it was by this same Order that England was converted.'

While he was being butchered Father Filcock called on him to have courage. When it came to his own turn, he said, 'Pray for me, blessed Father Mark. Pray for me to our Lord whose presence you now enjoy that I too may faithfully run my course.'

The martyrs' quartered bodies were thrown into the pit close by the gallows, but their corpses were secretly retrieved and a number of relics survived. Anne Line's body was reputedly taken to the Countess of Arundel, who arranged for a fitting burial. Where that took place is sadly unknown.

The Elizabethan Martyrs, 1577-1601

Notes to Chapter Four

[1] Blessed Thomas Ford came from Devon. He was an MA and Fellow of Trinity College, Oxford. Having studied at Douai he was ordained at Brussels in 1573 and returned to England in 1576, working on the mission in Oxfordshire. Having been captured with Edmund Campion he was sent to the Tower and tortured on at least three occasions. He was a tall man with a reddish beard. Condemned to death with Campion, his execution was postponed until 28 May 1582, when he was hanged, drawn and quartered at Tyburn.

[2] Robert Persons SJ (1546–1610) was a Fellow of Balliol College, Oxford, before being received into the Catholic Church in 1575. He joined the Jesuits and was ordained in 1578. It may have been Persons who initiated the idea of the Jesuit mission to England. He arrived in the country shortly before Campion but, having narrowly evaded capture many times, he escaped when Campion was arrested. He spent the rest of his life indefatigably working for the mission, encouraging the founding of English monasteries and seminaries on the Continent and getting involved in many dubious political schemes to further the Catholic cause. He was Rector of the English College, Rome, from 1597 until his death. The school he founded at Eu moved to Saint-Omer. During the French Revolution the College moved to Stonyhurst in Lancashire.

[3] Blessed William Hartley was born near Derby in 1551. He matriculated at St John's, Oxford, from where he was expelled by Tobie Mathew, the Vice-Chancellor. Having gone to Rheims he was ordained in 1580 and sent to England. He was sheltered at Stonor at the same time that the secret printing of Campion's 'Ten Reasons' was being undertaken. In June 1581 William took copies to Oxford University and secretly distributed them. Two months later, Stonor was searched and he was arrested along with the printers. Sent to the Marshalsea, he proved a recalcitrant captive, celebrating Mass for his fellow prisoners, who included Lord Vaux. This led to a letter of complaint about him in 1583 from Aylmer, Bishop of London, who informed Cecil that he had ordered William to be clapped in irons. Along with eight other priests, William was tried and condemned for some fictitious plot against the Queen. To everyone's surprise

The Elizabethan Martyrs, 1577-1601

William was not amongst those sent to Tyburn for execution. Instead he remained in the Marshalsea until banished in 1585. He was soon back in London where he was arrested in December 1587. Tried and condemned for his priesthood on 5 October 1588, he was executed at Shoreditch, outside the theatre, the first playhouse ever built in England.

[4] Brother Ralph Emerson was born in Durham about 1551. He was firstly the companion of Edmund Campion and then was designated to accompany Father William Weston to England in 1584. Ralph had charge of the baggage, which contained a large number of books. The day after his embarkation, Ralph was left to arrange for the books to be transported by river from Norwich to London. Ralph and the baggage arrived safely in the capital and he met up with Father Weston; but the books, which included copies of the Douai-Rheims New Testament as well as volumes by Cardinal Allen, were detained at the inn and it was dangerous to make a fuss about getting them released. On Ralph's return to the inn, the books had been discovered. Ralph was arrested on 26 September 1584 and questioned by Topcliffe and others. He was held prisoner without charge in the Counter in the Poultry for three years. Ralph was described as 'a very slender, brown little fellow…a great dealer for all the papists'. In 1587 he was transferred to the Clink, where he spent the next six years and where Father John Gerard met him. In 1600 he was transferred to Wisbech and remained a prisoner for the rest of Elizabeth's reign. He was in a bad way, by all accounts, having suffered a stroke that left him severely paralysed. After serving twenty years he was released on the accession of James I and died at Saint-Omer in 1604.

[5] Blessed William Filby was born at Oxford in 1555. After his conversion he went to Rheims and was ordained in March 1581 and sent to England. His brother, who had been ordained two years earlier, was already working on the mission. Captured with Campion, he was sent to the Tower and tried and condemned with Campion; but the sentence was delayed for six months, which he spent loaded with heavy chains before he was hanged, drawn and quartered at Tyburn with his three companions on 30 May 1582. He was just twenty-seven years old.

[6] Blessed Thomas Cottam was born at St Michael's on Wyre, Lancashire in 1549. Educated at Brasenose College, Oxford, he

The Elizabethan Martyrs, 1577-1601

worked as a schoolmaster before being converted. He went to Douai and was ordained deacon in 1577. He travelled to Rome and became a novice of the Society of Jesus. After a break because of ill health, he was ordained priest at Soissons in May 1580, shortly thereafter returning to England with three other priests. Sledd, the spy, described Thomas as lean and slender of body, his face full of freckles, his beard red and thin, and he had a mole on his right cheek. Spies had warned of their coming, and Thomas was quickly arrested and sent to the Marshalsea. He was transferred to the Tower and brutally tortured. Tried with Campion and his companions, he was condemned but not executed with them. When told he was to die the next day he cried out, 'Give thanks to God with me, for tomorrow is my day!' He was hanged, drawn and quartered at Tyburn on 30 May 1582.

[7] Blessed Robert Johnson came from Shropshire. He studied at the German College, Rome, where he apparently found the work hard, not helped by his poor health. He went to Douai and was ordained at Brussels in 1576. By 1580 he was in London and was arrested in July of that year. Sent to the Tower, he was tortured before being tried with Campion and his companions. Accused of plotting with them he protested that he had never even met any of them until brought to court. He was condemned and kept for six months in prison before being hanged, drawn and quartered at Tyburn on 28 May 1582.

[8] John Hart came from a strongly Catholic family in Oxfordshire. He went to Douai and was ordained in 1578, returning to England in 1580, but was arrested on disembarking at Dover. Unsuccessful efforts were made by Walsingham to get him to conform. He was sent firstly to the Marshalsea and then to the Tower, where he was left for days with only the bare ground to sleep on. He was cruelly racked and then tried with Campion and condemned to die. On 28 May 1582, the day of the execution, John's fear got the better of him. He wrote to inform Walsingham that he would conform and offered to act as a spy; so at the last minute a stay of execution was ordered, and he was actually taken off the hurdle he was sharing with Campion and returned to the Tower. All the evidence suggests that his offers were never fulfilled and John remained steadfast under continued brutal treatment in prison. He was kept in irons for twenty-one days and regularly incarcerated in the dreaded Pit. His

constancy was praised by fellow prisoners Luke Kirby and Edward Rishton. In 1583 he joined the Jesuits and two years later was banished. He ended up in Poland and died there in 1586.

[9] Blessed Lawrence Richardson, real name Johnson, was a native of Lancashire and educated at Oxford. After his conversion he went to Douai and was ordained in 1577, returning to England the same year. Arrested in Lancashire in 1581, he was sent to Newgate. He was tried and condemned with Campion but remained in the Tower until his execution with Luke Kirby and Thomas Cottam on 30 May 1582.

[10] Edward Rishton came from Lancashire and after becoming BA at Oxford went to Douai. He was ordained in 1577 and returned to England in June 1580. Robert Persons records that Edward was arrested that winter in Holborn, London. He wrote an account of his trial with Campion, at which he was sentenced to death. He also kept a diary of his imprisonment in the Tower. He was not executed but kept in prison for three years until banished with twenty others in 1585. He is remembered for continuing the important work of the learned Father Nicholas Sander, *The Rise and Growth of the Anglican Schism*.

[11] Blessed John Shert came from Macclesfield, Cheshire, and was educated at Brasenose, Oxford. He became a schoolmaster but on his conversion he went to Douai in 1576 and then to Rome, where he was ordained. In 1578 he returned to England. He is mentioned by a spy as being in Holborn in 1580. Arrested in 1581, he was sent to the Tower. He was tried and condemned with Campion but not executed until 28 May 1582, with Thomas Ford and Robert Johnson.

[12] John Colleton was born in Somerset in 1548 and educated at Oxford. We have his own account of much of his life and ministry. In 1573 he joined the Carthusians at Louvain, but spent less than a year with them before concluding that this was not his vocation, partly because of his indifferent health making it difficult to cope with the lifestyle and partly, so he tells us, because he was absolutely tone deaf and utterly incapable of singing a note! He went to Douai in 1576 and was ordained in June of that year, returning to England a month later. He went home to Somerset and reconciled his father, brothers and sisters to the Church. His father was later to die in prison at Gloucester for his recusancy. Colleton was arrested at

The Elizabethan Martyrs, 1577-1601

Lyford with Campion and sent to the Tower. He was tried with Campion and his companions, charged with complicity in the fictitious plot to kill the Queen. He alone was able to call witnesses to prove that he had never been to either Rheims or Rome where the plot was alleged to have been hatched. It did not secure his release and he remained in prison until 1585, when he was banished. After a time spent in Rome he returned to England, and he was recognised in London in 1591. Although he firmly protested his temporal allegiance to Elizabeth and to James, it seems to have done him little good. He spent the next thirteen years in and out of various prisons. Left relatively in peace under Charles I, he retired to Kent where he died aged ninety in 1637.

[13] James Bosgrave went abroad at an early age. He joined the Jesuits in Rome in 1564 and was ordained in 1572. He taught in Poland for several years before returning to England, where he was taken prisoner as soon as he landed. He was sent to the Marshalsea and in 1580 to the Tower. Although condemned to death he was left in the Tower until 1585, when he was banished with a group of twenty-one priests. He returned to Poland and died there in 1623.

[14] Thomas Norton (1532–1584) was a London-born lawyer and Member of Parliament. He was secretary to Edward Seymour, Protector Somerset. He married the daughter of Archbishop Thomas Cranmer. A friend of John Foxe and a rabid Calvinist, Norton seems to have pervertedly enjoyed interrogating Catholic prisoners under torture. He became so fanatical that he was deprived of his office and committed to the Tower at the behest of the Anglican bishops, but was soon released on the orders of Walsingham.

[15] John Mush was born into a poor family in Yorkshire in 1552. Educated by the Jesuits out of charity, he was however deemed unsuitable for the Society of Jesus because of his blunt manners and temper, in which perhaps lay the seeds of his future resentment of that order. He went to Douai in 1576 and moved to Rome to complete his studies, being one of the first group of students at the English College. He was ordained at Rome in 1583. His younger brother was also a priest. He left Rome for England in 1583 and three years later was in York; he was arrested there at the home of Blessed Richard Langley, who was martyred at York for sheltering priests on 1 December 1586. Father Mush escaped and was reported working in

The Elizabethan Martyrs, 1577-1601

London and Surrey. In 1593 he visited Rome but returned to England in 1594 and became a prominent figure amongst the Catholic clergy, travelling widely at home and abroad and getting involved in all sorts of controversies. By 1610 he was back in York and died in the North of England in 1617. It is as the biographer of Margaret Clitherow that he will be chiefly remembered by posterity.

[16] Blessed William Lacey was born *c.*1531 at Horton near Settle. He married the widowed mother of Father Joseph Cresswell SJ. He and his wife suffered great harassment for their recusancy. After her death he went to the seminary at Rheims in 1580 and was ordained at Rome by Bishop Goldwell of St Asaph in 1581. He returned to England and was captured leaving York Castle in July 1582. He was hanged, drawn and quartered on 22 August.

[17] Blessed Richard Kirkman was born at Addingham, Skipton. Educated at Rheims, he was ordained in 1579 and sent to England. In 1582 he was caught near Wakefield and sent to York, where the assizes were then in progress. He was arraigned with William Lacey and executed with him on 22 August.

[18] Blessed James Thompson was a Yorkshireman. He went to Rheims in 1580 and was ordained at Soissons the following year, returning to England, although in very poor health. He was arrested in York on 11 August 1582 at the house of a Catholic man who was then in jail. When taken before the Council of the North he confessed to being a priest. He was condemned for persuading to popery and executed at York on 28 November 1582 with a group of common criminals, some of whom he had converted.

[19] Blessed William Hart was born at Wells, Somerset, in 1558. Educated at Oxford, he went to Douai in 1577 and then to Rome where he was ordained in February 1581. In May of that year he returned to England. A deeply spiritual man, he spent most of his ministry in and around York, where he carried on a secret apostolate for a time amongst the many Catholic prisoners in York Castle, hearing their confessions and saying Mass. On 22 July 1582 he was caught saying Mass but managed to escape by climbing down the walls and wading through chest-high mud in the moat. He was exceedingly in demand in the days prior to Christmas. Having said Mass at the home of William Hutton, then in prison, on the night of

The Elizabethan Martyrs, 1577-1601

Christmas Day he retired to bed but was roused from sleep, having been betrayed. He was imprisoned in York Castle and on one occasion was dragged in chains to take part in theological disputations with the Dean of York. He was kept in prison until 15 March 1583 when he was hanged, drawn and quartered. Father Hart had a winning personality and unbounded charity. His reverence and devotion when saying Mass were impressive. He and Margaret Clitherow seem to have had a particular spiritual affinity, so much so that the authorities tried to blacken his name to her.

[20] Blessed Richard Thirkeld came from Coniscliffe, County Durham. He was educated at Queen's College, Oxford. He was at Douai and Rheims and was ordained in April 1579. He came to England a month later and was arrested by one of the sheriff's sergeants at York on 25 March 1583 while visiting one of the Catholic prisoners in the Ousebridge Kidcote. Keys were found on him and turned out to be those of his room and a chest at the house of William Hutton. They took away all his 'Church stuff' and his books were burned in the market place. He admitted his priesthood and was tried at York Castle on 27 May 1583. He was hanged, drawn and quartered two days later.

[21] Blessed Francis Ingleby was born *c.*1550 at Ripley Castle in Yorkshire, the fourth son of Sir William Ingleby. He studied at Brasenose College, Oxford and then entered the Inner Temple, London, in 1577 to study law. He went to Rheims and was ordained at Laon in December 1583 returning to England in April 1584. Although poorly attired, suspicion was aroused when it was noticed with what great respect he was treated. He was arrested and tried before the Council of the North. Every time he tried to speak he was shouted down and interrupted. He was hanged, drawn and quartered at York on 3 June 1586.

[22] George Errington was born near Ashington, Northumberland, in 1554. He was an MA of Trinity College, Oxford. He spent his life carrying out the dangerous work of assisting priests, meeting them on arrival in England and escorting them to safe destinations. He also conducted students to and from the Continent, as well as acting as a courier carrying messages. He was first arrested in 1585 by the River Tyne and was imprisoned in the Tower until 1587. Captured again in 1591, he was committed to York Castle, from which he escaped.

The Elizabethan Martyrs, 1577-1601

Offered a pardon if he agreed to conform, he declared that he would pray for the Queen and serve her with his body and his life, but he could not go to her Church as his conscience would not permit him. Rearrested in 1593, he remained in prison at Durham and York Castle. The wealth of information he possessed about priests and their helpers would have been invaluable to the government – had he revealed any of it. In prison he met William Knight and William Gibson. William Knight came from Hemingbrough in the East Riding of Yorkshire. A tenant farmer, he served terms of imprisonment in York and Hull. He was only twenty-three years old when executed. William Gibson was born near Ripon. He was a lady's manservant and had spent many years in and out of prison at York. All three were tried and condemned in 1596 on the same charge of 'persuading to popery'. All three were beatified in 1987.

[23] Blessed Robert Sutton was born in Burton-on-Trent, Staffordshire, in 1544. He was an MA of Christ Church, Oxford, and although a layman he was given the rectory of Lutterworth, Leicestershire, in 1571. In 1576 he became an Anglican deacon but resigned his living the following year and went to Douai. He was ordained priest in February 1578 and returned to England. Here he found shelter at the London home of Sir Thomas Gerard, father of John Gerard SJ. Robert was arrested at Stafford, sent to London for questioning and then returned to Stafford to be hanged, drawn and quartered. Both of his brothers became priests. Abraham was ordained the same day as Robert. After his brother's execution he was able to retrieve relics, including a thumb, which he gave to Father John Gerard. The third brother, William, also lived in the Gerard household and taught the young John Greek. William later joined the Society of Jesus and was drowned in 1590 while en route for Spain.

[24] In addition to Blessed Thomas Holford who died on the same day (see note 32), these were:

Blessed William Dean, seminary priest, born at Linton in Craven, Yorkshire. He studied at Rheims and was ordained at Soissons in 1581 in the same ceremony as two other future martyrs, Blessed George Haydock and Blessed Robert Nutter. He was exiled from England in 1585 but soon returned. Condemned with five other priests and four laymen, he was hanged at Mile End Green after being violently prevented from speaking.

Blessed Henry Webley, a layman from Gloucester. Arrested in Chichester Harbour, he was hanged with Dean for assisting a priest.

Blessed Robert Morton, seminary priest, was born at Bawtry, Yorkshire, *c*.1548. He was ordained at Rheims in 1587 and condemned at Newgate on 26 August 1588. He was hanged at Lincoln's Inn Fields.

Blessed Hugh More, a layman from Grantham, Lincolnshire. He was educated at Oxford and Gray's Inn. Having converted aged twenty-five, he was hanged with Morton at Lincoln's Inn for being reconciled.

Blessed James Claxton (or Clarkson) came from Yorkshire and was raised as a Catholic. He was ordained at Soissons in 1582 and returned to England and worked in Yorkshire. Tied to a horse, he was taken to somewhere near Isleworth and hanged.

Blessed Thomas Felton was hanged with Claxton. He was the son of Blessed John Felton who was martyred in 1570. Born at Bermondsey, London, he had studied at Rheims and been tonsured as a Friar Minim in 1583 but, being only twenty years old, he was not yet ordained. He had returned to England because of ill health and had suffered two years in prison.

Blessed William Gunter was a Welshman born at Raglan and educated at Rheims. He was ordained in 1587. Arrested in London and condemned on 26 August, he was taken to Holywell Lane, Shoreditch, and hanged outside the theatre.

[25] Blessed Richard Leigh was a Londoner born in 1561. Educated at Douai, Rheims and the English College, Rome, he was ordained in February 1586 and in June returned to England under the alias Garth, but was arrested and banished almost immediately. In the wake of the Armada he was arrested and sent to the Bishop of London who called him a 'papist dog' and had him sent to the Tower in July 1588. He was condemned for his priesthood and suffered martyrdom with Margaret Ward and his companions on 30 August.

[26] These seven were:

Blessed Robert Wilcox was born at Chester in 1558. He was ordained priest at Rheims in 1585, returning to England in January 1586.

The Elizabethan Martyrs, 1577-1601

He was soon captured in Kent and imprisoned in the Marshalsea, where he remained for over two years. He was hanged, drawn and quartered at Oaten Hill, Canterbury.

Blessed Edward Campion, whose real name was Edwards, was born at Ludlow, Shropshire, in 1552. Educated at Jesus College, Oxford, he entered the service of Lord Dacre. Having converted he went to Rheims in 1586 under his assumed name. Following ordination he returned to England in March 1587. Arrested at Sittingbourne, Kent, he was committed to Newgate. He was hanged, drawn and quartered with Wilcox at Canterbury.

Blessed Christopher Buxton came from Derbyshire, where he was a pupil of Blessed Nicholas Garlick at Tideswell. Ordained in 1586, he was arrested almost as soon as he arrived in England. He was hanged, drawn and quartered at Canterbury with Wilcox and Campion. Being so young, he was left the last to die in the hope that he would break, having seen the gruesome deaths of his colleagues. He was offered his life if he would conform, but declared that he would not purchase a corruptible life at such a price.

Blessed Robert Widmerpool came from the town of that name in Nottinghamshire. He was educated at Oxford and became a schoolmaster. For a time he was tutor to the sons of the 9th Earl of Northumberland. He was hanged with the above at Canterbury for helping a priest.

Blessed Ralph Crockett was born at Barton-on-the-Hill, Cheshire, in 1552. He attended both Cambridge and Oxford and became a schoolmaster in East Anglia and then in his native county. He was ordained at Rheims in 1585 and set out to return to England in April 1586 in the company of three other priests: Thomas Bramston, George Stransham (alias Potter) and Edward James. They were all captured on board ship at Littlehampton and imprisoned in the Marshalsea, where they remained for two years without trial. Ralph was taken back to Sussex and hanged, drawn and quartered at Broyle Heath, Chichester.

Blessed Edward James was born at Breaston, Derbyshire *c.*1557. He attended Derby Grammar School and St John's College, Oxford. After converting he went to Rheims and was ordained at Rome in

1583 by Thomas Goldwell, Bishop of St Asaph. Together with Ralph Crockett and two other priests, the Welshman Francis Edwards and Oxford-born John Owen, he was sent from London for trial at Chichester on 30 September 1588. Owen saved himself by taking the Oath of Supremacy and was reprieved. He later apostatised. Edwards waited until he was at the scaffold before he too recanted and apostatised. Edward James was hanged, drawn and quartered with Crockett.

Blessed John Robinson was born at Ferrensby, West Yorkshire. He married, but after his wife's death in 1584 he went to Rheims and was ordained in 1585. He was captured after landing at Lowestoft, Suffolk, and committed to the Clink where he remained for three years. In the wake of the Armada, John was sent back to Suffolk for trial and was hanged, drawn and quartered at Ipswich. His son, Francis, became a priest in 1597.

[27] Blessed William Way alias Flower was born at Exeter, Devon. He was educated at Rheims, where he was ordained in 1586, returning to England in December of that year. By June 1587 he was in the Clink. He was tried at Newgate in September 1588 and was hanged, drawn and quartered at Kingston-upon-Thames.

[28] In addition to William Hartley (see note 3) these three were:

Blessed Robert Sutton was born at Kegworth, Leicestershire. He may have been educated at Oxford before becoming an Anglican clergyman. In 1575 he converted and for a time was at Douai. After his return to England he was arrested, condemned for being reconciled and hanged at Clerkenwell.

Blessed John Hewett was the son of a York draper. He was educated at Caius College, Cambridge, before going to Rheims where he was ordained deacon. He came back to England and in 1585 found himself in prison at Hull. He was banished and ordained priest later that year. After returning home once more he was sheltered by a Catholic at Gray's Inn before being arrested again and tried in 1587. It seems he promised to conform and was released. He was captured in Holland carrying relics of recent martyrs and was sent back to England and imprisoned in the Bridewell, where he remained until after the defeat of the Armada. He was hanged at Mile End Green, where he endured a slow and painful death,

The Elizabethan Martyrs, 1577-1601

hanging for a long time with the blood bursting from his mouth, nose, eyes and ears while trying to make the sign of the Cross.

[29] Blessed Edward Burden came from County Durham and was an MA of Corpus Christi College, Oxford. In 1583 he went to Rheims and was ordained at Soissons the following year. In May 1586 he returned to England and worked in Yorkshire. He was captured and sent to the Council of the North at York. Although very ill, he was tried and steadfastly refused to reveal any of the places where he had been. He was condemned and shouted down by Protestant ministers when he tried to speak before he was hanged, drawn and quartered at York on 29 November.

[30] Blessed Nicholas Woodfen was born at Leominster, Herefordshire, c.1550. A teacher, he was employed by Swithun Wells at his school in Wiltshire. He went to Rheims in December 1579 and was ordained there in 1581, returning to England in June of that year. Hungry and weary, he arrived at the home of Sir Thomas Tresham at Hoxton, seeking shelter. For a time he had lodgings in Fleet Street and carried on an apostolate amongst students and lawyers at the Inns of Court. He again had to go into hiding at Hoxton, where he narrowly missed being discovered in an intensive search of the house. He was captured, condemned, and hanged, drawn and quartered on 21 January 1586.

[31] Christopher Dryland came from Kent. He went to Douai in 1576 and was ordained in 1582, returning to England shortly afterwards. A priest of exemplary life, he was arrested with Wells and Rawlins and committed to the Counter in Wood Street. The spy Berden's request that he be released in order to boost Berden's credit with the papists was denied by Walsingham and Dryland was sent to Wisbech in 1588, where he became confessor to Father Weston. He was moved to Framlingham and was banished in 1603. He made his way to Rome, where he joined the Jesuits.

[32] Blessed Thomas Holford came from Cheshire, where his father was a minister. He was a tutor to the sons of Sir John Scudamore in Herefordshire, but on his conversion he went to Rheims and was ordained at Laon in April 1583. Having escaped capture near London he returned to Cheshire, where he was arrested and imprisoned at Nantwich in 1585. Interrogated by the Bishop of Chester he

acknowledged that he was a priest. The bishop sent a report about him to London which contains a fascinating and detailed description of Thomas:

> Holford is a tall, black, fat, strong man, the crown of his head bald ... his apparel was a black cloak with murrey lace open at the shoulders, a straw-coloured fustian doublet laid on with red lace, the buttons red, cut and laid under with red taffeta, ash-coloured hose laid on with lace trimming, cut and laid under with black taffeta. A little black hat lined with velvet in the brim, a falling band and yellow knitted stockings.

In 1587 Thomas was sent to London and was lodged with two pursuivants, who were rather the worse for drink, to guard him at an inn in the Strand. By acting the fool he managed to escape from the inn and ran in his bare feet all the way to Harrow, where he arrived in a terrible state and was sheltered at Uxendon by the Bellamy family. The following day the house was searched but he managed to evade capture until 1588, when he was spotted by Hodgkins, a pursuivant, leaving the house of Swithun Wells and was arrested. Sent to Newgate, he was condemned and hanged at Clerkenwell on 28 August 1588.

[33] By one of those ironies of history, Archbishop Mathews' son, Sir Tobie Mathew, converted to Catholicism and in 1614 was ordained priest by Cardinal St Robert Bellarmine.

[34] Blessed Christopher Robinson came from Carlisle. He went to Rheims in 1589 and was ordained there in 1592, returning to England that same year. We have his graphic account of the trial and execution of John Boste, at which he was present. He was caught in March 1597 while sheltering with a Catholic family in Cumberland and martyred that month at Carlisle. As the rope broke twice, his execution was particularly barbaric. He was thirty years of age.

[35] Blessed Joseph Lambton was born at Malton in 1568. At the age of sixteen he went to Rheims, later entering the English College, Rome, where he was ordained in 1592; for this, a dispensation had to be granted because he was under the canonical age. In April 1592 he returned to England, where he was arrested with Father Waterson in Newcastle. Tried and sentenced to death, his execution on 24 July 1592 was barbaric in the extreme. The hangman was a condemned

The Elizabethan Martyrs, 1577-1601

prisoner who, to save his life, agreed to carry out the execution. Lambton was cut down while alive and, while attempting to disembowel him, the hangman panicked and ran away, leaving the priest agonisingly bleeding to death. The sheriff paid a French surgeon twenty shillings to carry out the dismemberment. Joseph Lambton was just twenty-four years of age.

[36] Blessed Edward Waterson was born in London and converted while in Rome in 1588. He studied at Rheims and was ordained in 1592, returning to England in June of that year. By July he had been captured at Newcastle. Huntingdon delayed his execution and he managed to escape but was quickly retaken. Dean Tobie Mathew of Durham wrote to Huntingdon to tell him of the 'harm' Waterson had done in Newcastle, converting people and saying Mass. In an attempt to frighten him, one of Lambton's quarters was shown to him in prison. Waterson's response was to kiss it. He was executed at Newcastle on 8 January 1593.

[37] Robert Cecil, 1st Earl of Salisbury (1563–1612), was the son of William Cecil. He was described as of dwarf-like stature with a humpback and Elizabeth referred to him as 'her pygmy'. Cecil was trained in the arts of espionage and dissimulation by Francis Walsingham and after the latter's death Cecil succeeded him as Secretary of State in 1590. After the death of his father he took his place as Elizabeth's and then James's first minister; he managed James's peaceful accession to the throne and was accordingly rewarded with a peerage. Cecil 'nursed' the Gunpowder Plot to great advantage and his part in its timely 'discovery' remains a murky area for speculation.

[38] Blessed Alexander Rawlins was born at Oxford in 1560 and educated at Winchester and Oxford. He worked for a time as an apothecary. In 1586 he was arrested with Swithun Wells and twice committed to Newgate. He was banished and arrived at Rheims in December 1587. Ordained in March 1590, he returned immediately to England, landing near Whitby. He worked in Yorkshire and Durham until Christmas Day 1594 when, hidden in a secret hiding place at the house of Thomas Warcop at Winston, Co. Durham, he was betrayed by a woman neighbour and captured by pursuivants. Taken with his host to York, he was tried and condemned, and with Henry Walpole was martyred on 7 April 1595. Some of his letters

written from prison and the account of his trial are extant. Blessed Thomas Warcop escaped from custody in York Castle but was recaptured two years later. Found guilty of sheltering priests, he was martyred at York in July 1597.

[39] William Weston SJ was born at Maidstone, Kent, in 1550. He graduated at Oxford before going to Douai in 1572, where he knew Edmund Campion. In 1575 he travelled to Rome on foot and was received into the Society of Jesus at Saint Andrea, where his fellow novices were Robert Persons and Henry Garnet. He was sent to Andalusia, Spain, in 1576 and spent three years at Cordoba. Proficient in Latin, Greek and Hebrew, he acquired a reputation for holiness. In 1579 he was ordained and afterwards served at the Jesuit College, Seville, until 1584. In company with Brother Ralph Emerson he sailed from Dieppe to the Norfolk coast. As the senior Jesuit in England, he became Superior. One of his first lodgings was with the Bellamy family at Uxendon, Harrow. At other times he stayed at various inns around Holborn or with Sir Thomas Tresham. He had a number of close shaves while evading capture. He was finally betrayed by the priest hunter Nicholas Berden and apprehended in a City of London Street near Bishopsgate in August 1586. Held at first in a private house, he was sent to the Clink, where he remained for over a year. As he was acquainted with Anthony Babington every effort was made to implicate him in the Babington Plot. Anthony Tyrell had a particularly malicious desire to ensnare Weston but never managed to do so. In 1588 he was transferred to Wisbech Castle. Before going he was able to bribe his jailer to allow him some liberty in order to make a visit to say goodbye to Robert Southwell at Arundel House. His first six years at Wisbech were spent in close confinement, only meeting his fellow prisoners at dinner times; but under a later keeper life became a little more bearable. A prayerful community life was established and Mass was said regularly. The priest prisoners had to provide for themselves, relying upon the generosity of Catholics outside to fund them. Each one paid the keeper twelve shillings a month for food and other necessities which, as there were around thirty priests, provided a profitable sinecure. Towards the end of Elizabeth's reign a more severe regime was reintroduced and the prisoners struggled to pay for food and bedding and often went hungry. In the winter of 1597 Weston was moved to

the Tower, where he spent the next four and a half years as a close prisoner in intolerable conditions, sleeping on the damp floor. When he begged to be let out into the open air, his jailer took him up to the roof, locked him up there and left him all day in all weathers. Visiting the Tower one day, the Queen's favourite, the Earl of Essex, noticed the priest kneeling motionless in prayer on the roof. After watching him for some considerable time, Essex wondered aloud if Weston could really be the great traitor he was made out to be. The strain on his eyes trying to read in the dark cell caused his eyesight to fail. On 13 May 1603, after seventeen years in prison, he was released into banishment along with several other priests, including John Roberts. A crowd of Catholics waited outside the Tower for the famous priest, kissing his hands and begging for his blessing. He was accompanied by his guard as far as Calais and then left. Half blind and prematurely aged he made his way to Saint-Omer. When his health recovered somewhat he was sent to Seville, where his eyesight improved and he was able to resume lecturing in Greek and Hebrew. In 1614 he was appointed Rector of the English College, Valladolid, where he died on 9 April 1615 aged sixty-five.

[40] Jonas Meredith was born in Bristol in 1547 and graduated BA at Oxford, but had been unable to proceed to MA because of his religion. Ordained in France in 1576, he returned to England the following year but was soon arrested and sent to the Marshalsea, again being released. He was arrested for the fourth time and sent to the Gatehouse. He was then transferred first to Wisbech Castle and then to Framlingham. After seventeen years in captivity he was banished in March 1603. He was back in England for a short time in 1605 before returning to France.

[41] Anthony Tuchiner came from Wiltshire. While still a layman he had served five years in the Tower, where he had been racked. He went to Douai in 1599 and was ordained in 1600. He was caught at Oxford in 1604 and banished. He was back in England by 1607, working in Oxfordshire. By 1625 he had risen to be Archdeacon of Oxfordshire and died around 1640.

[42] Blessed William Thomson was born at Blackburn, Lancashire. He went to Rheims and was ordained there in 1584, returning to England that year. For a time chaplain to Anne Line, he was captured with that arch priest-shelterer, Robert Bellamy of Harrow, and both

The Elizabethan Martyrs, 1577-1601

were sent to Newgate. Bellamy was able to escape, but William was condemned and martyred.

[43] Blessed Francis Page, although born at Antwerp, came from the Harrow family of that name who had already given a martyr to the Church in the person of Blessed Anthony Page at York in 1593. While working as a clerk in London he came into contact with Father John Gerard SJ, who was a prisoner in the Clink at the time. He became devoted to Gerard, who mentions him many times in his autobiography. When Gerard was moved to the Tower in 1597, Francis aroused suspicion by his many visits to try and see him. He was arrested and imprisoned but was able to buy his freedom. He went to Douai in 1598, and was ordained on 1 April 1600 and sent to England. On 2 February 1601, while preparing to say Mass, he had to hide when the pursuivants raided Anne Line's house. Page was caught in a London street later that day and held in custody in the parish of St Andrew's, Holborn. He was rescued by a Catholic gentleman named Slyfield who was later granted a pardon for his 'crime'. In 1602 Francis was betrayed in the street by a Catholic woman. He tried to evade capture by stepping into a house with an open door. Closing the door behind him he asked the owner to let him out by the back door. Unfortunately for him the man was a dyed in the wool Protestant, who handed him over. Francis was sent to Newgate where he was admitted into the Society of Jesus. Later he was sent to the Tower and in the Beauchamp Tower can be seen the inscription he carved on the wall: *Dieu est mon espérance. F. Page*. He was martyred at Tyburn on 20 April 1602 with the Venerable Father Thomas Tichborne and Blessed Robert Watkinson.

A member of the famous Hampshire family, Tichborne had been ordained in Rome in 1592. Having returned to England in 1594, he worked in his native county until captured in 1597. He was kept prisoner in the Gatehouse, from where he was rescued in 1598 by his brother, Venerable Nicholas Tichborne. In 1601 Thomas Tichborne was arrested and while being led through the streets was rescued by a young man, Venerable Thomas Hackshott. Nicholas and Hackshott were both martyred at Tyburn in August 1601. Thomas was finally betrayed by the apostate priest William Atkinson and arrested for the third time. Although he was suffering from well-advanced tuberculosis, it did not prevent his trial and condemnation.

The Elizabethan Martyrs, 1577-1601

The Yorkshire-born Robert Watkinson also had serious health problems, and as a result had been ordained at the age of only twenty-three before being sent to England to seek medical help. He was betrayed to the Bishop of London by a youth who had been a spy at Douai and arrested on arrival in the capital. He was executed less than a month after his ordination and must be the youngest of all the priest martyrs.

[44] Blessed Roger Filcock was born at Sandwich, Kent, in 1572. He arrived at the English College, Rheims, in 1581 and was later sent to Valladolid in 1591. After his ordination he returned to England in December 1597. He asked Father Henry Garnet to be admitted into the Society of Jesus in 1600, but while preparing to return to Flanders for his novitiate he was arrested and sent to Newgate. At his trial at Newgate Sessions, he was subjected to vicious verbal attacks from Bishop Bancroft of London. Condemned, he was martyred at Tyburn with Anne Line and Mark Barkworth.

[45] Blessed Mark Barkworth was born in Lincolnshire in 1572. He went to Douai in 1593 and was received into the Church. He attended Douai University and was then sent to Valladolid in December 1596. While at Valladolid he expressed a desire to join the Benedictines, and while on his return journey to England was received as a novice at the Abbey of Hyrache, Navarre, with permission, if in danger of death, to profess himself as a member of the order. He was ordained in 1599 and left for England that summer in the company of Thomas Garnet. He was not long in London before he was arrested and confined in the Bridewell. He was described as a tall man, well proportioned with a yellow beard and rather heavy-eyed. Condemned without even a proper trial, he was incarcerated in the dungeon known as Limbo in Newgate to await execution. He was martyred at Tyburn with Anne Line and Roger Filcock. On the scaffold he wore the Benedictine habit and tonsure.

Chapter Five

The Jacobean Martyrs, 1603–1625

> Put not your trust in princes.
>
> Psalm 146

James VI of Scotland succeeded Elizabeth as James I of England on 24 March 1603. Although a convinced Protestant, before his accession, when he was anxious to secure all the support he could muster for a peaceful succession to Elizabeth, he had been secretly communicating with prominent English Catholics. The fact that James had a Catholic convert for a wife fuelled Catholic optimism. There seems to be no reason to doubt that James did give certain assurances about his benign attitude towards his future Catholic subjects. How genuine those promises were we shall never know, emanating as they did from a man referred to as 'One of the most secret princes of the world'. But then James would have promised anything to anyone if it helped ensure for him the prize of the English Crown. Just as was the case when he went through the diplomatic motions of making overtures to Elizabeth to get a reprieve for his mother, his foremost consideration was for himself. As Caroline Bingham wrote in her *James VI of Scotland* (1979), 'He was... intensely anxious not to jeopardise his own position'.

While on his journey from Scotland to London, James, profligately showering honours on all and sundry, had continued to give promises of toleration, which encouraged the despairing Catholics to believe that at last they would be granted some respite. On the one hand, determined to ingratiate himself with everyone, it suited James to raise the hope of toleration. On the other hand, the Catholics were so desperate for relief that they unrealistically took him at his word and exaggerated his promises out of all proportion because it was what they wanted to hear. Father Henry Garnet wrote:

> The Catholics have great cause to hope [for toleration]... in that the nobility almost all labour for it and we have a good promise thereof from His Majesty.

For the first few months of the new reign their hopes seemed justified. James declared, 'I acknowledge the Roman Church to be our mother church, though defiled with some corruptions. My mind was ever so free from persecution.' Some Catholics felt confident enough to openly profess their Faith – much to the alarm of the Puritans, for whom James, like his predecessor, had scant sympathy. The State Papers containing the official returns for recusants reveal that by the end of the first year of James's reign there were 10,000 more who had acknowledged themselves as Catholics than there were at his accession. Over 140 priests had landed in England in the nine months since the death of Elizabeth. James relaxed the heavy fines and ordered the release from prison of scores of priests, arranging for them to be taken to exile in France. In return, the Catholics pledged their loyalty to James. But their illusory hopes were soon dashed: the respite was short-lived. After all, he would not be the first or the last monarch to break his promises to others if he could profit by doing so.

By suspending the extortionate fines, James realised he was losing huge sums of money which he needed for rewarding his rapacious courtiers. He hit upon a brilliant plan to satisfy their greed. An individual was given permission to seek out as many wealthy recusants as he liked. Once they had been identified, James then 'granted' those recusants, known as 'the benefit of recusants', to the individual, who could pursue them for their recusancy fines due to the Crown then or in the future. Alternatively, he could extort from them payments or property in lieu: in short the King 'sold' Catholics to his cronies, leaving them at the mercy of ruthless, mercenary persecutors, for whom they were a source of profit. Many famous members of the Catholic gentry lost two-thirds of their properties in this way and a nouveau riche class came into being on the backs of their misery.

Robert Cecil counselled James to vigorously renew the persecution of Catholics, yet the King appears not to have fully appreciated the depth of mindless anti-Catholic prejudice in Parliament. When Parliament met in 1604 the Elizabethan penal laws were not only renewed but increased, including making fines retrospective, and when Viscount Montague had the courage to protest about it he found himself in prison. By now James felt secure in his possession of the throne and his attitude to his Catholic subjects changed. 'We'll nae need the papists now,' he remarked.

In July 1604 a fresh wave of executions began, the first martyrs of the reign being the priest Blessed John Sugar and his lay helper, Blessed Robert Grissold,[1] who were executed at Warwick. The Catholics felt bitter and betrayed and this renewed repression destroyed all their hopes. There can be no doubt that the reneging of the King on his perceived promises directly provoked the Gunpowder Plot and played into the government's hands. This is not the place to go into the labyrinthine complexities of the Plot, but it played such a pivotal role in the history of Catholicism in Britain that a brief digression is justified.

Today it is generally, though not universally, accepted that there was a genuine conspiracy to blow up Parliament, with the King and his two sons at the same time. Equally, not only today, but also contemporaneously with the Plot itself, there seems to have been no doubt that the government knew about it in advance from a mole; given the efficiency of the intelligence service, that is hardly surprising. How far in advance and who the informer was remains a matter for dispute. The conspiracy was carefully monitored by Robert Cecil, Earl of Salisbury, as it was put into operation by the group of inept and inane plotters. The 'cloud cuckoo land' Plot, lacking all pragmatism, was an absurdly unrealistic fantasy masterminded by the hot-headed Robert Catesby, and he drew in some of his relations and friends. Despite his notoriety, Guy Fawkes, the ex-soldier, was only the foolhardy 'frontman'.

In essence, the Plot aimed at destroying the whole Protestant government, to be followed by a general uprising of the Catholic gentry with the aim of installing a more compliant regime. The fact was that, other than the band of conspirators, the Catholic community at large did not share these aspirations, which shows just how self-deluded the plotters were. Catholics might be faced with denial of civil liberties, financial ruin and risk their very lives for sheltering priests in order that they might receive spiritual succour from the Sacraments; but they were loyal – loyal not only to their country, but also to the Pope, who urged them to bear their sufferings with patient endurance.

Whatever our sympathies with the desperate plight of seventeenth-century Catholics, the conclusion must be drawn that the plotters, who saw themselves as brave idealists striking a blow for their Faith, were in reality would-be mass murderers. In her *Gunpowder Plot: Terror and Treason in 1605* (1996), Antonia Fraser bluntly calls the plotters terrorists. They got their just deserts for their misguided zeal and wicked intentions. But as a direct consequence of their actions, incalculable harm was inflicted on their co-religionists. In the popular consciousness Catholicism became equated as never before with treason, an attitude recalled and reinforced with the annual 5 November commemorations.

James himself seems to have been oblivious to the measure of personal responsibility he bore for having raised the hopes of Catholics with his promises, only to callously dash them. He simply felt affronted that his 'tolerance' had been so ungratefully abused. The Plot unleashed a tempest of even greater oppressive and cruel persecution of Catholics. Dozens of priests were rounded up and imprisoned. George Abbot, Bishop of London and then Archbishop of Canterbury (1611–33), begged the King on his knees to treat Catholics with the utmost severity. Not content with persecuting Catholics, Abbot also had Protestant dissenters burned for heresy.

The historian David Starkey is right in saying that the Plot set back the cause of Catholic Emancipation more than one hundred years. Under James I, Catholics became virtually non-persons, pariahs without any legal rights from the cradle to the grave. For example, Catholics could not serve in the armed forces, practice law, take a degree or vote in elections. It took until 1829 before Catholics were given the right to vote. During James's reign, with the exception of a few months when he was negotiating for a marriage between the King of Spain's daughter and his heir, Charles, Prince of Wales, the persecution of Catholics was unremitting. The penal laws were mercilessly enforced. The sweeping powers given to the pursuivants to conduct unannounced raids, day or night, on the homes of recusants who had no redress, can only be compared to the modus operandi of the Nazis or the Stalinist regime. These villains had carte blanche to act with impunity and were given every incentive to be ruthless, as they were able to claim one third of the resulting proceeds from their victims. What is of relevance to our story is that the Plot resulted in exile for forty-six priests. It also cost the lives of twenty-four martyrs.

Nicholas Owen

Only a life lived for others is worthwhile.

Albert Einstein, 1879–1955

In spite of references in several works to Nicholas as a 'cockney', all the evidence supports the traditional supposition that he was born into a Catholic family in Oxford. We can deduce this only from known information about his siblings. He had three brothers: John became a priest and worked on the English mission; Walter was certainly already a deacon when he went to the English College, Valladolid, where he died, probably after priestly ordination; Henry, the third brother, was a printer of underground Catholic literature and suffered imprisonment for his activities. Nicholas followed his father's trade as a carpenter and builder, which became his vocation. Sometime before 1580 he was secretly received into the Society of Jesus as one of the first English lay brothers.

He spent twenty-six years travelling all over England constructing hiding places for priests in country houses with incredible skill and extraordinary ingenuity, disguising their construction in such a way that the access to them was virtually undetectable. Among the houses in which he worked were Harrowden Hall, Northamptonshire; Coughton Court and Baddesley Clinton, Warwickshire; Sawston Hall, Cambridgeshire; and Oxburgh Hall, Norfolk. Built into the walls, the chimney breasts, underneath staircases and between floors, many examples of his hiding places still survive. Some were only discovered in the nineteenth and twentieth centuries. No two hiding places were exactly alike, so as not to provide any clues that might lead to the discovery of others. Sometimes he made false hiding places to fool the searchers so that, having found the decoy empty, they would depart, leaving the real hiding place undetected. While pretending to be carrying out repairs to the property by day, his real work was carried out single-handedly, in great secrecy, at night. He was nicknamed 'Little John' because of his diminutive stature, which enabled him to get into very small spaces. By contrast Father Gerard, being a tall, well-built man, was known as 'Big John'.

It is thought Nicholas firstly served Edmund Campion. After Campion's execution, Nicholas was in trouble for speaking out openly and boldly about the Jesuit's, innocence, for which he was arrested and imprisoned. When he was released in 1586 he went to serve Father Henry Garnet, the Jesuit Superior in England, and was his faithful companion for twenty years. He also served Father Gerard. Nicholas transacted business for the two priests, such as renting houses.

At Easter 1594, thanks to Owen's skill, Father Gerard was saved from discovery by the pursuivants when he hid for several days in one of Nicholas' secret hiding places at Braddocks, the home of the Wisemans. It was a close shave because Gerard was hidden beneath the hearth and the searchers lit a fire! He was not to remain much longer at liberty. Deciding it was time to move house, Nicholas found him somewhere suitable in London. While the new house was being prepared, he and Owen lodged temporarily in Holborn, at the house of Mr Middleton. On 23 April, while Gerard and Owen were sharing a bedroom at the house, there was a raid in the middle of the night and both were captured. They had been betrayed by a servant.

Nicholas was taken first to the Counter in Poultry and then moved to Newgate where, along with Gerard's servant, Richard Fulwood, who had been apprehended separately, he was tortured by being hung up in the manacles for three hours at a time. As yet the government was unaware of Nicholas's role and neither man revealed anything incriminating. To the Catholic gentry, Nicholas

The Jacobean Martyrs, 1603–1625

was indispensable, and the secrets he possessed were so far-reaching in their consequences if ever disclosed, that they paid a large sum to have him released. Father Gerard spent three years in the Clink, where Nicholas was able to visit him and act as a go-between for him and Father Garnet. This activity was betrayed by a fellow priest in the jail and Gerard was moved to the Tower.

On the night of 5 October 1597 Father Gerard made his amazing escape from the Tower. Many sources believe that Owen was the mastermind behind the escape. Richard Fulwood and John Lillie, faithful servants of Gerard's who both became Jesuits, directly assisted the priest, rowing him down the Thames and thence to a house used by Father Garnet at Spitalfields, where Nicholas waited for them with horses. He and Gerard quickly mounted and galloped off into the country.

In 1599 Father Gerard and Nicholas were nearly caught again while he was constructing a hiding place at Kirby Hall, Northamptonshire, the planned new residence of Lady Elizabeth Vaux, to whom Father Gerard acted as chaplain at Harrowden Hall. Nicholas had already provided several hiding places at Harrowden, so skilfully contrived that one would-be searcher stated that unless the house was pulled down there was little chance of finding anyone. That same year Nicholas suffered a bad accident. A horse fell on him, breaking his leg. The leg was set badly and as a result he ever afterwards walked with a pronounced limp.

In 1605 a large party of Catholics made a pilgrimage to St Winifred's Well at Holywell in Wales. The group included Fathers Garnet, Gerard, Oldcorne and Tesimond, and the daughters of Lord Vaux of Harrowden, Anne and her widowed sister, Eleanor Brooksby. The Vaux sisters had made it their life's work to shelter priests, creating safe houses for them supplied with secret hiding places. Anne was devoted to and fiercely protective of Henry Garnet and was his steadfast helper for twenty years. Nicholas Owen travelled with the group. It is said that he took the opportunity to renovate some of his hiding places in the houses they passed or stayed at en route to and from Wales.

Father Garnet was at Coughton Court when he received the news of the failed Plot. Later that month, Garnet, together with

Nicholas, Anne Vaux and her sister Eleanor, set out for Worcestershire and took refuge at Hindlip Hall, a great house about three miles north of Worcester. The home of Thomas and Mary Habington, the house was full of hiding places, secret stairs, trapdoors and chimney breasts with false flues – eleven hiding places in all, constructed by Nicholas. En route they were joined by their fellow Jesuit, Father Edward Oldcorne, who had been the resident chaplain at Hindlip for fifteen years, and his faithful servant, Brother Ralph Ashley.[2] Six quiet weeks passed during which they were unmolested, Garnet spending most of his time in a secret chamber in daily expectation of a raid by the authorities. During this time he wrote a letter to the Privy Council protesting his loyalty to the King and condemning the Plot, in which he had played no part, but accepting that he had somehow been an unwitting accessory to it by giving Communion to those now known to be conspirators.

On 15 January 1606, Fathers Garnet, Tesimond and Gerard were declared traitors and warrants were issued for their arrest. Yet the Privy Council still delayed taking any action. On 20 January Sir Henry Bromley, the local Justice of the Peace and his brother, Sir Edward, finally arrived with a large posse to search the house. Nicholas and Ashley hid in one place and Garnet and Oldcorne in another. The searchers found Catholic literature and 'popish trumpery' but no sign of their quarry. They also found several hiding places and no doubt to their chagrin had to admit they were impressed by the amazing 'cunning art' of the constructions. Thomas Habington was away from home when they arrived, but on his return he flatly denied all knowledge of the Jesuits.

The two Jesuit brothers spent four days hidden without any food other than an apple between them. They could hear the searchers taking turns to patrol the gallery which extended around the house. They waited until they thought the coast was clear, when the searchers were furthest away, and in the silence they stealthily came out from hiding behind the wainscot 'secretly and stilly and shut the place again' so that they were not seen or heard. They made for the door of the gallery, but at that moment the searchers unfortunately turned back and they were caught. At first they tried to bluff their way out of the situation. They claimed to be two men who just happened to be in the house and were about to depart. Admitting when questioned that they were Catholics, they were asked where they had been. They confessed to having hidden themselves in order to avoid being apprehended, but denied all knowledge of other men being hidden.

The searchers thought that they had captured the two priests and Nicholas and Ralph did not disabuse them of their error. That same night Sir Henry Bromley, still believing that he had caught the priests, wrote to Lord Salisbury to inform him that he had never come across such impudent liars as he found at Hindlip: 'all recusants and all resolved to confess nothing, what danger soever they incur'. When Bromley realised that he had not found Garnet and Oldcorne the search was violently renewed, with the raiders rampaging all over the house throughout the weekend.

There are three relatively contemporary descriptions of the raid at Hindlip: an anonymous account written by one of the searchers some months after the event, a letter from Father Garnet and a slightly later version from Father Gerard. Following the interpretation put on his capture in the anonymous account, some authors have asserted that Nicholas voluntarily surrendered, fearing that the two priests in cramped hiding might starve to death. He hoped that if he surrendered the search would be called off. Father Garnet's letter shows that he was also under the impression that this was what had occurred and expressed his regret that the two brothers had come out of hiding so soon. He believed that they could have remained undetected. While not denying that this factor may well have played a part in Nicholas's decision, a careful reading of the accounts indicates that this was not necessarily the case. It seems more likely that Nicholas was attempting to escape, which is borne out by the manner of his emerging from hiding. Furthermore the two priests had marmalade and other provisions and were given hot drinks by means of a special device of Nicholas's: a reed placed through a little hole in the back of the false chimney piece that backed onto a chimney breast in the chamber of either Anne Vaux or Dorothy Habington, sister of Thomas.

The Jacobean Martyrs, 1603–1625

On Monday, 27 January, day twelve of the search, although their hiding place had not been discovered, Garnet and Oldcorne surrendered. They emerged, according to Garnet, 'looking like two ghosts'. They had been forced to crouch in a confined space, unable to stretch their legs, which were very swollen as a result. There were no toilet facilities, either closet or commode. The lack of hygiene and stench in those awful conditions must have been unbearable to someone of Garnet's sensitivities. Bromley had no problem identifying Oldcorne, but was unsure about Garnet until on 30 January a man named Anthony Sherlock, who claimed to be a priest who had now renounced his popery, gave a statement identifying Garnet. Sherlock is a mystery because there is no record of any such priest.

Bromley detained his captives at his home at Holt, just a few miles away, while awaiting instructions from the Council. Salisbury made sure he left them in Bromley's care until after the executions of the eight gunpowder plotters had taken place. This appears to have been a deliberate ploy on Salisbury's part. Under torture, the plotters had exonerated the Jesuits of any involvement in their plans. But that did not suit Salisbury's purpose; with the plotters dead it would be far easier for him to implicate the Jesuits – whom he particularly detested – in the Plot, as there would be no one left able to corroborate their denials that they had been involved. A little embellishing of the truth by Salisbury would not go amiss in order to achieve his ends.

Bromley and his family seem to have been captivated by Garnet's winning personality and the two priests were treated in a friendly manner by the whole household. Bromley declared that never in his life had he met a man like Garnet either for modesty, wisdom or learning. In early February Bromley received orders to bring his prisoners to London. Garnet was ill and still suffering badly with swollen legs, the after-effect of his hiding at Hindlip. He was treated courteously and provided with a good horse, and Bromley, out of consideration for his prisoner, took his time in getting to London.

Arriving on 12 February, Garnet and Oldcorne were sent to the Gatehouse where the Jesuit's nephew, Thomas Garnet, was then also a prisoner. Nicholas Owen was first imprisoned in the

The Jacobean Martyrs, 1603–1625

Marshalsea before being removed to the Tower, to which Garnet and Oldcorne had already been moved. The Council gave orders for Ralph Ashley, Father Oldcorne and Nicholas to be tortured following their incarceration in the Salt Tower. By then the Council had fully realised the value of their little captive and the importance of the information he could disclose. Salisbury wrote,

> It is incredible how great was the joy caused by his arrest... knowing the great skill of Owen in constructing hiding places and the innumerable quantity of dark holes which he had schemed for hiding priests all through England.

Nicholas was first tortured mercilessly on 26 February, during which he uttered nothing but 'Jesus' and 'Mary'. Legally, Nicholas should have been exempt from torture, not only because of his leg injury but also because he was already a sick man, suffering from a serious hernia. This may have been caused by his construction work or have been the result of earlier torture. For the second torture session, his persecutors took the cruel precaution of encasing him tightly in an iron girdle to prevent rupture while he was hung up by the wrists for hours at a time with heavy weights attached to his feet. Under this excruciating torture he admitted nothing except that he had worked for Father Henry Garnet at certain locations, facts already known to the government.

On 2 March 1606 the torture proved too much. A report on his death stated, 'They tortured him with such inhuman ferocity that his stomach burst open and his intestines burst out.' He died in terrible agony. To have literally tortured a prisoner to death reflected badly on the government, to say the least. So to hide their guilt the calumny was wickedly put out that Nicholas had committed suicide by stabbing himself in the stomach. Father Gerard pointed out that Owen's hands were so crippled he could not feed himself, let alone wield a knife – even if he had managed to obtain the weapon.

> This slander was so improbable that even his enemies did not believe it, much less his friends that were so well acquainted with his innocent life and long-continued practice in virtue.

The Jacobean Martyrs, 1603–1625

In his *Narrative of the Gunpowder Plot* Gerard recounts that the jailer had admitted that Nicholas 'died in our hands'. The precise date of Nicholas's death has been questioned because of the emergence of later circumstantial evidence suggesting that it may have taken place on the 12th but the traditional 2 March date seems most likely.

Blessed Ralph Ashley and Blessed Edward Oldcorne were also severely tortured, the latter for up to five hours a day for as many days, so that he could no longer sign his name. They were then returned to Worcester, where they were martyred together on 7 April 1607. Ralph kissed Father Oldcorne, thanking him for all his kindness and he blessed God for granting him such a happy end to his life in such good company.

Both Father Garnet and Father Gerard wrote eulogies on 'Little John'. Gerard paid this tribute to his work for the English mission:

> I verily think no man can be said to have done more good of all those who laboured in the English vineyard... he was the immediate occasion of saving the lives of many hundreds of persons, both ecclesiastical and secular... How many priests then may we think this man did save by his endeavours...

Nicholas Owen may have been a small man but he was great in heart and soul.

Which leaves us with Father Henry Garnet. Protestant imagination turned him into a stereotypical, sinister, scheming Jesuit. Nothing could be further from the truth. Garnet was a devout, gentle scholar, kind-hearted and courteous; violence was abhorrent to him. He was born in Derbyshire in 1555, the son of Brian Garnet, headmaster of Nottingham Free Grammar School. Educated at Winchester, it would be expected that he would progress to Oxford, but as a Catholic this was barred to him. His elder brother had already been expelled from the university because of his Faith. Henry became apprenticed to a legal printer in London before going to Rome, where he entered the novitiate of the Society of Jesus in 1575. In Rome one of his fellow students and close friends was William Weston. After his ordination in 1577, Henry became a professor of philosophy and Hebrew. In company with Robert Southwell he returned to

The Jacobean Martyrs, 1603–1625

England in 1586 and the following year succeeded Weston as the Jesuit Superior. Fearless and indefatigable, he served in that capacity for eighteen years with conspicuous success.

Garnet was not a conspirator. As we have already seen it was he who revealed to the government the Bye Plot, that mad conspiracy involving Father William Watson. Garnet's misfortune was to learn the bare outlines of the Gunpowder Plot from Father Oswald Tesimond SJ, under what he believed to be the seal of the confessional. One of the conspirators had revealed to Tesimond in confession that some violent plan was afoot and the priest had tried to persuade his penitent to abandon the idea. When Tesimond relayed all this to Garnet, he was horrified and tried at second hand to dissuade those involved from proceeding. Faithful to his calling, he was agonisingly unable to divulge what he had heard. 'I could never sleep quietly afterwards,' he said at his trial.

His critics allege that having got wind of the plot under the seal of the confessional he should have found some way of learning about it outside of confession. That is surely easier said than done; he was in a no-win situation. Firstly the conspirators were hardly likely to start voluntarily blabbing about their secret intentions, and secondly he was in no position to raise the matter with any of them, given that the knowledge he had acquired had been imparted in confession, of which he had to maintain the seal. Given the magnitude of the intended crime, one can argue from the moral imperative that this outweighed revealing information gained in confession, and that he should have disclosed what he had learned regardless of the confessional seal; but Garnet did not see it that way. Based on his belief that the seal was so absolute the Church required him to maintain it inviolate, rightly or wrongly he made his conscientious judgement. It was a view that was supported by most of his Catholic contemporaries.

Garnet was interrogated on twenty-three occasions by Cecil and the leading members of the government and judiciary. Filthy lies were spread abroad to impugn Henry's morality. He was especially anguished when they accused him of keeping Anne Vaux as his long-time mistress, and on the scaffold he made a point of praising his helper and stressing the purity of their relationship. He was threatened with torture but maintained his innocence. When tried at the Guildhall for misprision of treason, no real incriminating evidence was produced. There was none. As Father Gerard wrote, the judges were perfectly aware that Garnet was innocent; so the prosecution case, conducted by Sir Edward Coke, had to rest upon lies and prejudice against the Jesuits. It would have been simpler just to indict him with being a priest. That fact was unchallenged, but this did not satisfy the government which wanted a propaganda coup, branding him a traitor by pinning involvement in the Gunpowder Plot on him.

At his execution he protested that he had never approved the Plot, and that the plotters had not acted as true Catholics because the horrible crime that they had intended was contrary to the teaching of the Pope. He was executed in St Paul's Cathedral Churchyard on 3 May 1606, when stands were erected for the spectators who paid for their seats! As a result of the protests of the crowd, he was allowed to hang until he was dead. Eyewitnesses reported that he hung motionless without any sign of struggle. As for what they thought of the affair, no one responded when his heart was held up; there was just discontented muttering. His head, which remained amazingly lifelike for weeks afterwards, was stuck on a pole on London Bridge. There is no doubt that Garnet was seen as a victim and venerated as a true martyr by his contemporaries.

The Church's attitude to him remains a puzzle; she has canonized saints who died rather than break the confessional seal. Furthermore, the fact cannot be avoided that the Church has canonized men who by today's moral judgements may not be regarded by some as 'whiter than white'. For example, the incomparable Thomas More who, for all his luminous qualities of universal greatness, was nonetheless active in prosecuting Protestant heretics. It therefore remains pertinent to ask, why the double standards apparently employed in Garnet's case? His name was included amongst those submitted to Rome as martyrs by the English hierarchy in 1880, but his cause made no further progress. One can only conclude that this was due to timidity in the face of anti-Catholic propaganda; but it has resulted in a great injustice to the memory of a good man who died because of his faithfulness to his priesthood.

Thomas Garnet

Where life was slain and truth was slandered.

> *To F C, in Memoriam Palestine*, Gilbert Keith Chesterton,
> 1874–1936

Thomas was born in Southwark in 1574/75, the son of Richard Garnet who had been a fellow of Balliol College, Oxford, where he had been persecuted for his adherence to the old religion. He had been intended for the priesthood but married. He was in and out of prisons for about forty years and lost all his property. His son, prophetically named after St Thomas Becket, was educated at Horsham Grammar School. His uncle was Father Henry Garnet. Thomas became page to Lord William Howard, one of Philip Howard's half-brothers, before entering the newly opened Jesuit College at Saint-Omer at the age of sixteen.

In 1595 it was decided to send him with several companions to train for the priesthood at the English College, Valladolid. The students were accompanied by the Jesuit, Father William Baldwin. The party set sail for Spain but encountered terrible weather in the Channel and the ship's captain decided to make for shelter in The Downs, the roadstead between Deal on the East Kent coast and the Goodwin Sands. When the weather calmed the vessel was boarded and searched and Thomas and his companions were discovered sheltering in the hold. Father Baldwin pretended to be an Italian merchant who spoke no English but he and the students were placed under arrest and the ship was escorted round The Nore, into the Thames Estuary and up to London, where they were examined by the Lord High Admiral, Lord Howard of Effingham.

Father Baldwin was sent to the Bridewell, but as his real identity could not be established he was eventually released. The students were given into the custody of Archbishop Whitgift of Canterbury at Lambeth, who in turn sent them separately to different Protestant clergy with the object of converting them. Thomas seems to have been confined in the house of Dr Richard Edes, Dean of Worcester and Chaplain to James I, who resided at Oxford. Thomas was taken ill and sent home to recuperate under a bond to return to custody at Oxford on a specified date. But Thomas escaped and had to keep away from his family to avoid causing them further trouble. Taking ship, Thomas returned to Saint-Omer and made the journey to Valladolid, where he finally arrived on 7 March 1596, over a year since he had first set out.

Like so many other English students, Thomas experienced health problems in the Spanish climate. Having only just reached the canonical age, he completed his studies and was ordained priest in 1599. In August of that year, in the company of the future martyr, Father Mark Barkworth, he was sent to England, apparently primarily for the good of his health. Travelling via Hyrache in Navarre, the two priests took ship to La Rochelle, where they had a brush with the Huguenots and the Puritan English merchants who plied their trade there. Finally the opportunity came to cross the Channel. Thomas tells us that having returned he wandered 'from place to place to recover souls which had gone astray and were in error as to the knowledge of the true Catholic Church'. For a time he was chaplain to Ambrose Rookwood at Coldham Hall, Suffolk. On 29 September 1604 Thomas was received into the Society of Jesus by his uncle Henry. He planned to go to Belgium for his novitiate but his plans were thwarted by the Gunpowder Plot.

In the witch-hunt after the Plot in 1605 Thomas was arrested near Warwick under the unfortunately chosen alias of Rookwood. By then it was known to the authorities that Ambrose Rookwood was involved in the Plot. Thomas was imprisoned in the Gatehouse and then in the Tower. Given that he had been staying with Rookwood and that his uncle was Henry Garnet, it was hardly surprising that the Council believed he possessed important information. He was roughly treated and rigorously interrogated by Secretary of State Salisbury, who threatened him with the rack and other tortures. Another ploy was then tried: a letter alleged to have been written by his uncle was handed to him, but Thomas denounced it as a forgery. He could not provide any information because he did not have any to give. He was left in a damp cell in the Tower for eight months with only the bare ground for a bed, which caused him to suffer from back pain for the rest of his life.

In the meantime Henry Garnet and the conspirators had all

The Jacobean Martyrs, 1603–1625

been executed. Ambrose Rookwood, who expressed his repentance for his crime, was executed in Old Palace Yard, Westminster, for his part in the conspiracy on 31 January 1606. Since the authorities were unable to either extract anything incriminating from Thomas or to produce a shred of evidence against him, he was banished by the Council together with forty-six other priests in 1606. On board the ship that was taking them into exile, a royal proclamation was read to them declaring that they faced execution if they ever returned. They were taken across the Channel and set ashore in Flanders.

Thomas made his way to his old college at Saint-Omer and then to Brussels, where he visited his old mentor, the Jesuit Superior, Father Baldwin, who directed him to the newly opened English Jesuit novitiate of St John at Louvain in February 1607. In September he returned to England. Just six weeks later, while ministering in Warwickshire, he was petitioned for by the Catholics of Cornwall, desperate for a priest. Setting off for Cornwall in November 1607, he ran into Anthony Rouse, a priest who had been sent into exile with him. A convert of Father Gerard's, Rouse had been ordained at Douai in 1592. When he returned to England he was imprisoned on a number of occasions between 1593 and 1605, before travelling to Douai after his banishment. Up to that time he had not given any indication that he was untrustworthy, but when he returned to England he apostatised. Rouse betrayed Thomas, who was escorted back to London. There he was first examined by Thomas Ravis, Bishop of London (1607–10) on 17 November 1607. Thomas neither denied nor admitted being a priest, but he was offered the Oath of Allegiance, which he refused. After further examinations by Sir William Waad or Wade, Governor of the Tower, he was sent to Newgate.

He was tried at the Old Bailey, charged with treason under Elizabeth 27, having been ordained priest overseas and defiantly returned from exile. He was offered his life if he would take the oath but again refused. He suggested alternative wording of his own: 'I, Thomas Garnet, sincerely heartily profess that I will pay to my rightful King James all fidelity and obedience due to him by the law of nature and the divine law of the true Church of Christ.'

His offer was treated with derision. Thomas was found guilty and sentenced to death, the judge insisting that he was condemned not for his religion but for refusing allegiance to the King. Thomas answered, 'He who is obedient to his prince is not faithless. The prince issues a command: "If any priest returns to England, let him be slain." I have returned here and I consent to be put to death; thus I give my body to Caesar and my soul to God.'

On 23 June 1608 he was taken to Tyburn, where an immense crowd had assembled, including many noblemen astride their horses or in their coaches. On the scaffold Thomas declared himself 'the happiest man alive this day' and forgave by name everyone who had persecuted him, including Anthony Rouse, the priest who had betrayed him, the Bishop of London who had him imprisoned, Sir William Waad who solicited his death and the Attorney General who had invented so many lies against him. 'May they all attain salvation and with me reach heaven.' He declared that he was a Jesuit priest and explained that he had not admitted this at his trial, as that would have meant he was his own accuser. Thomas was urged to save his life by taking the oath but he remained steadfast. He said the Lord's Prayer and the Hail Mary, and as he was saying the hymn *'Veni Creator Spiritus'* the cart was pulled away. The crowd insisted that he be allowed to hang until they were sure he was dead. Thomas is the protomartyr of Saint-Omer, the first of many martyrs of that college, of which Stonyhurst is the proud successor.

Justice requires that a note be added to the effect that Anthony Rouse deeply repented. He returned to Flanders in 1613 and was hospitably received and absolved by the Jesuits at Louvain, where Father Gerard was then Rector. He wrote a letter addressed to all the Catholics in England expressing his sorrow for what he had done.

John Roberts

Put nothing before the love of Christ.

Rule of St Benedict, Chapter Four

The life of the remarkable Welshman John Roberts is one of the most fascinating and adventurous amongst the martyrs. The eldest of the three sons of John Roberts, he was born in 1575/76 at

The Jacobean Martyrs, 1603–1625

Trawsfynydd. This ancient Welsh-speaking village, on the shores of the lake (*llyn*) of the same name, was then in the county of Merioneth, now in Gwynedd and part of the Snowdonia National Park. Nearby are the remains of a Roman fort and amphitheatre. In more recent times the village was disfigured by the Magnox nuclear power station, now closed down.

Although John's father was a merchant it would appear that his family could claim descent from the princes of North Wales. John stated that his parents were sympathetic to Catholicism but had conformed to protect their property, and John was baptised in the old parish church of St Madryn. Nonetheless he received his first education from an old, presumably Marian, priest. At the age of nineteen he matriculated at St John's College, Oxford, in February 1595/6. St John's was Edmund Campion's old college, and housed many Catholic sympathisers. John left Oxford two years later without taking his degree. Was this because he would not take the Oath of Supremacy? He moved to London and was admitted to Furnivall's Inn, one of the Inns of Court. However, his law career was brief because in 1598, wanting to see something of the world, he secured permission to travel on the Continent.

While in Paris he met an exiled English Catholic gentleman named Mr More, who was in the service of the Cardinal Archbishop of Bordeaux. More (was he related to Thomas More's family?) seems to have been instrumental in bringing about John's conversion. He was received into the Church by Canon Godebert at Notre Dame Cathedral. Various introductions were then given to John, one of whom was Father John Cecil, a relative of Sir Robert Cecil. Ordained at Rome in 1584, Cecil had at one time been a member of Cardinal Allen's household and had been sent by the Cardinal to help in the foundation of the English College at Valladolid. By the time he met John Roberts, Cecil was already working as a secret agent for the English government. Trusted with delivering letters from Father Robert Persons SJ, then the Rector of the English College, Rome, Cecil betrayed him and several priests mentioned in the correspondence. Back in France his superiors began to be suspicious about him, but he continued to enjoy their confidence while continuing to supply the English Government with information. Cecil had a colourful career in Spain, Italy, England and Scotland, but never seems to have formally apostatised.

Advised by Cecil and carrying letters of introduction from him, John decided to enter the English College of St Alban, Valladolid. Travelling via Madrid, John arrived at Valladolid on 15 September 1598. After only a few months he conceived a desire to join the Benedictine Order, but obstacles were put in his way. His Jesuit superiors at the college felt that the cloistered Benedictine way of life was not conducive to missionary work and that by joining the order outstanding young men like him would be lost to England. In the end, John and five other students literally ran away to enter St Benedict's Abbey, Valladolid, where they received the habit. He was then sent to the novitiate at the great abbey of St Martin in the renowned pilgrimage city of Santiago de Compostela, reputed resting place of the relics of the protomartyr of the Apostles, St James. Here he was known as Brother John of Merioneth. At the end of 1600 he was professed and sent to Salamanca, where the Benedictines had a college attached to the famous university. We do not know the date of his ordination but it seems to have taken place at Salamanca in 1602.

Papal permission had recently been given for the English Benedictines in Spain to work on the English mission, and despite suffering ill-health from the climate of Spain and the austerities of his monastic regime, on 26 December 1602 John set out to return to England with a companion, Dom Augustine Bradshaw. Making their way through Northern Spain, they arrived at Bordeaux and from there went to Paris. Here John met Father John Cecil again who, true to form, passed the information of John's return to an English spy; he in turn alerted the government. Although his movements were observed, John safely arrived in April 1603, having paid £3 for his passage across the Channel at night, and was put ashore while the rest of the passengers were asleep. He was the first Benedictine missionary to work in England since the suppression of the monasteries.

John made his way to London. The newcomer made contact with two priests imprisoned in the Clink: Francis Barnaby and Thomas Bluet. They both enjoyed considerable freedom at the Clink, but unknown to John they were 'plants' amongst the many

Catholics in the prison, supplying information to the government and the Bishop of London over many years. It was Barnaby, a malcontent anti-Jesuit agitator, who informed on Fathers William Watson and William Clark and led to their executions after the discovery of the so-called Bye Plot. Bluet ended his days in the service of Bishop Bancroft. A third person, a relative of John's, joined the conversation with the priests at the Clink, and it is conjectured that this was none other than Lewis Owen who was John's brother-in-law. Owen, a Protestant propagandist who later specialised in calumniating Catholics, was married to John's sister, Blanche. For a time he insincerely pretended to be a Catholic. Ironically, it is to Owen that we owe so much detailed knowledge about John Roberts. Owen informs us that John 'became very famous among the English papists and many resorted to him, some of them out of curiosity to see a Benedictine monk once again in England'.

The outcome of the meeting was that John was arrested having been in the country only a short time. However, following King James's arrival in London, John was released into perpetual banishment on 13 May along with a large group of priests, among whom was the venerable, almost blind Jesuit, William Weston.

John arrived at Douai on 24 May but soon returned to England, where the plague was once again raging that summer. Tens of thousands of people died and the coronation had to be postponed. John ministered to the sick and dying with incredible compassion, receiving the plaudits of his contemporaries for his heroic and selfless devotion and the number of those he reconciled to the Church.

He made a special point of actively encouraging young men with potential vocations. One of his most notable converts was William Scott of Chigwell, the future Benedictine martyr Dom Maurus Scott.[3] John's fame spread amongst the Catholics, who wanted to meet him if only for his curiosity value as a Benedictine, and he received many donations towards his work. In February 1604, King James issued a proclamation banishing all priests on pain of death. This coincided with John's attempt to return to Spain to attend the General Chapter of his Congregation. He was taking with him four young postulants, but

The Jacobean Martyrs, 1603–1625

they were all apprehended at the port of embarkation and John was imprisoned. Not knowing he was a priest, the authorities released him after a few months. During the course of 1604 many priests were sent into exile and some sources claim that John was banished with them, but there seems to be no supporting evidence. The claim is surely refuted by the fact that so soon afterwards he was known to be working in London, and in 1606 John himself refers to his 'second' exile, which seems to settle the matter.

Using the alias Richard Browne, John lodged with Master Knight, a lawyer's clerk, at a house in Holborn on the corner of Chancery Lane. We are told of his going out at times gaily apparelled in buff-coloured hose and a black silk doublet slashed with red taffeta and trimmed with silver lace, a sword at his side, something which, when they heard about it, somewhat scandalised his Benedictine brethren safe and secure in their Spanish monastery.

On 5 November 1605, the very day the Gunpowder Plot was 'discovered', John was arrested for the third time. It would appear that the actual owner of Master Knight's house was none other than the abandoned wife of Thomas Percy, one of the conspirators. She earned her living by teaching and she and John were good friends. Mr Justice Grange came to search her apartment for any evidence against Percy and John had the misfortune to return home while this was taking place. He admitted he was a Catholic and was detained by the constables. A great deal of his correspondence was seized in the hope of implicating him in the Plot. Some of the documents may still be read in the Public Records Office. The searchers must have been disappointed to find that they contained nothing of a political nature.

John was consigned by Archbishop Bancroft to close imprisonment in the Gatehouse, where he remained for nearly eight months. A fellow prisoner in the Gatehouse was Thomas Garnet, with whom John was able to regularly communicate in the later stages of his detention. By one of those quirks of fate, another prisoner was the Benedictine, Sigebert Buckley,[4] the last surviving monk of Westminster Abbey who, following the Plot scare, was again arrested and confined in the prison within the precincts of the Abbey. Dom Sigebert was eighty-eight years old and had spent forty years in and out of various prisons. At the end of July 1606 John, cleared of any complicity in the Plot, was released and banished at the instigation of the French Ambassador. Along with forty-six other priests, including Thomas Garnet, he was shipped to Dunkirk.

During his enforced exile of fourteen months, he was very active, visiting Paris, Valladolid, Salamanca, Santiago de Compostela and Douai. John and his companion, Dom Augustine Bradshaw, wished to establish a Benedictine house for the exiled English monks who belonged to Spanish monasteries. As so often with such enterprises, he encountered a great deal of opposition, much of it fuelled by pettiness, jealousy and rivalry. Sad to recall much of this came from the Jesuits who, for reasons best known to themselves, were still trying to discourage the Benedictines from working on the English mission. Thanks largely to the generosity of the abbeys of Flanders and the Abbot of Arras in particular, the house of St Gregory was established at Douai with John as its first prior. The house later became a monastery which is now St Gregory's Abbey, Downside, near Bath.

John returned to England in October 1607. In December he was arrested by a priest catcher close to St Dunstan's in Fleet Street and was sent to the Gatehouse, where he was rigorously examined by the Bishop of London, Thomas Ravis. It is from the extant record of that examination that much of our information about John can be corroborated. Once again his fellow prisoner was Thomas Garnet. John refused to take the oath and was left for some months in prison. But with the help of Francis Miles, a sixteen-year-old convert he had received into the Church during his last sojourn in the prison, he escaped from the Gatehouse prison by cutting through the window bars of his cell and climbing down with a rope.

Miles had spent a year studying with Thomas Garnet while he was in the Gatehouse. John managed to remain at liberty by staying hidden for nearly a year, despite the intense efforts that were being made to recapture him. By May 1609 he had been caught and was again in the Gatehouse, from where he was

The Jacobean Martyrs, 1603–1625

transferred to Newgate in preparation for his execution. He was again saved by the intervention of the French Ambassador and banished for the third time, along with a fellow Benedictine, Mark Broughton, and Francis Miles. The young convert went to Saint-Omer. After John's death he went to the English College, Rome and was ordained by Cardinal St Robert Bellarmine in 1616. He returned to England and worked on the mission, where he joined the Society of Jesus. He died in England in 1650.

While abroad, John again visited Spain and Douai, where he was able to set in motion plans to build a proper monastery for the community of St Gregory. Within a year John had returned to London, where the usual summer plague was raging, and his courageous ministrations were soon in demand. His final arrest, under a warrant from the newly appointed Archbishop Abbot of Canterbury, was on 2 December 1610, when he was taken at a house on the first Sunday of Advent. He had just finished saying Mass in the presence of five other priests when the pursuivants broke in, and they all had to hide in the cellar of the house. Soon discovered, John was carried off, still wearing his vestments, and dragged through the streets to Newgate. On 5 December he was tried in the Justice Hall of Newgate Prison before Sir Edward Coke, the Lord Chief Justice, the Recorder of London, and Dr Abbot, Bishop of London, a bloodthirsty, fanatical persecutor of Catholics. On trial with John was a fellow priest, Thomas Somers,[5] who had been captured by Lewis Owen in the summer, sent into exile and was newly returned.

From the extant accounts of the trial it is clear that John defended himself vigorously, protesting that the Bishop could not be his accuser and judge at the same time, nor should a man who called himself a bishop be sitting with judges in life and death cases. Using the opportunity to bear witness to the Faith, he disputed at length with the Bishop and put the Catholic case convincingly. John strongly objected when the Bishop introduced the subject of the Plot. 'It would be better for you to say not more about the Plot,' he remonstrated, 'as no one knows better than you do how entirely I established my innocence at the time before the Privy Council. So clearly was I justified that they declared me to be a man of good repute, and in liberating me testified that no imputation whatever rested on me.' This the Bishop had to acknowledge.

In the hope of saving the jurymen from having to find them guilty, John and Father Somers acknowledged that they were priests, but refused to take the oath.

'I am bound', John declared, 'by my priesthood to do the duty of a priest, and the reason I have returned to this country is to work for the salvation of souls.' Accused by the Bishop of deceiving the people, John responded, 'I do not deceive but try to lead back to the right path those… whom you have led astray… If I deceive then were our ancestors deceived by St Augustine, the Apostle of the English, who was sent here by the Pope of Rome, St Gregory the Great and who converted this country… the same faith which he professed I now teach. Nay, I am of the same religious order… as St Augustine.'

The Recorder told the jury, 'You have heard that he confesses he is a priest and this is enough for you to find him guilty,' to which John replied, 'If being a priest is equivalent to being a traitor then that would make Christ Himself a traitor.'

There were murmurings of discontent in the court, and John was ordered to be silent. He refused to be silenced. 'I must speak… St Matthew says go teach all nations, baptising them and teaching them to observe all that I have commanded you. I am here to speak in defence of my faith and I demand to be heard.'

The cut and thrust went on but it was of no avail. After a short time the jury returned the guilty verdict.

Three days later on Saturday, 8 December, the priests returned to court to receive their sentence. The Recorder made a violent attack on John, calling him the most dangerous priest in England, who had seduced more people to popery and reconciled more of His Majesty's subjects than any other priest for years. When the death sentence was pronounced, John responded by forgiving his persecutors and promising to pray for them, not only in the time left to him in this life but also after his death.

John was taken back to prison amongst the thieves and murderers. Doña Luisa de Carvajal y Mendoza[6] was a devout Spanish lady who had been living in London since 1605. Doña Luisa regularly visited imprisoned priests and had twice suffered

The Jacobean Martyrs, 1603–1625

imprisonment herself. Her confessor was Father Michael Walpole SJ, brother of Henry. Early in 1610 he was caught and imprisoned, but Doña Luisa persuaded the Spanish Ambassador to intervene and after great difficulty he was released and expelled from the country. On the night before their execution, Doña Luisa bribed the keeper of Newgate to transfer John and Father Somers from the condemned cell into the company of other Catholic prisoners. That evening she provided a dinner for more than twenty prisoners, at which she sat at the head of the table between the two priests. They were waited on by two young Catholic servant women from the prison: Margaret Ashe, a laundress, and Christian Darne. The eyewitness testimony relates that in a symbolic gesture the young women washed John's feet, then those of his fellow priests, several of them future martyrs, including John's convert, Dom Maurus Scott.

'Do you think,' asked John, 'that my feasting in this way may be a cause of disedification? Should I not withdraw myself for prayer?'

Doña Luisa replied, 'No, let them all see with what cheerful courage you are about to die for Christ.'

This episode caused a great stir. King James wrathfully fulminated about the 'idolatrous' goings-on at such length that an official government enquiry was held. Its findings, containing detailed descriptions of all that had taken place at the dinner, can be read in the State Papers. Everyone involved was severely punished. Keeper Houghton and his servant, Reynolds, lost their jobs and Doña Luisa was threatened with banishment; but this was not carried out after the intercession of the Spanish Ambassador.

On 10 December 1610, on a foggy morning, John, along with Thomas Somers and a group of sixteen thieves, was taken to Tyburn to die, before a dense throng. There are several eyewitness accounts of the martyrdom, one of them from a Protestant schoolteacher who stood close by the gallows. He recalled that 'Mr Somers had a sad, settled countenance as in strong meditation… sometimes seen to pray softly, his hands for the most part hid'. Roberts showed 'a most cheerful countenance, almost always smiling'. Untied from the hurdle, the two priests walked up to the gallows and John, who was weak and ill, had to be helped to climb up into the cart. He asked the Protestant ministers to kindly desist from troubling him.

Stretching out his manacled hands, he tried to bless the thieves who were already on the gibbet waiting to be hanged, and urged them to repent and embrace the Catholic Church. He asked the sheriff's permission to speak to the people and this was granted, but as soon as he began the ministers started loudly singing psalms. He asked them to cease as he could not be heard above the noise. He spoke at length explaining again how, as a Benedictine, he simply followed in the footsteps of St Augustine and for that he was to lose his life.

Father Somers was then brought forward and John gave him a helping hand into the cart, greeting him with, 'Welcome, brother and companion in the same glorious triumph.' They embraced and blessed one another with great affection, and they were allowed to exchange a few words secretly, no doubt to impart absolution to each other. As he looked at the fire that was being prepared to burn his entrails, John cheerfully joked, 'I see you prepare a hot breakfast for us in the cold weather.'

A kindly spectator offered him a cap with which to cover his head as he had been standing in the cold so long in just his loose gown. 'Do not trouble yourself, sir,' said John. 'Hereafter I shall never suffer from headache.'

Father Somers then spoke briefly maintaining his loyalty to the King but not in matters of faith. 'Outside the Catholic Church there is no salvation: out of Noah's Ark not one was saved,' he concluded. Suddenly they were simultaneously turned off the cart and left to hang amongst the thieves.

Thanks to the protestations of the crowd they were allowed to hang until they were dead. It was now after noon, and when the barbarities had been carried out on the corpses the severed heads were taken to be displayed on London Bridge. The quartered remains were thrown into a pit near the gallows along with the criminals. Two nights later, a small group of Catholics undertook the ghastly task of retrieving the remains and taking them to the house of Doña Luisa, who had prepared fine linen shrouds to receive them. The relics were taken across the Channel. Portions were given to Valladolid and Santiago de Compostela. The largest relics were kept at St Gregory's at Douai, where they remained until the French Revolution when they disappeared; but Downside Abbey still possesses a finger of Dom John Roberts, as well as a relic of Thomas Somers.

John Almond

> Love is a greater law.
>
> *The Knight's Tale*, *The Canterbury Tales*, Geoffrey Chaucer,
> *c.*1340–1400

John was born into a recusant family at Allerton near Liverpool in 1577, although Bishop Challoner claimed it was ten years earlier. His father had been heavily fined for years for his refusal to conform. John went to school at Much Woolton, but while still a boy was sent to Ireland to be educated. Interestingly, John had an earlier namesake who also died for the Faith. John Almond was a Cistercian monk in the time of Henry VIII. Under Elizabeth he was tried at York for his priesthood and imprisoned in Hull Castle, where he suffered greatly. He went blind and by all accounts became rather senile; yet was treated inhumanely by his keepers. Two Yorkshire Catholic laymen, John Fletcher, a former schoolmaster and Michael Tyrye, a BA of Oxford who had both served over twenty years in prison, performed the charitable task of looking after sick prisoners. They had already cared for Thomas Mudd, an old priest monk of Jervaulx Abbey expelled under Henry VIII, who had died in Hull Castle in 1583. Fletcher and Tyrye also tended Almond as best they could in the appalling conditions. He died in prison on 18 April 1585 of extreme old age. As he came from Cheshire it would be fascinating to know if he was distantly related to our martyr.

There is some dispute amongst sources as to whether or not John studied at the English College, Rheims. There may have been a confusion of identity between him and another priest called Almond, but there can be no dispute that John arrived at the English College, Rome, on 14 April 1597. The College

The Jacobean Martyrs, 1603–1625

records state that he was twenty years old at the time, thus disproving Challoner's dating. John was an outstanding student. On 21 April 1601 he was ordained priest at St John Lateran. He publicly defended his theses, covering the whole course of theology and philosophy, to much acclaim, before two Oratorian cardinals, Francesco Tarugi, nephew of two popes, and Cesare Baronius, the great Church historian. Because of his theological brilliance he was awarded a doctorate in divinity. On 16 September 1602 he left Rome for Douai, from where he departed on 10 November for England.

He worked in London using the aliases of Latham and Molineux. In 1607 we find him visiting George Blackwell in the Clink prison. Blackwell was born in 1547 and educated at Trinity College, Oxford, where he converted. He went to Douai in 1574 and was ordained the following year at Arras. Sent to England in 1576, he was in prison within two years but was released. He then travelled widely, spending some time with the Gerard family in Lancashire. In March 1598 he was appointed the first Superior of the secular clergy in England with the odd title of Archpriest. It was a highly controversial and divisive appointment and some of the clergy refused to accept his authority, appealing to Rome against him. One must feel sympathy for the man trying to cope with an impossible situation, albeit not very successfully. He exercised his authority harshly and censoriously and was described as severe, indiscreet and immodest. After the Gunpowder Plot, Blackwell was one of a group of priests who publicly defended the permissibility of taking the new Oath of Allegiance, in spite of the oath having been condemned by Rome. This put him into conflict with the Jesuits. Blackwell was arrested in June 1607 and imprisoned in the Gatehouse, where he took the oath in July. He was then moved to the Clink, where John Almond is recorded as giving him absolution in August. Blackwell's action was seen as a betrayal. It proved to be the last straw and on 1 February 1608 he was deposed. He remained in the Clink, where he died in January 1612.

John was arrested in February 1608 and imprisoned in the Gatehouse. He was freed sometime in 1609 and worked mainly in Staffordshire for the next few years. He was back in the London

The Jacobean Martyrs, 1603–1625

district in 1611, proving to be an energetic and successful missionary, stiffening the resolve of wavering Catholics and making many converts. He was so highly regarded that the government was determined to capture him. He was arrested again on 22 March 1612. He was described as, 'of stature neither high nor low but indifferent; a body lean either by nature or through ghostly discipline; a face lean; his head blackish brown'.

He was imprisoned at Newgate in appalling conditions. For twenty-four hours he was given nothing to eat or drink, and then only bread and water. Because of his reputation for learning and holiness the Anglican bishops especially wanted to obtain a recantation from him. Archbishop Abbot of Canterbury and Dr King, Bishop of London since 1611, both interrogated John; but while declaring his allegiance to King James, John refused to conform in matters of religion. 'I do bear in my heart and soul so much allegiance to King James (whom I pray God to bless now and evermore) as he or any Christian king could expect by the law of nature, the law of God, or the positive law of the true Church.'

Dr King seems to have had a particular grudge against John and pursued him relentlessly. The record of his examination of John is so puerile and pettifogging that one marvels at how he ever managed to attain his position. To give but one example: the Bishop questioning John about the circumstances of his birth, sarcastically asked him if he could not remember being born in a house. Turning the question back on him, John asked, 'Can you?'

The Bishop replied that his mother had told him so, to which John responded, 'Then you remember not that you were born in a house, but only that your mother told you so; so much I too remember.'

Conditions in Newgate had gone from bad to worse and the priests in custody refused to give their word that they would not try to escape. In November 1612 seven of them did escape and poor John appears to have borne the brunt of King's anger following that event. He was incarcerated in a filthy dungeon, loaded with chains in total darkness and had only the damp ground to lie on. After nine months in prison John was brought to trial, a long and detailed account of which has survived. Almond comes across as courageous and prudent in his own defence. Dr King was one of the judges, and although John never admitted to being a priest and no proof was offered, he was nonetheless condemned for his priesthood. On 5 December 1612 John was dragged to Tyburn. On the scaffold he answered the arguments of the assembled ministers. One of them asked how he, being a priest, could come into the country against the King's laws. John told him, 'Christ is the greater King. Laws made against Christ's laws are not binding. In case I were a priest, which has not been proved, I should have a commission derived from Christ who said, "Go and teach all nations," to come and teach in England.'

John told the crowd of the continuous ill treatment he had endured in Newgate. He threw the remaining coins in his pocket, about three pounds in silver, to the crowd and addressed them. 'One hour overtaketh another and though never so long cometh death. And yet not death; for death is the gate of life for us, whereby we enter into everlasting blessedness. And life is death to those who do not provide for death, for they are tossed and troubled with vexations, miseries and wickedness. To use this life well is the pathway through death to everlasting life.' He asked someone in the crowd to pass him a handkerchief with which to cover his eyes and died bravely with the name of Jesus on his lips.

His corpse was retrieved at night and put in acid at the house of the Spanish Ambassador, Don Diego Sarmiento, Count Gondomar. Later his bones were smuggled to Spain and deposited in a Franciscan convent. Rediscovered in 1912, with full authenticating documentation, they were re-buried by the Count's descendants in the Gondomar chapel. Some of the bones have since been given to Downside Abbey. Dr King is said to have later regretted his treatment of John but Catholic reports showing that he was reconciled to the Church on his deathbed seem to be totally unfounded. King James had been misled by his Archbishop into believing that John Almond was a rough, unlearned man and when he discovered the truth he was angry. Perhaps this was one reason why no other priest was executed for another three years; the longest period of relief since Cuthbert Mayne.

The Jacobean Martyrs, 1603–1625

Notes to Chapter Five

[1] Blessed John Sugar and Blessed Robert Grissold. John was born near Wolverhampton *c.*1558. After studying at Merton College, Oxford, he became a minister in the Anglican Church but in 1599 he went to Douai and was ordained at Tournai in 1601. He returned to England. Robert, a farm labourer who came from Rowington, Warwickshire, became Sugar's faithful servant. Robert's brother, John, was a servant to Father Henry Garnet. In July 1603 John and Robert were arrested on the highway by a cousin of Robert's who was willing to let Robert go but not the priest. Robert chose to stay with John and they were both imprisoned at Warwick. They were tried and condemned but were left in prison for a year. On 16 July 1604 they were summoned for execution. Robert insisted on walking through the mud behind the hurdle dragging John to the gallows saying, 'I have not followed him thus far to leave him now for a little mire.' The executioner was only about eighteen years old, and when he asked for the priest's forgiveness John replied, 'I forgive thee, boy.' Sugar was hanged, drawn and quartered, and before he was hanged Robert declared, 'I die here not for theft, nor for felony, but for my conscience.'

[2] Blessed Edward Oldcorne and Blessed Ralph Ashley. Edward was born at York in 1561, the son of a bricklayer. His whole family were recusants who suffered and died in prisons for their faith. He went to Douai in 1581, moved to Rome in 1582 and was ordained at the Lateran in 1587. In August 1588 he joined the Society of Jesus at the same time as Father John Gerard. He returned to England with Gerard and worked in the Midlands until the discovery of the Gunpowder Plot. Ralph Ashley was a Jesuit brother who had been a baker and servant at Valladolid. He met up with Father Oswald Tesimond in Brussels and in 1598 made the adventurous journey to England with him – vividly described in Tesimond's autobiographical memoir. Ralph became the faithful companion to Father Oldcorne. The two were captured together at Hindlip Hall and were executed for alleged complicity in the Plot at Worcester on 7 April 1607.

[3] Blessed William (Maurus) Scott came from Chigwell, Essex. He was educated at Cambridge and became a Catholic. He went to Spain in 1604 and joined the Benedictines at Sahagun, taking the name of

The Jacobean Martyrs, 1603–1625

Maurus. He returned to England and worked for a year before being arrested and banished. This was repeated a number of times until 1612 when, thanks to the fanatical fury of Archbishop Abbot, he was condemned and hanged, drawn and quartered at Tyburn in the company of a Northamptonshire priest, Blessed Richard Newport.

[4] Dom Sigebert Buckley (1517–1610) is the link between the medieval monastic world and today's English Benedictines. He had been clothed as a monk in 1558 by Abbot Feckenham of Westminster. In 1607 two monks, Sadler and Mayhew, sought out Buckley in the Gatehouse prison where they were professed by Dom Thomas Preston their superior. Dom Sigebert then aggregated them to Westminster and the English Congregation. In 1609 this was ratified by the general chapter of the Congregation and confirmed by Pope Paul V. By 1612 there were seven of these monks, and in 1615 they occupied as their monastery the abandoned church of St Lawrence at Dieulouard in Lorraine. Mayhew became prior of St Lawrence's which, as a result of the French Revolution, is now represented by Ampleforth Abbey in North Yorkshire. Dom Sigebert, by now blind, spent his last years in Hampshire, dying in 1610 at the age of ninety-three, and was secretly buried.

[5] Blessed Thomas Somers was born in Westmorland and became a schoolmaster. He went to Douai in February 1605 and was ordained at Arras in March of that year. He returned to England in June 1606. In 1610 he was arrested and banished but was back in England by October. He was soon arrested again, sent to Newgate and condemned to death.

[6] Doña Luisa de Carvajal y Mendoza (1568–1614) came from a noble Spanish family. She felt especially drawn to England and, much moved by the martyrdom of Henry Walpole in 1596, she decided to learn English. She used her share of the family fortune to found the English Jesuit College at Louvain. This was transferred to Watten near Saint-Omer in 1612. She went to England in 1605 and carried on a charitable ministry, winning converts partly by giving help to poor women and taking care of their children. Arrested in 1608, the intervention of the Spanish Ambassador soon obtained her release. Following the martyrdom of Maurus Scott and Richard Newport, she organised the retrieval of their bodies at night and had them taken to her house. Father Michael Walpole, the future Jesuit Superior,

used Doña Luisa's house as his headquarters and acted as her confessor. It may have been in the hope of capturing Father Walpole that her house was violently raided in 1613 by pursuivants sent by Archbishop Abbot of Canterbury. The priest evaded capture by pretending to be a Spanish servant. Although arrested again, Doña Luisa was released through Spanish influence. The Spanish government was beginning to fear Doña Luisa was becoming a source of friction between their country and England and ordered her to return to Spain. Before she could do so she died in London on 2 January 1614: her 46th birthday. Father Walpole accompanied her body to Spain in 1615 and it is believed he never returned to England.

Chapter Six

Charles I and the Civil War Martyrs, 1625–1649

Adversity is not without comforts and hopes.

Essays, Francis Bacon, 1561–1626

The twenty-five-year-old Charles I, with his elevated and unshakeable belief in the divine right of kings, succeeded to the throne in March 1625. With his humane and cultured outlook and a new Catholic wife, hopes were once more raised of toleration under the new monarch. Two years earlier, in 1623, a most significant event had occurred when seventy-year-old William Bishop[1] was ordained at Paris in June to serve in England as Vicar Apostolic, the first Catholic Bishop since the deposition of the hierarchy by Elizabeth. He was given the titular title of Chalcedon. He landed at Dover and despite his age walked in stages to London. At the time Prince Charles was in Spain, hoping to win the hand of the infanta, so there was a breathing space of toleration while the delicate negotiations were taking place. Bishop set up a Chapter of twenty-four canons headed by a dean and divided the country into archdeaconries. The Chapter was to be source of much division and controversy for years to come. Bishop spent the summer travelling around administering confirmation, but by April 1624 he was dead. His successor, Richard Smith,[2] was ordained bishop at Paris in January 1625 and arrived in England one month after Charles's accession. Opposition, both from the government and from within his own flock, led to his retirement to France in 1631, although he never relinquished his authority until his death. His lasting legacy was his 'Chalcedon' catalogue of the English martyrs. The forerunner of all later works, it was based upon prison and court records that disappeared long ago. England had to wait thirty years before it received another bishop under Charles's younger son, James II.

Charles I and the Civil War Martyrs, 1625–1649

The early years of Charles's reign were a time of relative peace for Catholics, and the numbers of priests steadily increased. Many in the Established Church began to regret the executions. Charles certainly found the idea of executing people for their religion abhorrent, but he had to tread cautiously. Although he had made promises at the time of his marriage to Henrietta Maria of France to repeal the most oppressive penal laws, Parliament had forced him to break his word. But Charles tried to circumvent the continued persecution of Catholics by Parliament. He did his best in his own dithering way to reprieve priests, often at the request of the Queen, whom he came to love deeply. She was a great benefactor of Douai College, as well as being the god-daughter of Pope Urban VIII.

The Queen had her own public chapel at Court served by several chaplains. Such open practice of Catholicism outraged the Protestants, who saw it as thinly disguised proselytising. There were a significant number of conversions by prominent figures of the reign, although Charles made known his disapproval. At Somerset House in 1632 Henrietta Maria had built a splendid chapel staffed by a small community of resident French Capuchin Franciscans. They maintained a full round of daily services from 6 a.m. to compline. The Catholics of the capital flocked to the chapel, where they knew they would be able to worship in security. On the occasions when the morally chaste, music and art-loving Charles visited his wife at Somerset House, he would inspect the chapel and once joined her and the company of Capuchins in their simple supper. It infuriated the Puritans. Their fanaticism blinded them to the fact that this was nothing more than a reflection of the King's innate courtesy towards the priests, whose cultivated conversation he appreciated. Such socialising may have been unwise and indiscreet but because Charles did not share the popular prejudices of many of his subjects, he fatally did not understand them or make allowances for them.

Catholics were able to readily frequent the chapels at the Catholic embassies in London, which they did in large numbers. Mary Ward, a Yorkshire woman born near Ripon in 1585 into a Catholic family, was educated by a Jesuit priest. A woman of vision, in 1609 she established a religious congregation on the

Continent modelled upon the Jesuits, with whose order she hoped to amalgamate. This being denied her, she returned to England in 1639 and, defying the prejudices of the time, she courageously organised a community of unenclosed sisters in London. Their work concentrated on the education of girls; Mary's ideas about the role of women were centuries in advance of her time and came in for much criticism. Mary died in 1645. Known as the English Ladies or later the Institute of the Blessed Virgin Mary, today Mary's foundation is called the Congregation of Jesus and still flourishes at the famous Bar Convent at York.

Papal agents were received at Court, ostensibly as envoys to the Queen. First was the Italian Father Gregorio Panzani in 1634, whose commission was to investigate the state of English Catholicism. He was followed from 1636 to 1639 by Father George Conn, a Canon of St John Lateran and, like the Queen's confessor, Dom Robert Philip OSB, a charming Scotsman whose company Charles particularly enjoyed. He was succeeded by the youthful Count de Rossetti who was expelled by order of Parliament. The Pope sent gifts to the King to add to his already impressive art collection, but it did not stop Charles from using his influence to get Rome to quash all attempts to inaugurate proceedings for the canonization of Father Henry Garnet as a martyr.

Charles, a sincerely religious King, was far from being Catholic; indeed, he achieved the nearest thing to unofficial canonization in the Church of England for his faithfulness to the Church of which he was Supreme Governor. The first monarch to be raised as a member of the Church of England, it was perhaps this certitude about his own Church that enabled him to be more tolerant of Catholicism. So sure was he of his position that when his Scottish subjects rejected all attempts to impose the Church of England Prayer Book on them he took up arms in 1639 and marched towards Scotland, with the aim of forcing the Anglican liturgy on them. He demanded that his Catholic subjects heavily contribute to the cost of the expedition with men and money. His forces were defeated and Charles had to make concessions to the Scots. As we know with hindsight, this ill-conceived venture was the start of his undoing and ultimately cost him his life.

In his liturgical tastes, Charles was what today would be described as High Church. He personally accepted many of the Catholic Church's doctrines and reverenced the Virgin Mary and the saints. In York he had restored the shrine of St William at the Minster. Like many Anglicans then and in later times, he called himself a Catholic, but that did not mean embracing the papacy; although he regretted the break with Rome and wished that more time could be spent in working towards reunion than in acrimonious controversy. The problem was that Charles was surrounded by those who shared his religious views, but they were in a minority.

It was all grist to the mill for his Puritan opponents who, in their ignorance, viewed the King's position as pseudo papistry. He was supported (or was it the other way around?) by his Archbishop of Canterbury, William Laud (1573–1645), who also eventually paid for his convictions with his life. Laud, who used all his authority to try and enforce his doctrinal and liturgical ideas, seems to have genuinely sought better relations with Rome. If the Civil War had not erupted, how different could the history of the Catholic Church in England have been? The question will remain one of those tantalising 'might have beens' of history.

By 1628 Parliament demanded that the King rigorously enforce the penal laws and an act came into force forbidding anyone to send their children abroad for a Catholic education. This was the only year in which Catholics were put to death. These were the Jesuit Edmund Arrowsmith and Richard Herst, a layman. After their condemnations, the executions were deliberately carried out with all speed to ensure that the royal reprieve would arrive too late. During the years of the King's personal rule without a Parliament from 1629 to 1640 there was an extended period of toleration. The penal laws remained in force, but although priests were condemned to death by the courts, thanks to Charles and his wife they were not executed. All that being said, we must not paint too rosy a picture. Catholics were made to pay – literally – for their comparative toleration, and were frequently reminded that the favour of toleration they were enjoying was merely toleration, not approval. There was no change in policy, and Catholics remained subject to iniquitous fines for their recusancy.

Charles I and the Civil War Martyrs, 1625–1649

Charles hit upon the idea of selling licences, allowing the practice of their religion to those Catholics wealthy enough to be able to afford them. An instance of this is the licence granted to the ancient Chichester family at Arlington Court, Devon, who maintained a domestic chapel. The fact was that this revenue had become an integral and indispensable source of government income, much as alcohol and petrol duty are today. Charles had inherited enormous debts from his profligate father, so the Catholics were squeezed even harder. The King was no doubt most gratified to find that his efficient finance minister had exacted a fivefold increase in recusant revenue.

The Long Parliament, which met in November 1640, was dominated by Puritan fanatics hell-bent not only on punishing Catholics but also on ridding the Church of England of its bishops and imposing Calvinism. Persecution was renewed and a proclamation was issued banishing all priests from the realm under pain of death. Charles continued to try and protect priests and the plight of Father John Goodman in 1641 became a test case in the struggle between the King and Parliament. Goodman, a Welshman who happened to be first cousin to Godfrey Goodman, Bishop of Gloucester, was a convert Anglican minister. He had worked on the English mission since 1631 and had been imprisoned several times. He was finally condemned to death at the Old Bailey; but a few days later his reprieve by Charles at the Queen's request caused ferocious protests. Parliament petitioned the King for the execution to be carried out, sending unedifying delegations to meet Charles in order to vilify Catholics in general and demand Goodman's death. There was a bitter battle between the two parties and rather than be a cause of strife Father Goodman volunteered to submit to execution. The priest's courageous offer impressed the House of Lords and caused a split between the Lords and Commons – of which Charles took advantage. He would not give way, even when the City of London refused him a loan to enable him to pay his army. Father Goodman remained a prisoner in Newgate, where he died in 1645.

Soon the King was embroiled in another tussle with his Parliament involving priests. Father Cuthbert Clapton was a chaplain and interpreter serving the Venetian Ambassador. On July 3, while walking in the City of London, Clapton was accosted by Francis Carpenter, who had once been a fellow student at the English College, Rome. He hauled Clapton before the local Justice of the Peace, accusing him of being a priest, whereupon Cuthbert was committed to Newgate. On 23 July he and Father William Ward were indicted at the Old Bailey before the Recorder of London for their priesthood, which they did not admit, insisting that it was the Court's job to prove it; furthermore, as the servant of a foreign ambassador Clapton claimed immunity. False testimony was given against Cuthbert by the pursuivant James Wadsworth and against Father Ward by Wadsworth's colleague, Thomas Mayo, both of whom we shall meet again. The two priests were found guilty and condemned to death.

The Venetian Ambassador appealed to the King, who apologised for the infringement of diplomatic privilege and instructed that the priest should be reprieved and released. The King's wishes continued to be ignored for several days, and as Charles was about to leave for Scotland the desperate Ambassador had a personal interview with him, when he expressed his anger that his instructions were being thwarted. Only after the King had exerted all his authority with both Houses of Parliament was Father Clapton finally released – on condition that he was sent abroad, where he died in 1644.

The eighty-year-old Blessed William Ward, whose real name was Webster, was not so fortunate. Born in Westmorland, he had served in England for thirty-three years, twenty of which he had spent in various prisons. He was arrested at midnight on 15 July by the priest hunter Thomas Mayo, acting on a warrant from the Speaker of the House of Commons. Condemned with Clapton on 26 July, he was hanged, drawn and quartered at Tyburn, the first priest to be executed for thirteen years; the first of many victims of the Long Parliament.

The numerical strength of Catholics at this time is difficult to quantify, but what figures are available suggest that in the counties of Lancashire and Durham and in South Wales Catholics could have made up approximately twenty per cent of the population. In Northumberland and Yorkshire the proportion was slightly less, whereas the great majority of the inhabitants of London were Protestant.

When the King left London at the outbreak of the Civil War, nothing could save the priests who were apprehended, and in a six-year period from 1641 to 1646 over twenty-two priests and laymen were executed by Parliament and nine priests died in prison. Just how limited the King's powers had become is illustrated by the case of two priests from the North Riding of Yorkshire: eighty-one-year-old Blessed John Lockwood and thirty-seven-year-old Blessed Edmund Catterick or Catherick. Lockwood had studied in Rome and was ordained there in 1597. He returned to England in 1598 and ministered there for forty-four years on the mission. He was imprisoned at least twice, once in 1610 when he was in Newgate and was condemned to death. His final arrest was at Thirsk, where he had lived for several years. Catterick was educated at Douai and ordained in 1630. He returned to England in 1634 to work in Yorkshire. Both priests were martyred at York on 13 April 1642 while the King was in residence in the city and had been prevailed upon to sign the death warrants. The execution went ahead despite Charles's protests at the barbarity. To show contempt for the King's authority, Lockwood's head was impaled on the North Gate at Bootham Bar, close to Charles's house so that he couldn't avoid seeing it.

Not surprisingly, during the Civil War the Catholics staunchly supported the Royalist cause. Whether or not Charles was entirely deserving of such wholehearted support is debatable. Their numbers should not be exaggerated, but without the Catholic gentry the King would not have had officers of calibre experienced in warfare on the Continent, or been able to raise enough troops to form an effective army. This included priests who served as army chaplains, some of whom were killed or maimed in the conflicts, such as the West Yorkshireman Father Francis Pavier, who was killed while attending the wounded at the Battle of Marston Moor in July 1644. Catholics flocked to the royal standard, especially in Yorkshire and the rest of the North, and contributed huge sums to the war effort. It was probably a case of 'better the devil you know', because for certain the Puritan

Charles I and the Civil War Martyrs, 1625–1649

alternative was too ghastly for them to contemplate.

It all backfired on the King, who was accused by his opponents of raising a papist army against the God-fearing Protestants. A taste of things to come was experienced in 1645 when Parliament ordered that two-thirds of all the property of papists was to be seized just because they were papists. It was a licence to plunder, and no one was spared the depredations, from the aristocracy to the humblest labourer.

In 1648 Parliament approved 'Articles of Christian Religion' in which Catholic doctrine, especially the Mass, was ridiculed and condemned and the Pope was described as the Antichrist. It was an additional sharp thorn in the crown they already had to bear when the Catholics found themselves on the losing side at the end of the Civil War. Charles was beheaded in Whitehall on 30 January 1649. As Parliament had already abolished the Anglican *Book of Common Prayer*, no prayers were permitted to be said at his burial. With his passing the Catholics were once more plunged into despair.

Edmund Arrowsmith

My loss may shine yet goodlier than your gain, when time and God give judgement.

Marino Faliero, Algernon Swinburne, 1837–1909

Edmund, the son of Robert and Margery Arrowsmith, was born at Haydock, near St Helens, Lancashire, in 1585. His father, born in 1559, was a yeoman farmer. He married Margery Gerard in 1584. Born in 1563, the daughter of Nicholas Gerard, she came from the same family as Father John Gerard of Bryn, just north of Haydock. The Arrowsmiths were also a well-known Catholic family. Edmund's grandfather died in prison for his faith. Robert and Margery's first child was baptised Brian but took the name Edmund, by which he wished to be known, at his confirmation. Being recusants who sheltered priests, his parents suffered a great deal of persecution because of their religion. Once, while still a small child, Edmund was left shivering in his nightshirt with his three younger siblings when the pursuivants took his parents and their servants off in the middle of the night to Lancaster jail. The children were taken in by kindly neighbours. Edmund had an earlier Lancashire namesake who was probably his uncle. The first Edmund was born in 1563 and was ordained priest at Rheims in 1587. He did not enjoy good health and never returned to England, but taught at Douai and Rheims until his death in 1601.

It is thought that Edmund attended the grammar school at Senely Green. His father having died while he was still a boy, Edmund's education was entrusted to an old priest. Obviously a pious child, Edmund is said to have often recited the Jesus Psalter or Our Lady's Office on his journey to and from his lessons. At the age of twenty, Edmund crossed the Channel and entered the English College, Douai, but his studies were dogged by ill health. He was ordained at Arras on 9 December 1612, and the following year he returned to his native Lancashire. There, under the aliases of Bradshaw and Rigby, he became famous for his fearless and forthright mission. Reportedly small and unprepossessing in appearance, a contemporary recalled him as being 'zealous, witty and fervent and so forward in disputing with heretics that I often wished him merrily to carry salt in his pocket to season his actions'. He was described as a man 'of great innocency in his life, of great sincerity in his nature, of great sweetness in his conversation and of great industry in his function. And he was ever of a cheerful countenance'.

In 1622 he was arrested and brought before Dr John Bridgeman, Bishop of Chester, who was at supper with some of his clergy. Edmund had a lively theological dispute with them, in which he was reported to have got the better of the argument. He was soon freed on the orders of King James. The King was anxious to promote a Spanish marriage for his son and needed to create a favourable impression, so he ordered all priests then in custody to be released. In 1623 the General of the Society of Jesus erected England into a Province, with Oxford-educated Father Richard Blount[3] as Provincial. He organised its members into colleges covering different areas of the country. In 1624, after making the Spiritual Exercises, Edmund joined the Society and made a long retreat in Essex. He went to London to undertake a

Charles I and the Civil War Martyrs, 1625–1649

short novitiate at the secret Jesuit house at Clerkenwell rented from the Earl of Shrewsbury. Unfortunately, it was not secret enough, for in 1628 it was raided and destroyed, but at least none of the priests present lost their lives. The Attorney General and future Lord Chief Justice, Sir Robert Heath (1575–1649), released them on bail and was censured by Parliament for doing so, but he was acting on the direct instructions of King Charles.

Charles I had succeeded his father while Edmund was carrying on his ministry in Lancashire. In 1628 Edmund was in the neighbourhood of Brindle, when he had occasion to severely reprove a young Catholic man called Mr Holden. He was the son of the landlord of the Blue Anchor inn, Hoghton. Edmund often used the old, half-timbered inn as a secret refuge. Mr Holden had married his Protestant first cousin before a Protestant minister and the couple were now living at the inn. Edmund was in the process of obtaining a dispensation for them to be validly married and suggested that they separate until the marriage ceremony. Resentful of Edmund's reprimand, Holden betrayed him to a Justice of the Peace, informing him that Edmund was likely to be at the Blue Anchor.

The JP, Captain Rawsthorne, unwilling to cause problems for the landlord, sent a message to warn him of the imminent search, urging him to get the priest to leave quickly. So Edmund packed up hastily and left the house on horseback. He made his dramatic escape through the lanes and fields of Brindle, but the Captain's young son and one of his servants caught up with him. Edmund's horse refused to jump the Moss Ditch, so he dismounted and ran along the course of the ditch hoping to find a narrower place, but was overtaken and apprehended. He was escorted to the Boar's Head inn in Hoghton Lane. What follows is taken from Edmund's own account of his arrest given at his trial.

> As I was upon the road that very man... rushed out upon me with a drawn sword. He was meanly dressed and on horseback. I made what haste I could from him, but being weak and sickly I was forced by him at last to the Moss where I dismounted and fled with all the speed I was able, which was not very great seeing I was loaded with heavy clothes, books and other things. At length he came up to me at the Moss Ditch and struck at me, though I

had nothing to defend myself with but a little walking stick and a sword which I did not draw. With a blow he cut the stick close to my hand and did me some little hurt. I then asked him if his design was to take my purse and my life. He answered that perhaps it was; upon which I fled from him but was soon overtaken. Then up came this youth... and others to assist him. They used me with much indignity and took me to an alehouse, and searched me to the skin, offering indignities which modesty forbids me to relate and which I resisted as far as I was able. That done they fell to drinking and spent nine shillings of my money in an hour; they told me that the Justice of the Peace, by whose warrant I was apprehended, was there in person, but that I would not believe. Upon this occasion I began to find fault with this man's wicked and rude behaviour, who seemed to be the ringleader and I besought him for Jesus' sake to give over his disordered life, drinking, dissolute talk and whatever might offend Almighty God.

Edmund was imprisoned in Lancaster Castle, where he continued to expound the Gospel to his fellow prisoners. Indicted for being a priest and a Jesuit on 26 August, he was sent for trial at the assizes before the rabidly anti-Catholic former Attorney General, Sir Henry Yelverton. The trial coincided with Parliament's order for the stricter application of the penal laws. Wasting no time, Yelverton immediately demanded of Edmund, 'Are you a priest?'

It was no part of Edmund's role to act as his own prosecution; it was up to the court to prove his guilt as charged, so he answered equivocally, 'I would to God I were worthy.'

After trying a number of times to lead Edmund into an incriminating admission, Yelverton then changed tack by asking if he was not a priest, to which Edmund made no answer. Incensed, Yelverton launched into an attack on the prisoner. At this point a clergyman called Leigh, who was sitting as a Justice of the Peace, joined in the attack, accusing Edmund of seducing the people to popery. Edmund requested a public debate in which he would be allowed to defend his faith. This was refused, and Edmund responded that he was prepared to defend his religion not only with words but with his blood.

'You shall seal it with your blood,' retorted Yelverton. 'I will not leave this town before you see your bowels burned before your face.' He repeated this and similar threats several times.

'And you, my Lord, must die,' said Edmund.

He was ordered to answer directly how he justified going overseas to be ordained in defiance of the law.

'If any man can lawfully accuse me, I stand ready here to answer him,' replied Arrowsmith, knowing full well that they did not have sufficient evidence against him.

Apart from the accusation of Mr Holden, the only witnesses they could produce were the youth and the servant who had apprehended him. They swore that Edmund had tried to convert them. It was at this point that Edmund asked leave to give his account of his arrest as quoted above, which he concluded thus: 'Upon my word and upon my life this, or to this effect, is all I said to him. Let him look on me and gainsay it if he can. As for that youth I deny not to have told him that I hoped when he came to riper years, he would look better into himself and become a true Catholic, for that and that alone, would be the means to save his soul: to which he made no answer at all. And I hope, my Lords, that neither they, nor any other can prove ill against me.'

This produced further invective from Yelverton, who told the jury that they should show no favour to Edmund. This made Arrowsmith smile, at which he was reproved for being a saucy fellow who had no better manners than to laugh at those who sat there in judgement for the King. On his knees Edmund begged them not to have such an opinion of him and prayed for the King and his judges, asking God in His mercy to confound heresy.

'Gentlemen of the jury', Yelverton said, 'look you how he wishes God to confound us all and root out heresy, by which he means our religion.' He then proceeded to harangue the jury to find the prisoner guilty.

Despite the lack of any real evidence it did not take the jury long to find Edmund guilty of being a priest. When the dreadful sentence was passed he dropped to his knees, made the sign of the Cross, said simply, '*Deo gratias*,' and repeated it in English; 'Thanks be to God.'

The jailer was ordered by Yelverton to treat the condemned man harshly. Edmund spent two days without food, loaded with heavy chains in a dark hole in which he could neither stand upright nor lie down but only sit crouching. The jailer provided him with a little pillow to put behind his back. No one was allowed to communicate with him except a Protestant minister, who pestered him. The pending execution became a matter of public controversy. The townspeople of Lancaster were sure that the King would reprieve Edmund. At first no one could be found willing to carry out the execution, not even the prisoners in the jail. The gruesome task fell to an army deserter under sentence of death. This man was offered his liberty, a payment of forty shillings and the prisoner's belongings.

On 28 August 1628 Edmund was told he was to die that midday. 'I beseech my Redeemer to make me worthy of it,' he exclaimed.

A large crowd had assembled as Edmund was led out to die. As he crossed the castle yard he raised his hand. This was a pre-arranged signal to a fellow priest and prisoner, John Southworth, who from his cell window above gave him absolution. Fastened to a hurdle, Edmund was dragged through the streets to the gallows. When he arrived at the scaffold he found Mr Leigh the vicar-cum-JP, who pointed out to him the boiling cauldron. 'Look you what is provided for your death,' was his callous greeting. 'Will you conform and lay hold of the King's mercy?'

Patiently, Edmund answered, 'Good sir, tempt me no more. The mercy I look for is in heaven through the death and passion of my Saviour, Jesus Christ; and I humbly beg Him to make me worthy of this death.'

He knelt and prayed, all the while plagued by the Protestant ministers, whose interruptions he tried to ignore. The sheriff told him to make haste and so he rose with the words, 'God's holy will be done,' kissing the ladder as he climbed up resolutely. He prayed for the King and freely forgave all his persecutors. Standing on the ladder he addressed the crowd.

'Bear witness… that I die a constant Roman Catholic; and for Jesus Christ His sake, let not my death be a hindrance to your well doing and going forward in the Catholic religion, but rather may it encourage you thereto. For Jesus' have a care of your souls, than which nothing is more precious; and become members of the true Church, as you tender your salvation; for hereafter that alone will do you good… nothing grieves me so much as this

England, which I pray God soon to convert.'

He then drew his cap over his eyes in readiness, but the persistent Mr Leigh made one more attempt to shake him, urging him to take the Oath of Allegiance and his life would be spared. 'You may live,' he cried, 'if you conform to the Protestant religion!'

Wearily, Edmund replied, 'Tempt me no more. I am a dying man. I will do it on no condition,' at which some of the ministers called out, 'Away with him!'

Covering his eyes again he was heard to say, *'Bone Jesus,'* as he was thrown off the ladder. He was permitted to hang until he was dead before the rest of the sentence was carried out. His head and four quarters were displayed on Lancaster Castle. The next day they executed Blessed Richard Herst or Hurst,[4] a young layman from near Preston on a trumped up charge of murder.

Edmund's right hand was rescued and today rests in a silver casket at the church of St Oswald, Ashton-in-Makerfield, close to Haydock where he was born. The 'Holy Hand' has been an object of continuous veneration and many miraculous cures have been attributed to Edmund's intercession through his relic.

Ambrose Barlow

> A holy-minded man of good renown... Christ's law he taught, but first he followed it himself.
>
> *The Parson, Canterbury Tales*, Geoffrey Chaucer, *c.*1340–1400

We are fortunate in possessing a good deal of contemporary biographical information about Ambrose. Bishop Challoner used manuscripts from St Gregory's Monastery, Douai, as his source, including one written by Ambrose's brother in 1642. Another manuscript entitled *The Apostolical Life of Ambrose Barlow* was written by an anonymous friend in the form of a letter to the martyr's brother. Ambrose was born at Barlow Hall, Chorlton-cum-Hardy, near Manchester, in November 1585. His pedigree was long and impressive; he was the fourth son of Alexander Barlow and Mary Brereton, daughter of Sir Urian Brereton of

Handforth Hall, Cheshire, by his second wife, Alice Trafford, daughter of Sir Edmund Trafford. Alexander and Mary had fourteen children: eight boys and six girls. The Barlows were a very ancient family who took their name from the place of their abode. Their history probably stretched back to Saxon times and they were recorded as living at Barlow as far back as the early thirteenth century, when the original hall was built near the River Mersey by Roger de Barlow in the reign of Edward I. They rose to prominence over the years and were related to every gentry family of note in Lancashire and Cheshire. The Hall in which our martyr was born had been rebuilt *c.*1574 by Alexander Barlow senior. He was Member of Parliament for Wigan several times but, as a Catholic, did not sit again after Elizabeth's accession. In 1583 the pursuivants raided the Hall in search of priests. None were found, but Alexander was arrested and sent to Salford jail, where he died in 1584.

His son, Alexander Barlow junior, along with his eldest son, a third Alexander, was knighted in the coronation honours of James I in 1603. In spite of the honour, Sir Alexander suffered grievously for his faith, being made to pay extortionate fines for the recusancy of himself, his wife and many children. He eventually fell foul of the law, enabling the King to refuse the monthly fines and take instead two-thirds of his estate. In 1609 the 'benefit' of his estate was bestowed on two of the King's favourites. When Alexander died in 1620 he asked to be buried with his ancestors in Didsbury Church, but was instead buried at night, probably without any service, in what is now Manchester Cathedral. As we have already noted, the persecution extended to the dead, and it was not unusual for a recusant to be so treated.

In order to comply with the law, Alexander and Mary presented their son for baptism in the fourteenth-century St James's Parish Church, Didsbury, on 30 November 1585. He was given the name Edward. The entry in the baptismal register is still to be seen. It is certain that as staunch Catholics they would first have had him privately baptised by a priest. The Barlows were closely related to the ancient Legh family; Elizabeth Legh was his paternal grandmother. Where Edward attended school is unknown, but at twelve years of age he was sent to Cheshire as page to his relative, Sir Urian Legh. Although it was customary for sons of the gentry to serve their apprenticeship in the homes of a nobleman, it seems an odd choice in Edward's case because Sir Urian was a Protestant. It seems that in this environment the young Edward conformed. The *Life* informs us that he was reclaimed through the influence of the widowed Lady Margaret Davenport, a neighbour of the Barlow family.

Edward's elder brother, William, had been educated at Douai and had joined St Gregory's Monastery, where he was ordained in 1608 taking the name Rudesind. He became famous as a scholar and canonist and served as prior of St Gregory's from 1614 to 1621, when he became President of the English Benedictine Congregation until 1629. He died in 1656 aged seventy-two. A younger brother, Robert, was also to enter St Gregory's where he was professed in 1630, dying in England a few years later.

At the age of twenty-three Edward left for the English College, Douai. He made good progress and was sent to the English College, Valladolid, where he arrived on 20 September 1610. After two years he returned to Douai, partly for reasons of ill health, but also it seems because he wanted to follow his brother and join the Benedictines. However, instead of remaining at Douai he was sent to the English Benedictine house at St Malo for his novitiate. He took the name of Ambrose, by which we shall henceforth call him. He did not stay long at St Malo but returned to St Gregory's, Douai, maybe because his brother, Dom Rudesind, had by then become Prior. On 5 January 1615 he made his solemn vows as a monk. Dom Ambrose was ordained priest in 1617 and shortly afterwards returned to work in England under the aliases of Brereton and Radcliffe.

His first call was at Barlow Hall to visit his family and no doubt he often went back to see his parents while they were alive. Evidently the ill health he suffered was the onset of consumption, because shortly after returning home he consulted a doctor about it. The doctor's advice was that he should drink new milk in the morning and eat a roasted apple at night. The advice must have been effective because Ambrose spent the next twenty-four years as a missionary in a relatively small geographical area, working around Manchester and south Lancashire. His life was orderly, dividing his time between spending one week touring the area and three weeks at home at his base. This was usually Morleys Hall, Astley, in the parish of Leigh. About seven miles from Manchester, the Hall was the home of the Tyldesleys, a notoriously recusant family. Sir Thomas Tyldesley later became a Major General in the Royalist army. Ambrose's other regular base was at Wardley Hall, Worsley, the seat of the Downes family, who were his cousins. Ambrose's annual allowance was £8, which was paid from a pension left by Elizabeth Tyldesley for this purpose. He gave back £6 of the allowance for his board and lodging, even though he was away from his base for long periods.

He travelled a great deal, always on foot with a long countryman's staff on his back and often said Mass in several different places on the same day. In the circumstances in which he and other priests ministered this was not an unusual practice. No matter how busy he was, he never neglected his own prayer and meditation. He always had a servant to tend him on his journeys. They were all volunteers who were expected to pay for their own food and for that reason they mostly served for only short periods. Ambrose would present each of them with enough cloth to make a suit. He was noted for his humility, kindness, good humour, wit and patience. He could be strict with his penitents, reproving those Catholics who failed to give a good example; but never as strict as he was with himself. He criticised those among the Catholic gentry who were fearful of being seen to attend Mass, saying he did not like those who were simply 'peeping at God'. He would deflect slanders and insults – and he had to suffer plenty of them – with a joke. He had a hearty laugh and was described in the *Life* as 'so witty and cheerful in his conversation that of all men I ever knew he seemed most to represent the spirit of Thomas More'. He never allowed anything to rob him of his cheerfulness.

The poor, towards whom he showed great love, were always his first concern and his house was a refuge for them. Unlike other people, who could be condescending, he never stood on ceremony with the poor but gave a priestly example in the simple and frugal manner of his life. His outmoded grey clothes attracted attention for their plainness:

> ...the fashion thereof for the oldness might be the same that was in use when he first did leave or return into England; a long wasted jerkin and doublet, his breeches tied above the knees. The best hat that I ever saw him wear I would not have given him two groats for; the band about his neck of the country folks fashion, as poor as one is ordinary worn by any... as I remember no cuffs at all. Instead of pantofles, a pair of scurvy old slip-shoes which he continually wore indoors.

The *Life* tells us that Ambrose was careless of his beard, which he never bothered to trim or shave but let it grow as nature intended. He had naturally short curly hair, chestnut in colour. The writer of the *Life* was clearly something of an amateur artist and he painted a picture of Christ crowned with thorns for the altar. Ambrose asked him to teach him how to paint and he turned out to be an apt pupil.

Ambrose never drank wine and when asked why he abstained he replied, 'Wine and women make the wise apostatise.' Although personally austere and abstemious he was a good host. At Christmas, Easter and Pentecost he held 'open house' for all. At Christmas there would be boiled beef and pottage, goose and mince pies. Ambrose would serve his guests, and when everyone had eaten enough he would make a meal out of the leftovers; then, if anything remained, he would divide it amongst the poorest to take home with them. It was also his custom to give each man a gift of a grey coat and he encouraged the wealthier members of his flock to similar acts of charity. The writer of the *Apostolical Life* gives a vivid description of how Ambrose celebrated Mass. The foulest weather did not deter the Catholics, young and old, from coming to him, either day or night.

> Being come they hasted to the chapel, where the men having laid their hats upon a round table... they passed by a fair coal fire to the altar; which upon the eve was ready dressed with clean linen and a venerable old vestment laid thereon, which came out but upon great days, with all other things poor and clean. The old picture before the altar was the arraignment of our Blessed Saviour. Against that time he used to prepare great wax candles, which he did help make himself... how much I was edified in that place... who seemed to represent the good Catholics in the

primitive Church. They so truly united in charity, rejoiced to meet one another... they spent the night modestly and devoutly, sometimes in prayer before the altar, otherwhiles singing devout songs by the fireside in another room... that their singing might not disturb those that would be praying in the chapel. On great Holidays and most Sundays... he used to preach... in every place that he lodged at in his circuit. He had a singular talent therein and could perform it with great facility without penning it. His style in preaching... was the likest unto Scripture phrase of any that I ever heard; brief, plain and pithy.

Ambrose suffered his fair share of persecution, having evaded many narrow escapes from capture. He was imprisoned four times. Challoner states that while a prisoner in Lancaster Castle in 1628 Ambrose managed to gain access to Edmund Arrowsmith and administer the last rites to him. He was released before Arrowsmith's execution and was unaware that the Jesuit was already dead when, on 28 August, the very night of Edmund's execution, his fellow priest seemed to appear to him by his bedside and warned him that he too would one day be called to similarly suffer. It did not deter Ambrose, who continued travelling as before, passing openly through Leigh, where he was said to be 'as well known as their Parson'.

In March 1641 King Charles, who had just reprieved seven priests under sentence of death, was forced by Parliament to issue a proclamation banishing all priests from the country within one month. Those who disobeyed would pay the penalty for treason. Ambrose was urged by his friends to go into hiding but he refused, saying, 'Let them fear that have anything to lose which they are unwilling to part with.'

His continual ill health was giving cause for concern but he would not consult a doctor. The *Life* tells us that 'he was to himself Dr Diet, Dr Quiet and the only Dr Merriman that I ever knew'. Early in 1641 he suffered a stroke, which caused a certain amount of paralysis down one side, and he was greatly concerned that if anything happened to him his flock would be deprived of the Sacraments.

The period fixed under the royal proclamation for Ambrose's banishment had long expired and on Easter Sunday, 25 April

1641, Mr Gatley, the Vicar of Leigh, apparently having nothing more edifying to do on such a holy day, came with an armed gang to Morleys Hall to arrest him. The reverend gentleman had proposed to his congregation that instead of holding their Easter service they should proceed en masse to the Hall and catch the papists and their priest in their idolatrous worship.

So without any legal authority, armed with clubs and swords, gathering support as they went, about 400 of them marched on the Hall. When they arrived they could be heard crying out, 'Where is Barlow?' and shouting threats. Ambrose was still preaching after Mass and he ordered that the doors be opened to them and calmly surrendered. The congregation were allowed to leave after their names had been taken. The mob searched the house but found nothing of interest to them. Ambrose was taken to a Justice of the Peace at Winwick, who ordered him to be sent under armed guard to Lancaster, accompanied by the insults and jeers of the mob. He was put on a horse but because of the weakening effects of the stroke he had to be supported to prevent him from falling off. Some of the local Catholics would have tried to rescue him, but Ambrose told them to go home peaceably and not interfere, explaining that 'to die for this cause was more desirable than life'.

He was imprisoned at Lancaster Castle, during which time his friends tried to get him removed to London or sent into exile; but Ambrose was content to let matters take their course: he had to die sometime, he said, so what better cause could there be? In prison he found solace in reading *Consolations of Philosophy* by the Christian Roman statesman Severinus Boethius (480–524), written during his own imprisonment. King Alfred the Great had translated the *Consolations* into Anglo-Saxon and it was a work that had a profound influence on the medieval world. Boethius discourses on the transitoriness of all earthly greatness. Tradition has it that Boethius died a martyr and the relevance to his own situation would have been keenly appreciated by Ambrose. He was, however, deprived of the book when it was confiscated by his jailer.

After four months in prison he was brought to trial on 7 September before Sir Robert Heath, former Solicitor General and

Attorney General, and future Lord Chief Justice. Heath was a reasonable and fair-minded man who had shown sympathy for religious prisoners, but he had received direct instructions from Parliament to ensure that the extreme penalty of the law was imposed on any priest caught in Lancashire in order to cow the papists, who were numerous in the county.

When the indictment was read, Ambrose immediately acknowledged that he was a priest and that he had carried on his priestly ministry for over twenty years. The judge asked why he had not obeyed the proclamation and left the country. He excused himself on two counts. Firstly, the proclamation specified Jesuits and seminary priests, whereas he was neither of these; he was a Benedictine monk. Secondly, he said that his poor health and his recent stroke had made it impossible for him to undertake such a long journey within the time allowed, as was known to those who had captured him. This elicited some sympathy in the court so the judge tried a different approach. He asked the prisoner his opinion of the justice of the law that sanctioned priests being put to death.

Ambrose replied that the law was unjust and barbarous. 'For what law can be more unjust than this by which priests are condemned to suffer as traitors merely because they are Roman, that is true priests? For there are no other true priests but the Roman; and if these be destroyed, what must become of the divine law, when none remain to preach God's word and administer His Sacraments?'

Heath then asked Ambrose what was his opinion of those who made such laws and of those who were charged with putting them into execution. Sensible of the pitfalls inherent in the question, Ambrose said that he prayed God would forgive all involved.

The judge accepted the priest's illness in mitigation and informed him that he would set him free if he promised not to seduce the people any more.

'It will be easy to pledge my word to this since I am no seducer but a reducer of the people to the true and ancient religion. I have laboured to disabuse the minds of those who have fallen into error and I am resolved to continue until death to render this good office to these strayed souls.'

Heath could not help admiring Ambrose's honesty and courage. 'You speak boldly,' he said, 'to a man who is master of your life and who can either acquit or condemn you as he shall judge proper.'

Ambrose answered that he could not deny the judge's powers, adding, 'You have power given to you over me through a wicked policy, but be aware, although I appear before you in quality of a criminal, being as I am a minister of Jesus Christ and a priest of the New Law, in spiritual matters I am judge and I declare to you that if you continue to condemn the innocent and remain in the darkness of heresy it will be to my salvation and your damnation.'

To this Heath responded that he had the advantage, since Barlow's sentence would be carried out first. Then he directed the jury to find the prisoner guilty.

The next day Ambrose was taken back to court to be sentenced to death, to which he responded with great serenity, 'Thanks be to God.' He then prayed that God would pardon all those who had been accessory to his death.

Heath seems to have genuinely regretted the priest's death but recognised that once Ambrose had openly confessed his priesthood there was nothing he could do to save him from the penalty of the law, especially in the face of demands from Parliament. Nonetheless, he acceded to Ambrose's request that he be given a cell to himself in order to prepare for his execution. Unknown to Ambrose, his fellow monks, meeting in General Chapter, had elected him to one of the English Benedictine titular offices as Prior of Coventry.

On Friday, 10 September 1641, carrying a wooden cross that he had made, Ambrose was placed on the hurdle and taken to his place of execution. Arrived at the gallows, he walked around it three times while reciting the *Miserere*. The Protestant ministers were all for entering into a dispute with him, but he told them that this was neither the time nor the place, for he had 'something else to do at present than to hearken to their fooleries'. He suffered with great fortitude as the dreadful sentence was carried out. His head was impaled on the tower of the Collegiate Church, Manchester, now the Cathedral. When the news of his martyrdom reached his brother monks at Douai, a celebratory Te

Deum was ordered and Masses of thanksgiving were offered.

Many relics of the martyr survived. His left hand, once kept at Knaresborough, Yorkshire, is preserved by the Benedictine nuns at Stanbrook Abbey, Worcester. His skull was obtained by Francis Downes of Wardley Hall, where it was kept for many years. The Downes family died out and the Hall passed into other hands. The whereabouts of the skull was forgotten. It was only in 1745, during the time of the Jacobite Rising when 'Bonnie Prince Charlie' reached Manchester, that the skull, still with an amount of chestnut hair, was accidentally rediscovered when part of the old Hall was demolished. The skull was subsequently enshrined in a niche of the staircase. To clear up all doubts, in the twentieth century scientific tests were carried out at St Bartholomew's Hospital, London, which authenticated the relic. Wardley Hall, where the skull has appropriately remained, has been the residence of the Bishops of Salford since 1930.

What of the Barlow family? They were loyal to King Charles and supported him in the Civil War. Sir Alexander, the martyr's brother, died in 1642 and was succeeded by his son, a fourth Alexander, who died without issue in 1654. He was followed by his half-brother, Thomas, and in turn by his son Anthony. The family remained faithful to the Church, and Anthony appears in the lists of recusants under George I. Anthony's son Thomas died of jail fever in Lancaster Castle in 1729. The last male heir of the family, Thomas, inherited Barlow and when he died in 1773 without issue, over seven hundred years of family history came to an end.

Alban Roe

Stone walls do not a prison make.

To Althea, Richard Lovelace, 1618–58

Bartholomew Roe was born at Bury St Edmunds, Suffolk, in 1580 or 1583. He was educated at Cambridge University and apparently, being of a naturally pugnacious disposition, he grew up an aggressive Protestant. The turning point in his life came while he was visiting friends at St Albans who told him about a recusant who was in prison there. Bartholomew resolved to visit him in order to persuade him of the error of his papist beliefs. It did not work out as he had intended. The prisoner was so sincere and resolute in his beliefs and argued his case so convincingly that Bartholomew himself began to have doubts.

In 1607 he became a Catholic and the following February he went to Douai, entering the English College as a 'convictor' – that is, a student who financially supported himself. In 1611 he was expelled from the College for insubordination, i.e. he was critical of the principal. He then decided he wished to become a Benedictine. He may have been familiar with the recently established Benedictine monastery at Douai but, perhaps discretion being the better part of valour, he sought admission in 1612 to the order not at Douai but at another English Benedictine monastery: St Lawrence at Dieulouard near Nancy in Lorraine, of which Ampleforth Abbey, North Yorkshire, is the successor. In 1614 Bartholomew was professed under the name of Alban. In 1615 he was ordained priest and was sent to Paris to help in the foundation of the third community of the re-established English Benedictine Congregation. This was the monastery of St Edmund, King and Martyr. After the French Revolution this monastery moved to Douai and in the hostile, anticlerical political climate in France at the start of the twentieth century it moved to England where it has remained as Douai Abbey, Woolhampton, near Reading.

From Paris, Alban returned to England and worked zealously in London for three years before being arrested and sent to the New Prison, Maiden Lane, in 1618. Here he remained for five years until at the request of Count Gondomar, the Spanish Ambassador, he was included in King James's general amnesty of 1623 and sent into permanent exile. He made his way to the Benedictines at Douai, but after only four months he was back in England to resume his work. In 1627 he was arrested by a professional priest hunter called Francis Newton.

This despicable man had once been an attorney-at-law but had been expelled from the legal profession for dishonesty. He and three equally disreputable cronies, James Wadsworth, Robert

Luke and Thomas Mayo, formed a priest-catching cooperative purely for profit. They later boasted to have been responsible for the apprehension of thirty-seven priests, several of whom died in prison, as well as the execution of thirteen of them. Newton had Roe imprisoned at St Albans in the very cell – still to be seen – in the abbey gatehouse where he had first been led to the Catholic Faith.

Conditions at the prison were terrible and after two months, through the influence of friends, Alban was transferred to the Fleet Prison in London, where he was to spend the next fifteen years. The Fleet, built beside the – now underground – river of the same name was one of the most ancient prisons, and the post of Keeper had been hereditary for hundreds of years. Principally for debtors, it was a notoriously corrupt institution, with the Keeper receiving the prisoners' payments for their food and lodging; the larger the amount they paid to the Keeper, the better the accommodation they were allocated. If inmates were willing and able to pay enough they were allowed out of the prison on parole, provided they gave their word to return before nightfall.

Alban was to take full advantage of this laxity. In spite of suffering from the pain of kidney stones he was the life and soul of the prison. His gaiety and holiness endeared him to everyone and he soon won the hearts of his jailers, who were invited to join him in games of cards while he told them amusing stories. There was a deeper purpose underlying all this socialising. As a result he was able to carry on an effective ministry, and not only amongst the prisoners. He was allowed to receive visitors, as well as being frequently allowed out on parole to minister to the Catholics of the city, returning to the prison at night. While he was permitted to follow this regime, what need was there for him to try and escape? Presumably through his influence, his brother James converted and joined the Benedictines and his sister became a nun. While in prison, Alban translated Latin works into English, including St John Fisher's treatise on prayer.

The Long Parliament put an end to such tolerance. In 1641 Alban was moved to Newgate, and on 19 January he was brought to trial at the Old Bailey charged under Elizabeth 27 with being a priest and a seducer of the people. When the barbarous sentence was pronounced he replied, 'How little this is in comparison to what Christ suffered for me.'

He spent the remaining two days asking his friends to pray that he might be worthy of martyrdom. On the morning of 21 January 1642, Alban and a fellow priest known as Richard Reynolds said Mass at Newgate. At its conclusion Alban spoke to those present. 'When you see our heads up on London Bridge, take it that they are there to preach to you, to proclaim that Faith for which we are about to die.'

There is some discrepancy or confusion in the sources about his companion. Known to posterity as Blessed Richard or Thomas Reynolds, his real name was Thomas Green, his maternal family being called Reynolds. Some claim he was born *c.*1560 and ordained in 1592, that he had worked on the English mission for fifty years and was aged eighty at the time of his death. The documentary evidence indicates that he was born at Oxford in 1579 and was ordained at Seville in 1602, afterwards returning to England, from where he was banished in 1606. He soon resumed his work on the mission and was imprisoned again in 1628 and condemned to death. He was reprieved by the King at the request of Henrietta Maria. Imprisoned in Newgate in 1632, he was released two years later. He was in the Gatehouse in April 1635 but discharged a few days later, only to be rearrested. He spent the next *seven years* in prison waiting for the death sentence to be carried out. Said by a contemporary to be a 'remarkably mild and courteous' man, he was now very infirm and rather corpulent. Father Reynolds confided to Alban that he was fearful of his execution. Alban strengthened him with powerfully comforting words. As they set out for Tyburn, Alban asked him how he was. 'In very good heart,' replied Reynolds, 'blessed be God for it and glad I am to have for my comrade in death a man of your courage.'

The road to Tyburn was lined with Catholics who ran forward to kiss the hands of the two priests and beg their blessing as they were drawn on the same hurdle. On the scaffold the two priests gave each other absolution and Alban helped Thomas up into the cart, from where he spoke to the crowd. He forgave his enemies and prayed that the sheriff would merit the 'grace to be a glorious saint in heaven', at which that official was much moved. He addressed the executioner. 'Pray do your duty neatly, I have been a neat man all my life.' Alban had been speaking words of comfort to three felons who were also to be hanged, and he now turned to the people with a cheery, 'Well, here's a jolly company!'

He gave away all the money he still had to the executioner, asking him to drink to his health, but cautioning him not to get too drunk. He asked God to pardon his many sins and expressed the hope that his death would be satisfaction for them. He forgave his persecutors and asked the sheriff if his life would be spared if he conformed. The sheriff swore that if he abjured his Catholicism even at this late stage he would be freed.

'See then,' said Alban, 'what the crime is for which I am to die, and whether my religion be my only treason... I wish I had a thousand lives then I would sacrifice them all for so worthy a cause.'

The two priests said the *Miserere* psalm in alternate verses and both called out the name of Jesus as they were simultaneously turned off the ladder. They were allowed to hang until they were dead, but the crowd made clear its displeasure at their deaths. In *Acts of the English Martyrs* by J H Pollen SJ, we read that on this occasion, as on so many others,

> The Catholics piously vied with each other in taking away relics of the martyrs. Many dipped their handkerchiefs in the dismembered bodies; others carefully collected the bloodstained straw from the ground.

Count Egmont, later Duke of Gueldres, who was the Spanish Ambassador in London from 1640 to 45, collected a huge number of relics of the martyrs. He was present at the deaths of eleven priests, including Roe and Reynolds, and among his relics was a piece of the executioner's apron soaked in their blood. It is now preserved at Downside Abbey.

Henry Morse

> All the bright company of Heaven hold him in their high comradeship
>
> *Into Battle*, Julian Grenfell, 1888–1915

Henry was born in 1595 in the village of Brome, Suffolk, just south of Diss, close to the border with Norfolk. He was the seventh of the nine sons, out of fourteen children, of Robert Morse of Tivetsall St Mary, Norfolk and Margaret Collinson, whose home was at Brome. Robert was a man of some wealth, owning land and property, granaries and cattle. In his will he left a legacy to all his surviving children. Henry's share was £300 plus an annuity of £27 and the 'silver bell salt with cover' that had belonged to his maternal grandmother. In spite of his actual place of birth Henry always described himself as a Norfolk man. He may have attended Norwich Grammar School as a boy, but in May 1612 he entered Corpus Christi College, Cambridge. For whatever reason, whether religious or not, he did not remain long at Cambridge, leaving to study law at Barnard's Inn, one of the Inns of Court in London. He later joined the Gray's Inn chambers of Richard Ross, who was his cousin by marriage. He appears to have conformed to the extent that he attended church occasionally. We know a great deal about his life from two contemporary biographies, the first written by his friend Father Ambrose Corby, the second by Father Philippe Alegambe, who had been one of Henry's professors in Rome. We are also fortunate that the detailed journal which Morse kept in prison has survived. It is an invaluable record, especially for the last months of his life.

What made Henry decide to become a Catholic is unclear. All he tells us is that while at Gray's Inn he began to have religious scruples. The Inns of Court were full of Catholics or fellow travellers and he may have begun to have doubts from contacts he must have made among them. Henry's father, Robert, appears to have been a secret Catholic, or at least very sympathetic to the

Church. He was certainly reported for recusancy and sheltering a priest. Perhaps he was reconciled to the Church before he died, and this had a deciding influence on Henry. One of his older brothers, William, who was also a lawyer, had converted and gone to Douai. William is known to have been in London in the autumn of 1613 and it is surely not too fanciful to imagine that it was he who helped convert Henry. William was ordained at Arras in 1617 and returned to work in England in 1618 where he became a Jesuit. Furthermore, another brother, Robert, had married into the Bedingfeld family. Perhaps the most famous Catholic family in Norfolk, their home was (and is) the beautiful moated Oxburgh Hall, in which the priest hole believed to have been constructed by Nicholas Owen can still be seen. It is inconceivable that Robert, yet another lawyer, had not converted when he married.

Whatever the deciding factor, in 1614 Henry obtained a licence allowing him to go abroad. He sailed to Dunkirk and arrived at Douai on 5 June, where he was formally received into the Catholic Church. Having decided to become a priest he returned to England to obtain the inheritance left him by his father, no doubt to pay for the cost of his priestly education. Unfortunately he was arrested on disembarkation. In spite of being in possession of a travel licence, when he refused to take the oath he was sent to London and put in the New Prison, Southwark, where he remained for the next four years, along with many other Catholics.

The Spanish marriage proposed for Prince Charles was causing enormous anger around the country, and during the period of Henry's imprisonment six priests and a layman[5] were executed, while others died in prison. Morse benefited from the amnesty to placate Spain granted by King James in June 1618, when he was included amongst the one hundred imprisoned priests sent into exile. He arrived back at Douai in early August where he was greeted by his brother, William, who was about to return to England. In December it was decided to send Henry to study at the English College, Rome, where that remarkable and holy priest Father Thomas Fitzherbert SJ[6] was Rector. Morse later acknowledged his debt of gratitude to Fitzherbert, who exercised great influence over him as well as being his good friend. He also formed lasting friendships with fellow students who later worked with him on the English mission and were to share his imprisonments. While in Rome, Henry used the alias Cuthbert Claxton, a name he retained and by which he was known in England.

Although reported as being quick-tempered, Henry was a very conscientious student who was always willing to help in the domestic chores of the college. He enjoyed acting as a tour guide to the English visitors to the Eternal City. He was ordained deacon in July 1620 and afterwards made a short visit to England. The precise date of his priestly ordination is not recorded but it was probably in May 1624. The following month he left for England. Before doing so he had asked permission to enter the Society of Jesus, and the Jesuit General had written to the Order's English Provincial, Richard Blount, advising him to receive Henry if he persisted in his desire. Henry wrote an account of his journey to Father Fitzherbert in Rome. Travelling via Brussels with two companions, they ran out of money because of the high cost of meals and Henry, having lent his companions money, had to borrow from the Jesuits at Liège. He eventually reached Saint-Omer and was provided by the College with all he needed to complete his journey home.

Henry was listed amongst the novices at the newly-established Jesuit novitiate at Edmonton, north of London, but he cannot have been there for very long because he was sent to Northumberland to undertake his first year's training under Father Richard Holtby. Henry took up residence at St Anthony's, the home of Mrs Dorothy Lawson at Byker, on the north bank of the River Tyne. Mrs Lawson was the second daughter of Sir Henry Constable and his wife Margaret Dormer, of Burton Constable Hall, Holderness, East Yorkshire. In 1596 Dorothy married Roger Lawson, a barrister of the Inner Temple, the son of Sir Ralph Lawson, but she had been left a widow in her thirties. The Lawsons had been Lords of the Manor of Byker for generations. Dorothy's house was one of the great Catholic centres of the North. She had her own chapel and library and there were plenty of hiding places. In addition to the local

Catholics, foreign seamen engaged in transporting coal from Newcastle were welcomed at St Anthony's.

The house was the chief residence of the septuagenarian Father Richard Holtby,[7] once tutor at Oxford to Alexander Briant. Holtby, who had succeeded Henry Garnet as Superior of the Jesuits, had spent most of his priestly life in the North. He was a skilled carpenter and the hiding places at St Anthony's were his work. He also made and embroidered the liturgical vestments. In this congenial environment Henry acted as chaplain, celebrating Mass daily and looking after the spiritual needs of the Catholics in the area. Soon the plague had broken out in Newcastle and Morse had his first taste of caring for its victims among the coal miners. King Charles had been forced to bow to the will of Parliament and priests had to be more cautious with so many pursuivants actively engaged in seeking them out.

Henry's arrest in April 1626 was the result of an unlucky set of circumstances. He had been working in and around Durham and had collected a boy from Jarrow who was being sent to Douai to complete his education. Henry and the boy waited by the Tyne until a coal boat on its way to Calais came into view. By previous arrangement, they hailed the captain and asked to be taken on board, where they changed into seamen's clothes. Somehow the customs officers at Newcastle had got wind of their plans and the boat was ordered to drop anchor; it was then boarded and Henry and the boy were taken prisoner. Examined by the mayor, at first Henry tried to pretend he was a foreigner who did not understand English, but when that did not work he tried to bluff his way out of the situation. In the end he had to admit that he was a Catholic and refused the oath when it was offered. But he would not admit to being a priest and nothing could be proved against him.

While he was in custody, another ship had been boarded and its passengers arrested. Among them was Father John Robinson SJ, posing as a Dutch merchant. Father Robinson had been a student in Rome with Morse and the following day he was sent to join him in jail. Here they were visited by the steadfast Mrs Lawson, who provided them with a few comforts. Soon they were removed to the appalling York Castle jail which was full of Catholics, men and women, kept in disgusting conditions in unventilated cells which

Charles I and the Civil War Martyrs, 1625–1649

often flooded; no wonder the death rate at the prison was so high. The two priests set about doing what they could to relieve their fellow sufferers, begging alms to provide sustenance and in the process converted a good number of the criminal inmates, which roused the ire of the Protestants of York. It was here, in his dark cell, that Henry served out his novitiate. Under the guidance of Father Robinson he managed to make a retreat, complete the Spiritual Exercises and take his first vows.

Three years passed and then in March 1630 Henry was released and banished in perpetuity. At the same time Father Robinson was put on trial and sentenced to death. He was reprieved and left to spend a further eleven years carrying out his apostolate in the prison. When eventually released Father Robinson continued to work in Yorkshire where he died in old age. Morse made his way to the English Jesuit novitiate at Watten, where Father Henry Bedingfeld was Rector. In the autumn he was given employment as chaplain to the British mercenary soldiers fighting in the Spanish army in the Low Countries. He worked so hard, travelling about unceasingly ministering to the troops that he fell seriously ill and for a time he was not expected to live. Thanks to the care of the Jesuit Fathers he recovered, but was not considered fit to return to arduous duties in the field so he was given an administrative post looking after all the temporal needs at Watten as well as serving nearby churches. He gave special attention to looking after the sick in the community. In 1633 Henry was moved to the Jesuit College at Liège where he undertook similar duties. By now he had recovered his health and Father Blount asked for him to return to England to work in the London district.

Henry laboured in and around the poorest areas of Holborn and Bloomsbury, visiting the Catholics crowded together in the squalid slums of the parish of St Giles-in-the-Fields. In the autumn of 1635 London was again hit by an outbreak of the plague, and this time it was virulent and widespread. By the following spring the capital was in the throes of a major epidemic. The usual precautions were ordered, including sealing infected persons together with their families in their homes. Henry will always be remembered for his heroic work in London during the plague, where he devoted himself to the sick with enormous courage. As Catholics were legally 'non-persons' they were not entitled to any assistance from the parish relief funds and depended entirely upon their co-religionists for help. In the absence of a bishop, the Chapter of secular priests governed the Church in England. Sadly, they and the Jesuits were often at loggerheads, usually as a result of mischief-making amongst some in the Chapter. In this dire situation, in 1636 the Jesuits and seculars agreed to cooperate in relieving sick Catholics. The Jesuits appointed Henry as their representative and the seculars nominated Father John Southworth. The two priests were to be responsible for the relief of Catholics in the panic-stricken city, whose civic leaders had all fled and where lawlessness reigned.

The conditions in which the two priests laboured were indescribably foul, horrific and dangerous. Henry had a list of around 400 infected families, both Catholic and Protestant. Carrying a white stick to signify that he visited plague-infected houses, day and night Henry attended to the spiritual and physical needs of the Catholics, including laying out the putrid and disfigured corpses for burial at night in the specially dug communal pits. It was work that Henry understandably found particularly repellent but, forcing himself to overcome his aversion, he courageously struggled on. At his later trial, many witnesses gave testimony to his administering the Sacraments to the Catholic sick and dying plague victims, as well as to the many converts he made through his equal kindness to poor Protestant families.

As conditions worsened, anxiety increased about the lack of money to continue providing relief. In October 1636 Henry and Father Southworth issued a joint public appeal entitled *To the Catholickes of England*, begging them for funds. From the Queen downwards the response was generous and undoubtedly saved the lives of many who would otherwise have perished for lack of sustenance. When Father Southworth was arrested, Henry had to continue his work alone, assisted by two brave Catholic doctors. For the second time Henry felt ill and it was realised he had contracted the plague. With the help of his doctor he almost miraculously recovered and after only a week's rest, despite his weakness, forced himself to resume his work during the winter months.

In November 1636 Henry was arrested on the evidence of a nurse that he had received a dying Protestant couple into the Church. The constable who interrogated him was impressed by his dedication and let him go. However, Henry's fame was such that there were those determined to see him imprisoned; but in spite of being harassed he managed to evade being arrested, sometimes by bribing his would-be captors. Francis Newton, the disgraced lawyer who was responsible for the arrest of Alban Roe, together with his cronies – one of them an apostate priest – was intent on pursuing Henry. Morse himself described Newton as 'a man of infamous life and behaviour, being for many dishonest practices... expulsed from the profession of an attorney-at-law... and has been convicted of many abuses and corruptions'.

Newton's chance came in February 1637 when he accosted Henry in the street and detained him in solitary confinement at the Sun tavern, Westminster, for several weeks. In March, Henry was brought before the Privy Council, accused of reconciling many people to the Church. He was removed from the tavern to Newgate. His already fragile health deteriorated but he tried to keep up his Lenten devotions, as well as carrying on a ministry amongst the prisoners.

After four weeks in Newgate, on 24 April he was taken to the Old Bailey to stand trial. Although the trial followed the familiar pattern, Morse defended himself well. Many accusations were levelled against him of converting Protestants. It was clear that at least some of the evidence for this was fabricated, as several brave Catholics testified that they had always been of that religion and were not converts. Thanks to the honest intervention of one of the judges, Sir William Jones, this resulted in him being found not guilty on the charge of persuading to popery but guilty of being a priest. He was returned to Newgate to await sentence and during Easter week made his solemn profession as a Jesuit before Father Edward Lusher. Called to the Old Bailey, instead of being sentenced he was ordered back to prison, the King having given instructions for sentence to be deferred and that the prisoner be treated with respect. (Father Lusher was to emulate Morse many years later. He died, aged seventy-six, in 1665, a victim of the Great Plague, having contracted the disease while caring for the sick.)

Henry wrote a personal letter to the King informing him of the circumstances of his arrest and trial and asking for clemency, especially in view of his state of health. Henry's doctors also sent a report to the King confirming how desperately ill he was. After three months in Newgate, Henry was released by the King through the intervention of Queen Henrietta Maria on bail of 10,000 florins. Henry remained in London for about a year, but as his health was still giving cause for concern he was sent to minister to the Catholics of Devon and Cornwall.

By June of 1640 Morse was back in London and at the instigation of the tenacious Newton was arrested with Father John Goodman, whose story has been told earlier in this chapter. Henry was brought to Lambeth before Laud, the beleaguered Archbishop of Canterbury, who ordered him to be confined in Newgate. In July the two priests were released. A royal proclamation ordered all priests to leave the country by April 1641, so Henry voluntarily left England. This was not only for the sake of his health, but also because his exile was considered prudent following the cause célèbre of Father Goodman's condemnation and reprieve by the King.

In 1641 Morse became chaplain to the English regiment in Flanders under the command of the Catholic Colonel Sir Henry Gage. His fellow chaplain was another future Jesuit martyr, the Northamptonshire priest Father Peter Wright. Henry also gave retreats at the convents of the English Carmelites and Benedictine nuns in Flanders, where he met two of the daughters of Mrs Dorothy Lawson whom he had known as children. The Civil War having begun in England, Gage, accompanied by Father Wright, had returned home to fight for the King. Morse was also anxious to return home and in 1643 to his great joy, filled with happy premonitions of his probable martyrdom, his request was granted. He landed in the North of England and was assigned to work in Cumberland, where he ministered for about eighteen months. Given the terrain and the distances to be travelled, it cannot have been easy missionary territory.

Charles I and the Civil War Martyrs, 1625–1649

Late one night while he was answering a sick call he accidentally ran into a troop of Parliamentary soldiers and was immediately arrested and taken to the house of a local magistrate. The magistrate's wife happened to be a Catholic. Regardless of the risk to herself, she secretly conducted Father Morse through the woods to safety, but the whole area was full of troops. He remained at liberty for six weeks, during which time the Parliamentary troops gained control of Northumberland and Durham. When recaptured, Henry was sent to Durham and lodged in filthy conditions before being transferred to Newcastle prison. In November he was put aboard a coal boat bound for London. He complained of being brutally ill-used by the crew on the voyage. Finally arrived in London, Morse was imprisoned at Newgate while his brother Robert tried every means at his disposal to save him.

It was a forlorn hope. Parliament was in the ascendant and without the King the Catholics in London no longer had any protection. They were at the mercy of the pursuivants and many priests were arrested and imprisoned. Only days after Henry had been brought before the magistrates, Archbishop Laud was executed and the Anglican services were abolished. Morse was again brought to court but there was no trial. On the strength of his conviction nine years earlier, he was sentenced to death.

During the few days left to him before his execution Henry was in great demand from a constant stream of visitors. A contemporary writer recorded that it was an amazing sight to see hundreds of people, Catholics and non-Catholics, from morning until night, wanting to see him and ask for his prayers and his blessing. Among them were the ambassadors of the European powers, who came to see this hero of the Faith. On his last day Henry fasted; moreover, he got no sleep, as he continued to receive visitors.

At 4 a.m. on the morning of 1 February 1645, Henry offered a votive Mass of the Holy Trinity in Newgate, surrounded by many friends. Afterwards he had a brief rest before visiting all the condemned prisoners and speaking a few words of comfort to each. All were astonished at his calm and smiling countenance. At 9 a.m. Sheriff Gibbs came to conduct him to his execution. Henry was tied to a hurdle before being dragged through the muddy streets to Tyburn, escorted by fifty mounted guards. Here he was made to wait for the arrival of a cartload of common criminals who were also to die. It was a memorable occasion. The ambassadors of all the European Catholic powers were present in their coaches, along with their diplomatic suites, to witness the priest's execution.

The rope having been placed around his neck, Henry asked permission to address the crowd. He told them that he was to die solely for his religion, the religion founded by Christ and continued by His Church to the present time. 'I have a secret to declare,' he said. 'Gentlemen, take notice, the kingdom of England will never be truly blessed until it returns to the Catholic Faith.'

Asking forgiveness for his sins and pardoning all who had injured him, he committed his soul into God's hands. He was left to hang until he was dead before the butchery began. The servants of the ambassadors dipped their master's handkerchiefs in Henry's blood while Sheriff Gibbs expressed his regret at such a shameful proceeding. Henry's four quarters were displayed on the city gates and his head on London Bridge. The great historian of the period, Dame C V Wedgwood OM, in *The King's War 1641–47*, wrote of Henry Morse, '… and there ended a life of patient devotion and self-sacrifice by a death of exalted fortitude'.

Charles I and the Civil War Martyrs, 1625–1649

Notes to Chapter Six

[1] William Bishop was born at Brailes, Warwickshire, in 1553. His family had remained loyal to the Old Faith and many of their monuments, including members of the family who were priests through to the nineteenth century, may be seen in the magnificent parish church, among them that of William's father who lived to the age of ninety-two. William was educated at Oxford and when he returned home he relinquished his interest in the family estate in favour of his brother and went to Rheims. After completion of his studies at Rome he was ordained in 1581, setting out for England at the end of the year. He was arrested on arrival at Rye, Sussex, early in 1582 and after interrogation was sent to the Marshalsea. Condemned to death in 1583, he remained in prison until banished in January 1585. He went to Paris and became Doctor of Divinity at the Sorbonne. He was back in England in 1591 and in 1598 travelled to Rome to present the grievances of the English clergy about the Archpriest Blackwell. He was back in England by 1603 where he was one of the signatories of a Protestation of Allegiance to Elizabeth. It had little effect because he was arrested again in 1603 but released. In 1605 he was recorded as working in Herefordshire and by 1610 was in Oxfordshire. In 1611 he was once more a prisoner in the Gatehouse. When he was released he went to Paris and in June 1623 he was consecrated Bishop there and set off for England; the first Bishop for over forty years. After spending his time administering the Sacraments he died in Essex in April 1624.

[2] Richard Smith (1567–1655) came from Lincolnshire. He was educated at Trinity College, Oxford. He went first to Rheims and then Rome, where he was ordained in 1592. From there he went to Valladolid and taught philosophy for several years. In 1598 he was sent to Seville, and despite his desire to return to England he was engaged in teaching for four years, followed by a period at Douai. In 1610 he at last returned home, but stayed for only two years before leaving for Paris as Superior of Arras College, established for higher studies by the clergy. When William Bishop died, Smith was appointed his successor. He was consecrated in Paris and returned to England in 1625. The Anglican bishops were incensed at his daring to

exercise his episcopal functions and warrants were issued for his arrest. In the teeth of opposition from among the ranks of the Catholic clergy as well as the Protestants, he retired to France in 1631 and was financially supported by Cardinal Richelieu. Deprived of that support when the Cardinal died in 1642, he took refuge with the Augustinian nuns in Paris and died there in 1655.

[3] Richard Blount (1563–1638) came from a well-to-do Leicestershire family. Educated at Balliol College, Oxford, in 1583 he entered the English College first at Rheims and then at Rome, where he was ordained in 1589. He returned to England via Spain in 1591, posing as a returning prisoner of war sailor. In 1596 he joined the Society of Jesus and spent many years sheltered at Scotney Castle, Sussex, from which he made a dramatic escape in 1598 during a raid searching for him. He moved into secret lodgings in London, only going out at night. He was legendary for his rich apparel while dressing very simply when at home. In 1617 he became Superior of the Jesuit Mission, and when England was made into a Province, Blount became the first Provincial. He died in London in May 1638 having been Superior for twenty-one years. By a special privilege he was buried late at night in the Queen's chapel at Somerset House, normally reserved for the Catholic members of her household. It was the only Catholic cemetery in London.

[4] Blessed Richard Herst was born near Preston. He was a yeoman farmer but also a well-known recusant. The Bishop of Chester sent pursuivants to arrest him, and in doing so a scuffle ensued with Herst's farm servants. In the course of the fracas one of the three pursuivants called Dewhurst fell and broke his leg. Unfortunately the leg turned gangrenous and Dewhurst died. Before he did so he made a statement confirming that it was the result of an accident, absolving Herst and his servants from blame. In spite of that, Herst was accused of murder and brought to trial. Hearing of Dewhurst's statement, the jury was unwilling to convict him, but the judge told them that as the authorities were determined to convict Herst they must deliver a guilty verdict. The real reason for his condemnation was apparent on the scaffold on 29 August 1628, when he was offered his freedom if the took the Oath of Supremacy. When he refused he was hanged. He was beatified in 1929.

[5] The six priests and a layman were:

Blessed Thomas Atkinson, born in Yorkshire, probably at Leeds, c.1545. After studying at Douai he was ordained in 1588 at Laon. After twenty-eight years on the mission in Yorkshire he was martyred at York on 11 March 1616.

Blessed John Thules, the son of the master of the local grammar school, was born at Whalley, Lancashire, in 1568. He was sent to Douai at a young age. From there he went to Rome and was ordained in 1592 by special dispensation as he was still under the canonical age. His elder brother was also a priest. He worked on the mission all over England for twenty-two years before being caught on 29 September 1615. He was imprisoned at Lancaster with Roger Wrenno (see below), and the two of them joined in a mass escape from the jail. They walked all night but discovered in the morning that they had gone in a circle and were recaptured. At their trial they denied breaking out of prison, stating that they had simply walked out when the opportunity arose. Offered their lives if they took the oath, they refused and were sentenced to death. They were martyred together at Lancaster on 18 March 1616. Thules' head was displayed on Lancaster Castle and his quarters hung up in four different towns.

Blessed Roger Wrenno, a weaver from Chorley, was hanged with Father Thules at Lancaster for assisting him. This is not the correct spelling of his surname, which was most likely Wrennal, and he may be identified with the Roger Wrennal baptised at Chorley in 1576. Executed with a group of criminals, all the bodies were cut up in pieces and thrown into a heap so that it was impossible to identify which remains were those of the martyrs.

Blessed Thomas Maxfield was born in prison at Stafford c.1585, as his parents were in jail for recusancy. His father, William, was condemned to death for assisting Father Robert Sutton, who was martyred at Stafford in 1588. He had spent almost twenty years in prison before buying his release in 1606. Thomas went to Douai and was ordained in 1614, returning to England in 1615 where he was arrested in London shortly afterwards. He refused to take the oath before Bishop King of London and was sent to the Gatehouse. A few months later he made an escape bid by climbing down from a high window but was quickly recaptured and put in chains in an underground cell. He was moved to Newgate in a terrible state of health and condemned to death. The pleas of the Spanish Ambassador on behalf of Thomas fell on deaf ears. Accompanied by the Ambassador, Thomas was martyred at Tyburn on 1 July 1616, little more than one year after his ordination. His remains were salvaged by English and Spanish Catholics and eventually found their way to Spain with the relics of John Almond.

Blessed Thomas Tunstal came from Westmorland. He went to Douai in 1606, was ordained in 1609 and returned to England the following year. Around 1615 he joined the Benedictines. He was imprisoned in Wisbech Castle from where he escaped, but was recaptured and martyred at Norwich on 13 July 1616.

Blessed William Southerne was born in Co. Durham in 1579. He was educated by the Jesuits in Poland, from where he went to Douai and then to Spain before ordination in 1604. He worked mainly in Northumberland. He was martyred at Newcastle-upon-Tyne on 30 April 1618.

The Benedictine, Father Robert Edmonds, was one of those who died in prison in 1615.

[6] Father Thomas Fitzherbert (1552–1640) came from the famous recusant family of that name. He was educated at Oxford where he served a year in prison for recusancy. In 1580 he married, but two years later, wanting freedom to practise his religion, he retired to France. He then moved to Spain, where for many years he served Philip II on various diplomatic missions. After his wife's death in 1588 he went to the English College, Rome, and in 1602 was ordained. In 1613 he joined the Society of Jesus. He became superior of the English Jesuit mission, living at Brussels from 1616 to 1618, and then Rector of the English College, Rome, from 1618 to 1639. He died in Rome in 1640 aged eighty-eight.

[7] Richard Holtby was born at Hovingham, North Yorkshire, in 1552. Educated at Oxford and Cambridge, he went to Douai in 1577 and was ordained in 1578, returning to England the following year. Early in 1581 he played host to Edmund Campion for several quiet days, during which time the Jesuit made the finishing touches to his book 'Ten Reasons'. No doubt influenced by his famous guest, he decided

to join the Jesuits at Verdun in 1582 and did not return to England until 1589. Although very active on the English mission, he was never once apprehended. Father John Gerard described him as 'father of all the Churches' from Yorkshire to the Scottish border. The venerable priest died in 1640 at the age of eighty-seven.

Chapter Seven

Puritan Parliament and the Commonwealth

Oppression stretches his rod over our land.

Samson, William Blake, 1757–1827

Many historians have tended to the opinion that generally speaking Catholics fared better under the Commonwealth than they had done for decades. Insofar as only two of them paid the ultimate price on the scaffold, that is true, but it is all a matter of relativity. Parliament was supposedly in control but power lay with Oliver Cromwell and the army. Before the execution of the King a more austere Puritan regime had been introduced. The celebration of Christmas had already been abolished and in the Articles of Christian Religion passed by Parliament in 1648 the Catholic Faith was specifically attacked. The Mass was described as abominable and the Real Presence in the Eucharist condemned as superstitious gross idolatry. A new catch-all oath was introduced: the Oath of Abjuration. This required Catholics to renounce papal primacy, to deny the Real Presence, deny Purgatory, deny that good works were meritorious towards salvation and condemn the use of crucifixes and other objects of piety. Echoing the reputed words of Elizabeth I, Cromwell said he wished to 'meddle not with any man's conscience'. This is an honourable statement of an ideal, and he may have sincerely meant what he said, but in practice it was a very different story of intolerance.

In 1650 the law requiring attendance at the services of the Anglican Church was repealed. The Anglican Church was no longer recognised, its deprived clergy forced to worship secretly in private. Anything of beauty that still remained in the churches was vandalised; even the ancient tombs were desecrated. By the act that made Cromwell Lord Protector in 1653, religious liberty was granted – with the exception of 'popery'. Cromwell – no doubt genuinely – believed that he was an instrument of divine retribution. Vide the Irish situation, which although it is not strictly within the ambit of this book illustrates his religious policy. Nowhere was Cromwell's messianic delusion more vividly illustrated than in Ireland, where Catholics were denied all mercy, being cruelly massacred, including women and children. The 'lucky' ones were transported as slaves to the sugar plantations of the West Indies. Bishops and priests were executed. In 1653 Catholicism was banned in Ireland. Statute 27 of Elizabeth, making it a treasonable offence simply to be a priest, was extended to Ireland. Priests were banished or sent to camps specially set up in the Arran Islands. Cromwell's treatment of the Irish will for ever be a stain upon his memory.

Under the Commonwealth and the Protectorate of Cromwell – an autocratic and dictatorial monarchy in all but name – the Catholics were made to suffer severely for their support for King Charles. A man of contradictions, Cromwell, somewhat surprisingly, had friendly relations with a number of Catholics, and the Protector toyed with the idea of entering into discussions with Rome about toleration for private Catholic worship. However, Catholics continued to be denied all freedom of worship and the penal laws were vigorously applied against them. Shockingly, there are cases of Catholic children being flogged for refusing to attend Puritan religious instruction. There are countless appeals recorded from Catholics begging for relief from the crippling fines imposed on them or the forfeiture of their entire estates. In spite of that many priests continued their ministry; Catholics flocked to the chapels of the foreign embassies to hear Mass and the number of conversions reportedly increased. It became such a problem that in 1655 the government passed a law forbidding English Catholics to frequent the chapels of foreign embassies.

During the period of the Civil War, when the Puritans in Parliament were in the ascendant, in addition to the five martyrs (Roe, Reynolds vere Green, Lockwood, Catterick and Morse) we have already described, twelve other priests[1] were martyred in the years between 1642 and 1646. To give him due credit, Cromwell was not by nature a persecutor and he was genuinely reluctant to execute priests. As a result only two, John Southworth and Peter Wright,[2] were martyred during the eleven years of the Commonwealth, which no doubt had a bearing upon the judgement of historians. However, this gives a false impression because under the Commonwealth there was no let-up in the persecution and dozens of priests were sentenced to death and reprieved, only to be left to die in harsh prison conditions.[3]

John Southworth

> The path of duty... the way to glory.
>
> *On the Death of the Duke of Wellington*, Alfred, Lord Tennyson, 1809–92

John Southworth (pronounced 'Suthearth') was related to the famous Catholic family of that name whose seat since the fourteenth century was Samlesbury Hall near Preston. Sir John Southworth had been prominent during Queen Elizabeth's reign. A staunch adherent to the Old Faith, he suffered the penalties for being a recusant. Edmund Campion had been his guest at Samlesbury, and for this offence Sir John had been imprisoned at Manchester and then London. Bishop Challoner tells us that John Southworth was 'a younger son of the ancient family of Samlesbury', from which we may infer he meant a junior branch; but neither the precise year of John's birth nor his birthplace is known for certain, though it may have been Samlesbury Hall. The saintly Bishop suggests 1592 as the year of John's birth, but if John's age was indeed seventy, as claimed by some at the time of his death, the martyr must have been born *c.*1584. It is more probable that Challoner is correct and John was sixty-two years old at the time of his death.

John entered the English College, Douai, on 14 July 1613 to begin his priestly studies. His health gave cause for concern and he went home to Lancashire for several months before returning to Douai at Easter 1617. He used the alias Lee, which may well have been his mother's maiden name. On 14 April 1618 John was ordained priest by the Archbishop of Cambrai, offering his first Mass on Easter Sunday. In April 1619 he left Douai to try his vocation as a Benedictine, but clearly this did not suit him and on 13 December of that year he was sent to England, where for the next five years he worked in the London area.

In March 1624 he was banished and shortly after arriving at Douai he was assigned as confessor to the Benedictine nuns at Brussels. By 1626 he was back in Lancashire. The following year he was arrested and imprisoned in Lancaster Castle at the same time as Edmund Arrowsmith and Ambrose Barlow. In September 1628 he was tried and condemned to death, but he was reprieved by the King and ordered to be detained in Wisbech Castle. The move never took place and he remained a prisoner at Lancaster for three years where, looking down from his cell window, he was able to give Edmund Arrowsmith absolution as he was led out to his execution.

On 24 March 1630 orders came for John to be banished by royal warrant, along with fifteen other priests, and he was moved to the Clink prison in Southwark in readiness. It is doubtful if John ever left the country as he was recorded as still being in the Clink in 1632, where his prison conditions were much ameliorated as a result of the interest shown in him by Queen Henrietta Maria. This led to complaints to the Privy Council from the pursuivants that John enjoyed too much liberty, being allowed to leave the prison. John's name also appears as a signatory to a number of appeals and petitions between 1630 and 1636. For the next twenty-five years John carried on his ministry in London, usually from secret lodgings in and around Westminster, which was in those times an area of some of the most appallingly filthy slums in the capital.

When the plague broke out in 1636 we have already seen how he worked with Henry Morse, heroically tending the sick. One gets the impression that in common with many 'northerners' John said what he thought, and in the early days of their collaboration he had occasion to chide his fellow priest for showing signs of timorousness in anointing the sore-ridden bodies of plague victims. When Morse succumbed to the plague it was John's turn to struggle on alone until Henry recovered. The

Puritan Parliament and the Commonwealth

curate of St Margaret's, Westminster, lodged a complaint that Southworth was using his charitable work to proselytise, and in April 1637 he was arrested and imprisoned in the Gatehouse, close to Westminster Abbey.

John addressed an appeal to King Charles via the Queen, protesting that his only care was for the poor and sick, and begging not to be kept in jail for the sake of those who depended upon his help. The appeal was successful. He was set free after only a few days because of the intervention of Father George Conn, the Scotsman who was the papal agent to the Queen.

John and Father Goodman were then apprehended by Newton, the priest catcher, and, like Morse, were held by him at the Sun tavern at Westminster. Newton hoped to make even greater money out of such detentions if the priests or their friends could be persuaded to buy their freedom. The situation must have come to the attention of the Secretary of State, Sir Francis Windebank, because in November 1637 he ordered the two priests to be removed to the Gatehouse, swiftly followed by orders for their release. John was again arrested and sent to the Fleet Prison in June 1640, only to be quickly set at liberty on Windebank's orders. For the next fourteen years John was continuously harassed in his work, being regularly imprisoned and released, usually through the intervention of the Queen. In 1653 the Chapter appointed John, along with Father Andrew Knightly, as a Collector for London and Middlesex, with the task of raising money for the maintenance of the clergy.

With the execution of the King, Southworth lost his protector, and the renewed persecution under the Commonwealth rendered his position even more vulnerable. Following information from a pursuivant called Jefferies, on 19 June 1654 John was taken from his bed and arrested by Colonel Worsley. On 21 June he was brought to trial at the Old Bailey. The magistrate begged him to plead 'Not guilty' to the charge, but John felt this was dishonest and a denial of his priesthood, so he readily confessed to being a priest. Despite all the pleadings and delaying tactics employed by the magistrate and his promise that John's life would be spared, he could not prevail upon John to plead not guilty to the charge. In the end, Serjeant Steel, the Recorder of London, had no

Puritan Parliament and the Commonwealth

alternative but to pronounce the death sentence, which he did in a voice choking with emotion and tears running down his face. The foreign ambassadors in London made strong representations to Cromwell to grant Southworth a reprieve. It appears that the Lord Protector was personally inclined to accede to their request, but was overruled by the Council which advised him that the law, which he had sworn to uphold, should be allowed to take its course.

On 28 June John was dragged to Tyburn to face death with several common criminals. A detailed eyewitness account of the execution was preserved by Bishop Challoner. Despite it being a stormy day with heavy rain, the crowd was huge, numbering several thousand. Over two hundred coaches containing important personages, ambassadors and their retinues attended. John insisted on wearing his cassock and his four-cornered cap on the scaffold. He read out a speech that he had prepared.

'Good people, I was born in Lancashire… now being about to die, I gladly witness and openly profess my faith for which I suffer. And though my time be short, yet what I shall be deficient in words I hope I shall supply with my blood, which I will most willingly spend to the last drop for my faith… I was sent by my lawful superiors to teach Christ's faith, not to meddle with any temporal affairs. Christ sent His apostles; His apostles their successors; and their successors me… I had a care to do my own obligation and discharge my duty in saving my own and other men's souls. This, and only this, according to my poor abilities I laboured to perform… I die for Christ's law, which no human law, by whomsoever made, ought to withstand or contradict it… our Blessed Saviour Himself said, "He that will be my disciple, let him take up his cross and follow me." To follow His holy doctrine and imitate His holy death, I willingly suffer at present. My faith is my crime, the performance of my duty the occasion of my condemnation.'

He then pleaded for liberty of conscience for the poor persecuted Catholics and asked them to pray for him. Raising his eyes and hands to heaven in silent prayer, he submitted quietly to execution. He was cut down while alive and the butchery was carried out but he made no sound.

After the execution, de Cardenas, the Spanish Ambassador, bought the mangled remains from the hangman for forty shillings. The head and quarters were sewn together by a surgeon and the body, embalmed with rich spices, was smuggled to Douai, where it was eventually encased in a lead coffin and placed under the altar of St Augustine of Canterbury in the college church. It was the object of great local veneration and at least one inexplicable cure took place. There the body remained until the outbreak of the French Revolution, when Douai College was suppressed in 1793. The college treasures, including Southworth's coffin, were all buried in the basement for safety.

In 1927 the former college buildings were sold to Douai Town Council, which decided to demolish them. While excavations were taking place the workmen found a lead coffin of about 5'8" in length. When it was opened a body wrapped in discoloured linen was found within. Steps were taken to identify the body, which was quite well preserved, especially the head. There were still traces of a beard and moustache, but the eye sockets were empty. By means of X-rays and other tests it was established that the body had been quartered and it was identified beyond doubt as John Southworth. The body was brought back to St Edmund's College, Ware, in Hertfordshire. After John had been beatified in 1929 it was decided to move his relics to Westminster Cathedral.

Clothed in a 'Roman-style' red chasuble, a black four-cornered cap on his head, his face covered by a silver mask, John's body was placed in a glass reliquary. On 1 May 1930 the relics were solemnly placed in the chapel of St George and the English Martyrs in Westminster Cathedral, where they still rest.

Notes to Chapter Seven

[1] The twelve other priests were as follows:

Venerable Edward Morgan, a Welshman, was born in 1584. He converted in 1601. He was educated at Douai, Rome and Valladolid but his ordination, which took place at Salamanca, was delayed until 1618 because of mental health problems. In 1628 he was in prison in Wales for refusing the oath. He was moved to the Fleet in 1632 and remained a prisoner for ten years until the Puritan Parliament decided to execute him. Condemned to death on 23 April, he was martyred at Tyburn on 26 April 1642, when he made a lucid and memorable speech offering his life for the good of his country, for 'God loves a cheerful giver'.

London-born *Blessed Hugh Green* was the son of a goldsmith. Educated at Cambridge he converted and went to Douai where he was ordained in 1612. Most of his ministry was based with the Arundell family in Dorset. When the order came for the banishment of all priests he set out for Lyme Regis to take ship, but was arrested and imprisoned at Dorchester, where he was martyred with unspeakable barbarity on 19 August 1642.

Blessed Thomas Bullaker was a doctor's son born in Sussex *c.*1602. His was a Catholic family that suffered for its recusancy. He went to Spain but joined the Franciscans and was ordained at Valladolid in 1622. He returned to England in 1630 and was soon captured at Plymouth. Transferred to Exeter, he was tried in 1631 but after a few days in prison was released. He was arrested again in London in 1641 but released on bail. He was finally apprehended by Francis Newton and his gang in London in 1642 in the home of Mrs Margaret Powell. Thomas was interrogated by a special parliamentary committee. He and Mrs Powell were tried together and both sentenced to death. Mrs Powell was reprieved but Thomas was martyred at Tyburn on 12 October.

Blessed Henry Heath was born at Peterborough in 1599. He was educated at Cambridge but converted and went to Douai, where he entered the English Franciscans at St Bonaventure's. After ordination he remained at Douai, serving his monastery in various offices including that of Superior. He desperately wanted to work on the English mission, and in 1643 he sailed to Dover with nothing but what he stood up in and walked to London. Caught sheltering in the doorway of a house, he was arrested and when found to be a priest was martyred at Tyburn on 17 April 1643.

Blessed Arthur Bell, born in 1591, came from a wealthy Worcestershire family. He studied at Valladolid and was ordained at Salamanca in 1618. That same year he joined the Franciscans. He worked in Brussels and at Douai, where he was Superior for two years. Having returned to England, he worked on the mission for nine years until arrested at Stevenage – another victim of Newton. He was martyred at Tyburn on 11 December 1643.

Blessed Thomas Holland came from Lancashire. He was educated at Saint-Omer and Valladolid. He joined the Society of Jesus in 1624. He was martyred at Tyburn on 12 December 1642.

Blessed John Duckett, born in 1614, was a North Yorkshireman from Sedbergh. His parents were 'church papists' but he was reconciled by a seminary priest. He went to Douai in 1633 and was ordained at Cambrai in 1639. He returned to England in 1643 and worked mainly in County Durham, where he was captured. Sent to Newgate, he was martyred at Tyburn on 7 September 1644.

Blessed Ralph Corby, real name Corbington, was born in 1598 at Maynooth, into a deeply religious family from Durham. His parents had moved to Ireland to escape the persecution. They returned to England and lived in Lancashire before emigrating to Flanders. Here Ralph was educated at Saint-Omer along with his brothers, who like him became Jesuit priests. Ralph completed his education at Valladolid and after ordination joined the Society of Jesus in 1625. He was martyred at Tyburn with Duckett. Ralph's mother and sisters became Benedictine nuns.

Blessed Philip Powel was born at Trallong, Wales, and educated at Abergavenny Grammar School before reading law at the Middle Temple. He joined the Benedictines in 1614. He served on the English mission mainly in the West Country and was martyred at Tyburn on 3 August 1646.

Blessed Edward Bamber came from Blackpool. He was born about 1600 and studied at Saint-Omer and Seville, where he was ordained in 1626. When he returned to England he disembarked at Plymouth and was arrested but soon released. He made his way to his native Lancashire, where he worked until 1643, when arrested and imprisoned at Lancaster for three years. He was martyred at Lancaster on 7 August 1646.

Blessed John Woodcock was born near Preston, Lancashire, in 1603. He studied at the English College, Rome. He finally got his wish to join the Franciscans at Douai and was ordained priest in 1634. He did not return to England until 1643. Landing at Newcastle upon Tyne, he made his way to Lancashire but was soon arrested and imprisoned at Lancaster for two years without trial. He was martyred with Bamber.

Blessed Thomas Whitaker, a schoolmaster's son, was born at Burnley, Lancashire in 1611. He studied at Saint-Omer and Valladolid, where he was ordained in 1638. He worked in Lancashire for five years, based at St Michael's-on-Wyre. Arrested at Goosnargh, he managed to escape while being taken to Lancaster Castle. He was soon recaptured and spent two years in jail awaiting trial. He was martyred at Lancaster with Bamber and Woodcock.

[2] Blessed Peter Wright was born into a recusant family at Slipton, Northamptonshire, in 1603. As a young boy he went to work as a clerk in a lawyer's office at Thrapston, where he had to conform, at least outwardly. He crossed to the Netherlands and eventually made his way to the Jesuit College at Liège. In 1629 he entered the Society of Jesus at Ghent, serving his novitiate at Watten, followed by years of study at Liège, where he was ordained probably in 1636. He became a military chaplain, serving the English Regiment of Colonel Henry Gage in the Spanish Netherlands. Here he met Henry Morse. In 1643 he returned to England and ministered to the soldiers during the Civil War. In 1645 he became chaplain to the Marquis of Winchester, based at his house in London. While preparing to say Mass on 2 February 1651 he was arrested and sent to Newgate. He was tried at the Old Bailey before Lord Chief Justice Henry Rolles. Evidence was given against him by the apostate former Dominican priest Thomas Gage. Condemned for his priesthood on 19 May 1651, he was hanged, drawn and quartered at Tyburn before a huge throng of carriages and horsemen. He was beatified in 1929.

[3] *... harsh prison conditions.* To give the lie to the general perception of leniency towards Catholics in the period, there follows just a representative selection of priests who suffered during the rule of Parliament and under the Commonwealth. Those who died in prison in those years were:

1642: Edward Wilkes, died York; Boniface Kemp OSB, died Yorkshire; Ildephonse Hesketh, died Yorkshire.

1643: Venerable Brian Cansfield SJ, aged sixty-one, died at York on 3 August from beatings and ill-treatment.

1644: Thomas Vaughan, died Cardiff.

1645: The Welshman, Venerable John Goodman, whose story has been told, died Newgate, aged fifty-three.

1646: Richard Bradley, died Manchester; John Felton SJ, died Lincoln; Peter Wilford OSB, sentenced to death 1642, died in Newgate, aged sixty-two.

1647: Thomas Blount, condemned to death and died in Shrewsbury jail, aged thirty-one.

1648: Thomas Foster SJ, died Lincoln, aged fifty-eight; Andrew Waferer OSB, condemned to death 1641, reprieved by the King but died in Newgate, aged seventy-two.

1650: John Abbot, Bridgettine, a nephew of George Abbot, Archbishop of Canterbury, condemned to death 1641, died in Newgate aged sixty-two; Robert Cox OSB, died in the Clink.

1652: George Gage, brother of the apostate Thomas, imprisoned Newgate and died there.

1660: George Anne SJ, aged sixty-five, died in York Castle, as did his recusant grandfather before him in 1600.

Other priests imprisoned/condemned included:

Charles Cheney, who shared a cell in Newgate with Peter Wright;

Sixty-four-year-old George Machell, condemned 1651 and left in Newgate;

Basil Norton, imprisoned Newgate, 1642, where he remained until 1661;

Richard Worthington, a great-nephew of Cardinal William Allen, condemned to death 1643 but saved by the Venetian ambassador.

Chapter Eight

Charles II and the 'Popish Plot', 1660–1685

> Truth sits upon the lips of dying men.
>
> *The Scholar Gypsy*, Matthew Arnold, 1822–88

The restoration of Charles II to his throne in 1660 aroused fresh optimism amongst English Catholics. Charles was conscious of owing a debt of gratitude to his Catholic subjects for their loyalty to his father in the Civil War. Furthermore, in 1651, as Prince of Wales, he had attempted to claim his throne. A Benedictine priest, Father John Huddleston, who had served as a chaplain in his father's army, saved his life by sheltering him after his defeat at the Battle of Worcester. It was an act of bravery the King never forgot. He relaxed the persecution and priests were released from prison. Most Catholics were allowed to live in peace and many priests were allowed to work discreetly. Charles, although brought up amongst Catholics, was a pragmatist when it came to matters of religion or indeed any other matters. Having spent his youth in exile he was determined, as he declared, never to go on his travels again, so all his policies were designed to ensure his continued tenure of the throne. He was personally sympathetic to the Church, having a Catholic mother, a beloved Catholic sister and dependence upon the Catholic Louis XIV for financial support. He had a Catholic wife, Catherine of Braganza; his brother James, Duke of York, converted and married a Catholic princess, Mary of Modena.

During Charles's reign the Chapter was able to set up a more formal organisational structure of archdeaconries covering England and Wales. No slander was too foul or allegation too farfetched to level at the Catholics, who in turn had been accused of being responsible for the Great Plague of 1665 and the Great Fire of London the following year. Despite his public religious ambivalence and scepticism, Charles made an effort to protect the Catholics from molestation by the Puritan bigots. His room for manoeuvre was, however, limited because the Civil War had so weakened the authority of the Crown. He tried to honour his nuptial contract to ensure that his consort, Queen Catherine, was allowed free practise of her religion. Father Philip Thomas Howard OP,[1] great-grandson of St Philip Howard, had a position of influence at Court. He was Grand Almoner to the Queen and lived at St James's Palace in receipt of a salary. During Queen Henrietta Maria's exile, the Puritans had imprisoned and then banished her Capuchin priests and desecrated their chapel. On her return to England in 1663 she reinstated the Capuchins.

In 1670 Parliament complained to the King about the 'Growth of popery'. Much to the resentment of the Protestants, he brought prominent Catholics into his government. While Parliament was prorogued in 1672, Charles issued a Declaration of Indulgence allowing toleration to Catholics; but when Parliament reconvened he was forced to withdraw it. Parliament retaliated by passing the Test Act, which disbarred anyone from holding any public office who did not take an oath insulting the Catholic Church and specifically denying the Real Presence of Christ in the Eucharist; thus all Catholics were effectively excluded from Parliament. Although aimed ostensibly at all Catholics, the act was a further swipe at James, Duke of York, who was banished to Scotland.

Our final six martyrs were all victims of the fierce anti-Catholic persecution of 1678–81 that amounted to nothing less than a pogrom against Catholics. The infamous so-called 'Popish Plot' unleashed a reign of terror. It was invented and fomented by the son of a former weaver and self-appointed Anabaptist preacher, Titus Oates, in collusion with his cronies: the deranged clergyman Dr Israel Tonge and, later, the Chepstow-born William Bedloe. There was a large measure of personal spite and revenge against Catholics not only in Oates's accusations but in the fabrications of other so-called witnesses. Deeply saddening though it is to recall, there were also a number of Catholics who were terrorised into providing false information, for example Miles Prance, a London goldsmith whose two brothers, Thomas and Charles were priests and two sisters nuns. Even worse were the apostate priests, such as John Travers SJ, who jumped onto the bandwagon and turned on their former colleagues by supplying false evidence against them.

The nub of the 'Plot' was the assassination of the King and his replacement by his Catholic convert brother James, Duke of York, who would then bring in a foreign Catholic army to massacre the Protestants and force the nation back to Catholicism. The whole affair would have been farcical were it not for the appalling consequences. The last persecution in which Catholics were actually put to death for their faith, it is one of the most shameful episodes in the whole of British history. The eighteenth-century statesman Charles James Fox called it 'an indelible disgrace upon the English nation'.

The physically unprepossessing Oates, with his jutting jaw and slobbering mouth, had been a failure at everything he attempted. Expelled from the Merchant Taylors' School, expelled from Cambridge, he became an Anglican vicar in Kent but was dismissed for theft, drunkenness, blasphemy and sodomy. For false allegations against a schoolmaster he was imprisoned at Hastings. In 1677 he began service as a naval chaplain before being ousted for sodomy. Unemployed, he moved to London and ingratiated himself with the Jesuits, who charitably supplied him with funds and found him a job. Purportedly converting to Catholicism, he entered the Jesuit College at Saint-Omer but was dismissed. Then he tried being a seminarian at Valladolid from where, when his true character was discerned, he was quickly thrown out. Returned to London, he fell in with Israel Tonge, another former Anglican vicar, now turned fanatic Puritan, who appears to have spent most of his time writing anti-Catholic, particularly anti-Jesuit, pamphlets. Feigning penitence, Oates once more wormed his way into the Catholic community and was given a second chance by being sent to the seminary at Saint-Omer. Needless to say he was very soon ejected. Oates later claimed he had only joined the Jesuits in order to spy on them. Teaming up with Tonge again in London, the pair of them began to concoct the 'Plot'.

Their far-fetched farrago having been given short shrift by officers of the government, in September 1678 Oates and Tonge sought out a Justice of the Peace, Sir Edmund Berry Godfrey, and presented to him their spurious allegations of a Catholic plot. The mysterious death of Sir Edmund in October was the catalyst they needed to lend some semblance of credence to the allegations when 'the Catholics' were accused of his murder. The rabidly anti-Catholic Anthony Ashley Cooper, Earl of Shaftesbury, and leader of the Whig opposition to the King, together with other bigots, eagerly seized the opportunity to ruthlessly exploit the 'Plot' for their political ends. Not content with fanning the flames of fanaticism, Shaftesbury actively connived with Oates and his cohorts to tailor their false information to the advantage of the exclusionist cause – that is excluding the Duke of York from the succession to the throne and supplanting him with the Protestant Duke of Monmouth, King Charles' illegitimate son. Shaftesbury did not stop at supplying false evidence when it suited his purpose. He also resorted to imprisonment and brutal treatment to compel so-called witnesses to provide lying testimony. Carried away on a tide of his own notoriety and influence, Oates's allegations mushroomed alarmingly in number and scope. He was bold enough to raid the Jesuit residence which was attached to the Spanish embassy. The ambassador, Count Egmont, prevented the soldiers from taking away Venerable Edward Mico SJ, his chaplain who was ill in bed with a fever. The priest was brutally treated by the raiders and placed under house arrest. He died a few weeks later.

King Charles, under no illusions as to the true purpose of the allegations, never believed in the existence of any Catholic plot. Finding it all too preposterous to be taken seriously, he made the mistake of treating the whole affair too light-heartedly at the outset. When the full import of the 'Plot' was realised, the King's efforts to mitigate its terrible consequences proved ineffectual. The real plot, as Charles knew very well, was the conspiracy against his brother. Charles personally exposed Oates as a liar when he questioned him before the Council and advised that he should be ignored. It was of no avail, as people who had been whipped up into an anti-Catholic frenzy were prepared to believe anything, however ludicrous. In spite of frequently contradicting himself, his so-called evidence being demonstrably false and his documentation forged, Oates was praised as the saviour of the nation, and his wicked perjury was only revealed when it was too late.

Blessed Edward Coleman, secretary to the Duchess of York, was the Catholic convert son of an Anglican minister. He was accused of planning to kill the King. The often indiscreet and overzealous Coleman had been warned by Sir Edmund Berry Godfrey that he had been accused by Oates. Purely on the flimsy evidence of intercepted correspondence with Father La Chaise, confessor to Louis XIV of France, and the lies of Oates, Coleman was martyred at Tyburn on 3 December 1678. Even the name of the non-Catholic Samuel Pepys was dragged into Oates's farrago of nonsense, presumably because he maintained his loyalty towards his former employer, the Duke of York.

The conspirators were bold enough to try and draw the King's Catholic consort, Queen Catherine, into the 'Plot' by attacking those attached to her court. Her physician, Sir George Wakeman, was accused of plotting to poison the King. He was tried for treason but acquitted. One of her chaplains, Father Thomas Tilden, commonly called Dr Godden, fled to France. His servant, Lawrence Hill, was not so lucky; nor was his fellow employee at Somerset House, Robert Green, an elderly married Irish Catholic whose job was to place the cushions in the Queen's chapel. Miles Prance, placed in irons and threatened with torture, falsely accused Hill and Green of involvement in the death of Sir Edmund Berry Godfrey. By the time Prance asked to see the King and confessed that his evidence was false – 'upon his salvation' – it was too late. These two humble Catholics were found guilty and martyred at Tyburn on 21 February 1679. Years later Prance voluntarily admitted that his testimony was a pack of lies. Another of the Queen's chaplains was Father John Huddleston OSB.[2] He was the one priest whom the conspirators dared not touch. As the saviour of the King's life after the Battle of Worcester, he was specifically exempted by royal proclamation from all harassment.

Aside from the King, there seem to have been few contemporary personages of any cool common sense or intelligence inclined to view the proceedings dispassionately. The diarist and author John Evelyn was one. He wrote of Oates as a vain, insolent man: 'Such a man's testimony should not be taken against the life of a dog'. Today it is difficult for us to grasp the extent of the incredible public hysteria and panic engendered by the 'Plot'. Scores of priests made their escape to the Continent, including the future bishop and Vicar Apostolic of the Eastern District, Bonaventure Giffard. In the witch-hunt hundreds of totally innocent lay Catholics suffered imprisonment in the countrywide round-up of well-known Catholics. Many of them died in prison the victims of the insanitary conditions and disease.

A typical case is that of Sir Henry Tichborne of the ancient Hampshire family which had given two martyrs to the Church: Venerable Nicholas Tichborne in 1601 and Venerable Thomas Tichborne in 1602. On 21 November 1678, having been accused by William Bedloe, Sir Henry was arrested on a warrant from Lord Chief Justice, Sir William Scroggs, and committed to Winchester prison for high treason. In December he was removed to the Tower where he was kept in close confinement for eighteen months. Throughout that time he was never examined or questioned or formally charged. Eventually he was released on a writ of habeas corpus and told to return home. It is a story that could be multiplied many times.

In addition to Edward Coleman, Lawrence Hill and Robert Green, three other laymen were put to death,[3] including William Howard, Viscount Stafford, the grandson of Philip Howard. Over thirty priests, most of them Jesuits, were condemned to death. Fifteen priests were executed,[4] including the six who are numbered among the Forty Martyrs, plus a Benedictine brother, Thomas Pickering. This tragedy was described by Jane Lane (the pen name of Elaine Kidner Dakers) in her biography of Titus Oates (1949) as 'a series of judicial murders without parallel in the story of these nations'.

No one indicted could remotely expect to receive even a faint semblance of a fair trial; the proceedings were a travesty. Sir William Scroggs (1623–83), who presided at most of the earlier trials, discriminated against, scurrilously abused and vilified the accused Catholics. Even those Catholics brave enough to give evidence for the defence found themselves insulted and their veracity impugned. Scroggs enunciated two absolutely incredible

Charles II and the 'Popish Plot', 1660–1685

principles as the basis for the proceedings at the trials: 1. Although it was true that the witnesses against the accused had committed serious misdemeanours, none of these should be admitted in court as in any way impairing the value of their testimony, especially as they had received royal pardons for their crimes; 2. No Catholic witness for the defence was to be believed, as it should be presumed that they had received dispensations to lie under oath. So even though the priests on trial defended themselves ably and through cross-examination clearly demonstrated that their accusers were manifestly guilty of blatant perjury, it was of no avail.

The tide began to turn with the trial of Sir George Wakeman, when Scroggs questioned the veracity of Oates's evidence and Wakeman was acquitted. One wonders at what stage Scroggs began to examine his conscience over his judgment in the cases of around fifteen innocent men he had already sent for execution. Shaftesbury openly revealed his hand when, taking advantage of the general hysteria, he brought forward an Exclusion Bill to remove the Duke of York from the succession. In 1681 the conspirators finally overreached themselves in seeking to impeach the Duke of York as a recusant and, on the strength of the change in public mood, the King decided that countermeasures had to be taken and he dissolved Parliament. So came to an end what, to quote Jane Lane again, was 'the bloodiest hoax in history'.

In the face of the baying Protestant extremists in Parliament, the powers of the King to stop the bloodshed were limited. It became politically expedient for him to allow the executions of condemned priests whom he believed to be innocent, and while he managed to reprieve many others they remained in prison, where sixteen died from ill usage.[5] Those who had managed to survive were released on the accession of James II in 1685. On his deathbed, the cynical Charles II finally honoured the long-standing promise he had made, and the night before he died he was received into the Catholic Church by the old Benedictine, Father Huddleston, who had saved his life thirty-four years before. There is no reason to believe that Charles was not perfectly sincere.

And what became of the conspirators? Shaftesbury was

charged with treason in 1681 and forced to flee to the Continent, where he died in 1683. Most of the others were later found guilty and punished for their perjury, including the arch-villain Titus Oates. In 1685 he was tried and condemned by Lord Chief Justice, Sir George Jeffreys, the selfsame judge who had sent innocent priests to their deaths on the strength of his testimony. Jeffreys concluded that Oates's testimony contained 'so many great contradictions, falsities and perjuries upon which so much innocent blood has been shed'. He proclaimed Oates a 'shame to mankind' and a 'monstrous villain' who had 'pawned his immortal soul', and pronounced him guilty of perjury. Oates was sentenced to be whipped, put in the pillory and imprisoned for life.

When William of Orange came to power he knew he had to keep his Protestant promoters sweet, so he ordered Oates's release and paid him a pension. He became a Baptist preacher until he was thrown out for being a hypocrite and defrauding that dissenting organisation of the proceeds of a rich old lady's will. He died in obscurity in 1705 and was buried in an unknown grave.

John Plessington

> Deeds of a purer lustre given to few, made for the perfect glory that remains.
>
> *The Call*, W N Hodgson, 1893–1916

John was born *c.*1637 at Dimples Hall, Garstang, Lancashire. He was the son of Robert Plessington or Pleasington and Alice Rawstone. Royalist Catholics, the family had suffered much because of their beliefs. John was educated by the Jesuits at their secret school at Scarisbrick Hall near Ormskirk. He went abroad to study for the priesthood firstly at the English College of St Alban, Valladolid, in 1660 and then at Saint-Omer. He was ordained at Segovia on 25 March 1662. The following year he was sent to England.

He ministered in Lancashire and at Holywell, North Wales,

Charles II and the 'Popish Plot', 1660–1685

where St Winifred's Well had remained a place of pilgrimage throughout the penal times. Using the alias William Scarisbrick, he then worked for the next sixteen years in Cheshire, using Puddington Hall near Burton, on the Wirral, as his base. The Hall was the ancestral home of the Massey family. The head of the family, Edward Massey, with his wife Alice Braithwaite sheltered John. When Edward died in September 1671 leaving John £5 in his will, Plessington remained with his son and heir, William. In 1679 when the Oates 'Plot' was at its height, Plessington was betrayed by a Catholic and arrested by a man named Thomas Dutton, who was paid for his trouble. John was imprisoned for two months in Chester Castle. He was never accused of being implicated in the 'Plot' but was charged under the old Elizabethan law solely with being a priest. He was tried in May 1679 and condemned to death. The judges who condemned him wrote to inform Parliament, asking if John should be reprieved. Parliament ordered the execution to be carried out.

On 19 July 1679 John was taken from Chester Castle to be hanged, drawn and quartered on Gallows Hill – now known as Barrel Well Hill – at Boughton, beside the River Dee near Chester. The speech full of love and forgiveness that he made from the scaffold was afterwards printed and circulated. The full text is in Bishop Challoner's *Memoirs of Missionary Priests*.

'I am here to be executed neither for theft, murder nor anything else against the law of God, not any fact of doctrine inconsistent with monarchy or civil government. Nothing was laid to my charge except my priesthood and you will find that priesthood is neither against the law of God, nor monarchy, nor civil government.' John then delivered a logical if barbed thrust at his persecutors. He declared, 'I know it will be said that a priest ordained by authority derived from the See of Rome is, by the law of the nation, to die as a traitor, but if that be so what must become of all the clergymen of the Church of England, for the first Protestant bishops had their ordination from those of the Church of Rome, or not at all, as appears by their own writers so that ordination comes derivatively from those now living.' He went on, 'I protest in the sight of God and the court of Heaven that I am absolutely innocent of the plot so much discoursed of, and abhor such bloody and damnable designs. I have deserved a worse death; for though I have been a true and faithful subject of my King, I have been a grievous sinner against God... But as there was never a sinner who truly repented and heartily called to Jesus for mercy to whom He did not show mercy, so I hope by the merits of His passion, He will have mercy on me, who am heartily sorry that I ever offended Him... I profess that I undoubtedly and firmly believe all the articles of the Roman Catholic faith and for the truth of any of them, by the assistance of God, I am willing to die; and I had rather die than doubt any point of faith taught by our holy mother the Roman Catholic Church... God bless the King and the royal family and grant His Majesty a prosperous reign here and a crown of glory hereafter. God grant peace to the subjects and that they live and die in true faith, hope and charity... I recommend myself to the mercy of Jesus, by whose merits I hope for mercy. Jesus, be to me a Jesus.'

His quartered remains were wickedly returned to the Massey family at Puddington Hall; they were instructed to hang them from the four corners of their house. But the local people buried the remains in nearby Burton churchyard, the location of the grave being handed down from generation to generation. Today a memorial plaque in the churchyard commemorates John Plessington and since 1980 his name has also been commemorated on a memorial plinth at the Gallows Hill site alongside that of George Marsh, who in 1555 was burned to death in that place for Lutheran heresy.

Philip Evans

> 'Bring me my harp... I would play one more tune before I die. Last night an angel called... play, and come through the gates of death.'
>
> *Dafydd Y Gareg Wen*: David of the White Rock

Philip was born at Monmouth, Wales, in 1645 and was educated at Saint-Omer. In 1665 at the age of twenty he joined the Society of Jesus and served his novitiate at Watten. Philip was highly thought of by his superiors, who praised him for his frankness, modesty and cheerfulness, qualities that remained with him all his life and won him universal affection. In 1675 he was ordained priest at Liège in Belgium and sent back to work in South Wales. He laboured zealously without molestation until November 1678. As everywhere else, the situation of the Church in South Wales at this time was fraught with difficulties and missionary conditions were hard, but the number of priests was maintained and the Franciscans were active in the area.

Following the scare of the 'Plot', the Calvinist John Arnold, of Llanvihangel Crucorney near Abergavenny, Member of Parliament, Justice of the Peace and tireless hunter of priests, offered a reward of £200 for Philip's capture. The youngest of the Jesuits on the mission, he was advised to flee but would not hear of deserting his post. He was caught at Sker House, Porthcawl, the home of his friend Christopher Turberville, and taken prisoner to Cardiff Castle. Here he was put in an underground cell, refusing to take the Oath of Supremacy. He spent five months in jail while the authorities scoured the countryside trying to find evidence against him. They finally found a poor old woman and her daughter and a deformed dwarf named Trott, who had once been at the Spanish Court but was now an apostate in the service of John Arnold. They were suborned to testify at the Spring Assizes that Philip was a priest. Trott's evidence was intended to implicate Philip in the 'Plot' but it was unsupported, so the court had to rely upon the evidence of the two women that they had seen him celebrating Mass and had received Communion from him.

The trial took place on Monday, 5 May at the Shire Hall, Cardiff. The judge, Mr Justice Owen Wynn, was a kindly man. He indicated to Philip that if he would deny the evidence he would go free. Philip, knowing it would be perjury to deny the truth of the evidence, remained silent. The judge told the jury that if they believed the evidence of the two women they must find Evans guilty under the Elizabethan statute 27, which they quickly did. After receiving his sentence with head bowed, Philip thanked the judge and jury.

The execution was delayed for eleven weeks during which

Philip was treated reasonably and allowed a great deal of liberty out of his cell. He wrote a short letter to his superior, Father David Lewis, who being in prison himself was most grateful and derived comfort from the message. We learn in these weeks of Philip's skill at games and music. It was during a game of tennis that the news was brought to him by the undersheriff that he was to die the following day; Philip calmly finished the game. He spent his last hours playing the Welsh harp and talking cheerfully to the many people who came to say goodbye.

On 22 July 1679 he was taken, with Father John Lloyd, to Gallows Field in Cardiff. Philip addressed the crowd in Welsh and English. Giving his final speech, he declared that this was the best pulpit any man could ever have to preach in: 'I die for God and religion's sake and I think myself so happy that if I had never so many lives, I would willingly give them all for so good a cause. If I could live it would but be for a little time, though I am but young. I think myself happy that I can purchase with a short pain an everlasting life.' He forgave his persecutors and, turning to his fellow priest, he said, 'Adieu, Mr Lloyd, though for a little time, for we shall shortly meet again. Pray for me and I shall return it when it pleases God that I shall enjoy the beatific vision. If any of you that see me willingly die for my religion have any good thought upon it, I shall think myself happy.'

As he climbed the ladder it proved to be too short. When he reached the top rung the ladder turned around with him so that one of the sheriff's officers grabbed hold of his legs and twisted them round after his body so that he would hang from the rope. Spoken in a clear voice, Philip's last words were, 'Into Thy hands, O Lord, I commend my spirit.'

John Lloyd

> All at rest thou liest and the fierce breath of tempests can no more disturb thy ease.
>
> *The Timber*, Henry Vaughan, 1622–1695

John, a native of Breconshire, Wales, was born in 1630. He was probably a nephew of his namesake, a Jesuit priest who studied at the English College in Valladolid and took the missionary oath there in 1649. John had a sister, Margaret, who was in the convent of the Blue Nuns in Paris. He studied humanities at Ghent, Belgium, before entering the English College of St Alban, Valladolid, in 1649. He was very popular because of his lovable innocence and humility. Having completed his theology and philosophy studies he was ordained priest on 7 June 1653 and the following year returned to South Wales, where he laboured for the next twenty-four years. He was known to frequent and say Mass at Trivor, the home of the James family in the parish of St Maughans, north of Monmouth.

A few weeks after the arrest of Philip Evans, John was apprehended at the home of Mr Turberville at Penllyn near Cowbridge, Glamorgan, and sent to join Philip in Cardiff Castle. He was tried with Philip, being convicted on similar evidence, and condemned. The two priests enjoyed each other's company while awaiting execution and were taken to the gallows together. Arrived at the place of execution they asked which of them was to die first and on being told that it was Philip they embraced each other and John gave him absolution as he watched his comrade suffer.

When it came to his own turn he kissed the gallows and gave a short speech, which was later printed. Claiming that he had never been a good speaker he said, 'My fellow sufferer has declared the cause of our death, therefore I need not repeat it... I shall only say that I die for the Catholic and Apostolic faith, according to these words in the Creed, I believe in the holy, Catholic Church; and with those three virtues, faith, hope and charity. I forgive all those that have offended me; and if I have offended anybody I am heartily sorry for it and ask their forgiveness. I beg the prayers of all and in particular of the Catholics here present, desiring them to bear their crosses patiently and to remember that passage of Holy Scripture, "Happy are they that suffer persecution for justice, for theirs is the kingdom of heaven".'

He then climbed the ladder and thanked all who had been kind to him, in particular Mr Carne, the sheriff. Striking his breast three times, he said 'Lord have mercy upon me a sinner,' and as he was saying, 'Into Thy hands, Lord, I commend my spirit,' he was turned off the ladder.

John Wall

> Now there is waiting for me the prize of victory awarded for a righteous life.
>
> Second letter of Paul to Timothy

John, the son of William Wall and Dorothy Reynes, was born into a wealthy recusant family, possibly at Chingle Hall, Kirkham, Lancashire, in 1620. Although the family originated from Norfolk, being connected with the Wall family at Chingle, they moved to Lancashire, which would explain why John and his brothers were born there. John was baptised by Edmund Arrowsmith. He was sent to Douai at an early age, and on 5 November 1641 entered the English College, Rome, under the name of John Marsh. He was ordained in the chapel of The Apostles Peter and Paul in the Vatican on 3 December 1645. His brother William also studied at Douai and arrived at the English College, Rome, just two days before John's ordination.

After completing his studies in May 1648, John returned to England, paying a visit to the Holy House shrine at Loreto en route. He returned to Douai in 1650 and on 1 January 1651 he joined the Franciscans at St Bonaventure's Convent, which had been founded by John Gennings, brother of the martyr. Father Gennings, now an old man, was still living at the convent. The new novice was given the name Joachim of St Anne. He was appointed Father Vicar and later novice master at St Bonaventure's, where he remained until 1656, the year in which, accompanied by a group of friars, he returned to England.

We have considerable information about his apostolate from an account written by an anonymous priest friend. John laboured on the mission for twenty-three years, mainly in Warwickshire and Worcestershire under the name of Francis Johnson, eventually settling his headquarters for his final years at Harvington Hall, near Kidderminster. This was the home of the widowed Lady Mary Yate, the daughter and heiress of Humphrey Pakington, Lord of Chaddesley Corbett. Her family had remained faithful and had been constantly in trouble with the authorities for their recusancy since Elizabethan times. There is a fascinating connection between the Pakingtons and one of the earliest Henrician martyrs, Blessed John Haile. Not long before he was arrested in 1535 there is a record of his having sold land in Worcestershire to John Pakington. The land was confiscated by the Crown before the sale was complete and Pakington asked Thomas Cromwell to use his influence to ensure that the land was transferred to him. Harvington Hall had several hiding holes in which priests could be concealed. They can still be seen today and are considered some of the best surviving examples of the work of Nicholas Owen.

There is the heartening story told of how John, shortly before his capture, was visiting Kings Norton and would have been caught had it not been for the goodness of a Protestant named Thomas Millward who bravely hid him in his house. In gratitude John told Millward that if he was ever required to die for his faith he would offer his life's blood for the Protestant's soul.

In October 1678, when the tumult of the 'Plot' burst out, John happened to be visiting London as a guest of the Queen's Capuchins at Somerset House. While in the capital he also called on the French Jesuit Claude de la Colombière. Claude had been confessor to the visionary of the Sacred Heart, Saint Margaret Mary Alacoque. On the recommendation of King Louis XIV, in 1676 he had been sent to London as preacher to the Duchess of York, Mary of Modena. He lived frugally at St James's Palace and, being subject to Father Thomas Whitbread, the English Jesuit Provincial in London, he knew all the fathers of the Society of Jesus who were soon to be martyred. John sought out Claude at St James's Palace, announcing himself as a poor Friar Minor come to seek the strength and counsel of the Sacred Heart of Jesus. John spent the day in conversation with Claude, stayed to supper and was persuaded to remain overnight, Claude giving up his bed to his guest while he slept on the floor. The following morning, the Feast of All Saints, John said Mass in Claude's oratory. John obeyed the order that required all Catholics to leave London. In the middle of the night on 24 November Claude was dragged from his bed at St James's Palace and arrested. He was sent to the King's Bench Prison, where he was very ill. It was feared that he would be executed but the French Ambassador intervened on the direct orders of Louis XIV and Claude de la Colombière was sentenced to banishment, which took place in January 1679. Claude died in 1682 and was canonized in 1992.

John returned from London to Worcestershire but not to Harvington. He took up residence at the home of the Finch family at nearby Rushock Court, near Bromsgrove. In December he was arrested there by a sheriff's officer who had come during the night to apprehend a defaulting debtor. While conducting the search the officer found John in bed. His status being suspect, he was taken to the nearby Justice of the Peace, Mr Townsend, who asked him to take the Oath of Supremacy. When he refused, the justice's compassionate wife tried to persuade him to save himself from further trouble, but John responded that he would not be moved by any fear of danger to go against his conscience. Mr Townsend then accompanied John to the magistrate at Westwood Park, Sir John Pakington, who happened to be a relative of Lady Mary Yate. He was questioned at length by Sir John, assuring him that he was and would be to his last breath as faithful a subject to the King as any subject whatsoever; but he refused to take the oath. Under guard, John was then taken to prison in Worcester Castle where he remained for five months.

At the January Quarter Sessions in 1679, he was brought before Mr Justice Street under the name of Johnson. He denied all guilt but the magistrates sent him back to prison and committed him for trial at the Lent Assizes where, they told him, there would be enough evidence to send him to the gallows. Much of John's life and suffering is known to us from his own account written while in prison. He wrote:

> Imprisonment in our times, when none can send to his friends, nor friends come to him, is the best means to teach us how to put our confidence in God alone in all things... We all ought to follow the narrow way, though there may be difficulties in it. It is an easy thing to run the blind way of liberty, but God deliver us from all broad, sweet ways.

On Tuesday, 25 April he appeared before Mr Justice Atkins and from the account of the protracted proceedings he defended himself under examination with great skill and dexterity. We

Charles II and the 'Popish Plot', 1660–1685

know what was said in detail because John himself wrote a lengthy account of the trial. Four witnesses were called: three of them had to be subpoenaed and stated that they knew of nothing with which to accuse John. On the strength of the evidence of a man who had a personal grudge against him, John was found guilty – not of any connection with the 'Plot' but simply for being a priest under the Elizabethan statute. After hearing his sentence, John bowed courteously to the judge and responded, 'Thanks be to God. God save the King, and I beseech God to bless your Lordship and all this honourable bench.' Later he wrote:

> I was not, thank God, troubled with disturbing thoughts and I esteemed the judge and jury the best friends that ever I had in my life. I was so present with myself, whilst the judge pronounced sentence, that at the same time I offered myself to God.

The judge, who told John he had spoken well, indicated that he did not intend John should die without knowing what were the King's wishes regarding his fate. Before being conducted back to prison, John tells us he was approached by a number of Protestant gentlemen who had been present in court. In a conversation lasting about half an hour, they expressed their regret and sorrow for his plight; but John assured them that they should not grieve for him for he was quite joyful, being ready to die tomorrow if required.

By order of the Privy Council in May, John was sent on horseback to London for interrogation by Oates and Bedloe. He was put in Newgate, where his brother William was already a prisoner, accused of aiding and abetting Sir George Wakeman of plotting to poison the King. To their sorrow, the brothers were denied the opportunity to meet. John tells us that he was 'very strictly examined' several times during the month he was detained in London, but Bedloe publicly pronounced him innocent of any plotting. John was offered his life on more than one occasion if he would renounce his religion. After a spell in Newgate, the Council ordered him to be sent back to Worcester, whither he returned on 18 July to await execution. In a letter to a friend who had sent him some money, he gave an account of his London interrogations. He wrote, 'I could not buy my own life at so dear a rate.' He added, prophetically, 'This is the last persecution that will be in England; therefore I hope God will give us all His holy grace to make the best use of it.'

Sir William Scroggs and Mr Justice Atkins arrived in Worcester in August for the Summer Assizes. They sent for John and told him bluntly that he would die in a few days for being a Roman priest unless he would secure his reprieve by taking the oath and conforming. John thanked the judges for their trouble but refused their offer. He was returned to prison and kept in close confinement. On 18 August he was informed that he was to die on the 22nd. What comfort it must have been for him to be allowed a visit from a fellow Franciscan, Father Francis Leveson, who was permitted to see him on the 20th and found him cheerful. Venerable Francis Leveson was at the time a prisoner at Worcester and died in February 1680, aged thirty-four, after fourteen months in jail. Contrary to their expectations, Leveson was allowed access to him again on the 21st for four or five hours. He heard John's confession and gave him Communion. John must have been extraordinarily composed, judging from the letter he wrote to the English Franciscan Provincial, in which he speaks so lovingly of himself as a child of the Virgin Mary.

On Friday, 22 August 1679, John was taken with two common criminals to Redhill, overlooking Worcester, to be executed. John remarked upon the appositeness of being executed with two thieves, just as Christ had been. Father Leveson managed to stand close to the scaffold and again gave John absolution before he died. Leveson informs us that while the criminals were hanged, John kissed the ladder, kissed the rope, kissed the hangman's hand and gave him ten shillings. While in prison John had written a long and beautiful speech, a copy of which he had given to Father Leveson and was later printed. The sheriff allowed John the time to read the speech in full. In it he discoursed on the three virtues of faith, hope and charity, speaking of the third virtue as the greatest.

'It has pleased our Saviour to declare that no man has greater charity than that he lays down his life for his friend. I therefore willingly undergo this death I am to suffer now, to testify that I love my friend and neighbour as myself; whilst I undergo this death for myself and them, seeing that it is for the profession of my faith I die… I testify I love God above all, because I forsake the world and myself in death, rather than offend Him by doing anything against my conscience.' He asked God to bless the King and give him a long and happy reign, to bless the nation and Parliament. 'I will offer my life in satisfaction for my sins and for the Catholic cause. I beseech God to bless all my benefactors and all my friends… and all those that suffer under this persecution; and to turn our captivity into joy; that they that sow in tears may reap in joy.'

Having placed the rope around John's neck, the hangman asked him to give a sign when he wished to be turned off, but John declined to give any sign, simply saying, 'Do it when you will,' and closed his eyes. The ladder was quickly removed and John was left hanging, presumably dead. His body was disembowelled and quartered and his head cut off.

Father Leveson obtained the head which was later conveyed to St Bonaventure's at Douai. Sadly, the treasured relic was lost after the suppression of the convent in the French Revolution. The body was buried in the churchyard of St Oswald's in Worcester, where there is now a memorial inscription, and it remains a place of pilgrimage for Worcestershire Catholics. In 1879 a memorial cross was erected to commemorate John in the churchyard at Harvington. It reads:

> In memory of Father John Wall OSF, in religion Father Joachim of St Anne, who obeying God rather than man, for twelve years ministered the sacraments to the faithful in this and other parts of Worcestershire in daily peril of death.

Since 1923 Harvington Hall, as a result of a generous benefaction, has belonged to the Catholic Archdiocese of Birmingham, which has carried out extensive conservation and restoration.

John's brother, William, was sent to England in 1650. In 1668 he joined the Benedictines, taking the name Dom Cuthbert. Arrested during the 'Plot' he was tried with Sir George Wakeman at the Old Bailey in July 1679 and, despite Oates giving evidence against him, he was acquitted, but remained in prison. He was brought to trial again the following January accused of being a priest and condemned to death. He was reprieved by the King, although still confined to prison; but, contrary to some authorities who assert that he died there, he survived until freed on the accession of James II. He died at the Abbey of Lambspring, Germany in 1704. As a postscript it may be added that five years after John Wall's martyrdom, his Protestant shelterer, Thomas Millward, became a Catholic.

John Kemble

> In the days of my youth I remembered my God! And He hath not forgotten my age.
>
> *The Old Man's Comforts*, Robert Southey, 1774–1843

John was born in 1599 into a Catholic family at Rhyd y Car farm in the parish of St Weonards, Herefordshire. His father, John Kemble, came from an old Wiltshire family. Why some of the Kembles moved to Monmouthshire is unclear, but it has been surmised that it was to enable them to practise their religion in greater safety in a rural area where Catholics remained numerically strong. In King James's time, John senior was well known to the authorities, being reported as a dangerous recusant who harboured priests. John's mother, Anne Morgan, came from a prominent family at Skenfrith. Her grandfather had been the last governor of Skenfrith Castle and his tomb may still be seen in Skenfrith parish church as well as the seventeenth-century Morgan family box pew. So John's ancestry was a mixture of Welsh and English. While he was a boy, his family moved into the parish of Llangarron. Although there is no written record of his arrival we know that at a young age, following in the footsteps of his elder brother, Walter, he was smuggled to Douai to be educated; a perilous undertaking for all concerned. Walter eventually became a Benedictine priest at Douai.

At the age of eighteen John entered the seminary at Douai and was ordained by the Bishop of Arras on 23 February 1625. On 4 June of that year he was sent to England to begin his apostolate in his native area of Hereford and the Welsh border country. He is unique among the martyrs for his extraordinarily long ministry of fifty-four years. The centre of his ministry was Pembridge Castle at Welsh Newton, the home firstly of his uncle, George Kemble, and then of his nephew Captain Richard Kemble. Today what remains of Pembridge is a farmhouse but the chapel has survived. In the adjoining parish of Llanrothal the Jesuits had established a community at the Cwm or Coombe, and with their help John founded mission centres around the Monnow Valley which delineates the border between England and Wales. Even today it remains a secluded, inaccessible area of narrow lanes, its medieval churches, such as those at Skenfrith, having strong defensive towers; a reminder that this was Marcher country. The Carmelites were also active on the Herefordshire borders and ran a secret school.

There were many Catholic families in Herefordshire and Monmouthshire who sheltered John and at whose houses he and other priests would have said Mass. During the Civil War Pembridge Castle was held for the King and was forced to surrender to the Parliamentary forces after a siege in 1646. It was severely damaged, but John continued to make it his headquarters. In 1649 John visited London on clergy business while back home many of the castle lands were seized as forfeit for the recusancy of the family. His nephew Richard Kemble distinguished himself at the Battle of Worcester in 1651 by helping Prince Charles to escape. In 1670 when Parliament complained to the King about the increase in Catholics, the Cym and the Jesuits operating from there were explicitly cited as an example of popish activities.

When the 'Plot' spread out its tentacles from London into the countryside, few places were more vulnerable than the Welsh borders where there was a concentration of Catholics. Priests were imprisoned in Monmouth, Cardiff, Brecon, Denbigh, Chester and many other towns. In the winter of 1678 priests in fear of their lives went into hiding or fled the country. Many hunted priests perished of hypothermia, hunger and exhaustion as they moved about the open country and mountains in wintertime trying to elude their captors. Catholic houses and property were ransacked and trashed by the authorities in the hope of finding a priest. The Cwm was raided and John was urged by his friends to flee. 'I'm too old now,' was his answer. He said he had but a few years to live and would remain at his post. After all, it 'will be an advantage to suffer for my religion.'

In spite of his wife and children being Catholics, Captain Scudamore of Kentchurch led the searchers to Pembridge Castle in November 1678. John calmly surrendered to his arrest and was dragged off through the snow to the county jail in Hereford. While John was in prison, the governor made a pen and ink portrait of him which has been preserved. He remained in prison over three months until sent for trial in March 1679, when he was condemned at the assizes to be hanged, drawn and quartered for being a seminary priest.

On 23 April he and Father David Lewis were sent to face examination in London for complicity in the 'Plot'. Too frail to ride properly, John was strapped to a horse, his face to the animal's tail 'like a bundle of merchandise', as one eyewitness described it, and taken on the painful journey to Newgate to join Father Roger Hanslepp, a priest who had been condemned at Gloucester. Oates, Bedloe and others were ordered by the House of Lords to interrogate the priests. Kemble was promised his life and liberty if he 'confessed' but Oates failed to implicate John in the imaginary 'Plot', or obtain any information from him. On 28 May the Privy Council ordered him to be sent back to Hereford, this time walking most of the way. He was returned to prison, sick and exhausted and in great pain, as witnessed by a fellow prisoner, Father Charles Carne, who was in Hereford jail at the same time awaiting his fate.

There is a most interesting relic in the form of a letter, albeit very damaged, between a lady and Kemble. The lady wrote to him in prison to tell him that she and her mother had endeavoured to persuade the keeper to let them in to see him, but without success; so she asked him for his prayers and blessings. On 13 June John wrote a short reply in the margins of the letter and returned it to her, enclosing a lock of his hair as a keepsake. The letter and the hair have survived. John's last letter, it reads:

> This poor old condemned man whom you so charitably visited in Newgate, to whom you delivered four pounds in the night before

Charles II and the 'Popish Plot', 1660–1685

our removal, came safely to Hereford on the Saturday following. But I have been so bruised in body that I have not been able to sit so long as to write to you according to your commands; be pleased therefore to excuse my want, not of dutiful respect to you and your worthy companions to whom I shall ever acknowledge myself unspeakably obliged, but to my miserable condition. You shall have of me as long as I live a true and faithful beadsman, but your full requiter must be the Almighty rewarder of all your good works. What I left in your hands I beseech you let be sent with what convenience may be. I am sorry I am able to do no more and had not been able to do so much had not you and your friends' extraordinary charity assisted me. I pray you expect no compliments from him that never knew how to make use of them and pardon this my shortness and bad writing which I perform in great pain.

In July the Privy Council ordered the death sentence to be carried out on all priests found guilty. John appeared before Lord Chief Justice Scroggs and Sir Robert Atkins at Hereford Town Hall on 4 August. His execution was ordered for the following month. While awaiting execution, he was allowed visitors, among them the children of Captain Scudamore, the man who had arrested him. With the children he shared the sweets sent in by friends. When asked why he treated them with such kindness, he replied that their father had been the best friend he had ever had.

On 22 August Mr Digges, the undersheriff of Hereford, came to tell him that he was to die that day. John asked for time to pray and smoke a last pipe. The undersheriff admired the old man and he and the prison governor joined John in smoking a pipe and drinking a cup of wine. The incident was the origin of the Herefordshire custom of referring to a parting pipe as a 'Kemble pipe'. John was drawn on a hurdle to Wigmarsh Common (now known as Widemarsh) outside the city to the gallows, where a huge crowd had assembled. As it was customary John spoke to the people while standing in the cart. His last words were taken down and printed.

> 'It will be expected that I should say something, but as I am an old man it won't be much, and not having any concern in the plot, neither indeed believing there was any: Oates and Bedloe

not being able to charge me with anything when I was brought up to London, though they were both with me, makes it evident that I die only for professing the old Catholic religion, which was the religion that first made this kingdom Christian... I desire God to forgive all those that have been anyways accessory to the bringing of me to this place. It is my prayer now, and shall be unto Almighty God not to punish them for so doing; and if I have offended any man in thought, word or deed, I am heartily sorry for it and beg his pardon as I pardon those that have anyways offended me.'

The hangman was greatly upset. John shook him by the hand and tried to encourage him saying, 'My friend, Anthony, be not afraid, do thy office well. I forgive thee with all my heart; you are doing me a greater kindness than discourtesy.'

He then pulled his cap over his eyes and prayed for a while in silence on his knees, after which he announced that he was ready and they might carry out their duty whenever they pleased. Three times he repeated, 'Into Thy hands, O Lord, I commend my spirit,' before the cart was pulled away. The hangman was clumsy and John hung for half an hour, slowly and painfully strangulating, the blood bursting from his mouth, nose and ears. No one had the heart to cut him down and so he was left to die. Such was the respect in which he was held that he was spared the disembowelling and quartering, but his head was cut off. John Kemble was eighty years of age. Even his persecutors declared that they had never seen anyone die so like a gentleman and so like a Christian.

His remains were begged by his nephew, Richard Kemble, and buried beside the churchyard cross at Welsh Newton, Monmouth, under a plain slab that reads:

JK Dyed the 22 of August Anno Do 1679.

The village, three and a half miles north of Monmouth, is situated on the A466, the main road between Hereford and Monmouth. The small Norman church of St Mary still retains its twelfth-century carved stone rood screen. John's grave immediately became and continues to this day to be a much loved place of pilgrimage and many miraculous cures have been attributed to the martyr's intercession at his resting place. In the early nineteenth century the great actress, Mrs Sarah Siddons, with her brother Charles, who belonged to the famous Kemble family acting dynasty, visited the martyr's grave and she sent a yearly donation to have it kept in decent order.

The martyr's left hand, being under his head, was accidentally severed at his execution. It was retrieved by a woman in the crowd who wrapped it in her apron. It now rests in St Francis Xavier's Catholic Church, Hereford, in a most beautiful silver-gilt reliquary. The hand lies in a crystal cylinder supported by the figures of saints and angels. Its base is set with the precious stones which the book of Revelation says adorn the foundation stones of the Holy City of God, the New Jerusalem. The reliquary was donated by a grateful father whose son recovered from a life-threatening illness after being touched by the hand. As recently as 1995 an inexplicable cure was attributed to the hand's healing powers. Father Christopher Jenkins suffered a massive stroke and lapsed into a deep coma; his life was despaired of. After the hand had been applied to his forehead he quickly made a full recovery. The Catholic Church at Monmouth possesses other relics of the martyr, among them his missal, with marginal comments in his handwriting, the oak benches that served as his altar and his portable altar stone.

David Lewis

> My soul, there is a country far beyond the stars… There, above noise and danger, sweet peace sits crown'd with smiles.
>
> *Peace*, Henry Vaughan, 1622–1695

David was born at Abergavenny in 1616. His father was Morgan Lewis, who had conformed, presumably for material advantage. His mother was Margaret Prichard, who remained Catholic. The Prichard family produced several priests. She was also a niece of the saintly Dom Augustine Baker OSB, lawyer, monk and famous mystical writer, who died of the plague in London in 1641. David, the eldest of nine children, strangely seems to have been the only one who was raised as a Protestant. He was educated at the Royal Grammar School, Abergavenny, of which his father was head. Another former pupil was Blessed Philip Powel OSB, who was martyred at Tyburn in 1646. Just like his Benedictine predecessor, when he left school at sixteen David was sent to study law at the Middle Temple in London. After three years in London he travelled to Paris and joined the household of Comte Savage as tutor to his young son. While in Paris he was received into the Catholic Church by Father William Talbot, procurator of the Jesuit mission. He returned home to spend two years with his family at Abergavenny and had the joy of seeing his father reconciled to the Church before his death.

Both his parents having died, David sought the advice of Father Charles Browne, Superior of the Jesuit mission in Wales, about his future. On 3 November 1638 he entered the Venerable English College, Rome, under the alias of Charles Baker. One of his fellow students was John Wall. After four years in Rome he was ordained priest at San Lorenzo in Damaso on 20 July 1642. Later that year, on the feast of the first Christian martyr, St Stephen, he preached a short sermon before Pope Urban VIII. On 19 April 1645 he joined the Society of Jesus and served his novitiate at Sant'Andrea. Immediately after he was professed in 1646 he was sent to the mission in Wales, but was quickly recalled to Rome to become spiritual director at the English College. This proved to be a short posting because there was a greater need for David's talents in his homeland, and in 1648 he returned to Monmouthshire to work in South Wales and Herefordshire for the next thirty years. This was not an easy task in the aftermath of the Civil War, when many priests were in great danger from the Parliamentarian authorities, and several of David's colleagues were imprisoned during the years of the Commonwealth.

His apostolate was carried out in the Jesuit missionary district known as the College of St Francis Xavier, with its headquarters at the Cwm, an isolated converted farmhouse near Llanrothal. The Cwm was not a college in any conventional sense of the name; it was an administrative centre and a place of rest and refuge for the priests serving on the mission. There were around

Charles II and the 'Popish Plot', 1660–1685

twenty-five priests on the mission when David joined them and they had to subsist on a communally shared meagre annual income. Some priests were attached as chaplains to the houses of prominent Catholic landowners from where they could minister to the Catholics in the surrounding area; for example, Father William Morgan SJ, who was chaplain at Powis Castle. Most led a peripatetic existence serving the area allotted to them. This was how David laboured, traversing the often mountainous country, mostly on foot. To avoid the persecutors he often took long, circuitous routes at night in order to visit and serve the poorest of his flock, for whom he evinced a special love and devotion. It earned for him the name *Tad y Tlodion*: the Father of the Poor. From 1666 to 1671 David was Superior of the South Wales district. He again held that post from 1674 until his death.

In 1678 the fanatically anti-Catholic John Arnold, Member of Parliament, presented to the Commons a report giving details provided by informers about Catholic activities in Monmouthshire and Herefordshire. It contained the information that David Lewis publicly said Mass in the chapel of the home of the Morgan family at Llantarnam, near Cwmbran, as well as other houses around Abergavenny, such as that of Thomas Gunter, who had also been host to Philip Evans. When the full fury of the 'Plot' burst upon Monmouthshire the hunt was on for every priest. Under the leadership of Bishop Croft of Hereford, the Cwm was raided and ransacked. The priests had managed to get away in time but a great deal of Catholic material was seized, including many books that were carted off to Hereford and still reside there in the famous cathedral library.

David went into hiding at Llantarnam, but his whereabouts were betrayed and early in the morning of Sunday, 17 November he was arrested while preparing for Mass. He was taken to Llanfoist, just west of Abergavenny, where Arnold and the magistrates awaited his arrival. All the details of his arrest, imprisonment and trial are known from the *Narrative* written by Lewis and published after his death. On that Sunday afternoon, escorted by twelve armed men, he was carried in a triumphal procession through Abergavenny to the Golden Lion inn; here Mr Jones, the Recorder, held a makeshift court. A former servant of the priest gave evidence that he had seen him say Mass many times, so he was committed for trial. Afterwards he was escorted to Arnold's house at Llanvihangel Crucorney, where he arrived at about midnight and was kept overnight under guard. The following morning he was conducted on horseback under armed guard to Monmouth prison, where he was kept in close confinement until 13 January 1679. David tells us that he was locked up by night and barred up by day so strictly that he was never allowed to leave his room, but friends managed to smuggle information to him.

It must have been heartbreaking to hear about the arrests of other priests and the destruction of his life's work in the mission. A few instances may be recalled of the fate of David's priestly friends and colleagues. Father Walter Price SJ fled his pursuers for two months, usually at night in the snow, with only the bare minimum of clothes to keep him warm. He succumbed to a fever and died. Not content with hounding the man to his death, the magistrate ordered his grave to be opened, ripped apart his shroud and removed the silver cross around the priest's neck. Father Charles Prichard SJ managed to evade capture for nearly eighteen months, hiding by day and emerging only at night. His health collapsed under the weight of strain and anxiety he endured. He suffered a bad fall, which hastened his end, and was buried secretly in the garden of a house where he had found shelter. The old Carmelite priest who ran their school, Father Nicholas Rider, was arrested but bailed by some local Protestants. Taken to London, he was again arrested and bailed but sought sanctuary in the Spanish Embassy, where he died. Father George Loop, a Herefordshire Carmelite, escaped from Captain Scudamore disguised as a farmer's wife. He successfully made his way through various villages all the way to Worcester. Father Thomas Andrews, who lived near Llantilio, hid in the woods before being taken in by a Catholic widow called Jane Harris. When the pursuivants raided her house Father Andrews had escaped. Mrs Harris was arrested and for a time was held in the same jail as David Lewis. Father Andrews, worn out by his hardships, died of exposure and was buried under the floor of a barn.

Not only the clergy but also the laity in South Wales had to

Charles II and the 'Popish Plot', 1660–1685

bear the brunt of the persecution. The penal laws were rigorously enforced against them for the first time in years. Their homes were raided and property confiscated. Many were thrown into prison for refusing to take the Test Oath, and reduced to penury by the iniquitous bail requirements to secure their release.

On 13 January 1679, on a bitterly cold day with heavy snow, David was transferred from Monmouth to Usk. In this jail he encountered a number of lay friends who had refused to take the Test Oath. On 28 March David was brought to trial at the assizes before Sir Robert Atkins. Having had legal training, he was able to conduct a worthy defence, challenging some of the jurors selected. After some difficulty, a jury was finally sworn which was to the satisfaction of Arnold – but not of Lewis, who feared that they were all ignorant men. The prosecution witnesses who were called testified to having seen David say Mass and carry out other priestly functions. David disputed the evidence, including evidence of his identity; he questioned the worthless character of some of the witnesses, a number of whom were motivated by malice, which he was able to expose, and vigorously refuted aspersions cast upon his good name.

However proficient his defence, the outcome of the trial was never in doubt: he was found guilty of being a priest under 27 Eliz. I, c. 2. When the death sentence was pronounced David bowed to the judge. Together with John Kemble, he was sent to London for questioning in Newgate by Oates and Bedloe. Neither being implicated in the 'Plot', nor persuaded to apostatise, Lewis, Kemble, John Wall and Roger Hanslepp were ordered on 28 May to be taken back to their respective prisons, and David was returned to Usk.

David spent three months awaiting his execution. During this time, thanks to the connivance of the jailer, Catholics were allowed access to him and he was able to administer the Sacraments to them. In prison David composed his final speech, a manuscript copy of which, written on jail paper, has survived. Sheriff James Herbert kept finding excuses to delay the execution in the hope that a reprieve might be granted. On 11 July the Privy Council issued orders that all condemned priests should be executed forthwith, but still the sheriff prevaricated. John Arnold, angry at the delay, asked Lord Shaftesbury to order the sheriff to carry out the execution.

Poor Sheriff Herbert, who was fined for neglect of duty, had to face further headaches on the day fixed for the execution, which took place on 27 August 1679 before a great crowd. The workmen refused to erect the gallows, so the sheriff had to bring a convict from the jail; this man, on a promise of securing his freedom, set up a makeshift effort of two poles with a crossbeam. However, they were not high enough to allow sufficient drop for a body, so a trench had to be dug beneath to create more space. The convict had to beat a hasty retreat when the crowd threw stones at him. The official hangman refused to carry out the execution and fled the town. A blacksmith was induced to perform the task when offered a handsome sum as a bribe.

Standing on a stool below the gallows, David delivered his eloquent speech in Welsh, which was afterwards published. He defended himself again from any imputations on his character and then explained what the cause of his untimely death was. He avowed himself a loyal subject of the King, for whom he prayed daily, and abhorred all plots, of which he knew nothing. He alluded to his interrogation at Newgate, in which he had been offered his life, proving that he died for reasons of conscience and his religion. He declared, 'Here is a numerous assembly; may the great saviour of the world save every soul of you all. I believe you are here met not only to see a fellow native die, but also to hear a fellow native speak. My religion is Roman Catholic; in it I have lived above forty years; in it I now die and so fixedly die, that if all the good things in this world were offered to me to renounce it, all should not remove me one hair's breadth from my Roman Catholic faith… A Roman Catholic priest I am; a Roman Catholic priest of that religious order called the Society of Jesus I am; and I bless God who first called me. I was condemned for saying Mass, hearing confessions and administering the Sacraments. As for saying Mass, it was the old and still is the accustomed and laudable liturgy of the holy Church; and all the other acts are acts of religion tending to the worship of God and therefore dying for this I die for religion.'

David forgave with all his heart those who had any part in

bringing about his death. He named his chief persecutor John Arnold specifically, declaring that he bore him no ill will but only love, and for whom he asked God to give the grace of true repentance. He said, 'Forgive and you shall be forgiven; I profess myself a child of the Gospel and the Gospel I obey.' Turning to his fellow Catholics he urged them, 'Fear God, honour your King; be firm in your faith... bear your sufferings patiently and forgive your enemies.' He made a humble act of contrition and then, as he uttered the words, 'Sweet Jesus, receive my soul,' the stool was pulled away.

A Protestant gentleman prevented the executioner from cutting Father Lewis down before he was dead. He was disembowelled, but the crowd protested that his body should not be quartered. He was, therefore, spared this indignity and all his remains were buried in the churchyard of old St Mary's Priory, Usk. They still rest there under an inscribed slab on the north side of the pathway close to the west porch of the church. His grave has continued to be a place of pilgrimage.

To those who may ask why pilgrimages should still be made to the places associated with the martyrs, the answer is eloquently supplied by the American poet, playwright and Nobel laureate T S Eliot, who in his verse drama *Murder in the Cathedral* wrote:

> Wherever a martyr has given his blood for Christ there is holy ground and the sanctity shall not depart from it.

Notes to Chapter Eight

[1] Philip Thomas Howard was the son of Henry, Earl of Arundel, grandson of the martyred Philip Howard. His mother was a daughter of the Duke of Lennox, so he was related to the Royal Family. At the age of sixteen he joined the Dominicans in Italy. Professed in 1646, he took the name of Thomas in religion. He was ordained in 1652. Devoted to the cause of the conversion of England, he founded a college for the education of English Catholic boys. Because he occupied a prominent position at Court he faced much hostility and opposition from the Puritan faction and returned to the Continent. In 1672 he was nominated by the Pope as Vicar Apostolic of England, but because of opposition from the Chapter of secular clergy, who wanted a diocesan structure restored, the nomination was withdrawn. In 1675 he was made a Cardinal and took up permanent residence in Rome where he tried to promote the interests of English Catholics, and in 1679 was named Cardinal Protector of England and Scotland. He rebuilt the English College at Rome. Through his influence, the number of Vicars Apostolic was increased to four at the accession of James II in 1685. He tried to exert influence, albeit from a distance, on the new King to be more cautious about pushing forward his policy of toleration in the face of Protestant opposition. He took part in three papal conclaves. He died in 1691, much mourned, and was buried at Santa Maria sopra Minerva, his titular church in Rome.

[2] Father John Huddleston OSB was born in 1608 at Leyland, Lancashire, one of the sixteen children of Joseph and Helen Huddleston, a recusant family. John studied at Saint-Omer and the English College, Rome, where he was ordained in 1637, returning to England in 1639. He served as a chaplain to the Royalist army in the Civil War. He seems to have spent most of his ministry in Staffordshire, but at what date he joined the Benedictines is unknown. It was Father Huddleston who hid Charles II at Moseley after the Battle of Worcester, thus saving his life. John's uncle, Richard, was also a priest, who as a boy had been taught by Blessed Thomas Somers. Richard Huddleston had written *A short and plain way to the faith and church*, which Charles had enjoyed reading while in hiding at Moseley. At his restoration, Charles appointed John a

chaplain to his mother, Queen Henrietta Maria, at Somerset House. After the Queen Mother's death he became attached to the chapel of Queen Catherine. He was the one priest who was safe from prosecution during the 'Plot' furore. He remained safe after James II fled in 1688 and continued in the service of Queen Catherine at Somerset House. He published his uncle Richard's book, along with his own account of his role in rescuing Charles II and the King's deathbed conversion. John died at Somerset House at the age of ninety in September 1698.

[3] The three other laymen put to death were as follows.

Blessed John Grove was the servant to Father William Ireland SJ. He lived at Wild House, which was part of the Spanish Embassy occupied by Jesuits. He was imprisoned at Newgate and Oates swore that Grove was to receive £1,500 for his part in the assassination of the King. He was hanged, drawn and quartered with William Ireland at Tyburn on 24 January 1679. On the scaffold he protested his innocence but forgave those who were the cause of his death. He was buried at St Giles-in-the-Fields.

Blessed Richard Langhorne was a married, Bedford-born barrister. He was the legal adviser to the London Jesuits, handling their property transactions. Arrested in October 1678 without any legal proceedings, he was kept in virtual solitary confinement in Newgate for eight months. In June 1679 he was tried at the Old Bailey, where Oates, Bedloe, Dugdale and Prance all gave false evidence against him. His dying words as he was hanged, drawn and quartered at Tyburn on 14 July 1679 were that he longed to be with Jesus. He was buried at St Giles-in-the-Fields.

Blessed William Howard, Viscount Stafford was born in the Strand, London, on 30 November 1612, the youngest of the three sons of Thomas, Earl of Arundel, only son of the martyred Philip Howard. At the coronation of Charles I in 1626 he was made a Knight of the Bath. In 1637 he married Mary Stafford, Baroness Stafford and he was allowed to take the title himself in 1640, when he was created a Viscount. They had eight children: three sons and five daughters. William naturally supported the King but in 1642 went into exile. When Charles II regained his throne William was restored to all his honours. As a Catholic he was excluded from the House of Lords under the legislation of 1673. He lived the life of a country gentleman, enjoying the company of his family, but was also somewhat litigious in asserting his rights. In 1675 he conducted his Dominican nephew, Philip, to Rome when he was made a Cardinal. In October 1678, for no apparent reason other than he was an easy target, Stafford was included in the list of Catholic peers accused by one Stephen Dugdale and Oates of involvement in the 'Plot'. Along with the Earl of Powis and Lords Petre, Arundell and Belasyse, William was sent to the Tower, where they were soon joined by Lord Aston. William was kept prisoner for a year before being suddenly taken for trial for treason at Westminster Hall in November 1680. No written evidence was produced and it appears no serious attempt was made to investigate the perjured testimony, but the cowardice of the Lords in the face of the popular frenzy ensured that William was found guilty. On Wednesday, 29 December 1680 he was beheaded on Tower Hill. He was full of confidence in the mercy of God, knowing he died for nothing more than his faith. He died with a quiet dignity and heroism, certain that one day the truth would be known and 'all the world will then see and know what injury has been done to me'. His last letter to his wife and the speech he made on the scaffold all confirm William's character as a 'generous, devout, charitable man' as stated in the 'Memoir' of him written by Dom James (Maurus) Corker OSB, his confessor. William Howard was the last Englishman to be put to death for his Catholic faith.

Dom Maurus had been one of three Benedictines arrested for the 'Plot' but the postponement of his trial saved his life. He was tried with Sir George Wakeman in July 1679 and acquitted. He was sentenced to death for his priesthood in January 1680 and remained in Newgate until 1685, when he was released by James II.

[4] The fifteen priests and the brother executed were as follows.

Blessed Thomas Pickering was born in Westmorland *c.*1621. He was a Benedictine lay brother who was professed at St Gregory's, Douai, in 1660 and returned to London in 1665. As one of a small group of Benedictines who were attached to the Queen's chapel at Somerset House, he was known to the King and Queen. In 1675 when Charles was forced by parliament to order the Benedictines to leave England, Pickering was allowed to remain, presumably because he was not a priest. In 1678 he was alleged to have skulked around St James's Park with concealed pistols waiting to kill the King. The accusations made against him by Oates and Bedloe – including that 30,000 Masses would be said for the success of his evil enterprise – were patently ludicrous, as the King and Queen said so, but he was found guilty. After a reprieve from the King his execution was delayed for several months; but Parliament demanded his execution and he was hanged, drawn and quartered at Tyburn on 9 May 1679 and buried at St Giles-in-the-Fields.

Blessed William Ireland came from a Yorkshire family, the eldest son of William Ireland of Crofton Hall, but was born in Lincolnshire in 1636. He was educated at Saint-Omer and entered the Society of Jesus at Watten in 1655 aged only nineteen. He was professed in 1673 and after ordination became chaplain to a convent of Poor Clares. He returned to England in 1677 and was appointed Procurator of the English Province. He was arrested by Titus Oates on 28 September 1678. Oates swore that Ireland had been in London at a Jesuit meeting plotting to kill the King. Thanks to the efforts of his sister, Anne, witnesses were able to testify that Ireland was in Staffordshire at the time of the alleged meeting, providing a solid alibi to discredit Oates's claim. However, Lord Chief Justice Scroggs virtually told the jury to ignore the witness testimony, and Ireland was found guilty and hanged, drawn and quartered at Tyburn on 24 January 1679 and buried at St Giles-in-the-Fields.

Blessed Thomas Whitbread, alias Harcourt, was born in Essex *c.*1618. Educated at Saint-Omer, he joined the Jesuits in 1635 and served on the mission from 1647 onwards, mostly in the eastern counties where he was at various times superior of the Lincolnshire and Suffolk districts. At the time of the 'Plot' he was the Jesuit Provincial and it was he who had dismissed Oates from Saint-Omer. Despite suffering serious illness, he was brutally treated after his arrest in London on Michaelmas Day in 1678. He was indicted at the Old Bailey on 17 December, but for lack of evidence against him he was sent back to prison. He was tried with four fellow Jesuits at the Old Bailey on 14 and 15 June 1679. Sir John and Lady Southcote and their children appeared as witnesses.

Their testimony included confirmation that Father William Ireland had indeed been in Staffordshire as he had claimed. It was too late to help Ireland, who had been executed six months earlier, but it served to discredit Oates. However, Lord Chief Justice Scroggs dismissed the evidence on the grounds that as the earlier jury had found Ireland guilty they must have believed Oates! Whitbread was hanged, drawn and quartered at Tyburn on 20 June 1679 and his remains were buried with his fellow martyrs somewhere near the north wall of St Giles-in-the-Fields church, which was on the road to Tyburn. When Oates was tried for perjury and found guilty in 1685, Lord Aston, newly released from the Tower, and Sir Edward Southcote repeated the testimony about Ireland's whereabouts in 1678 and were then believed.

Blessed William Harcourt, whose real name was Barrow, was born *c.*1610 at Kirkham, Lancashire. Educated at Saint-Omer, he joined the Jesuits at Watten in 1632 and returned to England in 1645 working in the London district for thirty-five years. He was elected Superior in 1678. He was hanged, drawn and quartered at Tyburn with Whitbread and his companions.

Blessed John Fenwick, whose real name was Caldwell, was born at Durham in 1628. Educated at Saint-Omer, he became a Jesuit in 1656. He was hanged, drawn and quartered at Tyburn with Whitbread. Had he not been executed, his leg would have had to be amputated as it had gone gangrenous from the heavy irons cutting into it while in prison.

Blessed John Gavan was born in London in 1640. Educated at Saint-Omer, he became a Jesuit in 1660 and served on the mission, mainly in Staffordshire. He had a reputation as an eloquent preacher. He was hanged, drawn and quartered at Tyburn with Whitbread.

Blessed Antony Turner was born near Melton Mowbray, Leicestershire, the son of a Protestant minister. He went to Cambridge and, after he, his brother and mother had converted he went to the English College, Rome. He joined the Society of Jesus in 1653 and was ordained in 1670. Returned to England, he served the mission mainly in Worcestershire. He was hanged, drawn and quartered at Tyburn with Whitbread. When the 'Plot's final

Charles II and the 'Popish Plot', 1660–1685

victim, St Oliver Plunket, Archbishop of Armagh, was executed at Tyburn on 1 July 1681, he asked to be buried at St Giles-in-the-Fields with the six Jesuits.

Blessed Nicholas Postgate was born either in 1598 or 1599 into a Catholic family at Egton Bridge, North Yorkshire. He went to Douai in 1621, was ordained at Arras in March 1628 and returned to England in June 1630. He worked selflessly on the mission in Yorkshire for almost fifty years, tramping the North York Moors in all weathers, his base being a cottage at Ugthorpe. A letter of his has survived, in which he gives an indication of the progress of his ministry, citing the number of baptisms, marriages, burials and converts made. In 1679 he was arrested at Sleights near Whitby; the man who apprehended him received £20 as a reward. When asked if he was a popish priest, he replied, 'Prove it.' Despite being interrogated, he could not be brought to divulge any information. However, he had on his person communion wafers and devotional books and was committed for trial at the York Assizes. He was condemned to death not for any complicity in the 'Plot' but simply for being a priest. He said that it was but 'a short cut to heaven.' Aged over eighty, he was hanged, drawn and quartered at York on 7 August 1679. In an extraordinary gesture, Catholics were allowed to take away his remains for burial; sadly where that took place is unknown. Few priests have been as much loved by their flock – a love that has endured to this day in the memory of the people of North Yorkshire. That Nicholas Postgate had to wait until 1987 to be beatified beggars belief.

Blessed Charles Meehan was born in Ireland *c.*1640. He became a Franciscan and was probably ordained in 1672. He lived for a time with the Franciscans at Louvain, in Germany and Rome. He set out to return to Ireland in June 1678. Fatefully for him, his ship ran aground on the North Wales coast and when he came ashore he was arrested at Denbigh. From his possessions it was determined that he was a priest and given the rampant anti-Catholic hysteria of the time he was condemned for his priesthood. He was hanged, drawn and quartered at Ruthin on 12 August 1679.

Blessed Thomas Thwing was born in 1635 at Heworth, near York, the son of George Thwing and Anne, daughter of Sir John

Gascoigne of Barnbow Hall, Barwick-in-Elmet. The Thwings were a great recusant family. It was at their house that Blessed Anthony Page of Harrow had been captured; he was then martyred at York on 20 April 1593. Thomas's family had already given a martyr to the Church: his uncle, Blessed Edward Thwing, had been executed at Lancaster on 26 July 1600. Thomas was educated at Saint-Omer and Douai. After ordination he returned to England in 1665 where he ran a school. In collaboration with his maternal uncle, Sir Thomas Gascoigne, he was responsible for inviting Mary Ward's Institute of the Blessed Virgin to settle in York in 1677 in a house donated by Sir Thomas. Three of Thomas's sisters were members of the community, which he served as chaplain. In July 1679 he was arrested with Sir Thomas at Barnbow Hall and spent a year in York Castle before being brought before the assizes in March 1680 in company with a number of men and women, all aristocratic Yorkshire Catholics. The jury was subject to so many challenges that the proceedings had to be abandoned until the next assizes in July. The 'evidence' produced against him was a list of names of Catholics willing to subscribe to defraying the cost of establishing the Institute in York. It was presented as a list of persons willing to kill the King. Judged even by the normal standards of the day, his trial under Sir Edward Atkins was a monumental farce, but he was condemned. Upon receiving the verdict, Thwing simply said, 'I am innocent.' The King ordered a stay of execution, but under pressure from the House of Commons this was withdrawn and Thomas was hanged, drawn and quartered at York on 23 October 1680. He was the last of the long line of seminary priests to suffer martyrdom.

[5] The list of all those priests who suffered in the 'Plot' is too great to detail, but a selection will serve to convey the extent of the endurance of the many who died in prison and/or from ill-treatment.

Venerable Thomas Bedingfeld SJ, real name Downes, chaplain to the Duke of York, died in the Gatehouse on 21 December 1678 while awaiting trial.

Venerable Francis Nevill SJ died in prison at Stafford in 1678.

Robert Pugh from Caernarvonshire was arrested in December 1678, and imprisoned in Newgate. While awaiting trial he died there of the harsh treatment to which he was subjected in January 1679.

William Lloyd was arrested in November 1678, condemned at Brecon, Wales, in April 1679 and died in prison there six days before his execution in 1679, aged sixty-five.

Thomas Jenison SJ came from a wealthy family and renounced his inheritance in favour of his younger brother, who apostatised and gave evidence against him. After spending nearly a year in prison he died in jail in London on 27 September 1679.

Venerable Francis Leveson, a Franciscan, died in prison at Worcester on 11 February 1680.

Placid Aldhelm, a Benedictine, was a convert minister. A chaplain to Queen Catherine, he died in Newgate 1680.

Richard Birkett died in prison under sentence of death at Lancaster in 1680.

Richard Lacy SJ (real name Prince) died in Newgate on 11 March 1680.

John Morgan was arrested and condemned in April 1679 but reprieved by the King. He died in Newgate in March 1680.

David Kemish or Kemys, Dominican, was an old man at his trial in 1679; he was too weak to stand and too deaf to hear. He died in Newgate a few days later. Tried with Kemish was the Benedictine Henry Starkey. Born in Cheshire, he had served in the Royalist army in the Civil War and had a leg blown off. Because of his disability, he was refused entry to Douai but accepted by the Benedictines in 1649, returning to England in 1661. He was condemned to death but remained in Newgate. After his release he lived in France, where he died in 1688.

William Atkins SJ died in prison at Stafford under sentence of death on 17 March 1680 aged eighty. Father Atkins was so feeble that he had to be carried into the courtroom and was so deaf that he could not follow the proceedings at his trial in August 1679. When the verdict was delivered it had to be shouted into his ear and he then thanked the judge.

Thomas Wilkinson SJ was ordained at Segovia with John Plessington. Arrested in 1679 he was imprisoned at Morpeth, where he was poisoned in January 1681.

Edward Turner SJ died in the Gatehouse on 19 March 1681.

William Allison died a prisoner at York Castle under sentence of death in 1681.

Benedict Constable, a Benedictine, died in prison at Durham on December 11 1683.

Anthony Hunter SJ died in Newgate in 1684.

John Bully came from Dorset. He fought for the Royalists in the Civil War and was ordained at Rome in 1654. He was arrested and imprisoned at Winchester in December 1678. Condemned to death, he was not executed but transported to the Scilly Isles, where he died in 1687.

Andrew Bromwich was condemned with William Atkins at Stafford in spite of taking the Oath of Supremacy. He remained in prison for ten years.

William Bennet SJ (real name Bentney) was born in 1609 in Cheshire. He joined the Jesuits and served on the mission from 1640. He was arrested and imprisoned in Leicester jail. He was tried at Derby in March 1682 and condemned to death, but remanded back to Leicester. It seems likely that he was released on the accession of James II in 1685, but was rearrested in 1688 and sent back to Leicester prison, where he died on 30 or 31 October 1692, aged eighty-four.

Epilogue

> They shall fight against you, but they shall not prevail against you, for I am with you, says the Lord.
>
> Jeremiah 1:19

There were great hopes when James II acceded to the throne. In spite of his Catholicism he enjoyed the support of the majority of the people. However, he was very unlike his brother in temperament. Hard-working and conscientious, honest and forthright to the point of tactlessness, he lacked Charles's facility for dissimulation, or put more bluntly, a capacity for telling lies when it suited political expediency. As a result he completely misread the mood of the times, believing that his welcome as King gave him a mandate to relieve and favour his fellow Catholics while at the same time continuing to protect the position of the Anglican Establishment. It did not. His determination to follow a policy of liberation for all, Protestant Nonconformists as well as Catholics, brought down upon him the wrath of his enemies. Emboldened by the defeat of the rebellion against him led by his bastard nephew, the Duke of Monmouth, he began to openly favour Catholics, appointing many to positions of authority. He attended Mass in public at Court in great splendour. The Church administration was divided under the Episcopal care of four Vicars Apostolic for the London, Midland, Northern and Western Districts, the latter embracing Wales. They supplanted the contentious Chapter which had governed the English mission since 1655.

Contrary to the caricature of him painted by his Whig opponents, James was not the bigot presented in Protestant propaganda, which had a vested interest in maintaining the falsehood. He had genuine friendships with dissenters, including the Quaker William Penn, one of the future Founding Fathers of America. Hundreds of Quakers were released from imprisonment

Epilogue

on James's accession. Penn probably influenced the drafting of the first Declaration of Indulgence for the Liberty of Conscience, which James issued on 4 April 1687. This first real step towards establishing religious freedom suspended all penal laws for failure to conform to the Church of England for Catholics, non-Anglican Protestant dissenters and Jews. It permitted everyone to worship wherever they saw fit and removed the requirement of taking religious oaths before being employed in government or military offices. Penn retained his affection and friendship for James long after he had lost his throne. Perhaps if James had adopted a more cautious, longer-term approach things might have been different. Even Queen Mary counselled moderation. On the other hand it might not have made any difference, as the anti-Catholic bigots were so implacable in their opposition. When James tactlessly sought to reinforce his Declaration in April 1688, Archbishop Sancroft of Canterbury and six other bishops opposed the King's wishes and were imprisoned. In today's more tolerant climate, James's policy strikes us as nothing more than long overdue common justice; but it was attempted far too insensitively and it proved to be his downfall.

After miscarriages and the deaths of four children in infancy, the last straw for many English people was the birth of a healthy Catholic son and heir to James and Mary. So the King's opponents entered into a conspiracy to dethrone him in favour of William of Orange, his dour Dutch Protestant son-in-law. James had been a conspicuously brave man all his life but when the so-called 'Glorious Revolution' was launched in 1688 his nerve inexplicably failed him and he fled. Three of the Vicars Apostolic were arrested; the fourth escaped to the north. With the departure of the King, the Catholic community was plunged into despair.

James's Declaration of Indulgence became void under William of Orange. In 1700 toleration was extended to non-Anglican Protestants, but not to Catholics. Parliament passed a new law bypassing priesthood as such but making the saying of Mass a crime punishable by life imprisonment. The same act forbade Catholics to own or inherit land, and Catholic heirs to property found themselves dispossessed. The early eighteenth century has generally been regarded as the nadir of the Catholic Church in

Epilogue

Britain, when the numbers of active priests declined and those remaining continued to be constantly harassed and imprisoned, some dying in jail under George II as late as the 1730s. The failure of the two Jacobite rebellions dashed any lingering hopes of a Catholic Stuart restoration. 150 years of persecution had taken its toll: worn down by the penalties inflicted upon them, many families finally conformed. Externally it appeared that the Church was dwindling into insignificance, but modern scholarship has tended to redress the balance of this depressing picture.

Internally the Church remained spiritually vigorous, developing its own very English devotional traditions, and although growth was very patchy, in some of the larger towns it actually showed a small numerical increase. Just how many Catholics there were is impossible to guess, but one estimate suggests that by the late eighteenth century there were between 50,000 and 60,000, about half of whom were in London. The Church was kept afloat largely by the remaining faithful gentry and the unassuming efforts of the Venerable Richard Challoner, by the time of whose death in 1781 at the age of ninety there was a glimmer of hope on the horizon.

There were still sporadic outbursts of active persecution such as that which took place in 1767, when several priests were prosecuted and one, Father John Baptist Maloney, convicted of saying Mass at Croydon, was condemned to life imprisonment but banished after serving a few years of his sentence. Although the old law carrying the death penalty was never again exercised, incredibly it remained on the Statute Book until 1843. The first Catholic Relief Act was passed in 1778, enabling Catholics to own land. In 1780 came the notorious Gordon Riots in London, organised by the Protestant Association led by the deranged Lord George Gordon. If anything the mayhem and wanton destruction only served to strengthen the resolve of those committed to Catholic relief. A new Relief Act followed in 1791 in which, momentously, priests were legally permitted to exercise their ministry. Religious refugees from revolutionary France and immigrants from Ireland swelled the numbers of Catholics, increased by a growing influx of converts. In 1829 came the Catholic Emancipation Act and finally, accompanied by 'No

Epilogue

popery' demonstrations and accusations of papal aggression from Parliament, in 1850 came the restoration of the Catholic hierarchy by Rome.

Today, in a world of ungodly scepticism, the Catholics of England and Wales enjoy the blessing of being able to openly practise their Faith. How little in these days of freedom can we even begin to imagine what the grinding tyranny of a century and a half of persecution meant to the faithful few.

The Forty Martyrs came from every walk of life from the highest nobility to the lowest of the poor. Regardless of their station, their Faith clearly meant everything to them, to the extent of ultimately giving their lives for it. Through all their vicissitudes they lived their Faith wholeheartedly, often full of humour; not always a noteworthy characteristic among the saints! May the sacrifices they and our Catholic forebears made never be forgotten.

Appendix 1

The Ikon of the Forty Martyrs of England and Wales

The ikon was 'written', i.e. painted, by Anna Dimascio, who came into the Roman Catholic Church from our sister Orthodox Church.

I had been researching the project of an ikon for many years ever since attending the canonization of the Forty Martyrs in Rome in October 1970. Anna and I collaborated to translate the fruits of that research into ikonography. Great care was taken to remain faithful to historical authenticity wherever possible. At the same time we had to ensure that this was not achieved at the expense of the ikon failing to maintain the integrity of true ikonographic traditions. A source of reference was the, albeit stylised, contemporary portraits and engravings of some of the martyrs, particularly those of the Stuart period, but not with the aim of reproducing an exact likeness.

Many hours were spent in composing harmonious groupings of the forty saints so that the historical and spiritual affinities amongst them were manifest. For example, the six Welsh martyrs are grouped together as are the three women; likewise those who shed their blood together or knew each other personally. The ikon took one year to complete and was solemnly blessed with the prescribed ritual of incense and holy water, by Bishop Alan Clark of East Anglia on the altar of his domestic chapel at Norwich in January 1992.

There are now reproductions of the ikon in many churches, abbeys and schools – both Catholic and Anglican – throughout England and Wales. The ikon has been featured in newspapers, magazines and diocesan yearbooks. A tribute, I hope, to the extraordinarily gifted Anna Dimascio, who sadly died of cancer at a tragically young age.

Appendix 2

Prayer to the Forty Martyrs of England and Wales

O God, almighty and everlasting, you fashioned the forty holy martyrs of England and Wales after the likeness of your Son, who is glorified through His death for the world's salvation: listen now to their prayers, and grant us the strength that their love and faith imparts, so that we may come to the fullness of life. Through Jesus Christ our Lord. Amen.

List of Sources

Abrami, J, O.Carm., *St Margaret Clitherow*, Carmelite Press, 1980

Ackroyd, P, *The Life of Thomas More*, Chatto & Windus, 1998

Acts of the Privy Council: New Series, Dasent, J R, [ed.], 32 vols., HMSO, 1890–1918

Allen, Cardinal William, *A Brief History of the Glorious Martyrdom of the Twelve Reverend Priests: Father Edmund Campion and his Companions 1582*, edited by J H Pollen, SJ, London, Burns & Oates, 1908

Anstruther, G, OP, *The Seminary Priests*

——, *vol. 1 Elizabethan*, St Edmund's College, Ware, 1968

——, *vol. 2 The Early Stuarts*, Mayhew-McCrimmon, 1975

——, *vol. 3 1660–1715*, Mayhew-McCrimmon, 1976

——, *A Hundred Homeless Years*, Blackfriars, 1958

——, *Vaux of Harrowden*, Newport, R H Johns, 1953

Ashley, M, *The English Civil War*, Sutton, Stroud, 1990

——, *Charles II*, Weidenfeld & Nicholson, 1971

——, *James II*, J M Dent, 1977

Atteridge, A H, *The Elizabethan Persecution*, Harding & More, 1928

Aveling, Dom J C H, OSB, *The Catholic Recusants of the West Riding of Yorkshire 1558–1790*, Proceedings of the Leeds Philosophical & Literary Society, 1963

——, *Northern Catholics: the Catholic Recusants of the North Riding of Yorkshire*, London, Geoffrey Chapman, 1966

——, *The Handle and the Axe: Catholic Recusants from Reformation to Emancipation*, Blond & Briggs, 1976

——, *Catholic Recusancy in the City of York 1558–1791*, Catholic Record Society, London, 1970

Baldwin Smith, L, *Henry VIII*, Jonathan Cape, 1934

List of Sources

Baskerville, G, *English Monks and the Suppression of the Monasteries*, Yale University Press, 1937

Bassett, B, SJ, *The English Jesuits*, Burns & Oates, 1967

Belloc, H, *James II*, Philadelphia, J. B. Lippincott Co., 1928

——, *How the Reformation Happened*, New York, R. M. McBride, 1928

Betts, J R, *Blessed Peter Wright SJ*, Northampton, The Becket Press, 1997

Bingham, C, *James VI of Scotland*, Weidenfeld & Nicholson, 1979

——, *James I of England*, Weidenfeld & Nicholson, 1981

Birt, H N, OSB, *The Elizabethan Religious Settlement*, Bell, 1907

Black, J B, *The Reign of Elizabeth*, Oxford Clarendon Press, 1959

Bossy, J, *The English Catholic Community 1570–1850*, Darton, Longman and Todd, 1975

Bridgett, T E, CSSR, and Knox, T F, *Queen Elizabeth and the Catholic Hierarchy*, Burns & Oates, 1889

Brooks, F W, *York and the Council of the North*, St Anthony's Press, 1954

Bruce, M L, *Anne Boleyn*, Harper Collins, 1972

Bryant, Sir A, *Charles II*, London, 1935, [rev. ed.], Cassell & Co., 1955

Budiansky, S, *Her Majesty's Spymaster: Elizabeth I, Sir Francis Walsingham and the Birth of Modern Espionage*, Viking, 2005

Burton, E H, and Pollen, J H, SJ, *Lives of the English Martyrs: 2nd series, the Venerable Martyrs 1583–88*, London, 1914

Butler, A, *The Lives of the Saints*, 4 vols., 1756–59, edited and revised by H J Thurston SJ and D Attwater, Burns & Oates, 1986 ed.

Calendar of State Papers, Domestic Series, of the Reigns of Edward VI, Mary, Elizabeth 1547–1580, preserved at the Public Records Office, edited by R Lemon, 2 vols., Longman, Brown, Green & Roberts, 1856

Camm, Dom B, OSB, *Forgotten Shrines*, Macdonald & Evans, 1910

List of Sources

——, *Courtier, Monk and Martyr: Blessed Sebastian Newdigate*, Art and Book Company, London, 1901

——, *A Benedictine Martyr in England: Dom John Roberts*, Bliss & Sands, 1897

——, [ed.] *Lives of the Martyrs Declared Blessed by Pope Leo XIII in 1886 & 1895*, 2 vols, London, 1904–05

Campion, E, SJ, *Ten Reasons Proposed to his Adversaries for Disputation in the Name of Faith*, transl. by J Rickely, SJ, London, 1914

Caraman, P, SJ, *A Study in Friendship: Robert Southwell & Henry Garnet*, India, 1991

——, *The Western Rising 1549*, West Country Books, 1994

——, *Henry Garnet 1555–1606 and the Gunpowder Plot*, Longmans, Green & Co., 1964

——, *Henry Morse: Priest of the Plague*, Longmans, Green & Co., 1957

——, [ed.], *The Other Face: Catholic Life under Elizabeth I*, Longmans, Green & Co.,1960

——, [ed.], *The Years of Siege: Catholic life from James I to Cromwell*, Longmans, Green & Co., 1966

Carlton, C, *Charles I: The Personal Monarch*, Routledge, Kegan Paul, 1983

Catholic Encyclopaedia, Robert Appleton Co., 1910

Catholic Record Society, *Documents Relating to the English Martyrs*

Catholic Record Society: x–xi, *The Douai College Diaries 1598–1654*, edited by Burton & T L Williams, 1911

xxx, *Registers of the English College, Valladolid 1589–1862*, edited by E Henson, 1930

xlvii–xlviii, *History of the English Persecution of Catholics and the Presbyterian Plot*, by Warner, J, edited by T A Birrell, 2 vols., 1953 & 1955

Chadwick, H, *St Omer's to Stonyhurst*, Burns & Oates, 1963

Chadwick, O, *The Reformation*, Pelican History Series, 1964

Challoner, Bishop R, *Memoirs of Missionary Priests Secular as well as*

Regular and of Catholics of Both Sexes that Have Suffered Death in England on Religious Accounts 1577–1681, issued 1741, new edition revised and corrected by J H Pollen, Burns, Oates & Washbourne, 1924

Chapman, H W, *Lady Jane Grey*, Jonathan Cape, 1962

Chauncy, Dom M, *The History of the Sufferings of Eighteen Carthusians in England*, translated from Latin, Burns, Oates & Washbourne, 1890

Clark, F L, *William Warham, Archbishop of Canterbury*, Oxford, 1993

Clark, J S, [ed.], *The Life of James II, collected out of Memoirs Writ of His own Hand*, 2 vols., London, 1816

Cobbett, W, *Complete Collection of State Trials*, vols. III and VII, London, R Bagshaw, 1809–1828

Connelly, R, *The Eighty-Five Martyrs*, McCrimmons, 1987

——, *No Greater Love: Martyrs of the Middlesbrough Diocese*, McCrimmons, 1987

——, *Women of the Catholic Resistance 1540–1680*, Pentland Press, 1999

Constant, G, *The Reformation in England. I The English Schism: Henry VIII*, transl. by R E Scantlebury, London, 1934

Cornwall, J, *The Revolt of the Peasantry 1549*, Boston, Routledge and Kegan Paul, 1977

Cox, J C, Rev., *Three Centuries of Derbyshire Annals*, Bemrose and Sons, London, 1890

Davey, F, *Blessed Cuthbert Mayne*, Longmans, 1960

Davies, M, *St John Fisher*, The Neumann Press, 1998

Devlin, C, SJ, *The Life of Robert Southwell, Poet & Martyr*, Sidgwick and Jackson, 1967

Dickens, A G, *The English Reformation*, Batsford, 1989

——, *Thomas Cromwell and the English Reformation*, English Universities Press, 1959

Dictionary of National Biography, Oxford University Press, 1921

Dodd, C [vere H Tootell], *History of England 1500–1688*, Wolverhampton 1742/London, 1839–40, with Notes,

Additions and a Continuation by Rev. M A Tierney, 5 vols., reprinted 1971

Dodds, M H & R, *The Pilgrimage of Grace 1536–37 and the Exeter Conspiracy 1538*, 2 vols., Cambridge, 1915

Duffy, E, *The Stripping of the Altars*, Yale University Press, 1992

——, [ed.], *Challoner and His Church. A Catholic bishop in Georgian England*, Darton, Longman and Todd, 1981

Edwards, F, SJ, *The Jesuits in England from 1580 to the Present Day*, Burns & Oates, 1985

——, *Guy Fawkes: The Real Story of the Gunpowder Plot?*, London, Harte-Davis, 1969

——, *The Gunpowder Plot. The Narrative of Oswald Tesimond alias Greenaway*, London, The Folio Society, 1973

Ellis, T P, *The Catholic Martyrs of Wales*, 1932

Elton, G R, *Reform and Reformation 1509–1558*, Harvard University Press, 1977

Emmison, F G, *Tudor Secretary: Sir William Petre at Court and Home*, Harvard University Press, 1961

Encyclopaedia Britannica

Erickson, C, *Bloody Mary*, John Dent, 1978

Evelyn, J, *The Diary*, Bray, W, [ed.], 2 vols., London, 1901

Farmer, D H, [ed.], *Oxford Dictionary of Saints*, 5th ed., 2003

Foley, H, SJ, *Records of the English Province of the Society of Jesus*, 8 vols., Manresa Press, 1877–1884

Fraser, A, *Mary, Queen of Scots*, Weidenfeld & Nicholson, 1969

——, *The Gunpowder Plot: Terror and Faith in 1605*, Weidenfeld & Nicholson, 1996

——, *King Charles II*, Weidenfeld & Nicholson, 1979

——, *Cromwell, Our Chief of Men*, Weidenfeld & Nicholson, 1973

Frere, W H, *The Marian Reaction*, SPCK, London, 1896

Gamache, Father Cyprien de OFM Cap, *Memoirs of the Mission in England of the Capuchin Friars of the Province of Paris from the Year 1630 to 1669, as Translated in the Court and Times of Charles I*, London, 1848

Gasquet, Cardinal F A, *A History of the Venerable English College, Rome*, London, Longmans, Green & Co., 1920

——, *Henry VIII and the English Monasteries*, G Bell, London, 1910

Gee, H, *The Elizabethan Clergy and the Settlement of Religion 1558–1564*, Oxford Clarendon Press, 1898

Gerard, J, SJ, *The Autobiography of an Elizabethan*, transl. and ed. by P Caraman, SJ, Longmans, Green & Co., 1951

——, *A Narrative of the Gunpowder Plot*, Morris, J, SJ, [ed.], in *The Condition of English Catholics*, 2nd ed., Longmans, Green & Co., London, 1872

Gillow, J, *A Literary and Biographical History or Bibliographical Dictionary of English Catholics*, 5 vols., Burns & Oates, 1885–1902 ed.

Haigh, C, *The English Reformation Revised*, Cambridge University Press, 1987

——, *The Last Days of the Lancashire Monasteries and the Pilgrimage of Grace*, Chetham Society, Manchester, 1969

Haile, M, *The Life of Reginald Pole*, New York, Longmans, Green & Co., 1910

——, *An Elizabethan Cardinal: William Allen*, Isaac Pitman & Sons, 1914

Handover, P M, *The Second Cecil 1563–1604*, Eyre & Spottiswoode, 1959

Harran, M J, *The Catholics in Caroline England*, Stanford University Press, 1962

Harting, J H, *Catholic London Missions*, Sands and Company, London, 1903

Haswell, J, *James II*, Hamish Hamilton, 1972

Hayward, F M, *Padley Chapel and Padley Martyrs*, Derby, Bemrose & Sons, 1903

Hay, M V, *The Jesuits and the Popish Plot*, Sands & Company, 1934

Hayley, K H D, *The First Earl of Shaftesbury*, Oxford, 1968

Haynes, A, *The Elizabethan Secret Services*, Sutton Publishing, 1992

——, *Walsingham, Elizabeth's Spymaster*, Sutton Publishing, 2004

List of Sources

Hemphill, B, Dom, OSB, *The Early Vicars Apostolic of England 1685–1750*, London, Burns & Oates, 1954

Hendriks, L, O. Cist, *The Carthusian Martyrs*, London, 1931

——, *The London Charterhouse: its Monks and Martyrs,* Kegan Paul, Trench, 1889

Hodgetts, M, *Secret Hiding Places*, Dublin, Veritas, 1989

Hope, W H Saint-John, *The History of the London Charterhouse from its Foundation until the Suppression of the Monastery*, W H Allen, London, 1925

Hopkirk, M, *Queen over the Water*, John Murray, 1953

Hughes, P, *Rome and the Counter-Reformation in England*, Burns & Oates, 1942

——, *The Reformation in England*, revised ed., New York, Macmillan, 1963

Janelle, P, *Robert Southwell the Writer*, Sheed & Ward, 1935

Jardine, D, *A Narrative of the Gunpowder Plot*, John Murray, 1857

Jessop, A, *One Generation of a Norfolk House*, Burns & Oates, 1879

Jones, J R, *The Revolution of 1688*, New York, Norton, 1972

Jordan, W K, *Edward VI: The Young King*, Harvard University Press, 1968

——, *Edward VI: the Threshold of Power*, London, Allen & Unwin, 1970

Knowles, Dom, D, OSB, *The Monastic Order in England*, Cambridge University Press, 1940, 1976 ed.

——, *The Religious Orders in England*, vol. 3, The Tudor Age, Cambridge University Press, 1948–59

Kelly, C, *Blessed Thomas Belson*, Gerrards Cross, Smythe, 1987

Kenyon, J P, *The Popish Plot*, William Heinemann, 1972

Kirk, J, *Biographies of English Catholics*, edited by J H & E H Pollen, London, Burton, 1909

Knox, T F, *Records of the English Catholics under the Penal Laws, 1st & 2nd Douai Diaries*, London, 1878

Lane, J, *Titus Oates*, Andrew Dakers, 1949

Lingard, J, *The History of England from the First Invasion of the Romans to*

List of Sources

the Accession of William and Mary 1688, 10 vols., James Duffy, Dublin, 1874

Loades, D, *The Reign of Mary Tudor 1553–58*, 2nd ed., Longman Group, 1991.

London Encyclopaedia, edited by B Weinreb & C Hibbert, Macmillan, 1983

Longley, K M, *Saint Margaret Clitherow*, Anthony Clarke, 1986 [being a revised and updated edition of the book published 1966 under the pen name Mary Claridge]

MacCulloch, D, *Thomas Cranmer: A Life*, Yale University Press, 1997

Mackie, J D, *The Early Tudors*, Oxford University Press, 1952

Magee, B, *The English Recusants*, Burns, Oates & Washbourne, 1938

Marks, A, *Who Killed Sir Edmund Berry Godfrey?* Burns & Oates, 1905

Marius, R, *Thomas More*, Alfred Knopf, New York, 1984

Marshall, A, *The Strange Death of Sir Edmund Berry Godfrey*, Sutton Publishing, 1999

Mathew, D, *Catholics in England*, Longmans, Green, 1936

——, *Catholicism in England: the Portrait of a Minority 1535–1935*, 2nd ed., Eyre & Spottiswoode, London, 1948

——, *James I*, Jonathan Cape, London, 1982

Mattingley, G, *Catherine of Aragon*, Little, Brown and Company, 1941

McGrath, P, *Papists and Puritans under Elizabeth*, Blandford Press, 1969

Meyer, A O, *England and the Catholic Church under Queen Elizabeth*, transl. from the German by J R McKee, Routledge, Kegan Paul, 1967

Miller, J, *Popery and Politics in England 1660–88*, Cambridge University Press, 1973

Monro, M T, *Blessed Margaret Clitherow*, New York, Longmans, Green, 1947

List of Sources

Moorhouse, Geoffrey, *The Pilgrimage of Grace*, Weidenfeld & Nicholson, 2002

More, H, *The Elizabethan Jesuits: Historia Missionis Anglicana 1606*, transl. by F Edwards, SJ, London, 1981

Morris, J A, *Richard Topcliffe: 'a most humbell pursuivant of Her Majestie'*, The Military College of South Carolina, 1964

Morris, J H, SJ, [ed.] *Troubles of Our Catholic Forefathers as related by themselves*, 1st, 2nd and 3rd series, including a transcript of *A True Report of the Life and Martyrdom of Mrs Margaret Clitherow* by Father John Mush, Burns & Oates, London, 1872–77

——, *The Catholics of York under Elizabeth*, London, 1891

——, *The Condition of Catholics under James I*, 1871

Muller, J A, *Stephen Gardiner and the Tudor Reaction*, London, 1926, 1970 ed., New Octagon

Neal, J E, *Queen Elizabeth*, Jonathan Cape, 1934

Neame, A, *The Holy Maid of Kent*, London, Hodder & Stoughton, 1971

Newton, D, *Catholic London*, London, Hale, 1950

Nicholls, M, *Investigating the Gunpowder Plot*, Manchester University Press, 1991

Oman, C, *Henrietta Maria*, Hodder & Stoughton, 1936

——, *Mary of Modena*, London, Hodder & Stoughton, 1962

Palmer, W, *Life of Mrs Dorothy Lawson of St Anthony*, Charles Dolman, 1855

Paul, J E, *Catherine of Aragon and Her Friends*, Burns & Oates, 1966

Pollen, J H, SJ, *The English Catholics in the Reign of Elizabeth 1558–1580*, Longmans, Green & Co., 1920

——, *Acts of the English Martyrs*, London, Burns & Oates, 1891

——, *Father Henry Garnet and the Gunpowder Plot*, London, 1888

Pollock, J, *The Popish Plot: A Study in the History of the Reign of Charles II*, London, Duckworth, 1903

Prescott, H F, *Mary Tudor*, revised ed., New York, Macmillan Company, 1953

List of Sources

Pritchard, A, *Catholic Loyalism in Elizabethan England*, University of North Carolina, 1979

Read, C, *Secretary Cecil and Queen Elizabeth*, New York, Knopf, 1955

Reid, R R, *The King's Council in the North*, Rowman and Littlefield, 1975

Reynolds, E E, *The Roman Catholic Church in England and Wales*, Anthony Clarke, 1973

——, *St John Fisher*, Anthony Clarke, 1955

——, *The Field is Won: St Thomas More*, Burns & Oates, 1968

Rhodes, W E, [ed.] *The Apostolical Life of Ambrose Barlow*, Chetham Society, 1909

Richards, D, *Britain under the Tudors and Stuarts*, Longmans, Green & Co., 1951

Ridley, J, *The Life and Times of Mary Tudor*, Weidenfeld & Nicholson, 1973

Rose Troup, F, *The Western Rebellion*, Smith & Elder, 1913

Rowse, A L, *Tudor Cornwall*, Macmillan, 1969

——, *The England of Elizabeth*, Macmillan, 1973

——, *The Tower of London*, Cardinal, 1972

Sander, N, *The Rise and Growth of the Anglican Schism 1585*, with a continuation by Edward Rishton, trans. by D Lewis, London, 1877

Scarisbrick, J J, *The Reformation and the English People*, Oxford, Blackwell, 1984

——, *The Jesuits and the Catholic Reformation*, The Historical Association, 1989

—, *Henry VIII*, Eyre Methuen, 1968

Simpson, R, *Edmund Campion*, J Hodges, London, 1896

Smyth, C H E, *Cranmer and the Reformation under Edward VI*, Cambridge, 1926

S.N.D, *William Howard, Viscount Stafford 1612–1680*, Sands & Co., 1929

List of Sources

Southwell, R, *An Epistle of Comfort*, edited by M Waugh, Burns & Oates, 1956

——, *An Humble Supplication to Her Majestie*, edited by R C Bold, Cambridge University Press, 1953

Stanton, R, *A Menology of England and Wales*, London, 1892

Steer, F W, *The Life of Philip Howard*, ed. from the 1630 anonymous *Life*, Howard Phillimore, 1971

Stonor, R J, *Stonor*, 2nd ed., Newport, R H Johns, 1952

Sturge, C, *Cuthbert Tunstall*, London, Longmans, Green, 1938

Thaddeus, Father, *The Franciscans in England 1600–1850*, London, 1898

Thomson, J A F, *The Early Tudor Church and Society*, Longmans, London, 1993

Thompson, E M, *The Carthusian Order in England*, SPCK, 1930

Todd, J M, *Reformation*, London, Darton, Longman & Todd, 1971

Trappes-Lomax, M, *Bishop Challoner*, Longmans, Green & Co., 1936

Trimble, W R, *The Catholic Laity in Elizabethan England 1558–1603*, Harvard University Press, 1964

Trudgian, R F, *Francis Tregian*, Alpha Press, 1998

Turner, F C, *James II*, Eyre & Spottiswoode, 1948

Waugh, E, *Edmund Campion*, Oxford University Press, 1980

Wedgwood, C V, *The King's Peace 1637–41*, Collins Fontana, 1972

——, *The King's War 1641–47*, Collins Fontana, 1973

——, *Oliver Cromwell*, Duckworth, 1973

Weston, W, *The Autobiography of an Elizabethan*, transl. and ed. by P Caraman, SJ, Longmans, Green & Co., London, 1955

Whatmore, L E, *The Carthusians under King Henry VIII*, University of Salzburg, 1983

Whelan, H, *Snow on the Hedges: A Life of Cuthbert Mayne*, Fowler Wright, 1984

White, F O, *Lives of the Elizabethan Bishops of the Anglican Church*, Skeffington, 1898

Williams, M E, *The Venerable English College, Rome*, London, 1979

Williams, N, *Elizabeth I*, Weidenfeld & Nicholson, 1967

Woodward, G W O, *The Dissolution of the Monasteries*, Blandford Press, 1966

Wriothesley, C, *Chronicle*, Camden Society, 1875–77

Yeo, M, *Claude de la Colombière*, Burns, Oates & Washbourne, 1940

Youings, J, *The Dissolution of the Monasteries*, Allen & Unwin, 1971

Pamphlets and Booklets

Arrowsmith, E, *A True Account of the Life and Death, 1630*, Vice-Postulation

Camm, Dom B, OSB, *The Life of Blessed [St] John Wall*, 1932, reprinted 1972

Caraman, P, SJ, *St Philip Howard*, CTS, 1985

De Rosa, P, *Blessed Alexander Briant*, Vice-Postulation

Edwards, G, *St Ambrose Barlow*, CTS, 1984

The Eighty-five Blessed Martyrs, Martyrs Office

Elvins, M T, *The Sussex Martyrs*, CTS, 1983

Fee, W, *Martyrs of Northumberland and Durham*, CTS, 1979

Fitzherbert, M, *St Philip Howard*, revised, M T Elvins, CTS, 1975

Foley, B C, *Blessed John Paine*, Vice-Postulation, 1961

——, *The Eighty-five Blessed Martyrs*, CTS, 1987

Forster, A, *Blessed Eustace White*, Vice-Postulation

Goulder, L, *Church Life in Medieval England and Wales. The Parishes*, Guild of Our Lady of Ransom, 1988 ed.

——, *Church Life in Medieval England and Wales. The Monasteries*, Guild of Our Lady of Ransom, 1990 ed.

——, *Westminster*, Guild of Our Lady of Ransom, 1967 ed.

——, *York*, Guild of Our Lady of Ransom, 1962 ed.

——, *London. The Tower and Environs*, Guild of Our Lady of Ransom, 1989 ed.

Hodgetts, M, *Harvington Hall*, Archdiocese of Birmingham, 1991

Johnston, F R, *St Richard Reynolds*, Syon Abbey, 1961

——, *Martyrs of England and Wales. Complete List of the Canonized and Beatified Martyrs*, CTS, 1979

McGoldrick, T A, *St Margaret Clitherow*, CTS, 1971

Morris, J, SJ, *The English Martyrs*, CTS, 1961

Nassan, M, *St Robert Southwell*, CTS

O'Dwyer, M, *Blessed Anne Line*, Vice-Postulation

Oxburgh Hall Guide, National Trust, 1990

Petre, Lord J, *Ingatestone Hall Guide*, Leighprint

Rice, F, *St John Boste*, Darlington Carmel, 1993

Stonor, Dom J, OSB, *Six Welsh Martyrs*, Vice-Postulation

Tigar, C, SJ, *Henry Walpole*, Vice-Postulation, 1970

Tyburn Convent, *They Died at Tyburn 1535–1680*, 1961

Walsh, J, SJ, [compiler] *The Forty Martyrs of England and Wales*, CTS, 1997 ed.

Waugh, M, *Blessed Ralph Sherwin*, CTS, 1962

——, *Blessed John Plessington*, CTS, 1961

Whatmore, L E, *Blessed Margaret Ward*, 1961

Whitfield, J L, *Blessed John Southworth*, CTS, 1959

Articles

Barry, P, 'The Penal Laws', in *L'Osservatore Romano*, English ed., 30/11/1987

Canning, J H, 'The Titus Oates Plot in South Wales and the Marches', in *St Peter's Magazine*, 1923–24

MacCulloch, D, 'The Myth of the English Reformation', in *Journal of British Studies*, 1991

Molinari, P, SJ, 'Canonization of Forty English and Welsh

List of Sources

Martyrs', in *L'Osservatore Romano*, English ed., 29/10/1970

Fiction

Benson, R H, *Come Rack, Come Rope*, Lepanto Press, 2001

Buchan, J, *The Blanket of the Dark*, Hodder & Stoughton, 1931

Fullerton, Lady G, *Constance Sherwood*, 1895

Prescott, H F M, *The Man on a Donkey*, Eyre & Spottiswoode, 1952

Taylor, Mother M, *Tyborne*, Neumann Press ed., 1994

Index of Persons

A

Abbot, George (5th Anglican Archbishop of Canterbury), 59, 249, 275
Abel, Thomas DD (priest martyr), 49, 54
Adams, John (priest martyr), 75
Agazzari, Alfonso SJ (Rector of English College, Rome), 124
Allen, William (Cardinal), 79, 84, 85, 108, 126, 209, 210, 264
Almond, John O. Cist, 273–74
ALMOND, ST JOHN (priest martyr), 273–76, 320
Aquaviva, Claudio (Jesuit General), 191
ARROWSMITH, ST EDMUND (Jesuit priest martyr), 283, 287–93, 298, 325, 346
Arundell, Sir John, 100, 101, 104, 105, 169
Ashby, Thomas (lay martyr), 49
Ashley, Ralph (Jesuit brother martyr), 253, 256, 277
Aske, Robert, 45
Atkinson, Anthony (apostate priest), 184, 185
Atkinson, Paul (Franciscan priest), xx
Atkinson, Thomas (priest martyr), 319
Atkinson, William (apostate priest), 244
Audley, Sir Thomas (Lord Chancellor), 35, 38
Augustine of Hippo (Bishop/saint), xvii
Aylmer, John (Anglican Bishop of London), 69, 95, 228

B

Babington
  Anthony, 74, 194
  Plot, 74, 173, 191, 194, 209
Bale, John (Protestant bishop), 48
Ballard, John (priest), 74, 75, 93, 210
Bancroft, Richard (4th Anglican Archbishop of Canterbury), 83, 93, 267
Barkworth, Mark (Benedictine priest martyr), 226, 245, 261
Barlow, Lewis (priest), 85, 96
BARLOW, ST AMBROSE (Benedictine priest martyr), 293–302, 325
Barnes, Robert (recusant), 217
Barton, Elizabeth (nun), 26, 50
Batmanson, John (Carthusian prior), 29
Bayne, Ralph (Bishop of Lichfield), 90
Beaumont, Sir Francis (judge), 186, 204
Beche, John (Benedictine abbot martyr), 49

393

Index of Persons

Bedloe, William (perjurer), 334, 338, 349, 354, 355, 361, 365, 367
Bedyll, Thomas (archdeacon), 31, 32, 38, 40
Belchiam, Thomas (Franciscan priest martyr), 54
Bell, Thomas (priest), 86
Bellamy family (recusants), 193, 240, 242
Bennet, John (priest), 145
Bennett, William (priest), 211
Berden, Nicholas (spy/pursuivant), 88
Bere, Richard (Carthusian priest martyr), 53
Beza, Theodore (Calvinist), 123, 139
Bickerdike, Robert (lay martyr), 183
Bickley, Ralph (Jesuit priest), 88
Bird, William (priest), 40
Bishop, William (Bishop, Vicar Apostolic), 280, 317
Blackwell, George (archpriest), 168, 274, 317
Blount, Richard (Jesuit priest), 194, 288, 309, 311, 318
Bold, Richard (recusant), 191
Boleyn, Anne (Queen of England), 24, 26, 30, 33, 45, 91
Bonner, Edmund (Bishop of London), 63, 90
Borromeo, Charles St (Archbishop of Milan), 123
Bosgrave, James (Jesuit priest), 117, 232
Bosgrave, Thomas (lay martyr), 87
BOSTE, ST JOHN (priest martyr), 165, 181–89, 204

Bourne, Francis (Cardinal), xix
Bourne, Gilbert (Bishop of Bath and Wells), 90
Bowes, Marmaduke (lay martyr), 156
BRIANT, ST ALEXANDER (Jesuit priest martyr), xiv, 117, 119, 128–33, 136, 310
Bridget of Sweden, St, 32
Brindholme, Edmund (priest), 49
Brookby, Anthony DD (Franciscan priest martyr), 54
Brooksby, Eleanor (recusant), 252
Brown, Mrs Dorothy (recusant), 81
Bruno, St, 28
Buckley, Sigebert (Benedictine priest), 267, 278
Bullock, Dr George (Master of St John's, Cambridge), 142
Burden, Edward (priest martyr), 168, 239
Buxton, Christopher (priest martyr), 94, 237

C

Campion, Edward (priest martyr), 237
CAMPION, ST EDMUND (Jesuit priest martyr), 83, 99, 105, 106–20, 122, 123, 126, 132, 136, 139, 140, 153, 193, 199, 208, 228, 229, 230, 231, 251, 264, 320, 324
Cantilupe, Sir Nicholas de, 28
Carey, John (lay martyr), 87
Carter, William (lay martyr), 82, 95
Carvajal, Luisa de, 270, 278

Index of Persons

Catherine of Aragon (Queen of England), 24, 52
Catherine of Braganza (Queen of England), 333
Catherine of Sweden, St, 32
Cecil, John (priest/spy), 264, 265
Cecil, Robert (Earl of Salisbury), 93, 196, 241, 247, 248, 264
Cecil, William (Lord Burghley), 65, 90, 92, 94, 107, 108, 241
Challoner, Richard (Bishop, Vicar Apostolic), xviii, xxiii, 131, 138, 215, 220, 223, 224, 273, 274, 293, 298, 324, 327, 341
Chapuys, Eustace (Imperial Ambassador), 37
Charles I (King of England), 232, 280–87, 289, 365
Charles II (King of England), 333–40, 364, 365
Chauncy, Maurice (Carthusian priest), 28, 30, 38, 39, 58
Cheney, Dr Richard (Anglican Bishop of Gloucester), 107
Clapton, Cuthbert (priest), 284, 285
Clapton, Mrs Grace (recusant), 189
Clapton, William (recusant), 184
Clark, Alan (Bishop of East Anglia), 377
Clark, William (priest), 168, 266
Claxton, James (priest martyr), 236
Clement VII (Pope), 25, 26, 43
Clement VIII (Pope), 216

Clement, Margaret (nun), 39, 53, 96
Clibburn, Gerard (priest), 181
Clinch, John (judge), 157, 159, 160, 183, 218
Clitherow, Anne (nun), 154, 160, 161, 163
Clitherow, Henry, 154, 163
Clitherow, John, 149, 151, 153, 154, 156, 157, 159, 163
CLITHEROW, ST MARGARET (lay martyr), 148–64, 233
Clitherow, Thomas (recusant), 163
Clitherow, William (priest), 149, 163
Cockerel, James (prior martyr), 46
Coke, Sir Edward (judge), 259, 269
Coleman, Edward (lay martyr), xxii, 337
Colet, John (Dean of St Paul's), 42
Colleton, John (priest), 111, 113, 117, 118, 231
Colombière, St Claude de la (Jesuit priest), 347
Comberford, Henry (priest), 151
Cook, Lawrence (Carmelite prior martyr), 40
Cooper, Anthony Ashley (Earl of Shaftesbury), 336
Corker, Maurus (Benedictine priest), 366
Cornelius, John (priest martyr), 87
Cottam, Thomas (priest martyr), 116, 117, 125, 126, 141, 229

Index of Persons

Covert, Thomas (Franciscan priest martyr), 54
Cranmer, Thomas (1st Protestant Archbishop of Canterbury), 25, 26, 36, 45, 53, 55, 56, 57, 60, 63, 80, 232
Crockett, Ralph (priest martyr), 237
Cromwell, Oliver (Lord Protector), 322, 327
Cromwell, Thomas (Ecclesiastical Vice-Regent), 31, 33, 35, 36, 38, 41, 43, 45, 47, 50, 347
Curry, John (priest), 87

D

Darbyshire, Thomas (Jesuit priest), 190
Davy, John (Carthusian deacon martyr), 53
Dean, William (priest martyr), 235
Dibdale, Robert (priest martyr), 75
Douglas, George (priest martyr), xxi
Dryland, Christopher (Jesuit priest), 173, 239
Dudley, John (Duke of Northumberland), 55, 62
Dudley, Robert (Earl of Leicester), 107
Duke, Edmund (priest martyr), 187

E

Ecclesfield, Francis (apostate spy), 183, 184
Edward III (King of England), 28

Edward the Confessor (saint and king), 47, 58
Edward VI (King of England), 51, 55–57, 61, 62, 142, 164
Egerton, Thomas (Solicitor General), 117
Eliot, George (pursuivant), 112, 114, 117, 119, 134, 135, 136
Elizabeth I (Queen of England), 60, 65–89, 107, 114, 167, 208, 322
Emerson, Ralph (Jesuit brother), 108, 112, 123, 229, 242
Epson, Thomas (Benedictine), 40
Erasmus, Desiderius (priest/scholar), 42
Errington, George (lay martyr), 164, 234
EVANS, ST PHILIP (Jesuit priest martyr), 342–44, 359
Exmew, William (Carthusian priest martyr), 38, 52
Eynon, John (Benedictine priest martyr), 49

F

Faringdon, Hugh (Benedictine abbot), 48
Fawkes, Guy (plotter), xiv, 248
Feckenham, John (Benedictine abbot), 58, 61, 63, 67, 68, 278
Felton, John (lay martyr), xxii, 72, 92
Felton, Thomas (Friar Minim martyr), 236
Fenwick, John (Jesuit priest martyr), 368
Fetherston, Richard DD (priest), 49, 54

Index of Persons

Filby, William (priest martyr), 114, 117, 140, 141, 229
Filcock, Roger (Jesuit priest martyr), 226, 227, 245
Fisher, John (Cardinal Bishop of Rochester, martyr), xvii, xix, 25, 26, 33, 39, 43, 50, 52
Fitzherbert, Anthony (recusant), 78, 79
Fitzherbert, John (recusant), 78, 79
Fitzherbert, Nicholas (recusant), 79
Fitzherbert, Richard (recusant), 78
Fitzherbert, Sir Anthony (judge), 35, 78
Fitzherbert, Sir Thomas (recusant), 78, 79
Fitzherbert, Thomas (priest), 111, 308, 320
Fleetwood, William (judge), 176
Flower or Floyd, Richard (lay martyr), 167
Ford, Thomas (priest martyr), 99, 111, 113, 118, 228, 231
Forest, John (Franciscan priest martyr), 47, 54
Foster, Mrs Isabella (recusant), 80
Foxe, John, 206, 232

G

Gage, Lady Margaret (recusant), 226
Gage, Sir Henry, 314
Gardiner, German (lay martyr), 49, 54
Garlick, Nicholas (priest martyr), xx, 78, 94, 237
Garnet, Henry (Jesuit priest martyr), 79, 168, 170, 180, 186, 191, 193, 196, 197, 202, 212, 213, 242, 245, 246, 251, 252, 255, 257, 258, 259, 282
GARNET, ST THOMAS (Jesuit priest martyr), 245, 260–63, 267, 268
Gavan, John (Jesuit priest martyr), 368
Geldard, Janet (recusant), 150, 153
Gellebrand, Nicholas (priest), 89
Gennings, John (Franciscan priest), 346
GENNINGS, ST EDMUND (priest martyr), 168–72, 173, 175
Gerard, John (Jesuit priest), 87, 94, 96, 179, 192, 195, 201, 202, 203, 214, 216, 217, 220, 222, 224, 225, 226, 244, 251, 252, 253, 257, 263, 277
Gibson, William (lay martyr), 164, 235
Gifford, Gilbert (priest spy), 74, 94
Gilbert, George (exiled recusant), xviii
Godfrey, William (Cardinal), xix
Godsalf, George (priest), 134, 135, 138
Goldwell, Thomas (Bishop of St Asaph), 90, 123, 233, 238
Goodman, John (priest), 284, 326, 332
Gordon, Lord George, 375
Grately, Edward (priest spy), 209, 210
Grayson, Thomas (priest), 148
Green, Robert (lay martyr), 337

Index of Persons

Green, Thomas (Carthusian priest martyr), 53, 305
Greenwood, William (Carthusian brother martyr), 53
Gregory XIII (Pope), xvii, xix, 42, 85, 109, 122
Grene, Christopher (Jesuit priest), xviii
Grenville, Sir Richard, 100, 101, 102, 103, 105
Grey, Lady Jane, 57, 62
Griffith, John (priest martyr), 49
Grimston, Ralph (lay martyr), 111
Grissold, Robert (lay martyr), 248, 277
Grove, John (lay martyr), 365
Gunter, William (priest martyr), 236
GWYN, ST RICHARD (lay martyr), 142–48

H

Habington family (recusants), 253
Haile, John (priest martyr), 34, 51, 347
Hanslepp, Roger (priest), 354, 361
Harcourt, William (Jesuit priest martyr), 368
Hardesty, William (apostate priest spy), 111, 187
Harrington, William (priest martyr), 110
Harris, Thomas (recusant), 102
Harrison, Richard (abbot martyr), 46
Hart, John (Jesuit priest), 117, 230

Hart, William (priest martyr), 155, 233
Hartley, William (priest martyr), 111, 228
Hastings, Henry (Earl of Huntingdon), 182
Haydock, George (priest martyr), xx, 235
Heath, Nicholas (Archbishop of York), 90, 206
Heath, Sir Robert (Attorney General), 289, 299, 300, 301
Heigham, William (recusant), 223, 224
Henrietta Maria (Queen of England), 281, 305, 314, 325, 365
Henry II (King of England), 28
Henry V (King of England), 30, 32
Henry VIII (King of England), 24, 27, 28, 30, 31, 42, 51, 52, 61, 62, 91, 190, 273
Heron, Giles (lay martyr), 40
Herst, Richard (lay martyr), 283, 293, 318
Hewett, John (priest martyr), 238
Hill, Lawrence (lay martyr), 337
Hill, Richard (priest martyr), 187
Hobbes, Robert (abbot martyr), 46
Hodge, John (recusant), 102
Hodgson, Sidney (lay martyr), 176
Hogg, John (priest martyr), 187
Holford, Thomas (priest martyr), 173, 239
Holiday, Richard (priest martyr), 187

Index of Persons

Holtby, Richard (Jesuit priest), 128, 202, 310, 320
Hopton, Sir Owen, 130, 135
Hore, Richard (recusant), 102
Horne, William (Carthusian brother martyr), 40
Horner, William (priest), 167
HOUGHTON, ST JOHN (Carthusian prior martyr), 28–32, 37, 38
Howard, Anne (Countess of Arundel), 193, 214
Howard, Philip Thomas (Cardinal), 334, 364
HOWARD, ST PHILIP (lay martyr), 93, 96, 193, 206–15
Howard, William (Viscount Stafford, lay martyr), 214, 338, 365
Huddleston, John (Benedictine priest), 333, 337, 339, 364
Huddlestone, Sir Edmund (recusant), 220
Hughes, John (recusant), 144, 145, 146
Humphreys, James (recusant), 102
Hutton, Mary (recusant), 154
Hutton, Matthew (Anglican Bishop of Durham and York), 186
Hutton, William (recusant), 154, 233, 234

I

Ingleby, Francis (priest martyr), xiv, 155, 156, 234
Ingram, John (priest martyr), 186, 187, 189
Ingworth, Richard (Bishop of Dover), 41

Ireland, John (priest martyr), 49, 54
Ireland, William (Jesuit priest martyr), 365, 367, 368

J

James I (King of England), xiii, 59, 85, 106, 168, 246, 247, 249, 260, 266, 271, 276, 294
James II (King of England), 280, 339, 352, 364, 366, 372, 373
James, Edward (priest martyr), 237
James, Roger (Benedictine monk martyr), 48
Jeffreys, Sir George (judge), 340
Jeffreys, Sir John (judge), 102, 103
Jenkins, David (pursuivant), 112, 113, 114
John of Bridlington, St (Austin Canon), xvii, xxiii
John Paul II (Pope), xxi
Johnson, Robert (priest martyr), 116, 125, 230, 231
Johnson, Thomas (Carthusian priest martyr), 53
JONES, ST JOHN (Franciscan priest martyr), 215–19

K

KEMBLE, ST JOHN (priest martyr), 352–57, 361
Kempe, John (recusant), 102
Kendall, Thomas (priest), 177
KIRBY, ST LUKE (priest martyr), 116, 117, 122, 125, 126, 138–42, 231

Index of Persons

Kirkman, Richard (priest martyr), 155, 233
Knight, William (lay martyr), 164, 235

L

Lacey, Brian (lay martyr), 176
Lacey, William (priest martyr), 155, 233
Lambton, Joseph (priest martyr), 189, 240
Lampley, William (lay martyr), 167
Langhorne, Richard (lay martyr), 365
Larke, John (priest martyr), 49, 54
Latimer, Hugh (Protestant Bishop of Worcester), 47, 60
Laud, William (6th Anglican Archbishop of Canterbury), 283, 314, 315
LAWRENCE, ST ROBERT (Carthusian prior martyr), 28–32
Lawson, Mrs Dorothy (recusant), 309, 310
Lee, Roland (Bishop of Lichfield), 31
Leigh, Richard (priest martyr), 167, 236
Leo X (Pope), 24, 43
Leo XIII (Pope), xix
Leveson, Francis (Franciscan priest), 350, 351, 371
LEWIS, ST DAVID (Jesuit priest martyr), 344, 354, 357–63
Linacre, Thomas (priest/physician), 42
Line, Roger (recusant), 223

LINE, ST ANNE (lay martyr), 87, 223–27, 243, 245
LLOYD, ST JOHN (priest martyr), 344, 345
Louis VII (King of France), 47
Low, John (priest martyr), 75
Ludlam, Robert (priest martyr), xx, 78, 94

M

Major, Anthony (apostate priest spy), 185
Maloney, John Baptist (priest), 375
Manny, Sir Walter, 28
Manwood, Sir Roger (judge), 102, 103, 105
Martin, Gregory (priest), 85, 96, 98, 99, 105, 108
Martin, Richard (lay martyr), 167
Mary I (Queen of England), 24, 26, 32, 54, 57, 58–61, 65
Mary Stuart (Queen of Scots), 70, 74, 76, 92, 197, 204, 207
Maskew, Mrs Bridget (recusant), 164
Mason, John (lay martyr), 170, 176
Mathew, Tobie (Anglican Bishop of Durham & York), 184, 228, 240, 241
May, Henry (Lord Mayor of York), 149, 153, 155, 157, 160
MAYNE, ST CUTHBERT (priest martyr), 98–106, 125, 133
Mayo, Thomas (pursuivant), 285, 304
Meehan, Charles (Franciscan priest martyr), 369

Index of Persons

Meredith, Jonas (priest), 209, 243
Middlemore, Humphrey (Carthusian priest martyr), 30, 38, 51
Miles, Francis (priest), 268
More, Hugh (lay martyr), 236
More, Sir Thomas (Lord Chancellor of England, lay martyr), xix, 24, 25, 29, 36, 39, 42, 50, 51, 52, 259
Morgan, Henry (Bishop of St David's), 90
Morgan, Polydore (priest), 175
Morris, Robert (recusant, 144, 145, 146
MORSE, ST HENRY (Jesuit priest martyr), 307–16, 325, 331
Morton, Robert (priest martyr), 236
Munday, Anthony (spy/pursuivant), 117, 132
Mush, John (priest), xiii, 150, 151, 152, 155, 157, 161, 163, 232
Mush, William (priest), 169

N

Neville, Charles (6th Earl of Westmorland), 184
Neville, Lady Margaret, 184, 189
Newdigate, Sebastian (Carthusian priest martyr), 38, 52
Newton, Francis (pursuivant), 303, 304, 313, 314, 326, 329
Nichols, John, 140, 141
Norton, Thomas (rack-master), 130, 232

O

Oates, Titus (perjurer), 334, 335, 337, 340, 349, 351, 354, 361, 365, 367
Oglethorpe, Owen (Bishop of Carlisle), 66, 90
Oldcorne, Edward (Jesuit priest martyr), 192, 252, 253, 255, 257, 277
Owen, Lewis (informer), 266, 269
OWEN, ST NICHOLAS (Jesuit brother martyr), 217, 250–59, 308, 347

P

Page, Anthony (priest martyr), 244
Page, Francis (Jesuit priest martyr), 225, 244
PAINE, ST JOHN (priest martyr), 99, 133–38
Parker, Matthew (1st Anglican Archbishop of Canterbury), 67, 91
Paschal, John, 122, 124, 125, 126
Paslew, John (abbot martyr), 46
Pate, Richard (Bishop of Worcester), 90
Paul VI (Pope), xi, xix
Paulet, Sir Amias (Keeper of Mary, Queen of Scots), 76
Percy, Thomas (Earl of Northumberland), xxii, 267
Persons, Robert (Jesuit priest), 108, 111, 112, 122, 124, 128, 139, 194, 228, 231, 242
Petre, Benjamin (Vicar-Apostolic), xxiii
Petre, Lady Anne, 112, 133, 134

Index of Persons

Petre, Sir William, 121
Phelippes, Thomas (forger), 88
Philip II (King of Spain), 58, 84, 166, 201, 320
Philips, John (recusant), 102
Philpot, Clement (lay martyr), 49
Pickering, John OSD (prior martyr), 46
Pickering, Thomas (Benedictine brother martyr), 338, 366
Pierson, Walter (Carthusian brother martyr), 53
Pius V (Pope, saint), 71, 92, 107
Pius XI (Pope), xix
PLASDEN, ST POLYDORE (priest martyr), 169, 170, 173, 175–77, 180
PLESSINGTON, ST JOHN (priest martyr), 340–42, 371
Plumtree, Thomas (priest martyr), xxii, 71, 91
Plunket, St Oliver (Archbishop of Armagh martyr), 369
Pole, Margaret (Countess of Salisbury, lay martyr), 49, 54
Pole, Reginald (Cardinal Archbishop), 54, 58, 62, 65
Poole, David (Bishop of Peterborough), 78, 90
Popham, John (judge), 95, 102, 117, 196, 211, 226
Postgate, Nicholas (priest martyr), xx, 369
Powel, Philip (Benedictine priest martyr), 330, 358
Powell, Edward DD (priest martyr), 49, 54
Prance, Miles (perjurer), 334, 337, 365
Pulleyn, Joshua (Jesuit priest), xiv

Pulleyn, William (priest), xiv

R

Raleigh, Sir Walter, 176
Rawlins, Alexander (priest martyr), 169, 173, 205, 241
Reding, Thomas (Carthusian brother martyr), 53
Reynold, William (recusant), 82
Reynolds, Richard (Thomas) (priest martyr), 305
REYNOLDS, ST RICHARD (Bridgettine priest martyr), 32–40
Rhodes, Francis (judge), 157, 159, 160, 183
Richard, Sir Rich (lawyer), 31, 50
Richardson, Lawrence (priest martyr), 117, 141, 231
Richardson, William (priest martyr), 84, 95
Ridley, Nicholas (Protestant Bishop of London), 57, 60, 61
RIGBY, ST JOHN (lay martyr), 219–23
Rishton, Edward (priest), 117, 118, 121, 122, 231
ROBERTS, ST JOHN (Benedictine priest martyr), 263–73
Robinson, Christopher (priest martyr), 189, 240
Robinson, John (Jesuit priest), 310, 311
Robinson, John (priest martyr), 238
Roche, John (lay martyr), 165, 166
Rochester, John (Carthusian priest martyr), 39, 53

402

Index of Persons

ROE, ST ALBAN (Benedictine priest martyr), 302–6
Rookwood, Ambrose (plotter), 261, 262
Roper, William (lawyer), 82
Roscarrock, Nicholas (recusant), 124, 125
Rouse, Anthony (apostate priest informer), 262, 263
Rugg, John (Benedictine monk martyr), 49

S

Sadler, Sir Ralph, 70
Salmon, Patrick (lay martyr), 87
Salt, Robert (Carthusian brother martyr), 53
Scott, Cuthbert (Bishop of Chester), 90
Scott, Maurus (Benedictine priest), 266, 271, 277
Scroggs, William (Lord Chief Justice), 338, 339, 350, 355, 367, 368
Scryven, Thomas (Carthusian brother martyr), 53
Sedbar, Adam (abbot martyr), 46
Seton, George (5th Lord Seton), 182
Seymour, Edward (Duke of Somerset), 55, 62
Shelley, Edward (recusant), 73, 167
Shelley, Richard (recusant), 73
Shelley, William (priest), 73
Shert, John (priest martyr), 117, 231
SHERWIN, ST RALPH (priest martyr), 87, 88, 116, 117, 119, 120–28, 132, 136, 139

Sherwood, Henry (priest), 169
Sherwood, John (priest), 169
Sherwood, Richard (priest), 88, 169
Sherwood, Richard (recusant), 169
Sidney, Sir Philip (Lord Deputy of Ireland), 107
Sledd, Charles (spy), 117, 132, 140
Smith, Richard (Bishop), xviii, 280, 317
Snow, Peter (priest martyr), 111
Somers, Thomas (priest martyr), 269, 270, 271, 273, 278, 364
SOUTHWELL, ST ROBERT (Jesuit priest martyr), 173, 190–98, 203, 211, 212, 257
SOUTHWORTH, ST JOHN (priest martyr), 292, 312, 324–28
Speed, John (lay martyr), 189
Stanihurst, Sir James (Speaker of the Irish House of Commons), 107
Stapleton, Brian (schoolmaster/priest), 156, 163
STONE, ST JOHN (Augustinian friar priest martyr), 40, 42
Storey, John (lay martyr), 72, 92
Sugar, John (priest martyr), 248, 277
Sutton, Abraham (priest), 235
Sutton, Robert (lay martyr), 238
Sutton, Robert (priest martyr), 167, 235

403

Index of Persons

Sutton, William (Jesuit priest), 235
Swallowell, George (lay martyr), 187, 189

T

Taylor, Hugh (priest martyr), 156
Tesh, Mrs Anne (recusant), 157, 163
Tesimond, Oswald (Jesuit priest), 252, 253, 258, 277
Thirkeld, Richard (priest martyr), 155, 234
Thirlby, Thomas (Bishop of Ely), 67, 90
Thirsk, William OCist (Prior martyr), 46
Thomas Becket, St (archbishop martyr), 47, 219, 260
Thompson, James (priest martyr), 155, 233
Thomson, William (priest martyr), 194, 223, 243
Thorne, John (Benedictine priest martyr), 48
Thwing, Edward (priest martyr), 370
Thwing, Thomas (priest martyr), 369
Tichborne, Nicholas (lay martyr), 244, 338
Tichborne, Sir Henry (recusant), 338
Tichborne, Thomas (priest martyr), 244, 338
Tonge, Israel (clergyman), 334, 335
Topcliffe, Richard (pursuivant/torturer), 79, 94, 95, 165, 170, 174, 176, 179, 180, 185, 186, 194, 195, 197, 202, 203, 217, 218
Towneley, John (recusant), 77
Trafford, William (abbot martyr), 46
Trafford, William (Carthusian prior), 39, 40
Tregian, Francis (recusant), 99, 100, 101, 103, 105
Tremayne, Richard (recusant), 102
Tuchiner, Anthony (priest), 215, 243
Tunstall, Cuthbert (Bishop of Durham), 90
Turner, Antony (Jesuit priest martyr), 368
Tynbygh, William (Carthusian prior), 29
Tyrell, Anthony (apostate priest spy), 74, 75, 76, 89, 92, 96, 102, 121, 167, 192, 210, 217, 242

U

Urban VIII (Pope), xviii, 358

V

Vaux, Anne (recusant), 191, 252, 253, 254, 258
Vaux, Lady Elizabeth (recusant), 252
Vaux, William (3rd Baron Vaux of Harrowden), 191
Vavasour, Dr Thomas (recusant), 150, 154
Vavasour, Mrs Dorothy (recusant), 150, 151, 154

W

Waire, John (Franciscan priest martyr), 49
Wakeman, Sir George (physician), 337, 339, 349, 351
WALL, ST JOHN (Franciscan priest martyr), 346–52, 358
Wall, William (Benedictine priest), 346, 349, 351
Walpole, Christopher (Jesuit priest), 201
Walpole, Edward (Jesuit priest), 201
Walpole, Michael (Jesuit priest), 201, 271, 279
Walpole, Richard (Jesuit priest), 200
WALPOLE, ST HENRY (Jesuit priest martyr), 199–206
Walsingham, Sir Francis (spymaster), 73, 74, 76, 88, 92, 94, 98, 112, 135, 191, 194, 204, 209, 230, 232, 239, 241
Walworth, James (Carthusian priest martyr), 39
WARD, MARGARET (lay martyr), 164–68
Ward, Mary (foundress), 281, 370
Ward, William (priest martyr), 285
Warham, William (Archbishop of Canterbury), 25, 50, 51
Waterson, Edward (priest martyr), 189, 241
Watson, Thomas (Bishop of Lincoln), 90

Watson, William (priest), 164, 165, 166, 168, 266
Way, William (priest martyr), 168, 238
Webley, Henry (lay martyr), 236
WEBSTER, ST AUGUSTINE (Carthusian prior martyr), 28–32
Wells, Mrs Alice (recusant), 172, 174
WELLS, ST SWITHUN (lay martyr), 170, 171, 172–74, 176, 239
Weston, William (Jesuit priest), 191, 208, 213, 229, 239, 242, 257, 266
Whitbread, Thomas (Jesuit priest martyr), 347, 367, 368
White, John (Bishop of Winchester), 65, 90
WHITE, ST EUSTACE (priest martyr), 177–81
Whitehead, Isabel (nun), 80
Whitgift, John (3rd Anglican Archbishop of Canterbury), 83
Whiting, Richard (Benedictine abbot martyr), 48
Whytford, Richard (Bridgettine priest), 33, 51
Widmerpool, Robert (lay martyr), 237
Wilcox, Robert (priest martyr), 236
William III (King of England), xx
Williams, John (recusant), 102
Wiseman family, 203, 217, 224, 251
Wiseman, Mrs Jane (recusant), 216, 217, 219, 224

Index of Persons

Wolsey, Thomas (Cardinal Archbishop), 27, 43, 50
Wood, William, (Prior martyr), 46
Woodfen, Nicholas (priest martyr), 172, 239
Woodhouse, Thomas (priest martyr), 72, 92
Woodward, John (priest), 121, 127

Wray, Sir Christopher (judge), 117
Wright, Peter (Jesuit priest martyr), 314, 324, 331
Wriothesley, Henry (3rd Earl of Southampton), 173

Y

Young, Richard (Justice), 75, 76, 89, 170, 223

Printed in Great Britain
by Amazon